ON THE FORWARD EDGE

*American Government and the
Civil Rights Act of 1964*

Robert D. Loevy

University Press of America,® Inc.
Lanham · Boulder · New York · Toronto · Oxford

Copyright © 2006 by
University Press of America,® Inc.
4501 Forbes Boulevard
Suite 200
Lanham, Maryland 20706
UPA Acquisitions Department (301) 459-3366

PO Box 317
Oxford
OX2 9RU, UK

Library of Congress Control Number: 2005932227
ISBN 0-7618-3327-7 (paperback : alk. ppr.)

⊖™ The paper used in this publication meets the minimum
requirements of American National Standard for Information
Sciences—Permanence of Paper for Printed Library Materials,
ANSI Z39.48—1984

CONTENTS

CONTENTS (CONTINUED)

ABOUT THIS BOOK

This book is a text-novel. It was written to teach the basic facts and ideas of an American Government textbook in the form of a novel.

The civil rights movement of the 1950s and 1960s provides the setting for this text-novel. It includes actual historical figures of the time as well as fictionalized young people working in behalf of enactment of the Civil Rights Act of 1964.

Quotations from actual historical figures are either direct quotes or extrapolations from direct quotes.

CHAPTER 1

MASS MEDIA:
WHO DECIDES WHAT'S NEWS?

The summer of 1957 found Clark Schooler with a freshly-minted bachelor's degree from Williams College. He also possessed a letter of acceptance to do graduate work in political science at the Johns Hopkins University in Baltimore, Maryland. Graduate school would not start until the fall, however, so Clark began searching for a summer job. Having been editor of the student newspaper when in high school, Schooler decided to "try his hand" working as a newspaper reporter.

He found a job at the *Baltimore Banner*. It was an afternoon paper. The *Banner* also was a Patriot newspaper. It belonged to a national chain of newspapers, known as the Patriot Press, which specialized in presenting news to the public in a flashy, interesting, and somewhat sensational style.

For the next seven summers, and on weekends throughout the remainder of the year, the *Banner* became Clark Schooler's principal means of economic support for getting himself through graduate school at Johns Hopkins University. But it became something more than just an additional source of money to add to Clark's all-too-meager graduate fellowship. It became the place where he learned about the city of Baltimore.

Clark met both the city's best citizens and its worst citizens. He observed the city's best neighborhoods and its worst neighborhoods. And, above all, the *Banner* was where Clark Schooler learned to write what he called "Patriotese," that fast-reading, hard-hitting, patriotic, common-person-loving style of newspaper writing for which Patriot Press newspapers were duly famous and, at the same time, infamous.

Clark Schooler was hired to be a police reporter for the *Banner*. It was his job to get in his car and cruise from one Baltimore police station to another, picking up small stories about petty crimes, such as fistfights, purse snatches, and burglaries.

These minor crime stories were not significant in themselves, but they came in handy when it was time for the city editor to make up the next edition of the newspaper. If there was an empty space in a newspaper column about one or two-inches long, the space could easily be filled with one of these short crime stories. These minor crime stories were referred to by the nickname "shorts."

Both the *Banner* and its big competitor, the *Baltimore Beacon*, had telephones in each of Baltimore City's police stations. Clark Schooler dutifully kept the telephone operator at the *Banner* informed as to which police station he was inhabiting at any given moment of his working day. That way, when the city editor or an assistant city editor wanted to give Clark a special assignment or send him to cover a fast-breaking crime story, the telephone operator could track Clark down at a police station and connect him to his editors as quickly as possible.

One Saturday, Clark Schooler was working the Eastern District police station when the *Banner* telephone rang demandingly. It was Frank Railley, one of the assistant city editors. It must have been a slow news day, because Railley's instructions to Clark were brief and to the point: "I want you to get me every 'short' there is in the city of Baltimore. Even if an old black man falls down and skins his knee, I want it for the paper."

Thus did Clark Schooler begin to learn that the newspaper business in the city of Baltimore in the 1950s was racially segregated. Neither the *Banner* nor the *Beacon* routinely covered social or business news about black people. As far as the major newspapers were concerned, the black community in Baltimore, which was fully 1/3 of the city's population, did not exist as a news source. The only way a black person could get his or her name or photograph in the paper was by committing a crime against a white person. When Assistant City Editor Railley said he would take a story about an old black man skinning his knee, he was being highly sarcastic.

Clark Schooler was surprised with himself and a little bit angry with himself. Throughout his junior high school and high school years, he had read the Baltimore newspapers virtually every day. It had never dawned on him, in all that time, that there was no news about black people, other than criminal news, in his daily newspaper. That fact became obvious to him, of course, once it was pointed out to him. But for years, he realized, he had been blissfully unaware that any favorable news about African-Americans was being carefully edited out of his hometown papers.

One day Clark was sitting in the Northwestern District police station. Northwestern was located in the center of Baltimore city's black ghetto, a racially segregated section of the city populated only by black people. Flora

Jane Simmons, a black policewoman who handled women's and children's cases in the Northwestern District, came up to Clark and gave him what she thought was a good tip.

"We just arrested a mother and father who, for the past three years, have kept their five children locked in the basement of their house over on McMechen Street," policewoman Simmons explained. "The children have been neglected. They've never been allowed to go to school, or to go out and play with the other children in the neighborhood. One of them was actually chained to his bed for a number of months for being disobedient and trying to escape out of the basement."

Policewoman Simmons showed Clark Schooler a copy of her police report on the incident and allowed him to take all the notes he wanted. The police report included photographs of the children as they appeared when police officers liberated them from their basement prison. Armed with what he thought was a very good story, Clark raced to the *Banner* telephone in the Northwestern District station house and called his editors.

The telephone was answered by Assistant City Editor Frank Railley. In an excited voice, Clark described the incident and suggested that the *Banner* should get a photographer up to McMechen Street to try to get a photograph of the children's basement prison. Frank Railley listened quietly while Clark explained the situation. When Clark finished his animated description of the potential story, Railley said curtly:

"Are these children white or black?"

Having seen the police photographs of the children in their basement prison, Clark quietly replied: "They're black."

Frank Railley's response was pointedly derogatory. "Who cares about a bunch of dirty black kids in a basement?" The assistant city editor then hung up the phone, leaving Clark Schooler standing there with a pile of notes on a story that was never going to get in the *Baltimore Banner.*

Clark often wondered what policewoman Flora Jane Simmons must have thought when she read that afternoon's *Banner* and saw there was no coverage of a story which, if it had involved white children, would have received top local news coverage. Once again, the "message" had been delivered to an educated, talented, caring, and successful black person. Flora Jane Simmons was graphically and directly reminded that she and her people were not of interest to the white community. She and her people did not matter. The news columns of Baltimore's daily newspapers were a world that black people were not permitted to enter unless they committed a dastardly crime.

As a police reporter, Clark Schooler soon learned there were an average of three murders a week in Baltimore. But only those murders that involved white people ever got in the newspaper. It soon became a routine part of Schooler's job to check murder reports to see if the persons involved where white or black. The murders involving white people became stories in the newspaper. The murders involving only black people were ignored.

During the summer of 1957 Clark Schooler helped to cover one of the more famous murder cases in Baltimore history. The story began when two police officers on routine patrol noticed a middle-aged man sitting on a bench in a remote section of Druid Hill Park, a large park in the city. The man was white, looked respectable, and ordinarily would not have been bothered by the police.

From a distance, however, the police officers noticed that the man had a butcher knife and was periodically placing it against his throat, as if he wanted to commit suicide but could not quite get up the courage.

The police officers, unobserved by the man, crept up behind him. Because the man apparently did not hear the police officers coming, the man was quickly overpowered, disarmed of his knife, and taken into custody. The man confessed on the spot to murdering his wife and leaving her body on the floor of the front hallway of their home.

The man was Charles Du Bois, the scion of one of the leading commercial families of Baltimore. His grandfather had founded a plumbing supply business in the 1880s that had grown into one of the largest and most profitable commercial operations in the city. Charles Du Bois was "old money." He and his wife were socially active in the country club set in Baltimore. Their home was a large mansion located in Homeland, an upper middle-class neighborhood just north of downtown Baltimore. Homeland had succeeded in resisting the urban blight and deterioration that had afflicted so many other neighborhoods in the city.

Apparently Charles Du Bois and his wife had been driving home from a dinner at the country club when they had an argument. Upon arriving in the front hall of their home, Mrs. Du Bois had turned and slapped Charles Du Bois across the face. Flying into a rage, Charles Du Bois ran into the kitchen, grabbed a butcher knife, ran back to the front hall, and brutally stabbed Mrs. Du Bois to death. The police report noted that she had more than 50 deep stab wounds in her body.

Both the *Baltimore Banner* and the *Baltimore Beacon* gave the story front page, banner headline, plenty of photographs treatment. The story had everything going for it. There was a socially prominent family, a brutal crime, and, of course, all the participants belonged to the white race. Instantly, public opinion in the city condemned Charles Du Bois and the brutal crime he had committed against his wife. The Du Bois murder quickly became the principal topic of conversation in almost every household in

Baltimore. The prevailing popular view was that Charles Du Bois was headed straight for the electric chair or a life sentence in the Maryland Penitentiary.

Clark Schooler was struck by the power which the news media in Baltimore, particularly the daily newspapers, wielded over this story. He later learned the process is called filtering the news or mediating the news. The news media does not control or make the news, but it definitely chooses the news, shapes the news, and defines the news. With three murders a week in Baltimore, every murder could not be given the front page, banner headline treatment. The news media picked out, for its readers and viewers and listeners, the murders that were important. And this murder was important because of the race, the commercial prominence, and the high social status of the people involved.

Clark Schooler thus came to see himself as a camera lens, an optical instrument through which the readers of the *Baltimore Banner* saw events in the police districts of their city. In the manner of a camera lens, Schooler limited his readers' knowledge of events, selecting for them what was important for them to read and know. As a human camera, Clark focused the attention of his readers on certain subjects and excluded their view from other, in his judgement less important, subjects.

Of course, Clark Schooler was only the first camera lens through which police news in Baltimore was filtered to the pages of the *Banner*. His city editors were a second camera lens through which the news he gathered had to be filtered. Between the two camera lenses, a lot of things happened in the police districts of Baltimore during the summer of 1957 that did not get in the newspaper.

This led to the promulgation of Schooler's First Law of the News Media: It is only important if the news media says it is important. Or, to put it in the vernacular: If it ain't in the newspapers, it didn't happen.

Clark Schooler was assigned by his city editor to cover the Charles Du Bois murder trial. Du Bois was indicted on a charge of second degree murder, which meant he was accused of killing his wife in an impulsive manner rather than a premeditated manner. He had, after all, not cunningly planned to kill his wife. He had knifed her to death spontaneously during a family argument. Testimony in court revealed that Du Bois had become angry with his wife because she was having a love affair with another man. Du Bois had killed her in a jealous rage.

A funny thing happened during the trial. The judge, who happened to live just down the street from Charles Du Bois in the Homeland neighborhood, reduced the charge from second degree murder to manslaughter. The judge took the position that Du Bois had never, in his sane moments, intended to kill his wife. Her death was thus accidental. An expensive team of defense lawyers and a highly-paid defense psychiatrist helped the judge arrive at this somewhat unconventional conclusion. And a very expensive private detective convinced the judge that Mrs. Du Bois had indeed been carrying on an extramarital affair.

Charles Du Bois was found guilty of manslaughter and sentenced to three years in the Maryland Penitentiary. Newspaper reporters covering the trial wrote in the newspaper that he would be out on parole in just two years.

At the same time he was following the Charles Du Bois trial, Clark Schooler had his eye on another trial working its way through the Baltimore City courts. Melvin Washington had come home unexpectedly from work one afternoon and discovered his wife in bed with another man, a neighbor from across the street. A floor installer by trade, Melvin unsheathed his linoleum knife, burst into the bedroom, pulled the neighbor out of the bed, and threatened his wife with the linoleum knife.

She cursed him and slapped him across the face. Melvin then began slashing at her, in a flailing manner, with the knife. He inflicted a multitude of long cuts in her skin that were painful and bloody but definitely not fatal. On one overly energetic slash, Melvin slipped and fell, and the knife punctured the jugular vein in his wife's neck. She bled to death in just the few minutes that it took a Baltimore City ambulance to get to the scene.

Because Melvin Washington, and his wife, and the neighbor were all African-Americans, not one word of this particular murder ever got into the Baltimore newspapers. Melvin Washington was tried and convicted of second degree murder. He was represented by a court-appointed lawyer, who Clark thought did a hasty and lackluster job. No psychiatric testimony was presented by an expensive defense psychiatrist. And there was no private detective to present detailed information about Mrs. Washington's marital infidelity.

The judge did not live in Melvin Washington's neighborhood. The judge did not decide to reduce the charge to manslaughter. Melvin Washington was sentenced to 18 years in the Maryland Penitentiary. No one bothered to note that he would probably be out on parole in just 12 years.

Clark made a mental note that the white man was sentenced to three years for murdering his wife, but the black man got 18 years for essentially the same crime.

In the fall of 1957, Clark Schooler began his graduate education at Johns Hopkins University. He ended his summer job at the *Baltimore Banner*, but not completely. The newspaper published a Sunday morning edition. It carried a large amount of advertising and thus required a great deal of local news to run with the advertising. Clark Schooler was hired to work every Saturday afternoon and evening to help gather and write all that additional local news.

Early in September of 1957, a "public opinion changing" event occurred in American politics. In the city of Little Rock, the capital of the state of Arkansas, the local school board had ordered the racial integration of Central High School, the main high school in Little Rock. But before nine black high school students, called the Little Rock Nine, could enter the previously all-white high school, a mob of segregationist whites formed outside the school building.

The white mob yelled curse words at the black students when they tried to enter the high school. The mob surrounded the automobiles bringing the black students to school, thereby threatening the black students' physical safety. The governor of Arkansas, Orval Faubus, supported racial segregation and refused to order the state police or the Arkansas National Guard to protect the black students and guarantee their safety while attending Central High School.

By refusing to support the peaceful and orderly racial integration of Central High School, Governor Faubus was openly defying a recent decision of the United States Supreme Court. In 1954, the nation's highest court had ruled, unanimously, that racial segregation of public schools was unconstitutional. In this court decision, the controversial *Brown v. Board of Education* decision, the justices concluded that having racially segregated school systems implied that one race was better than the other. As a result, racially segregated schools violated the Constitution's prescription that every citizen of the United States, black or white, receive "equal protection of the laws."

Orval Faubus's refusal to enforce the integration of Central High School in Little Rock presented a difficult problem to President Dwight D. Eisenhower. As president of the United States, it was Eisenhower's job to enforce the laws of the United States. For political reasons, however, Eisenhower did not want to override Governor Faubus and enforce racial integration in Little Rock with raw U.S. Government military power. Eisenhower was aware that the vast majority of white Southerners, similar to Governor Faubus, strongly supported racial segregation. Both President Eisenhower and his political party, the Republicans, would lose support in the white South if Central High School was forcefully integrated by U.S. military forces.

As a brand-new political science graduate student, Clark Schooler was fascinated by the dilemma facing President Eisenhower. The authors of the United States Constitution, meeting in Philadelphia in the summer of 1787, had created a government composed of both a national government and a number of individual state governments. This unique arrangement was called federalism, and both the national and the state governments were viewed as sovereign (having the power to rule). The various powers of government were divided between the national and the state governments. The police power, the power to enforce laws that maintain domestic law and order, was given mainly to the states, not the national government.

President Eisenhower did the logical thing. In the early stages of the Little Rock school crisis, he tried to convince Governor Faubus to use the state police or the Arkansas National Guard to forcefully integrate Central High School. That way, the police power would have been applied at the state level rather than the national level, just as the authors of the United States Constitution intended.

But Governor Faubus refused to act. The mob of white people continued to surround Central High School each morning, thereby preventing the black students from entering the school. The situation was deteriorating rapidly, and the *Brown v. Board of Education* decision clearly was not being enforced in Little Rock, Arkansas.

President Eisenhower was a former Army general. During World War Two, he had commanded all of the military forces of the United States and its allies in Europe. He knew what it was to be "in command," and he knew how to take swift and forceful action when necessary. The situation in Little Rock in 1957 was resolved when Eisenhower ordered regular troops of the United States Army, not the Arkansas National Guard, to take over Central High and racially integrate the school by force.

The entire situation was ready-made for television news. The event was largely visual. Scenes of the white mob surrounding the school building to prevent racial integration gave way to images of U.S. Army paratroopers, bayonets fixed to their rifles, taking command of the situation. The soldiers, moving at a double-time pace, took up positions inside the school and outside on the streets and athletic fields surrounding the school. Under armed guard, the Little Rock Nine were escorted into Central High School. The Army troopers stayed close by the black students all day long to make certain they were not physically harmed in any way.

Clark Schooler was impressed with the decisiveness and thoroughness with which President Eisenhower had sent the United States Army into Little Rock. Eisenhower made it clear that he was acting as commander in chief of the military forces of the United States, a power granted to him in the United States Constitution. Eisenhower specifically stated that he wanted the troops to occupy Central High School and enforce racial integration. Lastly, Eisenhower authorized the use of as many troops and as much equipment as necessary to carry out the mission successfully.

"Thanks to Eisenhower at Little Rock," Clark said in his graduate seminar in American Politics one day, "we now have a script for all future racial disturbances. The courts will order the local schools to be integrated. Mobs of white southerners, often unruly and sometimes overtly violent, will protest the action. The governor, or the mayor, or the police chief, or whoever is in charge of law and order, will decline to forcefully impose racial integration on white Southerners who so clearly do not want it. In the end, one way or another, the president of the United States will have to do what Eisenhower did at Little Rock. Send in the troops and enforce racial integration at the point of a bayonet."

Beau Stevens, a graduate student at Johns Hopkins from Albany, Georgia, immediately questioned Clark Schooler's statement. "President Eisenhower used one part of the U.S. Constitution to violate another part," Stevens argued. "True, as president, Eisenhower is commander in chief of the armed forces. But, under our system of federalism, the state of Arkansas has sovereign power over its own territory, particularly where police powers are concerned. The nation's Founders, who wrote the U.S. Constitution, intended for the states to work out these kind of local police problems themselves. Eisenhower should have shown more respect for our constitutionally-mandated federalism and kept the U.S. Army out of it."

Beau Stevens was known among his fellow graduate students as "the sane Southerner." It was a title in which Beau actually took a great deal of pride. Unlike most white Southerners, Beau supported racial integration and saw the inevitability of an end to legalized racial segregation in the American South. But, like many educated and intelligent white Southerners, Beau had found justification in the United States Constitution for the individual states, rather than the national government in Washington, D.C., to be the appropriate governmental units to end racial segregation in the United States.

"President Eisenhower should have read the *Brown* ruling more carefully," Beau continued, getting ever more committed to his position. "The Supreme Court said that racial integration in public schools should proceed with 'all deliberate speed.' Eisenhower could have argued that it was too soon to integrate Central High School in Little Rock. He could have slowed the process down. He could have argued the court's words 'all deliberate speed' did not mean 'right now.' That way he could have given Governor Faubus and the people in Little Rock more time to work things out."

At that moment, Candy Kaufmann, a graduate student from New York city and a party activist in the Democratic Party, decided to join the academic fray. "I think President Eisenhower was too slow in acting at Little Rock," Candy opined. "He let hours and days go by during which the black students trying to integrate Central High School were terrorized and intimidated and belittled by the white mob. At times, the black students were in physical danger of being roughed up or even killed in some accidental fashion by all those crazed white Southerners. President Eisenhower did not act dynamically or forcefully at Little Rock. He acted only after Governor Faubus, by refusing to enforce law and order at the state level, left Eisenhower no choice but to act. President Eisenhower sent in the troops because he had to, not because he wanted to."

The professor guiding the seminar was Michael Middleton, a recognized national expert on United States voting behavior. Professor Middleton joined Clark Schooler in defending Eisenhower's actions at Little Rock. "It's true this is a federal state," Middleton pontificated, "with powers divided between a national government in Washington and a number of individual state governments. But what about the supremacy clause of the Constitution. It states very specifically: 'The Constitution and laws of the United States shall be the supreme law of the land.' Doesn't that take away completely Governor Faubus's right to defy the Supreme Court decision calling for racial integration of the public schools?"

Beau Stevens refused to back down, even in the face of Professor Middleton and the supremacy clause of the United States Constitution. "The Constitution calls for both national rights and states' rights," Stevens argued. "The Founders did not intend to create an all-powerful national government in Washington, D.C. They wanted some of the powers reserved to the states, particularly the police power. By sending U.S. troops into Arkansas, President Eisenhower upset the more or less even balance between the national and state governments that the Founders had in mind."

Professor Middleton felt constrained to further defend President Eisenhower's record on the issue of states' rights. "Eisenhower has been very careful," Middleton noted, "to only enforce racial integration where he clearly has the Constitutional power to do so. He racially integrated the United States Government bureaucracy with all the U.S. Government jobs because, as president, he is the executive head of the government. He integrated restaurants and snack bars in Washington, D.C., because the nation's capital is run by the national government and not by the states. He appointed the first black person to the White House staff because that clearly is his appointment to make. Eisenhower has been careful to act only in those areas where national law gives him the power and authority to act."

Middleton summed up his argument as forcefully as he could. "Eisenhower sent the troops into Little Rock because, in the *Brown v. Board of Education* decision, the Supreme Court made it national law that public schools have to be racially integrated. And President Eisenhower interpreted the phrase 'all deliberate speed' to mean sooner rather than later."

A true as well as sane Southerner, Beau Stevens continued to argue his point. "This was the first use of U.S. troops against the South since the Civil War," Stevens blurted out. "The United States Government militarily invaded one of its constituent sovereign states and imposed a law that the vast majority of Arkansas citizens strongly oppose. It was too much. It was a gross abuse of national government power."

"That it may have been," Clark Schooler chimed in, "but it accomplished something I believe is very important. Black people in America now know that, in the end, the American president will come to the aid of blacks and enforce school integration in the South. President Eisenhower has put the full power of the U.S. presidency behind the school integration movement. That is going to embolden American blacks in their quest for more equal treatment throughout the entire southern United States."

The graduate seminar ended, as most graduate seminars do, with nothing finally decided. But that day's discussions had confirmed in Clark Schooler's mind his favorite rule for analyzing human behavior: Judge people and politicians by their behavior, not by what they say or what others say about them. As far as Clark was concerned, Beau Stevens, Candy Kaufmann, and Professor Middleton could argue all day about President Eisenhower's motives at Little Rock and what other people were writing and saying about Eisenhower at Little Rock. To Clark, the important thing was that President Eisenhower had taken the appropriate action. All the palaver about motives and intentions and true feelings was just wasted time. "Judge people by how they act, not by what they say, or by what others say about them," was a rule of human behavior that Clark Schooler relied on constantly.

After President Eisenhower sent U.S. soldiers into Little Rock, Clark Schooler detected a new attitude on race relations on the part of his city editors at the *Baltimore Banner*. There was somewhat more willingness to pay attention to black people, particularly if those black people were aggressively picketing and demonstrating for African-American civil rights.

The impact of Little Rock was clarified for Clark at a subsequent graduate political science seminar at Johns Hopkins University. George Gallup, the famous public opinion pollster, was the guest lecturer at the seminar. "It is events," Gallup said, "that have more effect on public opinion than any other factor. Depressions. Wars. Important scientific discoveries. It is these kind of concrete events that create major shifts in public opinion. The millions of press releases ground out by the legions of public relations personnel have very little effect on public opinion when compared to real events."[1]

Little Rock had been a graphic national event, Clark realized, that began changing public opinion throughout the eastern and western United States. Little Rock even had changed, ever so slightly, the opinions of his city editors. The result was the promulgation, in Clark Schooler's mind, of Schooler's Second Law of the News Media: Events, not press conferences and press releases, are the major determinants of public opinion.

In The Interim

The news media are as influential in the 2000s as in the 1950s and 1960s. But there have been some changes. The three major television networks, ABC, CBS, and NBC, no longer dominate the news as they did in Clark Schooler's time. The rise of alternate news sources, such as cable television and internet web sites, provide a wider variety of means for politicians and political pundits to put their ideas before the American people.

Daily newspapers are still important sources of information for the public, but circulation and readership are generally holding steady or declining. Daily newspapers remain the main interpreters of state and local government news for those who are interested in the state and local political scene.

The news media continue to be the major filters that decide what news is presented to the public. As a key link between the public and government, the news media are sometimes referred to as a Fourth Branch of Government.

The unfavorable treatment of minority groups that Clark Schooler found in the Baltimore newspapers in the 1950s and 1960s is long gone. In the 2000s, with inexpensive desk top publishing and near-instantaneous e-mail communication, almost any new political idea or emerging political cause can find its way into some form of print.

But other aspects of American society continue to harbor racial prejudice. Police departments have been accused of racial profiling, stopping and checking higher proportions of African-American and Hispanic persons and looking for signs of criminal activity. Sadly, some forms of racial discrimination, often very subtle forms, are still evident in American life.

CHAPTER 2

MASS MOVEMENTS:
CONFRONTING THE ESTABLISHED ORDER

One Saturday afternoon in 1959, Clark Schooler was sent up to the Monarch, one of the first regional shopping centers constructed in the Baltimore area. The Monarch was located in northwest Baltimore. It was immediately surrounded by all-white neighborhoods. Just a few blocks away, however, was the outer edge of the largest black community in Baltimore, a black community that was constantly growing larger and progressively expanding into nearby white areas.

In Baltimore at that time, there was a chain of small restaurants called the White Dinner Plate. These restaurants all had tables and chairs, booths, and a long counter with stools. The food was nourishing, occasionally tasted good, and was quite modestly priced. A wide range of social classes ate at the White Dinner Plate. The restaurants were conveniently located in a variety of places around town, and everyone from a bum to a businessman could get a decent meal there in a relatively short time.

There was a brand-new White Dinner Plate in the brand-new Monarch Shopping Center. Similar to all the other White Dinner Plates, it had a white tile floor, white-painted walls, white tables, white counter tops, and white china. The overall color theme was pure white. And something else was all-white. In the traditional manner of restaurants and snack bars in the American South, the White Dinner Plate did not serve black people.

Baltimore and Maryland, of course, were not technically in the South. During the Civil War, Maryland had been a Border State, a state immediately adjacent to the South but which had remained in the Union during the Civil War. In the years following the Civil War, however, Maryland had chosen to follow the Southern example, rather than the Northern example, and segregate the two races. That meant that most restaurants, snack bars, hotels, motels, amusement parks, and swimming pools were open only to whites and were strictly off-limits to blacks.

Clark Schooler's boss at the *Baltimore Banner* was a grizzled city editor named Terry Songman. Middle-aged and slightly overweight, Terry Songman had the gruff but sympathetic manner that cub reporters expect from a city editor.

"Get right up to the Monarch," Terry Songman said to Clark Schooler, a note of urgency in his voice. "A group of protesters is sitting at the tables and demanding to be served. The White Dinner Plate won't serve them, and the protesters are refusing to leave until they do get served. Apparently some of the protesters are black, but others are white."

At that point, Terry Songman apparently detected Clark Schooler's enthusiasm for getting to cover a story about black people and write it up for the *Banner*. Terry Songman smiled at Clark, and then laid it on the line.

"Look, kid," the city editor explained, "all we want you to do is keep an eye on things. We're not going to do a story unless there is a riot, or something like a riot. Right now its pretty quiet, but we need to have someone up there if it doesn't stay quiet."

Clark Schooler jumped in his car, a 1951 Ford Victoria hardtop convertible, and drove out to northwest Baltimore. After parking his car in the shopping center parking lot, he walked into the center and had no trouble finding the White Dinner Plate. There was a small group of pickets, about six in number, walking up and down in front of the restaurant, quietly holding signs calling for racial integration of the White Dinner Plate. The pickets were nicely racially integrated. About half of them were white and the others were black. The pickets were making no effort to prevent anyone from entering the White Dinner Plate to get a meal.

Inside the White Dinner Plate, eight protesters were sitting down trying to get served some food. Four were sitting in a booth, and four others were sitting at a table. These protesters also were racially integrated. Some were white and some were black. A number of them, confident they would not be served, had brought along books or magazines and were quietly getting a little reading done.

The management at the White Dinner Plate was simply ignoring the protesters, not serving them anything to eat but, at the same time, not making any attempt to physically force them to leave. A small number of white persons, many fewer than you would expect on a busy Saturday afternoon, were sitting elsewhere in the restaurant eating their food. These white patrons appeared to be going out of their way not to notice the racial protest taking place near them in the restaurant.

A white Baltimore City policeman, in uniform and armed with his police revolver, was standing just outside the restaurant door. Similar to Clark Schooler, the policeman had been sent to simply keep an eye on things. He was bored. And he was only too happy to answer Clark's questions about what was going on.

"This is the third Saturday in a row that we've had this," the policeman said. "The protesters come promptly at 10 A.M. and quit about 4 P.M. Because this is a shopping center, the restaurant mainly does a lunch and afternoon snack business, so the demonstration is designed to drive away patrons at the busiest time of the day."

"They're quiet, though," the policeman said of the protesters. "The picketers are not trying to talk to or interfere with any of the people trying to get into the White Dinner Plate. The protesters are handing out a leaflet, but only to people who come up and ask for one."

"But it's working," the policeman concluded. "A lot of people are walking up as if they are headed to the White Dinner Plate to get something to eat. Then they see the pickets and their signs, and the people just stop dead in their tracks. They look things over for a while, wondering what to do, and then most of them walk away. I guess they figure they'll get a meal someplace else today. Who needs the hassle?"

One of the picketers outside the White Dinner Plate took notice of Clark Schooler talking to the policeman and writing down what the officer had to say. The picketer was a young woman. She was white. In terms of age, she looked as though she was in her mid-twenties. She was nicely dressed in a wool sweater and a Scotch plaid skirt. When Clark Schooler had finished talking to the policeman and was just standing there thinking of what, if anything, to do next, the woman approached him. She asked Clark politely: "Are you a newspaper reporter?"

Clark answered her inquiry in a somewhat smart-alecky tone. "How could you tell?"

"Well, it's Saturday," the woman said. "Most men don't go shopping on Saturday dressed in a suit coat and necktie. Also, most men don't talk to a police officer and take notes on what the officer has to say."

The woman's response had been friendly enough but very rational and businesslike. Clark sensed that she was very serious about what she was doing that day and was in no mood to fool around.

"I'm surprised to see a reporter here," she said. "The newspapers haven't bothered to cover any of our other demonstrations and protests. Would you mind telling me who you work for?"

"You should have said 'whom you work for,'" Clark said spontaneously. Then he added, "I work for the *Banner*."

"Actually," the young woman shot back, "I should have said 'for whom you work.'" Clark and the young woman had successfully demonstrated to each other that both of them knew something about how to speak and write the English language.

Clark quickly returned to his journalistic duties. He asked: "Are you the person in charge of this demonstration?"

"Yes, I am," the young woman replied. "I represent CORE, the Congress of Racial Equality. This is an official CORE demonstration."

Apparently the young woman wanted to be interviewed by the press, because she was willingly answering Clark's questions with some measure of enthusiasm. Clark asked: "What are you trying to accomplish here?"

"We are trying to racially integrate the White Dinner Plate at the Monarch Shopping Center," the young woman replied. "CORE's goal is to integrate restaurants, snack bars, lunch counters, and public rest rooms throughout the North, the Border States, and the upper South."

Clark interrupted her oration on the rationale for CORE with a quick question. "Why just the upper South? Why doesn't CORE try to integrate the entire South?"

"We know better than to attempt that," the young woman replied. The tone of her voice suggested she considered Clark naive for asking such a question. "We know better than to go into the Deep South. Places such as Georgia, South Carolina, Alabama, and Mississippi are just too dangerous. Furthermore, our nonviolent techniques are not likely to be successful in 'The Heart of Dixie.'" She said "The Heart of Dixie" with just a touch of malevolent sarcasm.

"So you're doing the easy part first," said Clark Schooler, "and I guess Baltimore and Maryland get classified as the easy part."

"There is an invisible and indeterminate line across the United States," the young woman responded. "Above that line, blacks can be served alongside whites in public places. Below, that line, everything is racially segregated. It's called the Jim Crow line. CORE is dedicated to pushing the Jim Crow line southward as quickly as reasonably possible, and right now the Jim Crow line sits just a little bit north of the city of Baltimore."

There was a pause in the conversation. Clark Schooler looked away from the young woman and at the pickets slowly walking up and down in front of the White Dinner Plate. It was getting to be later in the day, and the number of people shopping at the Monarch was beginning to diminish. There was a strange peacefulness to the scene, not at all what one would expect during a civil rights demonstration. Clark looked back at the young woman.

"Right now," he said, "there isn't much of a story here. What would happen if the manager of the White Dinner Plate asked the police to forcefully remove your CORE demonstrators? What if your people who are occupying the booth and the table inside the restaurant were told by the police to get out? What would happen then?"

"Our people are highly trained and know just what to do," the young woman replied. "If there's violence, they know how to curl up their bodies and put their arms around their heads so as to reduce the effects of a physical attack. No matter how hard someone might hit them, our demonstrators are taught to never strike back. CORE is nonviolent. But at the same time we are very determined."

"We try to be smart about it," the young woman went on. "Notice that only half of our demonstrators are breaking the law by occupying a booth or table inside the restaurant. If they get arrested, the people outside the restaurant, the picketers, can arrange for a lawyer to come and bail them out of jail. If the people inside are beaten up by segregationist toughs, the people outside can see to their medical needs and get them to the hospital if necessary."

While the young woman was talking, Clark Schooler caught himself looking at her left hand to see if she was wearing an engagement ring or a wedding ring. When she talked, the young woman's face became very animated. Clark tended to be drawn to talkative and animated young women.

Clark saw no engagement or wedding ring on her left hand, but he also suddenly remembered that he was working for the *Banner* that afternoon and was not at a social event. He quickly tried to assume a very professional and disinterested tone while talking with the young woman.

"Speaking about breaking the law," Clark said, "why do you think you have the right to break the trespass laws of the great state of Maryland? The owner of the White Dinner Plate has the right in this state to refuse service to anyone, for any reason, and he could get the police in here to enforce that law if he wanted to."

Clark had no difficulty making the private property argument for defending racial segregation in restaurants and other privately-owned properties that the general public patronizes. He had heard the argument made many times in his graduate school American Politics seminar by Beau Stevens of Albany, Georgia.

With this question, the young woman's tone and manner changed completely. She softened her stance, and lowered her voice, and looked Clark straight in the eye as she answered him.

"It's wrong," she said, "to put 'Keep Out' signs on restaurants and snack bars and have those signs apply to only one group of people. It's so demeaning to black people to have large parts of their world marked off as places where, because of their skin color, they cannot go. Have you ever thought about how long the list of segregated places is in Baltimore? Blacks can't go to restaurants, swimming pools, skating rinks, country clubs, movie theaters. They can't go to Ford's Theater in downtown Baltimore to see a Broadway play. They can't go to the Lyric Theater to hear the Baltimore Symphony. They are reminded of their second-class status everywhere they look and everywhere they go. It's unfair. It's unkind. It's immoral."

Listening to this impassioned plea, Clark Schooler was struck by the depth of the young woman's commitment to the cause of black civil rights. He also was aware of something else. When available young men and available young women talk and socialize with each other, a sense of elation and a great feeling of well-being and happiness can build within them. Clark was suddenly getting that feeling, on his part at least, with this young woman. As he and she had talked that afternoon, their conversation had accelerated and become animated in a manner typical of a man and woman who like each other.

But any thoughts Clark Schooler might have had of asking her for a date were quickly ruled out. Clark was, after all, giving the young woman a raw deal. He had been talking to her for almost an hour, pretending the whole time that he would be writing a story for the Sunday paper about CORE and the civil rights protest at the Monarch.

Since there had been no violence, not even harsh words, there was no way that even one word of the event would get in the next day's *Banner*. Even if Clark wrote such a story, his city editors would make sure it never saw the light of day.

The next morning, when the young woman searched the pages of the *Banner* for the story, she would find nothing. She and her white and black CORE compatriots were going to receive one more rejection. There would be no coverage in the Baltimore newspapers.

The sun was getting low in the western sky when Clark said goodbye to the young woman and walked away from the CORE demonstration at the Monarch Shopping Center. He turned back one time and saw that she was watching him leave. She did not avert her eyes or try to look away. It seemed to Clark she had a disappointed look to her. He could not tell what her look meant. Was she disappointed because perhaps she had failed to convince him of the importance of her civil rights demonstration and her political cause? Or was she disappointed because he had not asked her out?

Nothing ever came of the CORE demonstration at the Monarch. The manager of the White Dinner Plate shrewdly let the demonstrators continue to sit in his restaurant without having them arrested. There was no violence, and therefore no newspaper or television coverage. Clark never heard for certain, but he assumed the Congress of Racial Equality eventually gave up on that particular protest and quietly accepted, at least temporarily, defeat. This much was for certain. The White Dinner Plate stayed all-white.

Shortly thereafter, on a hot summer's evening, Clark Schooler was once again covering the police districts, this night on the south and west side of Baltimore city. By this time, Clark felt something of a kinship with the black community in Baltimore. For almost two years, he had driven and walked through their neighborhoods, searching out the facts on a variety of crime stories. He had seen black families sitting on the white marble steps of their brick row houses, enjoying a street life unknown to white families living in large, free-standing homes in the Baltimore suburbs.

This night was a particularly hot one, and it seemed that almost every black family in Baltimore had ventured out on to the sidewalks and into the streets to escape the blast furnace effect of staying indoors. Many adults had set up folding lawn chairs on the sidewalk and were sitting around chatting. Some children were playing baseball in the middle of the street, while other children were playing hopscotch and jumping rope on the sidewalk. The entire scene was lively yet peaceful. By forcing so many people out onto the sidewalk and street, the hot weather had given a genuine community feel to the black neighborhoods of Baltimore.

Three black girls, from ten to twelve years of age, were jumping rope on the sidewalk. Two of them were sisters. The third girl was one of their cousins. Two of the girls were holding and turning the rope while the third girl was jumping in the center.

An automobile, driven by a man who had imbibed much too much alcohol, came rolling down the street. He either lost control of the car, or passed out at the steering wheel, because the car veered away from the center of the street, climbed the curb, and roared across the sidewalk where the three girls were jumping rope.

As fate would have it, the car completely missed one of the girls who was turning the jump rope. It ran head-on into the girl jumping rope, however, and then, with the girl pinned to the front of the car, smashed into the wall of a house. In a split second, the car bounced off the wall and struck a glancing blow to the girl holding the other end of the rope. The automobile came to an abrupt stop when it slid sideways into a lamp post.

Both of the girls hit by the car were badly injured. The one who had been jumping rope was unconscious but breathing. The one who had been turning the rope and took a glancing blow from the car was covered with blood and screaming and crying loudly. Ambulances were called, arrived on the scene quickly, and both girls were rushed to the emergency room at West Baltimore General Hospital.

Clark Schooler arrived at West Baltimore General shortly after the ambulance did. As he walked through the waiting room outside the emergency room, he noticed that it was filled with about 20 African-Americans of all ages and all sexes. Clark quickly divined that these were the parents, other close relatives, and neighbors of the two injured girls. Exercising his prerogative as a newspaper reporter, Clark negotiated his way through the crowd of people and then walked through the door that led from the waiting room into the emergency room.

Clark took one step into the emergency room, stopped, and surveyed the scene. One of the black girls was lying on an operating table. She was receiving what looked like the best attention medical science could provide. One doctor and three nurses worked quickly, quietly, and efficiently to save her life. She was receiving a blood transfusion, and a variety of other tubes, wires, and machines were hooked up to her body. The doctor and the nurses spoke politely but urgently to each other, reporting on her condition and giving and getting instructions.

Clark had barely stepped into the emergency room when a high-ranking Baltimore City police officer, a lieutenant, walked past him and entered the waiting room. The people in the waiting room, seeing his uniform and knowing his position of authority, crowded up to him and asked him how the two girls were doing.

The police lieutenant raised his hands in the air. The motion both warned the people to stay back and, at the same time, quieted them down. "The doctors and nurses are doing all they can for the girls," the police lieutenant said. Then he looked at the crowd of people and added, "I need a member of Roberta Monroe's family, but not one of her parents, to come back here for a minute."

A black woman, about 40-years-old, stepped forward and told the police lieutenant that she was Roberta Monroe's aunt. The woman was nicely attired, in a dress, stockings, and high-heel shoes. Clark Schooler speculated that she had been getting dressed for a dinner, a dance, or a party when she had received word that her niece had been injured in an auto crash.

The police lieutenant took the woman into the emergency room. Before he could say anything, the woman said, in a concerned voice, "I hope Roberta's going to be all right." The police lieutenant turned, looked at her, and said matter-of-factly, "I am sorry to be the person to tell you this, but we think she is dead."

"Oh, no! Oh, no!" said the woman, bursting into tears. The police lieutenant gave her some time to absorb this gruesome news and get herself together. Then the police lieutenant looked her in the eyes and said: "I called you back here to identify Roberta's body. You can understand that I didn't want her parents to have to do that."

The police lieutenant then stepped up to a large green curtain hanging on a long curtain rod. He quickly pulled the curtain aside, revealing the dead body of a young black girl lying on an operating table. Her eyes were still open. Her arms and legs were somewhat askew on the table top. Apparently an emergency room doctor had pronounced her dead and then rushed off to see what could be done to help the other little girl, who was still alive. No effort had been to made to arrange the dead girl's arms and legs in an orderly manner.

"It's her! It's her! It's Roberta," the woman gasped. The tears started all over again as she looked away from the painful sight.

"She died in the ambulance on the way down here," the police lieutenant said. He then added somewhat brusquely, "Now, I want you to look at her one more time and be absolutely certain it is Roberta Monroe."

"I don't need to look," the woman blurted out. "It's Roberta!" But the woman responded to the police lieutenant's request, looked one more time, and then nodded her head up-and-down. The woman said softly, almost inaudibly, but with finality, "It's her."

The police lieutenant once again looked the woman in the eyes. "Now," he said, "you have to go back to the waiting room and tell Roberta's parents that she's dead."

"I can't do that," the woman said.

"You have to," the police lieutenant replied. "It will be better for them if they get the news from you rather than from me."

The woman accepted this particular bit of logic. She walked back with the police lieutenant to the waiting room. As she came through the door, the entire roomful of people turned in her direction. A voice cried out: "How's my Roberta?" It was obviously the voice of the girl's mother. "Oh, Annie," said the woman, again breaking into tears, "Roberta's dead."

The waiting room suddenly became a place of furious action and powerful emotion. Men and women stamped the floor in agony as they absorbed the news that the little girl had been killed in the accident. Some of them pounded the walls with their fists. There was a chorus of anguished words. "No!" "No!" "Oh, Lordy!" "Why, Lord?"

Clark Schooler had stood and watched the entire incident from beginning to end. It had not affected him emotionally at all until the African-American aunt had returned to the waiting room and told the African-American parents, relatives, and neighbors that the little girl had been killed. The room had exploded with the physical manifestations of pain and despair. There was foot stamping, fist pounding, and cries of anguish filled the air. As this was happening, certain ideas penetrated Clark's consciousness in a very powerful fashion.

Black people have and can freely express emotions.

Black people love their children and experience great depths of pain when their children die young.

Clark Schooler felt suddenly ignorant, unaware, and insensitive. Of course part of him, the intellectual part, the part that had gone to college in New England and become a racial integrationist, knew that black people had the same emotions as white people. But Clark had just been put in touch with another part of himself, a part he had not known about, that emotionally put black people in a completely different category than white people.

Simultaneously with these thoughts, Clark Schooler could feel himself becoming furious with himself. He realized that he had bought the myth. Raised in a racially segregated city, the product of a racially segregated school system, Clark had unintentionally absorbed the idea, pushed relentlessly by segregationists, that black people were different from white people. It was the stereotype that black people were happy-go-lucky, that black people did not have a care in the world, and that black people did not think or feel the same things that white people thought and felt.

Clark Schooler recognized, in this moment of emotional awakening, that he was consciously and intellectually a racial integrationist. Subconsciously and emotionally, however, he had just faced the reality that there still were elements of racial segregation in his outlook on life and his view of the world. At least, those elements were there up until this particular evening of his life.

Clark realized he had achieved racial integration of the mind. He still had some work to do on racial integration of the heart.

The other little girl was badly injured in the car accident, but she did not die. Clark Schooler telephoned the story to the *Banner*. As ever, Clark was asked by an assistant city editor whether the story was white or black. Clark said the three little girls were black, but he got up the courage to point out to his editor that two little girls being hit by a runaway automobile while jumping rope on the sidewalk was a very newsworthy story.

The assistant city editor put the story on the first local page of the next day's newspaper. A photographer was sent to West Baltimore General Hospital the next morning to get a photograph of the injured black girl in her hospital bed. Clark secured a photo of the little girl who was killed, Roberta, from her parents. The newspaper also printed that photograph.

To Clark Schooler's knowledge, it was the first time in history that photographs of African-Americans, except for wanted criminals, were printed in the *Baltimore Banner*.

Clark never found out why the *Banner* suddenly changed policy and began running news photographs of black persons who were not criminals.

Perhaps his city editors, racial segregationists though they might be, detected the changes in race relations that were in the wind in the late 1950s. Or perhaps it was just the high news value of little girls jumping rope and being killed and injured by a careening automobile.

The outright refusal of Southern and Border State newspapers and television stations to cover black people, except as criminals, was known as the Cotton Curtain. Suddenly, in the summer of 1959, the Cotton Curtain lifted in the city of Baltimore. The *Baltimore Beacon* and Baltimore's local television stations followed the *Banner* in giving appropriate coverage to major non-crime news events in Baltimore's African-American community.

Clark Schooler realized that a change in public opinion had helped to inspire newspaper and television news editors in Baltimore to start reporting news about black people. Out of this change, Clark Schooler developed his Seeing-Eye Dog Theory of United States Journalism.

"The news reporter," Clark would tell anyone willing to listen, "responds to the public and its wishes as well as to his or her own judgement about the news value of a story. The public is like a blind man, needing the help of a seeing-eye dog to get him where he wants to go. The press is the seeing-eye dog. Just as the seeing-eye dog gets its orders from the blind man, the press gets its orders from the public. The dog then decides what the blind man needs to know, and in the same way the press decides what the public needs to know."

"Many things happen as the blind man and the seeing-eye dog go down the street," Clark liked to say. "An automobile parks at the curb. A hot dog vendor and his hot dog wagon roll by. The dog sees these things. But the dog does not communicate these things to the blind man unless these things get in the way of the blind man and the dog getting to the blind man's chosen destination. In short, the seeing-eye dog chooses for the blind man what the blind man needs to know to get where the blind man wants to go."

"And so it is with the journalist," Clark would continue. "The public tells the press how it wants to be informed, to be entertained, to be touched emotionally, but the public leaves the decision as to exactly what the public reads in the newspaper or sees on television to the individual members of the press."

"The journalist picks and chooses information for the public," Clark would conclude, "exactly the way a seeing-eye dog picks and chooses information for the blind man, but never forget that it is the blind man, and not the dog, who makes the overall decision as to where the two of them are going to go."

On February 1, 1960, four black college students decided to do something about racial segregation in the restaurants and snack bars of Greensboro, North Carolina. After talking among themselves much of the previous night about the problem of legally enforced racial separation in the United States, the students walked from their college campus to a drug store in downtown Greensboro. They sat down on four stools at the snack bar in the drug store and refused to leave without being served.

The four demonstrators, all males, were students at North Carolina Agricultural and Technical College, an all-black school. They acted spontaneously. They did not bother to tell the news media, either in Greensboro or nationally, about what they intended to do. As a result, there was no television coverage of what quickly became an historic event. It was the first college student sit-in at a restaurant or snack bar in a college town.

There was newspaper coverage, however, and the idea of college student sit-ins rapidly spread to black and white college and university campuses throughout the nation. In the ensuing year, thousands of college-age youngsters of both sexes and all races organized and participated in sit-in demonstrations. A new civil rights organization, the Student Nonviolent Coordinating Committee, was formed to organize sit-in demonstrations in college and university towns throughout the South. This student organization soon was called by its initials, SNCC, which were pronounced Snick.

The four black students in Greensboro had not invented the sit-in demonstration. The Congress of Racial Equality (CORE) had been staging sit-ins to protest racial segregation since the 1940s. But CORE demonstrators were adults and easier to ignore. When the sit-in demonstrations began to involve college students, particularly large numbers of white college students, the news media began to give the protests extensive coverage. The coverage got very extensive when, as often happened, white segregationists would verbally taunt and physically assault the students who were staging the sit-in demonstration.

By the time of the 1961-1962 school year, Clark Schooler was one of the senior teaching assistants at Johns Hopkins University. In return for free tuition for his graduate school education, Clark taught "discussion sections" of major courses that were mainly instructed by the leading professors at Johns Hopkins. Although the graduate school was coeducational, the undergraduates were all men. But there was a women's college nearby, Goucher College, and Clark taught some undergraduate political science courses there as well.

There also was an African-American institution of higher learning in Baltimore. Morgan State College was a well established and highly regarded black college located in the northeastern section of Baltimore city. Morgan State had a large and attractive campus. It was landscaped with acres of green grass and many shrubs and trees. There were a number of substantial stone buildings, all of them accented with white-painted wooden trim.

Morgan State also had a nearby movie theater called the Montebello Theater. The theater was named for the neighborhood where it was located. The neighborhood was named for a nearby lake, a City water reservoir, called Lake Montebello.

Unfortunately for the students at Morgan State College, the Montebello Theater limited its clientele to white persons only. When Morgan State students wanted to go to the movies, they had to drive in their cars or ride the bus to one of the all-black movie theaters closer to downtown Baltimore.

Following the example set by the four young men in Greensboro, an example being emulated by college students all over the South, a group of black students from Morgan State College began a "line-in" at the Montebello Theater. The black students got in line to buy a ticket to the movie. Then they refused to step aside when the ticket seller refused to sell them a ticket. The Montebello Theater's ownership responded by calling the Baltimore City police and having the protesting students arrested and carted off to the City Jail in downtown Baltimore.

Men students from Johns Hopkins and women students from Goucher College, almost all of them white, quickly joined the Morgan State students, almost all of them black, in the line-in at the Montebello Theater. By the time Clark Schooler arrived on the scene, there was a line of more than 300 students stretching away from the theater box office out into the parking lot.

The Baltimore City police were politely, carefully, but ever so systematically arresting the students, white as well as black, when the students reached the ticket office. The white students were being arrested because, by standing in the long line of protesters, they were preventing the regular customers of the theater from being able to buy tickets and get into the theater. This was deemed to be denying the owners of the Montebello Theater the full use of their property, so all the students, no matter what their race, were being arrested and charged with trespassing on private property.

Clark Schooler had been sent to cover the story by the *Banner*. There was a festive atmosphere among the students waiting in the theater line, particularly the white students. They had no concern that being arrested might put them in physical danger or could result in their having a damaging criminal record. The fashionable place to be at that moment was in the line-in at the Montebello Theater demonstrating for civil rights. Clark quickly learned from the students that they were totally committed to their cause and enjoying every minute of it.

The arrested students were being carted off to City Jail in cruising patrol wagons. These were large panel trucks with barred windows and externally locked rear doors that were used to haul prisoners from the place where they were arrested to jail. In the daily language of Baltimore City police officers, the vehicles were referred to as "cruisin' 'trol" wagons. As soon as each vehicle was filled with arrested students, it would pull away from the movie theater parking lot amid good natured cheering from the not-yet-arrested demonstrators.

On the scene also were the three television stations in Baltimore and a reporter from the *Baltimore Beacon*. The whine of the television camera motors was incessant, as was the prattle of television reporters interviewing virtually everyone they could drag before their cameras. Periodically one could hear the click of a still camera as a photographer sought to capture exactly the right images for the next edition of a newspaper. One radio station, WFBR, was doing periodic news broadcasts live from the cement steps in front of the Montebello Theater.

Clark Schooler marveled at the scene. Where had all the cameras and reporters been some four years ago when CORE staged its sit-in demonstration at the White Dinner Plate in the Monarch Shopping Center? What had changed that made a civil rights demonstration a nothing story one day and, three short years later, the biggest story in town?

The *Beacon* reporter covering the Montebello Theater line-in was Roy Roost, a newspaper writer who only covered police stories when they had an unusual or extra dramatic angle to them. Roy was a good friend as well as a professional colleague of Clark Schooler. The two men discussed the fact that suddenly, for no apparent reason, civil rights sit-in demonstrations had become a top news story, not just in Baltimore but all over the nation.

"It's phenomenal," Roy Roost was saying. "We've got two reporters and three photographers on this story. I'm covering the demonstration here at the theater. A woman from the business section is getting the reaction of the Montebello theater ownership. She's also getting opinions from the Chamber of Commerce. The *Beacon* is all over this story."

"It's all because of those four black college students down in Greensboro," Clark responded. "They are the guys who gave this phase of the civil rights movement its critical mass."

"Critical mass," said Roy Roost quizzically. "What does critical mass have to do with it?"

"I can see that this is my opportunity to win another convert to my Atomic Theory of Mass Movements," Clark said playfully but with the serious intention of seeking another convert to the theory.

Roy Roost had spent some time sitting around Baltimore City police stations listening to a variety of Clark Schooler's theories about politics, journalism, and the nature of humanity. It was as good a way as any to pass the minutes and hours while waiting for new developments in a major crime story. Roy Roost relaxed his stance, put down his reporter's notebook, and prepared himself to hear what Clark Schooler had to say.

"You know how an atomic explosion takes place," Clark began. "Little chunks of uranium aren't dangerous at all when they are lying around in different places. But get enough of those chunks together in one place and there is a critical mass. The result of a critical mass is a chain reaction. The little chunks of uranium all start reacting with each other and, boom, there's an atomic explosion."

Roy Roost listened to this quasi-scientific explanation of an atomic explosion and said simply: "I think those little chunks of uranium you referred to are called atoms."

"You're starting to get it," Clark lectured on. "After Greensboro, there suddenly were so many civil rights demonstrators and so many newspaper reporters and so many television cameras that the entire situation reached critical mass and a chain reaction was set off. Here, before your eyes, in the parking lot of the Montebello Theater, is the Baltimore city version of the atomic explosion that started, relatively quietly, in Greensboro."

"I have one problem with your Atomic Theory of Mass Movements," Roy Roost said. "Greensboro eventually brought a new kind of uranium into the mix. The new kind of uranium was white college students. It was the presence of white college students that really got things going after Greensboro, and it's white college students who are making these demonstrations so newsworthy here today. How does your theory account for that?"

Roy Roost was smirking at Clark Schooler as he deliver his critique and question. Trying to debunk the various theories propounded by Clark Schooler was something Roy Roost relished doing. He criticized Schooler's theories with the same good natured attitude with which Clark Schooler propounded them.

"We have adjusted the theory for the white college students," Clark Schooler replied, thinking fast and pretending he had dealt with the question before when actually he had not. Thanks to an instant inspiration, Clark further perfected his theory while answering Roy Roost's question. Clark said:

"Have you heard of this new stuff they're developing for making nuclear bombs? It's called plutonium. It's supposed to be more powerful than plain old uranium. It gets to critical mass faster and produces a faster and bigger chain reaction. That's where the white college students come in. They are the new plutonium fuel of the civil rights movement."

Roy Roost pondered this latest addition to the Atomic Theory of Mass Movements and said somewhat seriously: "Your theory does sort of explain why civil rights protests went on for years without attracting press attention and then suddenly became a big story about the time of Greensboro. Civil rights demonstrations went from being no story to the big story of the moment. The newspapers and the television stations paid no attention, and now they are giving it all the attention in the world."

At that moment, as if to highlight Roy Roost's thoughts, another cruisin' 'trol wagon pulled away from the front of the Montebello Theater and began taking another load of college students on the long ride to the Baltimore City Jail. There were the customary cheers and shouts of defiance. Clark turned away from Roy Roost to study the crowd of demonstrators. Some of the college students, particularly some of the white college students, seemed to be making only a halfhearted effort to stay in line and advance toward the box office and get arrested. They were socializing. They were shouting and cheering each time another cruisin' 'trol wagon took off for the City Jail, but they also were surreptitiously moving backwards in the line and thereby avoiding arrest and a possible criminal record.

The next day both the *Baltimore Banner* and the *Baltimore Beacon* carried front page photographs of the scene at the Baltimore City Jail. Because so many college students had been arrested at the Montebello Theater, there was no cell space for them all. The jail authorities had simply herded the students, men and women together, into a large indoor recreation area with a hard cement floor. The students were standing or sitting around, passing the time and waiting to see what the authorities were going to do with them.

By incarcerating the students in the open recreation area, prison officials had sidestepped the problem of putting college students in the same jail cells with hardened criminals. But that decision had given the newspapers a tremendous photo opportunity. When the respectable, middle-class citizens of Baltimore looked at their newspaper the next day, they saw a giant crowd of college students in jail. Every conceivable type of student was visible in the photographs. They were male, female, white, black, well-dressed, not so well-dressed, etc. In the foreground, looking pert in their "poor boy" T-shirts and Bermuda shorts, were two women students from Goucher College. One of them was one of Clark Schooler's political science students.

But something else was visible in the photographs of all the college students in the City Jail. In the background of most of the photos one could see barred windows. Peering out from behind those bars were the hardened and threatening faces of the jail's regular clientele. The features on the jail inmates faces were indistinct, really only the suggestion of faces, but that made them appear even more threatening. The photographs in the newspapers left no doubt that the college students, although in one sense off on what appeared to be a great social and academic adventure, also were close to potential danger.

Soon after the photographs of all the students in City Jail appeared in the newspapers, the telephones began ringing in the Criminal Court building in downtown Baltimore. Just plain citizens were calling the various City judges and telling them what they thought of imprisoning college students protesting for civil rights.

Another kind of call began coming in also. These calls came from all over the United States. They were from the parents of the Johns Hopkins University and Goucher College students who had been arrested at the demonstration at the Montebello Theater. Many of these parents were doctors and lawyers, and some even were judges themselves. They complained long and loudly about their children being imprisoned. They also expressed genuine concern for their children's physical safety.

That day found Clark Schooler back out in the parking lot of the Montebello Theater. The word had spread to a myriad of university and college campuses that the thing to do was to demonstrate to integrate the theater. There were about 1,000 students in the parking lot, almost double the number from the day before. Some of them had come from as far away as the University of Pennsylvania and the University of Virginia.

There also was a definite change in mood. The festive atmosphere of the day before had been replaced by a palpable sense of dedication and sacrifice. Having seen the photographs of their compatriots in Baltimore City Jail in that day's newspapers, these students knew where they were heading and that the place they were going was none too pleasant.

Also, the student leaders of the demonstration had things better organized. The students were standing in a clearly defined line, and it would have been very obvious and embarrassing to move backward in the line the way some students had been doing the day before. Once a student took a place in this line, that student was going to move steadily forward toward the box office and face an inevitable arrest and ride to City Jail.

Something new had been added. Just outside the theater entrance, barely 50 feet from where the students were being arrested, a group of counter-demonstrators were waving signs in full view of the demonstrating students. The signs bore statements such as: "Every American Has The Right To Serve Whom They Want, When They Want, How They Want." Another read: "Private Property Rights Are As Important As Civil Rights."

These counter-demonstrators were mainly white males in their 20s and 30s. They were not directly disturbing anyone. They did not yell threats or curses at the demonstrating students. But these young men looked like they

could cause a great deal of trouble if they wanted to do so. Their numbers
were growing slowly as the day went by.

In the afternoon, a large luxury car, a black Cadillac sedan, pulled into
the parking lot at the Montebello Theater. Out stepped an older white man,
in his early 60s, who was dressed in a suit coat and necktie and appeared
to be a typical businessman. He walked up to one of the police officers and
identified himself as the owner of the Montebello Theater. He asked for a
bull horn, which was a battery-powered portable microphone and loud-
speaker, so he could make an announcement to the throngs of people in the
parking lot. A police captain went and got him a bull horn from a nearby
police car.

Clark Schooler and all the other news reporters and television camera
operators were caught completely off-guard by this man's sudden arrival.
There was a furious stir of activity as all the reporters, photographers, and
television people circled around the man to get his picture and hear what
he had to say. The various news personnel, acting in haste, got in each
other's way and, in some cases, inflicted mild damage on each other. Shoulders bumped, elbows were jammed into stomachs, ankles were struck
glancing blows by passing television camera tripods, and one newspaper
reporter was accidentally hit in the cheek by a fast-moving radio microphone.

The man took the bull horn and addressed the demonstrating students.
He stunned Clark Schooler and almost everyone else by beginning with a
joke. "Hello," he said. "I am the owner of the Montebello Theater. I want
to thank you all for coming out to see our movie presentation today."

A wave of reluctant and somewhat grudging laughter spread throughout
the crowd. Everyone present was in a serious mood, but the man's little joke
had reached the heights of biting sarcasm.

The man looked briefly at the counter-demonstrators and their signs,
but only briefly. He then looked directly at the parking lot full of demonstrating students. He was standing on the front steps of the theater, which
allowed the demonstrators to see him as well as hear him.

"The Montebello Theater is closed for the rest of today," the man said
slowly. "No movie will be shown. No more tickets will be sold. And there
will be no more arrests of student protesters by the Baltimore Police Department."

The man stopped speaking for a moment and let that message sink in.
His pause heightened the tension. The crowd of students stood motionless
and silent, waiting in high anticipation to see what he would say next.

"Tomorrow," the man finally continued, "the Montebello Theater will
open on an integrated basis. The Montebello will sell tickets to customers

without regard to race, religion, or . . ."

The man never got to finish his sentence. The crowd of students in the parking lot erupted in wild celebration. Young men and women yelled, jumped up and down, and grabbed each other and danced around. It was, Clark wrote in the *Baltimore Banner*, "a genuinely jubilant, truly heartfelt response."

The man gave the students about one minute to celebrate. He then used the bull horn, which was very loud, to quiet them down and, once again, get their attention.

"I have done this for you," the man said. His voice was on the edge of quivering with emotion. "Now I want you to do this for me. I want you to go home. And I want you to go home safely. I want you to leave this parking lot in an orderly fashion and go back to your lives as students. There is nothing more for you to accomplish out here today."

The students were still in a celebratory mood, but they began drifting away and returning to their respective college and university campuses. The protest at the Montebello Theater was over. The students had won.

At the same time, downtown, one of the judges of the Baltimore Criminal Court released all of the arrested students from the Baltimore City Jail. All charges against the students were dropped, simply because the owner of the Montebello Theater had decided not to press charges. There were no court trials of the protesting students. Therefore, there were no criminal convictions or criminal records for any of them.

When the owner of the Montebello Theater had finished speaking to the crowd of students in the parking lot, he handed the bull horn back to one of the police officers. He then walked over to the group of counter-demonstrators, shook a few hands, and thanked them for making their statement in behalf of private property rights. He then asked the counter-demonstrators to "go home" and "go home safely."

When the theater owner turned around, however, he found himself facing all the news reporters and the television personnel. An impromptu press conference took place on the spot. The first question was an obvious one: "What convinced you to racially integrate the Montebello Theater?"

"I became concerned about the physical safety of all the people gathered in the parking lot," the theater owner said. "Nothing bad was happening, but I became fearful that the situation could become dangerous and threatening."

The next question concerned other movie theaters in the Baltimore area: "Did you meet with the Theater Owners Association, and are they going to follow your example and racially integrate all the movie theaters in Baltimore?"

"I did meet with the Theater Owners Association," the owner of the Montebello Theater stated, "but there was no agreement on integrating all the city's movie theaters. Most of the owners argued strongly that letting black people into their movie theaters would cause them to lose their white clientele. They said they were not personally prejudiced, but they believed they could not afford the financial losses if white people stopped going to integrated movie theaters."

With all the reporters' and photographers' attention focused on the owner of the Montebello Theater, no one noticed that one of the students from Morgan State College, a young black woman named Vonda Belle Carter, had worked her way into the circle of news personnel. Standing next to the theater owner and looking him directly in the eye, she asked passionately and sincerely:

"Can you honestly say, in your own conscience, that racial segregation of movie theaters in Baltimore is morally right?"

There was absolute silence. Only the whir of the television cameras could be heard while the owner of the Montebello Theater absorbed Vonda Belle Carter's question. The theater owner looked down at his feet. Then he looked up at Vonda Belle Carter. "No," he replied firmly and clearly. "I cannot say, in my conscience, that segregating white movie theater patrons from black patrons is morally right."

That moment of revelation was the highlight on the 6 o'clock and the 11 o'clock news on every television station in Baltimore that evening. The television film of Vonda Belle Carter asking her question, and the theater owner answering her question so frankly, was played over and over again in the ensuing days. The following day, two of the three national television networks, ABC and CBS, used the film clip on their national evening newscasts.

That one news clip left the movie theater owners of Baltimore in a defenseless position. A businessman of the city had announced, for all to see and hear, his opinion that racial segregation of movie theaters was "immoral." Quietly, without fanfare or public announcement, all the movie theaters in the Baltimore area voluntarily became racially integrated over the next few months.

Clark Schooler had one last story to write on the demonstrations at the Montebello Theater. The next day, the four university and college students who had organized and led the protest made a symbolic trip to see the current movie at the theater. By prearrangement, they met with Clark for an interview in the lobby of the Montebello Theater after the movie was over.

One of the students was a man from Johns Hopkins University, one was a woman from Goucher College, and the other two were a man and woman from Morgan State College. The woman student from Morgan State was Vonda Belle Carter, the student who had confronted the theater owner the day before about the morality of racial segregation.

Clark began the interview: "How did you like the movie?"

"It was terrible," said the young woman from Goucher College. "It was 'The Moonspinners.' It was a Disney movie. It was for kids. I had to work hard to not fall asleep."

"Our having to go to see 'The Moonspinners' was the white segregationists' ultimate revenge," said the young man from Johns Hopkins. "But what else could we do? We had to show everyone that the Montebello Theater really is integrated now."

Clark tried to steer the interview in a more serious direction. He asked: "When all this started, did you ever think it would end this successfully?"

"It ended the way Mahatma Ghandi and Martin Luther King said it would end." The speaker was Vonda Belle Carter from Morgan State. "Nonviolent protest is aimed at the moral values of the ruling group. Once you reach the conscience of the ruling group, its members are required by their own moral code to grant you the rights you are seeking."

Vonda Belle Carter's statement sounded pre-written and rehearsed to Clark Schooler. It was obvious that her professors at Morgan State College had mentally armed her with the established intellectual and moral rationale for justifying sit-in demonstrations.

Clark widened his discussion with the students a bit: "How does it feel to be members of a mass movement? What you accomplished at the Montebello Theater is being accomplished by college students all over the nation. Students are racially integrating snack bars in Nashville and restaurants in St. Louis."

"It feels great," said the young man from Morgan College. "But it's just one more step down a long, long road. Sit-ins and line-ins and swim-ins are working in the Upper South and the Border States, but they aren't working at all in the Deep South. There's more work to be done. There's a lot more."

Clark Schooler saved his toughest question for last: "Do you think you could have won this battle without the tremendous news coverage you received from Baltimore newspapers and television stations?"

None of the four students was anxious to answer that question, but finally Vonda Belle Carter took a stab at it. "The news coverage was crucial," the young black woman said. "My mother told me it was the newspaper photos of all the college students in City Jail that turned the tide. She said she just held the newspaper and stared for several minutes at the photograph. She said she'll bet the man who owned the movie theater looked at it for a long time, too. She thinks that photograph made up his mind."

The incident at the Montebello Theater quickly faded from the Baltimore news scene. But the racial integration of all Baltimore movie theaters was an accomplishment of great permanence. In his concluding newspaper story about the event, Clark Schooler wrote these words:

"All over the United States, businessmen are responding to college student sit-in demonstrations the way the owner of the Montebello Theater responded. They are voluntarily integrating their privately-owned facilities."

"This is being done in hundreds of cities and towns. It is happening without the National Guard or U.S. troops having to be called to the scene."

"These many incidents of voluntary racial integration, after only slight prodding from the university and college youth of America, stand in sharp contrast to those few incidents, mainly in the Deep South, where voluntary acceptance of racial integration has not yet been achieved."

In The Interim

Periodically throughout United States history, mass movements have arisen at the grass roots which have led to major changes in government policy. One of the most famous and significant was the abolition movement of the early 19th Century, which worked to bring an end to human slavery.

The civil rights movement of the 1960s became something of a model for subsequent mass movements. The anti-Vietnam war movement from 1965 to 1975 directly copied the confrontational techniques of sit-in demonstrations and attention-getting public protests. The women's movement of the early 1970s used much of the language and logic of the civil rights movement, particularly the appeal to conscience to grant equality and dignity to a previously-oppressed group. The most recent mass movement of significance has been the gay and lesbian rights movement.

The U.S. Government is divided into the legislative, the executive, and the judiciary. Mass movements are most likely to occur when one of the three branches fails to respond to the needs and wishes of a substantial portion of the body politic. Some mass movements succeed while others fail, but the mass movement is definitely an important part of the United States system of government.

CHAPTER 3

FEDERALISM:
MISSISSIPPI, ALABAMA, AND THE U.S.A.

By the summer of 1962, Clark Schooler had gone ABD at Johns Hopkins University. ABD stood for All But Dissertation. It meant that Clark had completed the course work for his Ph.D. degree in political science, but he had not yet written the approximately 500 page manuscript, called a dissertation, which was the final requirement for the degree.

Being ABD at Johns Hopkins put some free time into Clark's work schedule. He had plenty to do to write his dissertation. There were long hours doing research in the university library and even longer hours pecking away at the keys of his Underwood portable typewriter. But he could do the work whenever it was convenient for him. If he needed to leave Baltimore for a few days or a few weeks, he could do so without seriously interrupting his dissertation writing schedule.

Which was fortunate, because the Patriot Press newspaper chain, owner of the *Baltimore Banner*, had plans for Clark Schooler. In the early 1960s, the Patriot Press had developed a news gathering and marketing technique called the Patriot Press News Squadron. Promising reporters from throughout the Patriot Press newspaper empire were sent as a two or three person team to cover important and fast breaking national news stories. These stories were published in all the newspapers owned by the Patriot Press throughout the United States. And right under each reporter's name, or byline, ran the words: "Member, Patriot Press News Squadron."

The city editor at the *Baltimore Banner*, Terry Songman, looked at Clark Schooler and spoke with animation. "Get yourself down there. Get yourself down there as quick as you can. There's a black guy trying to get into the University of Mississippi, which has been a pillar of racial segregation for as long as anyone can remember. The story is hotter than a Baltimore city row house on a hot August night."

"The Patriot Press is sending you down there with a reporter from the *New York Liberty* who is black himself," Terry Songman continued. "The black reporter is going to cover the black student and his efforts to get into the university. Your job will be to cover the response of the university officials and other government officials in Mississippi, particularly the governor. This is the first time the Patriot Press has sent out a racially integrated Patriot Press News Squadron."

The *New York Liberty* was the Patriot Press paper in New York City. Clark Schooler was excited that he was going to be a member of the Patriot Press's first integrated news team.

Then he thought about it for a second. The news team was going to be integrated, but the national executives of the Patriot Press were dividing up the assignment in a racially segregated fashion. The black reporter was going to cover the black student trying to get accepted to the University of Mississippi. The white reporter was going to cover the white university officials and the white Mississippi politicians. The news team may have been integrated, but the news assignments were handed out on the basis of strict racial segregation.

As he so often did, Terry Songman laid it on the line with Clark Schooler about the real purpose of his assignment. "Sending a black man as a reporter on a civil rights story is something new for the Patriot Press," Songman told Clark. "The big guys up in New York City are worried that a black reporter will only give them the civil rights supporters' side of the story. Your job is to make certain the white point of view gets reported."

Clark Schooler was not quite certain how to respond to being the "white reporter" assigned to cover "the white point of view." He solved the problem by not responding. He hurried home, packed some clothes, drove to Baltimore's Friendship Airport, and got on an airplane headed in the general direction of the University of Mississippi at Oxford, Mississippi.

The trip was time-consuming and required a change of planes in Washington, D.C. Although the early 1960s were the dawn of the jet age, the particular airplane Clark flew on for most of the trip was an older propeller driven job that flew low and slow. That gave Clark a great deal of time to chat with his seat mate on the flight. His seat mate was the black reporter from the *New York Liberty* who was the other half of this particular Patriot Press News Squadron.

The young African-American man had been covering a story in Washington, D.C., for the *New York Liberty*. He and Clark arranged to fly from Washington to Memphis, Tennessee, together. Memphis was the closest major city to Oxford, Mississippi, and the university there.

The black reporter's name was Bernard Martin. He had grown up in Washington, D.C., where his father had a Civil Service job with the U.S. Government. Bernard Martin was a graduate of Howard University, the predominantly black university in the nation's capital that had produced, over the years, a number of well-known African-American legal and political leaders. Bernard Martin had begun his career working as a reporter for a national magazine, published in Washington, D.C., that was written mainly for an African-American audience. The editors at the *New York Liberty* noticed his work there and hired him away to be the *Liberty's* first black newspaper reporter.

The airplane may have been old and slow, but the lunch served was a full meal and quite tasty. Clark Schooler and Bernard Martin were able to have a lengthy and lively luncheon conversation. Bernard Martin began by asking Clark if he had ever been to Mississippi before.

"No, I haven't," Clark replied. "I've spent time in Virginia. I've taken the railroad train through South Carolina and Georgia on my way to winter vacations in Florida. But I've never really spent any time in the Deep South, at least not long enough to get to know the people and the customs."

"It's different down there," Bernard Martin opined. "It's way different. The first thing you'll need to know about when you're down there is the willing suspension of law and order."

Clark's response was to immediately launch into a watered-down version of one of his political science lectures. "Equal protection of the laws and the right to live in domestic tranquility," Clark said, "are two of the most honored principles of the American democracy. Law and order exist in all places where the United States Constitution is the fundamental ruling authority."

"Somehow," Bernard Martin explained patiently, "that part of the Constitution never reached black people in the deepest parts of the American South. You are about to enter a world where blacks can be beaten and murdered and otherwise terrorized. And their white tormentors have no fear whatsoever of ever being caught, prosecuted, or punished for their criminal acts."

Clark Schooler was genuinely disturbed. He stammered: "But, how can that happen?" Clark was perplexed by even the thought that there could be a part of the United States where basic legal protections were not guaranteed to every citizen by the established state and local police authorities.

"As I said," Bernard Martin went on. "The key is the willing suspension of law and order. State and local police simply stop doing their jobs for a few minutes, or a few hours, or a few days. That allows private individuals who are white people to do whatever they want to black people. The whites, often acting in disorganized mobs, can carry out beatings, commit murders, or do anything else they feel like as long as their victims are black. And that's just fine with the state police, or the city police, or the county sheriff, or whoever is the local police power. They just look the other way."

Clark Schooler searched for a reasonable response to Bernard Martin's statements. Clark fell back on the part of the universe he knew best, which was the United States Constitution. "But the Constitution guarantees fundamental civil rights," Clark blurted out, "such as the right to trial by jury. Every citizen is guaranteed that, if they are charged with a crime, guilt or innocence will be determined by a jury of their peers, a group of their fellow citizens. Every Southern black individual is protected by . . ."

Bernard Martin cut Clark Schooler off in mid-sentence. "Every Southern black individual is protected by essentially nothing," the young African-American said. "The jury trial actually functions to protect the white people who beat and murder blacks. Even if they are identified, arrested, and tried for harming or killing a black, white folks are judged by a white jury that always finds a way to find them innocent. It's called the free white jury that will never convict."

Clark continued to struggle to prove that the U.S. Constitution protected all Americans, including African-Americans, even in the Deep South. "After the Civil War," Clark said in his beginning-teacher voice, "the United States adopted the 14th Amendment to the Constitution. The 14th Amendment guaranteed the civil rights of the newly-freed slaves. They were to have equal protection of the laws, the idea that laws would apply to all citizens equally, no matter what their race, even if they were former slaves."

"There also was the requirement for due process of law," Clark continued pedantically. "That was the idea that anyone who was to be punished for a crime had to be arrested, charged with a specific crime, given reasonable bail, and tried by a jury of their peers. Under the 14th Amendment, if black people are denied equal protection of the laws or due process of law, the U.S. Government can intervene and guarantee those rights." Clark made that final point as if he were winding up a classroom lecture just at the moment the bell rang, signaling the end of the class.

Bernard Martin was not ready for this particular class to end. "Have you ever really read the text of the 14th Amendment?" Bernard Martin asked that question and then looked at Clark Schooler as if he were a naive freshman in an introductory American Government course rather than an ABD political science graduate student. "The wording is exactly this: 'No state shall make or enforce any law which shall abridge the privileges or immunities of citizens of the United States.' It goes on from there."

"The problem is the use of the words 'no state shall,'" Bernard Martin continued. "The prohibitions against violating the rights of black persons are on the states but not on the citizens who live in those states. Therefore, if the state and local government officials are careful not to do anything, the 14th Amendment does not apply to whites who take the beating and murdering of blacks into their own hands. That's how the tradition grew up of Southern law enforcement officials looking the other way and letting private citizens do the threatening, beating, and, when deemed necessary, the murdering of uppity blacks."

"In this case," Bernard Martin concluded. "An uppity black is defined as one who joins the National Association for the Advancement of Colored People, participates in civil rights demonstrations, tries to get Southern blacks registered to vote, sneaks in a drink of water from the white drinking fountain down at the court house, or otherwise publicly attempts to do something about racial segregation in the South. They are immediately punished by private individuals. During this time, state and local police officials are very careful to do absolutely nothing, one way or the other."

Clark Schooler did the graduate student thing and tried to sum up the discussion so far. "Your point," he said, "is that the threat of being beaten or being murdered prevents Southern blacks from really doing anything about racial segregation. That's because private citizens, acting as lawless Southern whites, will punish them. The punishment may take the form of bombing the black person's home, or his business if he owns one, or even stringing him up at the end of a rope. And, while all this is happening, Southern law enforcement officials just look the other way. And, furthermore, the U.S. Government in Washington can do nothing about it because the 14th Amendment prohibits the states from denying rights to blacks. The 14th Amendment does nothing to stop private individuals from denying rights to blacks."

Clark had summed up the discussion thoroughly and, without his realizing it, loudly. Two people seated in the row of seats ahead of Clark and Bernard Martin turned around and looked at Clark to see who was doing all the talking.

Both Clark and Bernard Martin laughed at this, and the laughing provided a little relief from the seriousness of the discussion. "I have one last point," Bernard Martin said. "One thing is different now. Thanks to the United States Supreme Court decision in *Brown v. Board of Education* in 1954, the United States Government can intervene when the issue under discussion is the racial integration of educational institutions. If the president wants to send in troops to help integrate the University of Mississippi, he can do it, because public education is the issue."

In the fall of 1962, the president of the United States was John Fitzgerald Kennedy of Massachusetts. John F. Kennedy had succeeded President Dwight D. Eisenhower by winning the 1960 presidential election. Unlike Eisenhower, who was a Republican, Kennedy was a liberal Democrat who was serving as a United States senator from Massachusetts at the time he ran for president.

Dwight Eisenhower had served eight years as president. The two-term limit (two four-year terms and out) prevented Eisenhower from running for reelection in 1960. John F. Kennedy had been opposed by Eisenhower's vice-president, Richard M. Nixon, a Republican like Eisenhower. The presidential election contest between John F. Kennedy and Richard M. Nixon in 1960 had been very hard fought. John F. Kennedy defeated Richard M. Nixon by only a very narrow margin of votes. It was one of the closest presidential elections in United States history.

For the remainder of their airplane ride, Bernard Martin and Clark Schooler discussed whether President John F. Kennedy would end up deciding to enforce racial integration at the University of Mississippi by sending in U.S. Army troops. "The Southern white leadership in Mississippi will never give in voluntarily," Bernard Martin said. "They'll talk a lot, do nothing to maintain law and order, and in the end President Kennedy will have to send in the soldier boys. You can count on that."

"I don't know if I agree," Clark replied. "John Fitzgerald Kennedy is a Democrat, and no Democrat has ever been elected president of the United States without carrying the white South. The last thing in this world a Democratic president wants to do is send U.S. troops into a Southern state, because that Democratic president is probably going to want the white people in that Southern state to vote for him in the next presidential election. President Kennedy will try to find a peaceful way out of this situation at the University of Mississippi if he can."

Bernard Martin answered back by changing the subject slightly. He asked: "But what about the black vote in the North? Black voters in New York and Philadelphia and your own hometown of Baltimore supported John F. Kennedy strongly in 1960. He'll want their support again in the upcoming presidential election in 1964. President Kennedy could really nail down the black vote in 1964 by sending U.S. troops into the University of Mississippi and sending them in early."

Clark Schooler had a ready answer. "The white vote in the South is more important to a Democratic presidential candidate than is the black vote in the North. It all goes back to President Franklin D. Roosevelt. He fashioned a winning Democratic Party national majority by uniting the working class and minority voters of the North with the traditionally Democratic white voters of the South. The result was the Roosevelt Coalition, a winning combination of voters that enabled the Democratic Party to dominate American national politics from the early 1930s to the present day. A Democratic president has to carry the white South to get elected, and he has to hold the white South to get reelected."

"I'm beginning to think you may be right," Bernard Martin replied. "After all, it is the Solid South. White folks in the South have been solidly Democratic since the end of the Civil War. I hate it, but I can understand why even a northern liberal like President Kennedy would not want to antagonize the white South by sending troops into the University of Mississippi."

Clark Schooler had enjoyed his airborne visit with Bernard Martin while flying down to Memphis, Tennessee. Clark noticed that he and Bernard Martin were similarly dressed. Both were in grey flannel suits with white button-down shirts and a necktie. Furthermore, Bernard Martin wore his hair in the current crewcut style and sported a pencil thin mustache. It occurred to Clark Schooler, as he and Bernard Martin were leaving the airplane, that Bernard Martin was every inch an organization man, someone who dressed and acted to please those who were in charge of the establishment business organization for which he worked.

Clark Schooler and Bernard Martin parted company at the airport in Memphis, Tennessee. Bernard Martin said it would be dangerous for a white man and a black man to be seen driving from Memphis to Oxford, Mississippi, together. They would be all right in Tennessee, Bernard Martin guessed, but really bad things might happen to them in Mississippi. Bernard Martin also believed it would be exceedingly dangerous for him to be seen wandering around gathering news stories on a Deep South university campus, such as the University of Mississippi, that was about to be racially integrated.

Bernard Martin therefore elected to stay in Memphis, which was the place where lawyers from the United States Department of Justice were waiting with James Meredith, the young African-American man who was trying to get admitted to the University of Mississippi. As soon as the Registrar at the University of Mississippi agreed to admit James Meredith to the school, James Meredith and the Justice Department lawyers would drive the 87 miles from Memphis to Oxford and Meredith's days as a university student could begin. The Patriot Press had sent Bernard Martin down to cover James Meredith, and for the time being James Meredith was going to be based in Memphis.

Clark Schooler rented a car and headed down the highway to Oxford, Mississippi. The drive only took about two hours. As the car neared Oxford, Clark saw that the town was surrounded by cotton fields, most of which appeared to be farmed by African-American sharecroppers. Here and there were the small white shacks of the sharecroppers, most of them with the paint peeling off. Black adults and children were lounging and playing around outside the shacks in the comfortable warmth of a Mississippi September. They reminded Clark of the black adults and children he often saw lounging and playing around on the cement sidewalks in front of their red-brick row houses back in Baltimore.

Clark Schooler arrived at the University of Mississippi. It was the weekend, and the traditional Southern atmosphere of quietness and laziness seemed to dominate the campus. The university was best known, Clark was soon informed, by its historical nickname, Ole Miss. Clark stood in front of the school's signature building, the Lyceum, and admired its six white columns. Next he found, in the midst of the many beautiful trees on the campus, the university's monument to its Civil War veterans. It was a marble statue of a Confederate soldier.

That statue reminded Clark that the divisions between North and South in the United States were very real. He recalled his own alma mater, Williams College in western Massachusetts, where a bronze statue of a Union soldier graced the lawn in front of one of the major academic buildings, Griffin Hall. This statue soldier stood firmly, holding his long rifle, his resolute gaze pointed toward the South.

Clark later discovered that this particular bronze statue of a Union soldier had been mass-produced. He found additional copies of it on court house lawns and in municipal parks in cities and towns all over the Northern United States.

Clark Schooler returned his attention to the Confederate memorial at the University of Mississippi. The statue was striking in its similarity to the statue of the Union soldier at Williams College. A marble Confederate soldier stood looking outward, shading his eyes against the sun. With rifle in hand, he waited vigilantly for those invading Yankees. It occurred to Clark there probably were statues just like it, or something like it, all over the South.

Clark's final thought was that, although the Civil War was long over, there were two separate armies of bronze and marble monuments, one army in the North and the other in the South, that still stood and opposed each other.

But then it was time for Clark to do some work of a pleasant nature. It was a football weekend at Ole Miss. Many of the students were leaving the campus to go to the football game. The University of Mississippi was playing the University of Kentucky at the football stadium in Jackson, Mississippi, the state capital. Clark convinced himself he could better understand and write about the people of Mississippi if he made the drive from Oxford to Jackson and watched the Ole Miss football team play Kentucky.

That somewhat self-serving decision enabled Clark Schooler to witness one of the most important events in United States civil rights history. At half time at the football game, Ross Barnett, the governor of Mississippi, walked out onto the field to address the more than 40,000 persons in the stands. Governor Barnett had strongly opposed the entrance of James Meredith into the University of Mississippi. It seemed that everyone at the football game knew it.

A lone microphone on a thin metal stand had been placed on the football field for Governor Barnett to use. The governor let the immense crowd quiet down, thereby increasing the crowd's anticipation for what he was about to say. Barnett then clenched his right fist, raised it high in the air, and held it there to symbolize struggle and determined opposition.

His first words reverberated throughout the packed stadium. "I love Mississippi."

The crowd responded with loud cheering and shouts of support.

"I love her people," the governor continued. There was even more cheering and shouting.

Then Barnett told the crowd what it really wanted to hear:

"I love our customs."

Clark Schooler was amazed by the frenzied celebration that ensued. The all-white audience rose almost as one person and yelled its support for Governor Ross Barnett. It was support bordering on love. Feet stamped, pennants waved, and many persons reflected Governor Barnett's spirit of defiance by shaking their clenched fists in the air.

Governor Barnett had used the words "our customs" as political code-words. Because his football half time speech was being covered by newspapers and television, Barnett had not wanted to openly and directly speak out in favor of racial segregation. Everyone in the stadium knew, however, that the codewords "our customs" meant the peculiar Southern custom of strict racial segregation.

The next day was Sunday. Clark Schooler traveled back to the University of Mississippi in Oxford, arriving on campus in mid-afternoon. He found the Mississippi state police on the scene and reasonably in control. The police officers were working hard to see that only students, and not non-student troublemakers, were getting on to the campus.

But even the students seemed to be in a rebellious mood. A large crowd of them began to gather in front of the Lyceum building. They were talking to each other about their collective opposition to James Meredith being

permitted to join the Ole Miss student body. Occasionally, the more boister-
ous among them would yell an anti-racial integration epithet or two.

Clark Schooler had been sent to Mississippi to cover the Southern
white reaction, so Clark made it his business to mingle with the students and
interview those who were willing to give their opinions. He quickly got an
earful of deeply-felt opposition to racial integration at the University of
Mississippi. Quite a few of the students had been at the football game in
Jackson the night before and had been fired up by Governor Barnett's
implied defense of "our customs." If the governor was against having
Meredith on campus, one student pointed out, then "why shouldn't the
student body join the governor in resisting racial integration by every means
possible?"

Things livened up late in the afternoon when slightly less than 200 U.S.
marshals arrived on the University of Mississippi campus and stationed
themselves at the base of the white pillars on the Lyceum building. Their
arrival was unexpected by the student crowd on the grassy area in front of
the Lyceum. The word quickly spread among the students, erroneously, that
the marshals were guarding the Lyceum because James Meredith was in the
building. In reality, Clark Schooler learned later, the marshals had hidden
James Meredith in Baxter Hall, a dormitory located at a far-distant corner
of the campus.

When the U.S. marshals arrived at the Lyceum, the Mississippi state
police quickly took up positions between the marshals and the student
crowd. Now, when the students wanted to yell anti-integration curses and
epithets at the marshals, they had to do so over the heads of Mississippi state
police officers. However, the state police made no effort to quiet the crowd
or to disperse it.

As evening came on, Clark Schooler could feel a palpable change in
the mood and composition of the crowd massed outside the Lyceum building. The number of people present was well above 1,000 persons, and there
were now many older adults, mainly males, mixed among the students. Clark
could feel hatred beginning to emanate from the crowd. That hatred was
directed at the U.S. marshals, the visible symbols of United State Government authority currently invading the University of Mississippi campus.

Technically speaking, U.S. marshals are officers of the United States
Courts. Under normal conditions, they carry out routine functions such as
serving court papers and escorting prisoners. But these particular U.S.
marshals were anything but routine. They were dressed in riot vests which
were dyed a highly-visible orange color. The vests had deep pockets that
contained tear-gas canisters for crowd control. But the most distinguishing
feature of these men was their white-painted helmets with the words "U.S.

Marshal" prominently displayed on them.

Some of these specially-trained U.S. marshals were a gift from the Eisenhower administration to the Kennedy administration. Following the disturbances at Little Rock, President Eisenhower had ordered that a group of U.S. marshals be specially trained to help enforce nationally-mandated school integration in the American South. It was the hope of the Eisenhower Administration that, by using these specially trained U.S. marshals, future presidents of the United States could avoid using military troops to desegregate Southern schools.

Somehow sensing that what they were doing would not make flattering television coverage for the Southern cause, the crowd began attacking the television cameramen who were present and shooting film. Because the television crews were working with bright lights, they were easy for the more combative members of the crowd to spot and assault.

The sound of shattering glass could be heard periodically as television lights were smashed on the ground and trampled to bits by the mob. Clark Schooler could see cameramen struggling with various members of the crowd, the more aggressive rioters trying to wrest the cameras away from the cameramen so as to then destroy the cameras. In one instance, a group of young men were rocking and smashing and trying to tip over an automobile containing a newsperson.

The crowd was yelling anti-integration slogans and epithets. But then Clark Schooler began to hear other, more disturbing sounds. Nearby voices were saying: "Stop the newsmen!" "Kill a reporter!" "Get those integration-lovin' press people."

Suddenly Clark experienced a sensation that was totally new to him. He realized that, for the first time in his life, he was experiencing overwhelming feelings of personal vulnerability. He was amazed to find that he was genuinely fearful for his life. He quickly moved back out of the crowd and stood beside a tree. He slowly took off his suit coat and necktie, hoping no one would notice what he was doing. In an intentionally casual manner, he neatly placed the suit coat and tie beneath the tree. By getting rid of his suit coat and tie, Clark hoped to make himself look more like a student rioter and less like a newspaper man.

Clark looked worriedly around himself in all directions. So far, at least, no one was paying any attention to what he was doing. He next took his newspaper reporter's notebook out of his rear pants pocket and placed it and his pencil on top of the suit coat. He took his press card out of his wallet and hid it under his suit coat. He did not want to be carrying anything that would suggest to the angry crowd that he was a member of the news media.

After another furtive look around, Clark began drifting slowly away from his little pile of possessions under the tree. Then a very disturbing thought penetrated his consciousness. What if some of the students he had interviewed earlier recognized him and encouraged the crowd to attack him?

In an effort to effect an instant disguise, Clark did two things. He unbuttoned his top shirt button and opened the collar of his button-down shirt. This was a popular casual way of wearing a shirt in the late 1950s and early 1960s. Clark also rolled up his shirt sleeves to just below the elbow. That also was an au courant collegiate style of the time.

Then, in a final effort to alter his appearance and hide his identity, Clark took off his horn-rimmed eyeglasses and slipped them into his pocket. This was something of a calculated decision on Clark's part. He could see without his eyeglasses, and easily move around, but he could not see details very clearly. For the remainder of the evening, he would cover the riot at Ole Miss with his vision somewhat fuzzy.

Clark was so fearful of being identified and attacked by the mob that, in addition to changing his appearance, he changed his behavior. He occasionally shook his fist in the air as the more defiant students were doing. One time he passed a group chanting: "Two-four-six-eight; we ain't goin' to integrate!" Clark joined them in their pro-segregation yell. If a group of students went by Clark, running in a particular direction with some form of riot mischief in mind, Clark would run with them. Clark did not just fade into the mob. His disguise was to become an active part of the mob.

By this time, individuals in the crowd were attacking the U.S. marshals by throwing rocks and other convenient missiles at them. Items thrown included handfuls of gravel, empty beer bottles, and small pieces of asphalt and cement. Anything that could be picked up and hurled through the air at the marshals was being launched by the rioters. Clark made his contribution by throwing a handful of loose dirt. It made Clark appear to be as angry and rebellious as the other rioters, but Clark was confident that the small amount of Mother Earth that he threw at the marshals could not possibly have hurt anyone.

As Clark Schooler worked at effecting a good disguise and fading into the crowd, a disturbing thought occurred to him. A black person, caught in a similarly dangerous situation, would not have been able to "cast off" his or her skin color as readily as Clark had "cast off" the superficial indicators of being a newspaper reporter. It was easy enough for Clark to shed some of his clothing and hide his note pad and press card. It would have been impossible for a black to change or hide his or her skin pigmentation.

Suddenly the airborne attack on the U.S. marshals grew more serious and dangerous. Bricks began flying through the air. Some in the mob began throwing three-to-five-foot sections of metal pipe. One of the pipe sections struck a U.S. Marshall in the head, leaving a giant dent in his helmet. Fortunately, thanks to the protection of the helmet, the U.S. marshall was not seriously hurt.

Molotov cocktails were being thrown. These were small glass bottles filled with gasoline. A piece of paper or cloth was crammed into the neck of the bottle and lighted with a match or cigarette lighter. When the bottle smashed against a wall or a pillar of the Lyceum, the gasoline ignited and the Molotov cocktail caused a hot explosion and fire.

At this time, with the battle getting brutally serious and physically dangerous, the Mississippi state police were ordered to leave the scene of the riot. Up to this point, the state patrol officers had watched the growing riot but had done nothing to restrain or control it. In fact, it seemed to Clark Schooler, the state police had observed the melee with an attitude of mild amusement and unspoken support.

Concerned for his own personal safety, Clark believed that uniformed police officers would always do their duty to maintain law and order. But Clark was horrified to see the state police leave their posts, get into their patrol cars, and drive away from the Old Miss campus. The demoralizing sight of a line of state police vehicles disappearing down the campus streets was permanently seared into Clark Schooler's memory. Once the state police were all gone, only the U.S. marshals remained to defend the Lyceum building and continue the battle to get James Meredith admitted to the University of Mississippi.

It was happening, Clark Schooler suddenly realized, exactly the way that Bernard Martin had said it would happen. It was: "The willing suspension of law and order." Clark's African-American newsman colleague had called the shot perfectly. As if on cue, the Mississippi state police were removing themselves from the scene and leaving the fate of the U.S. marshals in the hands of the lawless mob. From here on out, it would be up to the U.S. marshals to protect themselves.

Clark Schooler later came to attribute great significance to that moment when the Mississippi state police intentionally departed the riot-torn Ole Miss campus. That moment, Clark concluded, was one of the great failures of the United States federal system.

By this time, the assault on the Lyceum had become a real battle. Larger objects, such as trash cans and chairs and directional signs, were being thrown at the marshals. The rioters were scavenging the campus, picking up and ripping out any object that might be turned into a missile to be hurled at the marshals. In desperation to protect themselves, the marshals attempted to push the crowd back from the Lyceum building by firing tear gas into the mob. Such periodic assaults would shove the crowd back for a moment. But, once the tear gas had cleared away, the mob would move in close again and resume pelting the marshals with any object that could be found and thrown.

Perhaps it was the tears in his eyes from an occasional whiff of tear gas. Perhaps it was the fact he did not have his eyeglasses on. For whatever reason, Clark had an academic mystical experience as he stood amidst the mob attacking the Lyceum building. Suddenly, it seemed to Clark, the U.S. marshals were Union soldiers of the Civil War era, dressed in the characteristic blue uniforms. They were lined up defending the Lyceum in the classic Civil War infantry maneuver of a straight line of troops directly facing the enemy. They were a small band, Clark saw, but nonetheless determined to hold their defensive perimeter at all costs.

The mob had turned into Confederate soldiers, some dressed in the classic Southern grey uniform and others in the butternut color that characterized Rebel uniforms in the later years of the Civil War. The Confederate troops were more numerous than the Yankees, but they were highly disorganized. The Southerners launched a skirmish here and a skirmish there but were never able to get all their troops together for one single, massive attack.

The vision lasted only for a minute or so, but from that vision developed one of Clark Schooler's most important insights. The civil rights movement was the renewal, both intellectually and physically, of the American Civil War. Once again, Northern troops (U.S. marshals) were having to come down South to enforce national values on recalcitrant Confederates (lawless Southern rioters). And the end result of the civil rights movement, Clark thought, would be the same as the end result of the Civil War. The South would be nationalized and coerced into following Northern values and Northern legal principals.

Clark Schooler was still moving about among the rioters. For protection, he continued to pretend he was one of them. But as he did so, Clark began to wonder where the U.S. troops were. It was now late in the evening, around 10 P.M., and the situation had been out-of-control for almost four hours. Where was President Kennedy? This was the moment when the script, first written by President Eisenhower at Little Rock, called for sending in the cavalry.

After all, those were President Kennedy's U.S. marshals under attack on the front porch of the Lyceum building. The president had ordered the marshals on to the Ole Miss campus. It was President Kennedy's job, now that it was clear a full-scale riot was in progress, to protect the marshals by sending in U.S. Army soldiers. Was President Kennedy so beholden to Southern white voters in the Democratic Party, Clark speculated, that he was not going to order in the troops?

Military troops were appropriate, Clark concluded, because now many of the rioters were armed and firing live ammunition at the Lyceum building. The sharp crack of a rifle shot was frequently heard, followed by the ping or thunk of the bullet hitting the red brick walls or the white trim of the Lyceum. Occasionally there would be the blast-like sound of a shotgun being fired. The rioters were overturning parked automobiles and setting them on fire. Clark's fears of being attacked for being a news reporter were strongly reinforced when he saw that a truck belonging to a television station had been engulfed by the rioters, flipped over, and set ablaze.

Somehow the mob had gotten a hold of a fire truck. There was an attempt to drive the fire truck through the line of marshals and then smash the truck into the front door of the Lyceum. The marshals stopped this assault by drawing their pistols and shooting the fire truck's tires flat. Clark noted that gunnery had now been used by both sides in the conflict, although the U.S. marshals had never fired their guns directly at the rioters.

Clark later learned the reason there were no U.S. soldiers yet at Ole Miss. President Kennedy tried until the last minute to get Mississippi Governor Ross Barnett to maintain law and order on the University of Mississippi campus. But the president finally gave up on Governor Barnett and ordered U.S. troops to leave Memphis and occupy the University of Mississippi at Oxford.

Slowly, after midnight, U.S. soldiers began to filter on to the Ole Miss campus and take military control of the territory. As more soldiers appeared, the rioters progressively disappeared. Within 24 hours there were more than 10,000 U.S. military personnel maintaining tight control at the University of Mississippi. James Meredith then was officially registered at the university without incident.

Clark took an airplane flight back to Washington with Bernard Martin, the African-American reporter who worked for the *New York Liberty*. From his post in Memphis, Bernard Martin succeeded in filing some very important stories. He did a good in-depth interview with James Meredith as the young black man waited in Memphis to leave for Oxford and the university. Bernard Martin also was able to report on the military's progress getting to Ole Miss once President Kennedy finally ordered in the troops.

Clark Schooler spent the 1962-1963 academic year teaching entry-level American Government courses at Johns Hopkins University and Goucher College. At least that was how he spent his mornings. He spent his afternoons completing the writing, correcting, and rewriting of his doctoral dissertation. By early April of 1963, Clark was putting the final coats of polish on a document that had grown to more than 350 double-spaced typewritten pages in length.

Also in April of 1963, a significant national event was taking place on Clark Schooler's television set. Every evening Clark, along with millions of other Americans, made it a point to sit down in front of his black-and-white TV set, watch the 6 P.M. news, and get the latest developments in civil rights events in Birmingham, Alabama.

Birmingham was a logical place for things to be happening. From 1957 to 1963, there were more than 15 racial bombings in the community, inspiring civil rights advocates to derisively call the city Bombingham. When a U.S. Court ordered Birmingham to desegregate the city parks, local political leaders closed the parks rather than allow black people to enter the parks and mix with white people. Even the local professional baseball team was disbanded rather than let racially-integrated opposition teams play ball in Birmingham.

In April of 1963, Martin Luther King, Jr., and the civil rights organization he led, the Southern Christian Leadership Conference (SCLC), launched a series of protest demonstrations in Birmingham. The protests were aimed at ending racial segregation in almost every aspect of community life in Birmingham, but the immediate goal was to integrate lunch counters and restaurants in downtown Birmingham.

The political establishment in Birmingham responded forcefully to these civil rights demonstrations. When African-American school children marched through the city center to show their support for civil rights, they were met by burly white police officers armed with clubs and police dogs. Suddenly Clark Schooler was witnessing, in two-dimensional black-and-white, police dogs leaping through the air and biting young black men. In the background, Clark could see wildly flailing billy clubs as police officers attempted to beat back and chase away the African-American demonstrators.

Then it was the Birmingham Fire Department's turn. High pressure fire hoses, powerful enough to strip the bark off trees, were turned on the parading demonstrators. The force of the water knocked many of the protesters off their feet and began washing them down the street. A number of the demonstrators being smashed by the water from the fire hoses were young black women, some of them wearing their white Sunday dresses.

The TV image would shift back to the white policemen. They had armed themselves with electric cattle prods. These instruments of animal control delivered a sharp electrical shock. They were customarily used to force reluctant cattle from the holding pen into the slaughter house. The police used the cattle prods on the African-American protesters, seeking to drive them back into the black sections of the city from which they came.

When the violent action of the demonstrations was not taking center screen on Clark's TV set, the face of Police Commissioner T. Eugene (Bull) Connor was. Bull Connor ordered his police officers to arrest the demonstrators for parading without a permit. When not supervising the arrest operation personally, Bull Connor was more than happy to give personal interviews to the national news media. His comments, delivered in a thick Southern accent, were laced with racial insults and determined insistence on the perpetuation of white supremacy. Slowly but surely, as his face and his ideas appeared day-after-day on the national network evening news, Bull Connor came to symbolize, to Clark Schooler and much of the rest of the nation, uncompromising Southern white opposition to racial integration.

Alternating with Bull Connor on Clark's TV set was the face of Martin Luther King, Jr. By the spring of 1963, Martin Luther King was known throughout the United States, and much of the rest of planet Earth, as the leading spokesperson for African-American civil rights. King projected an image of being just as determined to achieve racial integration in Birmingham as Bull Connor was committed to stopping it. "If we can crack Birmingham, I am convinced we can crack the South," King said confidently. "Birmingham is a symbol of segregation for the entire South." [2]

For days almost without end, it seemed to Clark Schooler, this continuing drama played on his television set. Just as interesting to Clark, however, was the accompanying drama in Washington, D.C. Despite the violent and compelling television images being generated in Birmingham, President Kennedy refused to allow the United States Government to intervene directly in the tense stand-off in that troubled city. The best John F. Kennedy would do was to send an assistant attorney general, Burke Marshall, to try to peacefully negotiate the dispute.

By mid-May considerable progress had been made in the negotiations, and it appeared that peace might be restored in Birmingham without the need for direct military intervention from Washington, D.C. On May 12, 1963, however, a bomb was hurled from a passing automobile into the home of the Reverend A. D. King, Martin Luther King's younger brother and a local civil rights leader in Birmingham. A. D. King, his wife, and their five children were fortunate to escape the dynamite blast that partially destroyed their home.

A short time later, a second bomb was hurled into the Gaston Motel. This was the motel where Martin Luther King, Jr., normally stayed when he was in Birmingham. Luckily, that particular night, he was visiting his family at his home in Atlanta. This dynamite bomb exploded in a downstairs motel room located just below a room previously occupied by Martin Luther King. "Bombingham" suddenly was living up to its nickname.

As word of the two bombings spread throughout the African-American neighborhoods in Birmingham, angry blacks began gathering in the streets. When police sought to disperse these unruly crowds, the black people began throwing rocks and bottles at white police officers. All at once, the African-American response to racial segregation in Birmingham was something other than nonviolent. Instead of staging a nonviolent civil rights demonstration, Birmingham blacks were having a violent black riot.

Despite the efforts of civil rights leaders to calm the crowd, black mobs rampaged through the city for more than four hours. The television cameras were there, so Clark Schooler and the rest of the vast United States television audience looked on from afar as the riot grew in violence and intensity. Two grocery stores, both of them owned by whites, were set on fire. As so often happens during an incendiary riot, the flames quickly spread to nearby homes owned by black people. Clark's television screen now was filled with the eerie sight of an entire city block burning down, with groups of people running about looting stores. The sound of wailing police and fire sirens poured out of the speaker on Clark's TV, along with the voices of frantic police officers trying to bring a mob-gone-mad under control.

One television image particularly effected Clark. The fire from the riot ignited a telephone pole, which quickly turned into a flaming cross, the symbol of the Ku Klux Klan and its ideology of white supremacy. Clark thought a great deal about this ironic mental picture. But this time, he realized, it was blacks, not whites, who had set the symbolic cross of racial hatred afire.[3]

Although he only witnessed them on television, Clark Schooler learned much from the nonviolent civil rights demonstrations in Birmingham, Alabama, that late one night turned into a violent black riot. Clark noted how the television camera tended to confine images to just a limited area of activity. This effect tended to make events appear larger and more significant. This confining effect was particularly pronounced when the TV cameras "zoomed in" and got "close-ups." Television viewers throughout the United States could see the fear on the faces of the African-American civil rights protesters. Seconds later, in sharp contrast, they could see the looks of determination on the faces of the white police officers.

Because there was plenty of action at a civil rights demonstration, or a riot, the television cameramen often turned their cameras rapidly from one event to another. This swift shifting of camera angles created a feeling of danger and instability for the television viewer. It occurred to Clark that jerky camera movements served to disorient the television viewer, thereby making the viewer feel somewhat threatened and insecure as a result of what he or she was seeing.

And, finally, Clark noted to himself, many of the television images from Birmingham were fuzzy, unclear, and out-of-focus. The water spray from fire hoses, or shifting crowds of people getting in front of the television cameras, often made it difficult for viewers to see exactly what was taking place. In such a situation, the viewer filled in the images for himself or herself, usually concluding that what the viewer was not quite seeing was the Birmingham police badly mistreating civil rights demonstrators.

Clark was not alone in concluding that television coverage of the demonstrations and riots in Birmingham had influenced, and moved, and in most cases infuriated, TV watchers all over the United States. Clark delighted in a newspaper article by Eric Severeid, a well-known political commentator, who wrote: "A newspaper or television picture of a snarling police dog set upon a human being is recorded in the permanent photoelectric file of every human brain." [4]

But the real importance of Birmingham, Clark Schooler later learned, was the effect it had on the brain and political strategizing of President John Fitzgerald Kennedy. As the dramatic and upsetting events in Birmingham progressed, demands for legislative action, at the national level, poured into the president at the White House. Intense pressure, from the Northern and Western United States, came to bear on President Kennedy to introduce a major civil rights bill in Congress. Maintaining support in the North and West soon became as big a concern to the president as hanging on to segregationist white support in the South.

There also were constant demands for action from President Kennedy on civil rights in the national press. Walter Lippmann, a noted political thinker and commentator, put the case succinctly: "The cause of desegregation must cease to be a black people's movement, blessed by white politicians from the Northern states. It must become a national movement to enforce national laws, led and directed by the national government." [5]

Suddenly Clark Schooler began to detect the subtle signs that there was about to be a major policy change on civil rights at the White House. A group of civil rights leaders reported that, at a strategy meeting with John F. Kennedy, one of those present had spoken about Bull Connor in a derogatory fashion. President Kennedy was quick to make a correction, noting that "Bull Connor has done more for civil rights than anyone in this room." [6] The president was later heard to say: "The civil rights movement should thank God for Bull Connor. He's helped it as much as Abraham Lincoln." [7]

By the end of May of 1963, Clark Schooler had completed his doctoral dissertation and turned it in to his professors at Johns Hopkins University. This gave Clark six-weeks or so of time off while the dissertation was being read and evaluated. Clark returned to his job at the *Baltimore Banner*. Shortly thereafter, the Patriot Press once again sent Clark southward to be a member of a Patriot Press News Squadron covering a major Southern civil rights story.

This time the scene of the action was the University of Alabama at Tuscaloosa, Alabama. The governor of Alabama, George Wallace, was an outspoken racial segregationist. He had based his campaign for governor on a platform of all-out opposition to civil rights. At the time of his gubernatorial inauguration, George Wallace defiantly challenged the U.S. Government to try to enforce racial integration in Alabama. Wallace said:

"From this very Cradle of the Confederacy, this very heart of the great Anglo-Saxon Southland, I draw the line in the Dixie dust. I toss the gauntlet before the feet of national tyranny. And I say: Segregation now! Segregation tomorrow! Segregation forever!" [8]

As for the University of Alabama, Wallace had pledged to "bar the school house door" rather than let any black students go to school with white students in Alabama. The time for Governor Wallace to keep that pledge came when two African-American students, Vivian Malone and James Hood, received an order from a United States Court admitting them to the University of Alabama.

One reason the Patriot Press selected Clark Schooler to go to Tuscaloosa was the experience he had gained reporting on the riot at Ole Miss. No one knew exactly what might happen if Wallace really did stand in the doorway and defy U.S. Government authority. Would there be another riot? Would President Kennedy once again, as he had done at the University of Mississippi some nine months earlier, have to send in the United States Army?

When he first arrived on the University of Alabama campus, Clark Schooler was surprised by the reception he and the other national news reporters received from university officials. An entire building had been designated the official press facility. University officials had thoughtfully provided the anticipated hordes of national press correspondents with desks, typewriters, and telephones. There even were teletype operators available so that, when the time came, the reporters could easily transmit their stories back to the newspapers and magazines that employed them.

It all symbolized to Clark Schooler just how much ground the civil rights movement had gained in just a few short years. The University of Alabama was acting as though it was doing the media puffery for a big football game, or perhaps a brand new fund-raising campaign. It made Clark suspicious that he was watching a rigged, made-for-the-media event rather than a real event. News reporters had taken to calling them pseudo-events.

Unwilling to risk another disaster such as the one at Ole Miss, President John F. Kennedy early on federalized the local National Guard troops.

In effect, this shifted the Alabama National Guard from Governor Wallace's control to President Kennedy's control. From the president's perspective, it was better to have federalized Alabama National Guardsmen forcefully integrate the University of Alabama rather than regular U.S. Army troops.

A whole set of other precautions made it virtually impossible for a riot to occur. The students were placed on a tightly-enforced curfew during the late evening and nighttime hours. Police roadblocks were set up at every entrance to the campus and only bona fide students were admitted to the university grounds. Soft drink bottles, which had proved to be dandy objects for throwing at U.S. marshals at Ole Miss, were quietly removed from soft drink machines and snack bars and replaced with paper cups. Contractors working on building projects at the university were ordered to temporarily haul away all bricks, stones, and pipes.

Despite all the pre-programming, the racial integration of the University of Alabama was a significant event when it finally occurred. Clark Schooler stood in a large clot of news personnel facing an open door in a major building at the university.

The scene in front of Clark was a media classic. Governor Wallace stood in the doorway, thereby fulfilling his pledge to "bar the school house door." He was standing behind a portable wooden podium. Facing him, and representing the United States Government, was Deputy Attorney General Nicholas Katzenbach, the man who had directed the U.S. marshals that defended the Lyceum building at Ole Miss. At that moment, a camera lens clicked. The Associated Press sent the resulting photograph to virtually every news outlet on the entire planet.

In the photograph, Wallace appeared to be short, which he was, but with a thick head of black hair. Nick Katzenbach, on the other hand, was tall with bare skin visible on the top of his balding head. The two men were looking straight at each other. The photograph perfectly symbolized state authority confronting national authority. The photo revealed clearly how the state of Alabama was defying the United States of America.

But the stand-off portrayed in the photograph did not last. Clark Schooler and the other reporters watched intently as a General Graham, the commander of the newly-federalized Alabama National Guard, approached the wooden podium. He was accompanied by four of his elite soldiers. General Graham came to attention. He then looked squarely at Governor Wallace and said softly, "It is my sad duty to ask you to step aside."

Wallace did not "step aside." He remained behind the wooden podium and began to read a short speech. The Southern governor remained defiant, even in the face of certain defeat. "The trend toward military dictatorship continues," he said. "But this is a constitutional fight, and we are winning.

God bless all the people of this state, white and black." [9]

Governor George Wallace then stepped aside, and the University of Alabama soon was officially racially integrated. The date was June 11, 1963. Wallace had given way to a National Guard general who, just a few hours earlier, had been under Governor Wallace's command rather than President Kennedy's command.

That evening President John F. Kennedy addressed the nation to defend his actions at the University of Alabama. Clark Schooler watched the speech on television in his hotel room in Tuscaloosa. President Kennedy used the speech to announce his intention to send a strong civil rights bill to the United States Congress and to use all his powers as president to get it passed.

To Clark Schooler, one of the most important roles of the U.S. president was to serve as a sort of Spokesperson for America. It was a big part of the president's job, Clark often said, to boldly express the common sentiments of the people of the United States. In so doing, the president would not only sum up the national mood but also help to lead the nation toward necessary actions.

"We are confronted primarily with a moral issue," President Kennedy told the nation. "It is as old as the scriptures and is as clear as the American Constitution. This nation, for all its hopes and all its boasts, will not be fully free until all its citizens are free."

"The fires of discord are burning in every city, North and South, where legal remedies are not at hand," the president concluded. "Next week I shall ask the Congress of the United States to act. I shall ask the Congress to make a commitment, [one that] it has not fully made in this century, to the proposition that race has no place in American life or law." [10]

In The Interim

The relationship of the United States Government to the fifty state governments has been a delicate one throughout American History. Debate continues to rage over exactly which functions should be carried out by the U.S. Government in Washington, D.C., and which should be executed only by the states.

When economic times are favorable in the United States and there is little disturbance in the social balance of the nation, most Americans prefer for state governments to become more active and to do more things. But during times of economic discord and social upheaval, pressure quickly mounts on the U.S. Government to step into the breach and try to solve problems from the nation's capital in Washington, D.C.

CHAPTER 4

THE CONSTITUTION:
DEMOCRACY AND MINORITY RIGHTS

Gilman Hall was the most prominent and historic building on the main campus of Johns Hopkins University in Baltimore. The red brick structure was accented with white wooden trim and topped with a picturesque cupola. Tall white wooden columns decorated the large porch at the front entrance. Clark Schooler considered himself privileged to have spent his graduate school career studying and writing in such an attractive and comfortable academic building.

On an afternoon in late June of 1963, Clark was sitting on a chair outside the main political science seminar room in Gilman Hall. For the past six years, through all the time Clark was a graduate student, that seminar room had been a major part of Clark's life. He had taken almost all of his graduate school classes in that seminar room. The political science seminar room also was the place where, as a teaching assistant, Clark had taught some of his first political science courses to undergraduate students at Johns Hopkins.

On this particular day, however, Clark Schooler was facing the final hurdle in his long dash to earn a doctoral degree in political science. In only a few minutes, he would enter the seminar room and take his Ph.D. oral examination. A committee of three faculty members at Johns Hopkins would ask Clark questions about his dissertation, the book-length manuscript which Clark had just completed writing, correcting, and proofreading.

As he sat in the chair outside the seminar room, Clark was actively applying his First Rule Of Meeting Attendance. That rule read: Never go to a meeting without a clear picture of what you want to accomplish at the meeting. Clark had long ago noted that many people go to a meeting with no set agenda of things that are to be achieved at the meeting. Clark tried never to do that. Before each meeting he attended, Clark worked hard to have clear in his mind the specific things he wanted done at the meeting.

For instance, this particular policy was to be adopted at the meeting. Or this particular man, or that particular woman, was to be hired at the meeting. The particular goal was not important. What was important was that Clark Schooler attend and participate in the meeting in such a way that Clark's particular goals and interests were clear in his mind. If they were, Clark's goals and interests stood a good chance of being advanced by the meeting.

In the case of Clark Schooler's Ph.D. oral examination, Clark's goal for the meeting was crystal clear. "Get the three faculty members to vote to award Clark Schooler his Ph.D. degree in political science."

But Clark wanted more from this particular meeting. Graduate students who performed unusually well in their Ph.D. oral examinations were awarded the degree "with distinction." The longer Clark sat in the chair outside the seminar room, the more he worked himself up psychologically to give a really good performance and get a Ph.D. diploma marked "with distinction."

Professor Michael Middleton, Clark's Ph.D. dissertation supervisor, emerged from the political science seminar room. This was the same Professor Middleton who taught the graduate seminar in American Politics at Johns Hopkins.

Professor Middleton previously had gathered the other faculty members together in the seminar room and briefed them on Clark's graduate school career and the subject matter of his dissertation. Professor Middleton gave Clark a sort of "This is it!" smile and then invited Clark to follow him into the seminar room.

As he entered the seminar room, Clark was struck once again with the room's attractiveness and comfortableness. The room was located in the southeast corner of Gilman Hall, with large windows on both the east side and the south side. Because of the abundant southern exposure, the room tended to be bright and sunny all day long. In the early fall and late spring, when the weather was warm, the windows could be opened to let fresh air into the room. That was the case on this particular June day. The sun was shining, the windows were open, and the seminar room was filled with the luxuriant feeling of a pleasant early summer afternoon.

Clark sat down at the end of an oblong conference table. Three copies of his dissertation were scattered around the table top. The three faculty members could pick up one of the copies and look up particular parts of Clark's dissertation if they wanted to do so. Clark noticed, with a little bit of discomfort, that one faculty member had stuck little pieces of paper at various points in one of the copies of the dissertation. Obviously, Clark deduced, Clark was going to be questioned on each portion of the dissertation that particular faculty member had marked.

Professor Michael Middleton opened the festivities. "Clark," he said, "tell us the title of your dissertation and why you selected that particular topic?"

Clark swallowed hard, and his oral exam began. "The title of my dissertation," Clark said clearly but not too loudly, "is 'Black Americans And The United States Constitution.' I selected that topic because I wanted . . ."

That was all the further Clark got. He was interrupted, somewhat officiously, by Professor Charles Brentwood, an expert in the U.S. Constitution and constitutional law. Professor Brentwood said: "I would have been happier if you had entitled your dissertation 'The United States Constitution And Black Americans,' thereby putting the Constitution first. The Constitution, as the fundamental written document of the United States Government, should automatically be placed before any constituent group in U.S. society, even a minority group as important as black people."

Clark responded quickly and confidently: "The reason I put American blacks first in the title was that black men and women were first brought to what is now the United States in 1619. That was exactly 168 years prior to the writing of the United States Constitution in Philadelphia in the summer of 1787. Black people were here in the U.S. quite some time before the Constitution was adopted."

Clark did not just answer Professor Brentwood's immediate question. He used the question as an opportunity to expound on the history of African-Americans in the English colonies in North America, a key part of the introduction to his dissertation.

"Jamestown, Virginia, was the first permanent English colony in North America," Clark said. "It was founded in May of 1607. Only twelve years later, in 1619, twenty African slaves were sold to the Virginians from a Dutch ship visiting the harbor. That was the beginning of 'slavery' and 'involuntary servitude' in the American South."

"Incidentally," Clark continued, "I used the words 'slavery' and 'involuntary servitude' because those are the words used in the U.S. Constitution."

That statement received a nod of approval from Professor Brentwood. It was legend among students at Johns Hopkins that Professor Brentwood knew the U.S. Constitution word for word and was delighted whenever he heard his students using exact constitutional language.

Clark continued with his presentation. "It is a great coincidence that African slaves were first brought to Virginia in 1619. That is the same year that the Virginia House of Burgesses, an elected legislature, held its first meeting in Jamestown. This was the first meeting of a legislature, elected by the people, in North America. How ironic that slavery began for Africans in America the same year that representative government began for white people."

It seemed to Clark that the panel of three professors was ready to let him talk for awhile and present some of the ideas from his dissertation. "The African slaves proved useful and profitable on the farmlands of the American South," Clark pointed out. "Meandering tidewater rivers made large plantations accessible to ocean shipping. The South became an ideal place for growing cotton and other agricultural products needed back in England and on the European continent. The African slaves were a cheap and reliable source of labor for the South's emerging agricultural economy."

"In the North," Clark went on, "the land was hillier and the climate more harsh. The use of human slaves was not economically successful. The Northern colonies mainly used the labor of yeoman farmers who owned the land they farmed. In the emerging factory towns and cities in the North, white men and women worked for wages."

"The end result," Clark continued, "was the creation of sectionalism in what is now the United States. The South relied heavily on slave labor. The North emphasized the work and industry of free citizens. These two sections of the nation, the North and the South, developed different economies, different social structures, and vastly different attitudes toward the institution of human slavery."

Clark was moving his presentation along and enjoying it. He could see the faculty members were listening intently and paying close attention.

"The irony of freedom developing for whites and slavery existing for black Africans continued throughout the colonial period," Clark explained. "In 1620, the Mayflower landed at Plymouth Rock. The Pilgrims adopted the Mayflower Compact, the first written plan of government to be adopted in the colonies. That plan created an orderly society roughly based on the consent of the governed. But it applied only to the Pilgrims. No such ideas were ever applied to the African slaves in the South."

"In 1639," Clark continued, "a group of Puritans left Massachusetts and founded Connecticut. They drew up and adopted the Fundamental Orders of Connecticut, the first written constitution in the colonies. It provided for a colonial legislature, with elected representatives from each Connecticut town. But no one even thought about drawing up a compact or a constitution to protect the rights and provide a role in self-government for the black slaves in the South."

"Or take our own state of Maryland," Clark said with hometown enthusiasm. "Maryland was founded in 1634 as a haven for Roman Catholics, a place where they could escape religious persecution in Protestant England. But George Calvert, the founder of Maryland, invited a number of religious groups to come and live together in his new colony. In 1649, Maryland adopted the Act Of Toleration, which guaranteed freedom of religion."

"But no one bothered to be tolerant of the rights and freedoms of the African slaves in Maryland," Clark went on. "It's true that Maryland is a Border State and did not secede from the Union during the Civil War. But it also is true that Maryland was a slave colony and, after the American Revolution, a slave state. Our hallowed and venerated 'toleration,' of which all Marylanders are justifiably proud, was clearly marked 'Whites Only.'"

Clark decided it was time to hammer home one of the main points of his dissertation. "In 1776," he noted with emphasis, "Thomas Jefferson, a Virginia slave owner, wrote the Declaration Of Independence. In his original draft, Jefferson included a stern condemnation of the international slave trade. That was the process by which blacks were captured in Africa, put in chains, and shipped to a life of bondage in the New World."

"But Jefferson's brave words condemning trading in human flesh were deleted from the Declaration," Clark said with the sound of condemnation in his voice. "Why? Because the free colonies in the North wanted to keep the support of the slave holding colonies in the South in the upcoming Revolutionary War with Great Britain."

Clark was certain this statement would get a rise from the assembled faculty members. He was not disappointed. William Carpman, professor of history at Johns Hopkins, was a published scholar in the field of 19th Century American history. A history professor had been brought in to give an interdisciplinary perspective to Clark's oral examination. "Are you implying," Professor Carpman asked with feigned amazement in his voice, "that Thomas Jefferson, one of our most admired historical leaders, was of two opinions on the subject of human slavery? Are you saying that he condemned slavery, or at least the international slave trade, in his political thought but continued to own slaves and defend slavery in his public life?"

"Yes, I am," Clark replied forthrightly. "But, for me, Thomas Jefferson established a model for well-meaning persons in both the North and the South. People like Jefferson were opposed to trading in human flesh in their hearts, but they were unwilling in their public lives to openly condemn slavery and thereby antagonize the white South. As I said, the white South was needed to win the Revolutionary War, or, later on, the white South was needed to win World War I and World War II."

"Some very well-intentioned and courageous people," Clark continued, "were unwilling to condemn slavery and, later on, racial segregation in the South. Why? Because they did not want to risk losing support from white Southerners for some other, often totally unrelated, political or governmental purpose."

Professor Carpman looked hard at Clark for a moment and then asked: "Do you condemn Thomas Jefferson for amending the Declaration of Independence, one of the great documents in the history of human freedom and liberty, so as to not mention the international slave trade and thereby not antagonize the South?"

Clark Schooler had to think about this question. Professor Carpman was a renowned expert on the period immediately prior to the American Civil War. Clark tried for a few seconds to divine the answer that Professor Carpman was seeking. When nothing came to Clark in that regard, he gave his own honest answer.

"I do not condemn Jefferson," Clark said with conviction. "Like so many United States political leaders, Jefferson was the victim of historical accident. For geographical reasons, the United States turned to slave labor in the South and free labor in the North. In order to keep the country united, good men and women, both South and North, had to put a muzzle on their condemnation of human slavery. Jefferson was just the first in a long line of political leaders who would feel the need to sacrifice freedom for African slaves on the altar of national unity."

Professor Carpman looked at Clark and muttered, somewhat to himself, "That's one way to look at it."

There was a brief pause, and then Clark went on with his defense of his dissertation. "That brings us to the Constitutional Convention in Philadelphia in 1787," Clark said. "Never before or since has there been such a gathering of great leaders. George Washington, of Virginia, the victorious commander of the colonial troops in the Revolutionary War, was chosen to be the presiding officer. James Madison, also of Virginia, kept the notes that are our major written record of what was debated, adopted, and discarded at the convention. Alexander Hamilton, of New York, provided many of the ideas concerning a strong national government that found their way into the Constitution."

Clark Schooler hesitated for a moment. He looked around the table at his faculty inquisitors. Very slowly and precisely, Clark said: "I now want to take each of the major governmental institutions created by the United States Constitution and show how those institutions affected black Americans."

"I'll begin with federalism," Clark stated in his most official voice, "because the creation of a federal system was the most important accomplishment of the Constitutional Convention. The thirteen colonies had evolved into thirteen states. These state governments were allowed to retain their sovereignty, their legal and governmental control, over state matters. But a new national government was created with its own sovereignty, mainly over national and international matters. This creation of two forms of sovereign government, thirteen governments at the state level and one government at the national level, was called federalism, or dual sovereignty."

"Federalism is a marvelous creation," Clark continued, "but it has made life miserable for black people in America. It permitted state governments in the American South to legalize slavery. After the Civil War and the emancipation of the slaves, federalism permitted the Southern states to legally institutionalize racial segregation. Rules segregating blacks from whites, particularly in public places, were codified in state laws. Long after there was a national consensus that racial segregation should be ended throughout the United States, federalism permitted the Southern states to legally preserve strict racial separation."

While Clark Schooler was making this definitive critique of American federalism, Professor Charles Brentwood, the constitutional expert, had grown increasingly agitated.

"Hold on a minute, Clark," Professor Brentwood snapped. "There's a strong historical precedent for federalism in the United States. England treated the thirteen colonies as thirteen individual governments. England never created a centralized colonial government for the thirteen colonies, say at New York or Philadelphia. The result was a tradition in the colonies of local self-rule."

"At the time of the American Revolution," Brentwood thundered on, "the thirteen individual colonies became thirteen individual states. True, the Continental Congress was created to fight the Revolutionary War for the thirteen states and signed the Treaty of Paris ending the war. But the Articles of Confederation, which were created to govern the new United States after the Revolutionary War, retained all sovereignty in the states. Participation in the Articles of Confederation, and obeying the decisions and programs of the Continental Congress, was purely voluntary on the part of the states."

"It's also true," Brentwood continued, "that the Articles of Confederation did not work very well. Individual states refused to tax their citizens to pay the cost of fighting American Indians on the western frontier. Individual states imposed tariffs on goods imported from other states that greatly restricted commerce between the states. At the Annapolis Convention, the forerunner of the Constitutional Convention in Philadelphia, the states wrestled with the question of whether Maryland or Virginia owned and controlled the Potomac River, and they could not reach a solution. After failing to make any progress at Annapolis, they decided to meet again later in Philadelphia."

Professor Brentwood's voice trailed off. He realized he had better get to the point of his oration. "What I am getting at," Professor Brentwood concluded, "is that state power was clearly established by the time of the Constitutional Convention in 1787. There was no way the convention was going to adopt anything but a governmental system in which the individual states retained a major share of their sovereign powers."

At this point the history professor, William Carpman, rejoined the discussion. "I agree with Professor Brentwood," Carpman began. "We are talking here about one of the great safeguards of United States democracy. Federalism created what I call the territorial balance of power. The possibly tyrannical power of the national government is checked by the power of the individual state governments. I have always thought of federalism as one of the great safeguards of liberty and freedom. But you, Clark, are presenting it as a great threat to the civil rights of racial and ethnic minorities."

There was a joke in academe that the best way to pass a Ph.D. oral was to get the examining professors riled up and doing all the talking. The more the professors talked, so the joke went, the less time there was for the Ph.D. candidate to talk, possibly make mistakes, and get into trouble. The joke had momentarily come to pass at Clark Schooler's Ph.D. oral. Professor Brentwood's defense of the strong position of state sovereignty in American history had used up some time. Professor Carpman's ideas on a "territorial balance of power" had used up even more time. The result was a brief but uncomfortable pause when Professor Carpman finished speaking.

Clark used the pause to advantage. "Of course," Clark said, "no one can deny the importance of federalism in the historical development of government in the United States. But also, no one can deny that the states' rights aspect of federalism has been the major reason for the reduced position of black people in American life."

"To understand my Ph.D. dissertation," Clark concluded firmly and loudly, "you have to understand that I have set as my task the following: The revelation of the racially discriminatory aspects of some of the most treasured and admired aspects of American Government. Federalism, and state's rights, is only my first case in point."

Making that point so forcefully had given Clark a feeling of power and control. He moved forward confidently with his presentation. "My second case in point," Clark said, "is separation of powers. During that hot summer of 1787 in Philadelphia, the Founders created a national government that was divided into three parts. Those were the legislative, the executive, and the judicial. Most people know the three branches of the U.S. Government by the more familiar titles of the Congress, the President, and the Supreme Court."

"In addition to separation of powers," Clark went on, "the Founders permitted the three branches of the national government to have checks and balances on each other. The president can veto laws passed by Congress. To override a presidential veto, Congress must repass the law by a 2/3 majority in both houses of Congress. On the other hand, the Congress possesses all the power to appropriate money. The president cannot implement his various governmental programs, at least not for very long, if the Congress will not appropriate the money to pay for them."

"The exact role of the Supreme Court took some time to emerge," Clark said, "but its powers in the national government were soon clear. The Supreme Court, by a process called judicial review, can declare laws of Congress unconstitutional, which means those laws are no longer in effect. Furthermore . . ."

At that point Clark was abruptly interrupted by Professor Michael Middleton, who had supervised the writing of Clark's dissertation. "Clark," Professor Middleton said somewhat testily, "everyone in this room knows how separation of powers works. Get to the point."

Clark responded immediately to Middleton's demand. "The point is," Clark said, "that separation of powers became an obstacle to American blacks gaining their civil rights. By the middle of the 20th Century, it was obvious that racial segregation in the American South could only be eliminated by national government action. But for the national government to act, all three branches of the United States Government have to be in agreement. And one branch of government, the U.S. Congress, has failed to act on behalf of civil rights for black men and women. The Congress has steadfastly refused, throughout the 20th Century, to pass a major civil rights bill guaranteeing freedom and equality to Southern blacks."

"When dealing with this question," Clark went on, "it is important to note that two of the three branches of the national government, the President and the Supreme Court, have progressively supported black civil rights. President Franklin D. Roosevelt issued an executive order in 1941 that racially integrated all the defense plants in the United States during World War II. President Harry Truman, in 1948, issued an executive order that racially integrated the armed forces, specifically the Army, the Navy, the Marine Corps, and the Air Force. And, of course, President Eisenhower in 1957 issued his famous order to use U.S. troops to integrate Central High School in Little Rock, Arkansas."

"And, in 1954," Clark said, "the Supreme Court placed itself firmly behind black civil rights when, in the *Brown v. Board of Education* ruling, it mandated the racial integration of public schools throughout the United States."

"But one branch of our tripartite national government, the Congress, has refused to pass a civil rights bill. As a result, black persons in the American South remain unprotected where their civil rights are concerned. And separation of powers is the admired and exalted principal of our national government that has permitted this situation to come into existence."

To Clark Schooler's surprise, none of the faculty at his Ph.D. oral exam questioned his description of separation of powers as harming African-American civil rights. The role of the U.S. Congress in killing all meaningful civil rights legislation was well-known in the mid-20th Century.

So Clark continued with his presentation.

"We come now to one of the most familiar events at the Constitutional Convention," Clark explained. "The adoption of a two house, or bicameral, national legislature. This legislative body, called the United States Congress, was composed of both a Senate and a totally separate House of Representatives."

"At the Constitutional Convention," Clark continued, "the state of Virginia proposed that representation in the national legislature be mainly on the basis of population. The larger the number of people that lived in a particular state, the larger would be its number of representatives elected to the Congress. This proposal was known as the Virginia Plan. It favored states such as New York, Pennsylvania, and Virginia, which had large numbers of residents."

"But a rival plan was presented by the state of New Jersey," Clark said. "This proposal called for equal representation of each state in the national legislature, no matter what a state's population might be. This New Jersey Plan favored states with small populations, such as Maryland, Delaware, and New Jersey."

Clark realized that he was once again telling his faculty examiners things they already knew. He got to the point as quickly as he could. "The resolution of these two plans was a compromise," Clark said, "the renowned Connecticut Compromise. A two house Congress was created with the upper chamber, the Senate, having equal representation that took the form of two senators from each state. The lower chamber, the House of Representatives, was based on population, with the more populous states having more representation in the House."

Clark moved to his main point with a rhetorical question and answer: "And how has this affected American blacks? The Senate, with equal representation, has become the great defender of Southern states' rights. The South had a smaller population than the North, but each Southern state, no matter how small its population, had the same number of senators as any populous Northern state. The result was the South came to rely on its power in the Senate, the power of less populous states over more populous states, to defeat civil rights bills for black Americans. In some cases, these were civil rights bills that had easily passed in the House of Representatives, where the more heavily populated North could make its pro-civil rights voice heard."

"The Senate thus became famous as the burial ground of all civil rights bills," Clark concluded.

At that moment, Clark Schooler got out of his chair and walked to the chalkboard in the political science seminar room. He took a piece of chalk and drew a large arch on the board. "What I am setting up here," Clark explained, "is an Arch Of Racial Oppression. Black people in America live under an arch of constitutional principles and state laws that greatly limit the black person's liberty and freedom. Tragically, federalism, separation of powers, and bicameralism are three of the major building stones in that arch."

Clark used the chalk to draw three stones in his Arch Of Racial Oppression. He carefully labeled one stone "Federalism," a second stone "Separation of Powers," and the third stone "Bicameralism." He then returned to his seat and continued his defense of his Ph.D. dissertation.

Clark Schooler reviewed the ideas which he and Bernard Martin, his African-American newspaper colleague, had discussed on their airplane flight to Memphis, Tennessee, and the riot at Ole Miss. Clark explained how the Constitution rested police powers in the state governments, and this gave state and local officials the option to willingly "suspend law and order" for United States blacks. Clark then stepped to the chalkboard and added a stone labeled "Police Powers" to his Arch Of Racial Oppression.

Next on Clark's agenda was the guarantee in the U.S. Constitution of trial by jury. Clark described how individual Southerners could harass, beat, and even murder African-Americans and be certain of being found innocent by a jury of their white peers. Giving verbal credit to Bernard Martin, Clark actually used the phrase: "The free white jury that will never convict."

As he added a stone marked "Jury Trial" to his Arch Of Racial Oppression, Clark detected a pained look on the face of Professor Brentwood. Charles Brentwood had spent his entire academic career studying and praising the United States court system. It appeared to hurt Brentwood to see one of the great protections of United States jurisprudence, the jury trial, being described as an instrument for protecting people who illegally persecute minority persons.

And then Clark described the peculiar wording of the 14th Amendment, that post-Civil War constitutional amendment that was supposed to guarantee civil rights to the newly freed slaves. "By using the words 'no state shall,'" Clark said, "the 14th Amendment left individual Southerners free to limit the rights and freedoms of blacks, often by beating them or killing them. The 14th Amendment to the United States Constitution limited the power of the states to harm blacks, but not the power of individuals to do so." Another stone went into Clark's arch, this one labeled "14th Amendment."

At this point William Carpman, professor of history, decided to question Clark carefully about the overall theme and tone of his Ph.D. dissertation. "Clark," Professor Carpman began, "you seem to be describing the Constitutional Convention as a plot against the black people of the United States. You give the impression that our exalted and admired Founders created an 'Instrument of Oppression' in the Constitution rather than, as most people think, an 'Instrument Of Liberty and Freedom.' Let's begin discussing this question by having you tell us exactly how the Constitutional Convention handled the immediate question of human slavery."

Clark was ready for this question. He answered it quickly and deftly. "One of the problems concerning black Americans at the Constitutional Convention was the international slave trade," Clark began. "Many Northern delegates were concerned about the continuing capture of free persons in Africa and their importation into the United States to be sold into bondage. The delegates solved this dispute with a compromise. The slave trade would be allowed to continue for only twenty years after the Constitution was adopted, at which time Congress could abolish it, which Congress did."

Professor Carpman nodded his head in agreement and gave a somewhat sarcastic smile. "You do acknowledge then," the historian said, "that the Constitutional Convention did something for the black person. It provided for Congress to abolish the slave trade as of twenty years after the Constitution was adopted."

Clark was forced to agree with Professor Carpman on this point. "Yes, the Constitution did authorize Congress to eventually do away with the slave trade," Clark said. "But let's not forget that, for twenty long years, from approximately 1788 to 1808, black men, women, and children were physically captured in Africa, were forced to cross the Atlantic Ocean in chains, were jammed into the holds of sailing ships, where thousands of them died from disease, and . . ."

"That's all true," Carpman interrupted, "but the slave trade was finally abolished. The Constitutional Convention was not, as you seem to be portraying it, totally hostile to the interests of American blacks."

There was a brief period of silence following this mildly heated exchange. Clark finally decided it was his responsibility to revive the conversation and continue his oral examination.

"Also at the Constitutional Convention in Philadelphia in the summer of 1787," Clark began hesitantly, "the delegates debated whether or not the African slaves in the South should be counted when determining how many representatives a state would have in the House of Representatives. The Southern states would have more votes in the House if the African slaves could be counted as well as the free white citizens."

"The end result was a famous compromise," Clark went on. "It was the Three/Fifths Compromise. For every five African slaves living within its borders, a Southern state could count an additional three persons for the purpose of determining representation in the House of Representatives. Thus three additional persons were counted for every five African slaves."

Once again Professor Carpman nodded his head in agreement and gave a sarcastic smile. "You do agree then," Carpman said, "that the Founders, meeting at the Constitutional Convention, at least gave some recognition to the slaves as human beings. The slaves were deemed, at least for counting purposes, as being similar to their white owners, even though the slaves rated only a three/fifths count for representation. For the summer of 1787, I would argue that partial recognition of the slaves as human beings was an important step forward."

Clark felt the need to respond to Professor Carpman's comment. "But the role of the Southerners on this point was so self-serving," Clark noted. "The Southerners were unwilling to extend any legal rights or privileges to the slaves, and certainly not the right to vote, but still the Southerners maneuvered to count the slaves for representational purposes. I have great difficulty seeing such a position on the part of the Southerners as a step forward of any kind. That's everything for the white Southerner, virtually nothing for the African slave."

"In fact," Clark said in a summary tone of voice, "it is interesting to take a second look at both the abolition of the international slave trade and the Three-Fifths Compromise on representation in the House of Representatives. In each case, the African slaves were victims of compromise. Some progress was made, the slave trade was finally abolished, and the slaves were acknowledged to be human enough to be counted as three/fifths of a person for the House of Representatives. But such unfair compromises became a pattern for the future. By being so willing to compromise with the Southerners on racial issues, the Northerners ended up agreeing to a final solution that always left the American black in a weakened, compromised position."

Clark's comments did not slow down Professor Carpman one bit. The history professor continued with his effort to put the framers of the U.S. Constitution in a more positive light where the treatment of black Americans was concerned. "Once the Constitution was written," Carpman said, "it had to be adopted by the states to take effect. Clark, please describe that process for us. Describe it the way you described it in your Ph.D. dissertation."

Clark Schooler was somewhat frightened by this question. At first thought, the question looked easy. It appeared that Professor Carpman was helping Clark out by asking a question that Carpman knew Clark could answer. But Clark worried about just why Carpman had asked that particular question. Carpman was driving at something. Clark worried that it might be something that could get Clark into a great deal of intellectual trouble.

"For the new Constitution to take effect," Clark answered somewhat nervously, "nine of the thirteen colonies had to officially adopt it. It was well-known, however, that the Constitution would not be very effective if the three most populous states of New York, Pennsylvania, and Virginia did not give their approval."

"The people who supported the new Constitution were called Federalists," Clark went on. "Those who opposed it were called anti-Federalists. The major criticism of the new Constitution by the anti-Federalists was that the new Constitution did not, in specific language, protect the rights of individual citizens from incursions and illegal acts by the new national government."

"In a political manipulation to gain anti-Federalist support for the new Constitution," Clark continued, "the Federalists agreed to add a Bill Of Rights to the Constitution. Thanks partly to this maneuver, the Constitution was adopted by the states. Shortly thereafter, the first ten amendments were added to the Constitution. Written mainly by James Madison, of Virginia, those first ten amendments were the promised Bill of Rights."

Professor Carpman was smiling while Clark was talking, which Clark took to mean Carpman wanted him to go on with this particular line of discussion. "The Bill of Rights spelled out what has become one of the great collections of human rights protections in human history," Clark said with something of a patriotic fervor. "The 1st Amendment, which some people argue is the most important, protected freedom of religion, freedom of speech, freedom of the press, and the freedom to assemble at political meetings and rallies. The 4th Amendment is also considered significant. It protected the people from unreasonable searches and seizures. The 5th Amendment protected a person from self-incrimination, being forced to testify against oneself in a court of law."

"We've already discussed some aspects of the 6th Amendment," Clark went on. "It's the one that mandates trial by jury."

Well aware that his examiners knew what was in the Bill of Rights, Clark quickly related that document to his Ph.D. dissertation. "The problem with the first ten amendments to the Constitution," Clark said matter-of-factly, "is they protect U.S. citizens from the national government but not from state governments. The black person in America did not and does not need protection from the national government in Washington, D.C. The black person in America needs protection from the state governments, specifically Southern state governments. In most cases, the Bill of Rights did not, and does not, provide such protections."

"In fact," Clark said, "the 1st Amendment begins with the words, 'Congress shall make no law,' and then goes on to spell out the rights protected. Courts subsequently interpreted that phrase as meaning the bulk of the Bill of Rights applied only to the United States Government, specifically the Congress, and not to the individual state governments. For instance, the U.S. Supreme Court ruled in the case of . . ."

Clark was stopped in his verbal tracks. Professor Carpman took command of the discussion abruptly and passionately. "True it may be," Carpman said somewhat loudly, "that the Bill of Rights applied mainly to the national government and not to the states. But, frankly, your dissertation misses the point that, no matter how it is applied, the Bill of Rights sets a standard for democratic government."

"The Bill of Rights has been a beacon of liberty and freedom from the very first day it was adopted," Carpman exclaimed. "No matter what the courts say, thanks to the Constitution and the Bill of Rights, all Americans expect to be treated as if they are equal. At school, at work, even in the privacy of their own homes, citizens of the United States expect to have the freedom of religion, the freedom of speech, and all the other freedoms mentioned in the Bill of Rights. Those rights have become part of the internal fabric of the American consciousness."

"I am as displeased with the Southern treatment of black people as you are," Professor Carpman said in a definitive manner. "But when Martin Luther King, Jr., and his followers demand the right to hold meetings in behalf of civil rights, to hold parades in behalf of civil rights, and so on and so forth, they are mainly telling the rest of us to live up to the promises made in the Constitution and the Bill of Rights."

"The recent unpleasantness in Birmingham, Alabama, was mainly over black demands for the 1st Amendment right to peacefully assemble and parade," Carpman went on. "If you ever decide to publish this dissertation, Clark, I suggest you add some positive points about the Constitution and the

Bill of Rights to it. In spirit if not in law, it is the Bill of Rights which is inspiring the current drive for black civil rights."

When Professor Carpman had finished speaking, Clark went up to the chalkboard and added a stone labeled "Bill of Rights wording" to his Arch Of Racial Oppression. Because of Professor Carpman's comments, Clark did not draw that stone with a great deal of verve and confidence. It occurred to Clark that, with his sharp criticisms, Carpman was living up to the nickname given to him by the students at Johns Hopkins, which was "Professor Carping."

As he returned from the chalkboard to his seat, it occurred to Clark Schooler that the assembled professors had taken charge of his Ph.D. oral examination. He was no longer making an orderly presentation of his ideas. As almost always happens in an oral examination, this one had hit the point where Clark was spending all his time responding to questions from his intellectual inquisitors. And they were probing questions at that.

The next attack was led by Charles Brentwood, the political science professor whose special field was American Jurisprudence. Brentwood was currently in the process of writing a book on the United States Supreme Court in the years just prior to the Civil War. Those were the years in the United States when, from roughly 1830 to 1860, the North and the South drifted progressively further apart over the issue of abolition, which was the proposed outlawing by Congress of the institution of human slavery.

"Prior to the Civil War," Professor Brentwood asked in a deprecating tone, "what was all the fuss about a man named Dred Scott?"

Clark was in luck. He had spent a number of pages of his Ph.D. dissertation discussing in considerable detail the case of *Dred Scott v. Sanford*.

"Dred Scott," Clark replied, "was an African slave who was taken out of the slave state of Missouri into the free state of Illinois and the free territory of Wisconsin. Scott was later returned to Missouri, where he sued for his freedom. Scott based his case on the argument that, the moment he stepped on to free soil in Illinois and Wisconsin, he was a free citizen. The time was the late 1840s and early 1850s."

Clark decided to impress Professor Brentwood by making a point that Brentwood had once made while Clark was taking Brentwood's course in American Jurisprudence. "We know nothing of the particulars of Dred Scott's life," Clark said. "His name is on one of the most important court cases in American history, but his name is all we know. It was typical of attitudes toward black people in the mid-1800s that no one considered it important to find out very many personal facts about Dred Scott the person. We know few of the details of where he was born, where he grew up, what work he did as a slave, whether he was married, and so forth and so on.

Even the abolitionists who supported his case did not bother to find out or write down very much about him. Ironically, what we do know are the names of the white persons who owned him and the dates when he was sold from one white person to another."

"The chief justice was Roger B. Taney of Maryland," Clark continued. "Taney was himself a slave owner, and he and a court majority of 7-2 dealt severely with Dred Scott. The court ruled that slaves were not citizens, and therefore Dred Scott could not sue for his freedom in U.S. courts. It was a major blow to the abolition movement for the Supreme Court to declare that, according to the United States Constitution, a slave was not a citizen but actually was a white person's personal property. The decision came at a time when a leading abolitionist, William Lloyd Garrison, was burning up copies of the Constitution in public."

"But Chief Justice Taney and the Supreme Court went even further," Clark pointed out. "The court ruled that, since slaves were personal property, Congress could not prevent white citizens from taking their slaves with them to United States territories, such as Kansas and Nebraska, that had been declared free territories by laws of Congress. This had the effect of declaring unconstitutional the Missouri Compromise, a congressional law that had created free territories as well as slave territories."

"For my Ph.D. dissertation," Clark concluded, "the point is that the Supreme Court, in the mid-1800s, found in the U.S. Constitution the justification for delivering a double insult to American blacks. First, the slaves were not citizens of the United States. Second, the slaves were the mere personal property of their white owners." With that firm remark, Clark went once again to the chalkboard and drew in a stone named "*Dred Scott* decision" on his Arch Of Racial Oppression.

Professor Brentwood was laying in wait for Clark when he returned to his chair at the conference table. "I get the impression," Brentwood said, "that you disapprove of the Supreme Court's decision in the *Dred Scott* case. Why is that?"

"It was a dramatic instance of judicial activism," Clark responded. "Chief Justice Taney and his Southern supporters on the Supreme Court attempted to use the court for political, not judicial, purposes. They wanted to legalize slavery in all the territories, a decision that should have been made by Congress, the legislative branch, rather than by the Supreme Court, the judicial branch."

"Furthermore," Clark continued, "I find nothing in the U.S. Constitution that says that slaves are not citizens. The Constitution refers directly to the slaves as other persons, not as noncitizens. The court was actively making law, which is what judicial activism is. In this case, I think the court should have practiced judicial restraint, following the exact letter of the Constitution and not trying to make new laws in the courtroom. In my view, the Supreme Court never should have ruled on the question of whether or not slaves were citizens, or whether slaves could be taken into free territories."

At this moment the historian, Professor Carpman, decided to get back into the action. He asked: "Whatever happened to the *Dred Scott* decision? Is it still the law of the land?"

"In practical terms," Clark responded, "the *Dred Scott* decision was reversed by the American Civil War. The South seceded from the Union over the issue of human slavery. However, the North invaded the South, defeated the Confederate armies, and forced the South to remain in the United States. During the Civil War, in 1863, President Abraham Lincoln issued the Emancipation Proclamation, which freed the slaves in those states that seceded from the Union."

"In legal terms," Clark went on, "the *Dred Scott* decision was reversed, immediately following the Civil War, by the three great Civil War amendments. The 13th Amendment freed the slaves. The 14th Amendment attempted to grant the newly freed slaves their civil rights. The 15th Amendment attempted to grant the newly freed slaves the right to vote."

"I used the word 'attempted,'" Clark continued, "because the 14th Amendment and the 15th Amendment never really worked the way their authors intended. We've already discussed the problems with the 'No state shall' wording of the 14th Amendment. That amendment protected black people from actions by state governments but not actions by individuals."

"As for the 15th Amendment," Clark said, "the Southern states got around it by finding other ways to keep blacks from being allowed to vote. One of the most popular techniques was the literacy test. Voting officials in the South required would-be voters who were black to read and analyze complex sections of the state constitution. When the blacks became confused, as anyone but a constitutional lawyer would become confused, the blacks were denied the right to register to vote. No such high standards were set for prospective white voters."

It occurred to Clark that he was now back on the main theme of his dissertation. That theme was that the U.S. Constitution and its amendments were oppressive to African-Americans. He stepped to the chalkboard and drew another stone for his Arch Of Racial Oppression. This stone was labeled "Literacy Tests."

Professor Carpman then asked Clark Schooler why state voting officials had been able to get around the 15th Amendment's clear stipulation that no one be denied the right to vote on account of "race, color, or previous condition of servitude?" Carpman commented: "I thought the Constitution and laws of the United States were the supreme law of the land."

Clark responded to the question swiftly and knowingly. "The problem lies in another part of the United States Constitution," Clark said. "In Article One, which sets up the Congress, anyone can vote for Congress who can also vote for 'the most numerous branch of the state legislature.' That appears to put the power to determine who can vote firmly in the hands of the states rather than the national government. A subsequent part of Article One gives the U.S. Congress the power to overrule the states where voting is concerned, but so far the U.S. Congress has declined to exercise that power to overrule the states."

Clark made yet another trip to the chalkboard, and added another stone to his Arch Of Racial Oppression. Because of space limitations, all he could get on that particular stone were the words "States Control Voting."

Before Clark had returned to his seat, Professor Carpman was once again biting at Clark's intellectual throat. "Clark," Carpman said. "You've taken my graduate course in 19th Century American history. What's my attitude toward the Civil War and the three Civil War amendments?"

"You think very highly of them," Clark responded cautiously. "In fact, you refer to the Civil War and the three Civil War amendments as the Second American Revolution. You see it as a time when an honest attempt was made to extend constitutional and Bill of Rights protections to minority Americans. The problem with that point of view is . . ."

Professor Carpman cut Clark off in mid-sentence. "Indeed I do see it that way," Carpman said authoritatively. "I see real progress being made. We've advanced from legal slavery in the 1600s and 1700s, to ending the slave trade in 1808, to abolishing slavery altogether in the late 1860s. I mean, the United States fought a bloody Civil War to end human slavery. Clark, it all depends on how you look at it, doesn't it? I see the Civil War amendments as genuine historical progress. You seem to see only the flaws in those amendments."

One of the professors at the Ph.D. oral exam had been essentially silent up to this time. Professor Michael Middleton, the political scientist who had directly supervised the writing of Clark Schooler's Ph.D. dissertation, stepped in and made a procedural comment.

"We're sort of starting to run out of time," Middleton said. "But, there are enough minutes left for Clark to describe a few more major points from his dissertation. Begin to wind it up, Clark, by just hitting some of your major conclusions."

"Well," Clark said, "let's quickly complete my Arch Of Racial Oppression. We have to include another Supreme Court decision called *Plessy v.*

Ferguson. Homer Plessy was only 1/8 black, but he was barred from riding in the white section of a railroad passenger car. Plessy sued, but the Supreme Court ruled that black persons could be racially segregated from white people as long as the facilities were equal in quality. This thus became the famous 'separate but equal decision.'"

"There was a constitutional basis for the court's finding," Clark continued, trying to hurry himself along. "The U.S. Constitution mandates 'equal protection of the laws,' the concept that the laws should apply evenly and equally to all citizens. After the Civil War, the 14th Amendment applied 'equal protection,' as it is usually called, to the states."

"The unusual thing about the *Plessy* case," Clark went on, "is that the court ruled that 'separate but equal' did not violate the constitutional mandate for 'equal protection of the laws.' The result was a more than 50 year period, from 1896 to 1954, that Southern states were allowed, under the U.S. Constitution, to forcefully segregate blacks from whites." Clark stepped to the chalkboard and added a stone marked *"Plessy v. Ferguson"* to his Arch Of Racial Oppression.

While Clark was still at the board, Professor Brentwood asked him a question: "How does the recent decision by the Supreme Court to racially integrate public schools affect your Arch Of Racial Oppression?"

Clark remained up at the chalkboard. *"Brown v. Board of Education* directly reversed the *Plessy v. Ferguson* decision," Clark said. "The Supreme Court ruled that segregation is inherently unequal." With that statement, Clark picked up a chalkboard eraser and erased the stone that he had marked *"Plessy v. Ferguson."* He redrew that part of the Arch Of Racial Oppression in such a way that the two remaining stones came together unevenly, thereby suggesting that the Arch Of Racial Oppression was now a slightly less stable architectural structure. "But *Brown v. Board of Education* is just a start in dismantling the Arch Of Racial Oppression," Clark concluded. "There is still a lot of arch left, and its holding together very well despite the current furor over civil rights."

When Clark had returned to his seat at the conference table, Professor Brentwood decided to pursue the subject of *Brown v. Board of Education* a bit further. "Would you say," Brentwood asked, "that *Brown v. Board of Education* was an example of judicial activism or judicial restraint?"

"Judicial activism," Clark said definitively. "The Supreme Court moved boldly forward to eliminate racial segregation in public schools in the United States."

Professor Brentwood gave a small smile of intellectual triumph. "There's a problem here, Clark," Brentwood said. "You criticized the Supreme Court for using judicial activism in the *Dred Scott* case. You said it was wrong for the court to try to legalize slavery in all the territories. You said that job should have been left to Congress. But you praised the court for its judicial activism in the *Brown* case, when the court ruled that racial segregation in public schools is unconstitutional. Shouldn't the job of integrating public schools have been left to the Congress?"

Brentwood did not give Clark a chance to answer that question. "Now, you cannot have it both ways, Clark," Brentwood went on. "You cannot condemn judicial activism in one case, such as the *Dred Scott* case, and then praise it in another, to wit the *Brown* case."

Clark had been skillfully caught in a trap of his own making. It was obvious he had no answer for Professor Brentwood's comment. Professor Middleton quickly rescued Clark by saying: "I guess we'll all have to spend some time thinking about that. I, too, condemn the *Dred Scott v. Sanford* decision and praise the *Brown v. Board of Education* decision. Go on with your presentation, Clark."

Clark took a few seconds to look around at the professors gathered for his Ph.D. oral exam. Then he said with great clearness and importance: "Gentlemen. It now is time for me to put the keystone in my arch. The keystone in the Arch Of Racial Oppression is the Senate filibuster."

"The rules of the United States Senate provide that no senator can be interrupted when speaking," Clark began. "The result is that Southern senators can talk to death a civil rights bill by holding the Senate floor and speaking endlessly. One of the most familiar images in American political history is the Southern senator with leather lungs talking forever on the Senate floor in order to keep a civil rights bill from ever coming to a vote. The filibuster prevents the Senate from acting on civil rights. The filibuster thus prevents Congress from acting on civil rights. And the filibuster thereby prevents the national government from acting, in a comprehensive and complete way, on civil rights."

"In my view," Clark said with sincere conviction, "the United States will not solve its civil rights problems until a way is found to overcome the Senate filibuster."

"There is a way to stop the filibuster," Clark went on. "It is called cloture. If 2/3 of the senators vote to stop debate, the filibuster ends and the bill can be passed. But, it is very difficult to get 2/3 of the Senate to vote for cloture. And the Senate has never been able to cloture a civil rights bill."

Professor Brentwood stopped Clark at that point. Brentwood said: "Your Ph.D. dissertation is entitled, 'Black Americans And The United States Constitution.' But the filibuster is not part of the Constitution. It is only a procedural rule in the Senate. You're straying off your topic here, aren't you?"

"Not really," Clark replied confidently. "Many prominent scholars have argued that the filibuster fits nicely with the intentions of the delegates to the Constitutional Convention in 1787. The Senate was created to protect the interests of the small states. In my dissertation, I quote Professor Lindsay Rogers of Columbia University. He gave an interpretation that I have memorized: 'The filibuster is a weapon that the constitutional framers who constructed the Senate failed to anticipate but one that they would view with favor.'" [11]

After delivering that line, Clark went to the chalkboard and, with studied deliberateness, drew in the keystone to his Arch Of Racial Oppression. The keystone was clearly labeled "Senate Filibuster."

Clark Schooler returned to his chair and sat down. There was a brief silence. It was getting to be late afternoon on this particular early summer's day. The air was still warm but beginning to cool down. The sunlight pouring into the room was now coming at a noticeable angle from the west. It was time to end Clark's Ph.D. oral examination and everyone knew it.

Charles Brentwood cleared his throat. He began to speak in a slow and deliberate manner. Professor Brentwood did not look at Clark as he spoke. Instead, Brentwood looked directly at Clark's dissertation. A copy of the dissertation was sitting on the table in front of Professor Brentwood.

"Every point you make in your dissertation is technically correct," Brentwood began. "There is some justification for every stone in your so-called Arch Of Racial Oppression. But there is an overall flaw in your work. You are trying to find values. You are trying to find values for racial equality in a document that was only intended to set up and operate a national government. The Constitution creates the machinery of democracy, but the Constitution does not tell that machinery what to do or what values to discover."

"Our Founders knew what values were," Brentwood continued. "But they also knew that values change over time. They also knew that values can vary from one person to another. The Founders therefore believed in right reason, the idea that human beings could learn together, could progress together, could grow intellectually and socially together. And as human beings change, so must governments."

"To facilitate right reason," Brentwood went on, "the Founders guaranteed freedom of speech, but they did not tell human beings what to say. They guaranteed freedom of the press, but they did not tell human beings what to write and put into print. In short, they created procedures for obtaining values but gave us very little advice as to what those values should be. That's why I and others refer to the United States as a procedural society."

Professor Brentwood decided to further develop this line of thought.

"The Constitution creates the Congress," Brentwood said, "but it does not tell the Congress what laws to pass. The Founders believed right reason would lead the Congress to pass the appropriate laws for the time. In the same way, the Constitution creates the presidency, but it does not tell the president how to execute the laws. The Constitution assumes the president will do what is appropriate at the time he is president. The Constitution contains the machinery for working toward utopia. It contains the machinery for working toward a more perfect human society. But it gives us no clue as to what that utopia should be like."

A temporary hush came over the room when Brentwood finished speaking. Clark's spirits fell. He believed Brentwood's critique had been intellectually devastating. Clark's dissertation had analyzed the Constitution looking for the value of protecting racial minorities. As Brentwood pointed out, the job of the Constitution was to create a national government, and not to tell it what to do.

The hush was short lived. Professor Michael Middleton, the faculty sponsor for Clark's dissertation, came rushing to Clark's rescue. "I think," Middleton said in a voice that rivaled Professor Brentwood's in authority, "that Clark's final conclusion will help clarify things for us. Clark, tell us what that big final conclusion is."

"It is simply this," Clark said, beginning to regain his intellectual confidence. "In order to reap the benefits of the United States Constitution, American blacks will have to overcome the negative effects of that Constitution as represented in the Arch Of Racial Oppression. To put it in more concise terms: In order to benefit from the Constitution, American blacks will have to overcome the Constitution."

Professor Michael Middleton ended this particular Ph.D. oral examination on the spot. Middleton escorted Clark back out into the hallway, instructing Clark to wait while the three professors evaluated his performance in the oral exam. The three professors were going to make the final decision as to whether or not Clark would get his Ph.D.

Clark wandered back to the hallway chair he had been sitting in before his Ph.D. oral examination began. He sat in the chair and realized that his original agenda for his Ph.D. oral exam had been completely derailed. He had gone in hoping to get a Ph.D. "with distinction." Professor Brentwood's and Professor Carpman's comments had made it clear that was not going to happen. Clark found himself hoping that, somehow, the three professors would just give him a plain old Ph.D from Johns Hopkins.

Sitting in his chair, Clark could hear the three professors talking inside the political science seminar room. He could not hear the exact words they were saying, but he could hear enough to comprehend the tone of the discussion. Periodically voices were being raised, sometimes almost in anger. The more he listened, the more disturbed and fearful Clark became. Clearly, a major argument was going on over whether or not Clark was qualified to receive his Ph.D.

By now it was very late in the day. It was well after 6 P.M., and Gilman Hall was practically empty. Clark's three examiners had to be in a hurry. They were surely going to be late getting to their various homes for dinner. But still the discussion went on. For Clark, one long minute stretched into another. And the muffled voices emanating from the seminar room continued to sound argumentative, combative, and divisive. Clark worried that, the longer the discussion went on, the less chance there was of Clark being awarded a Ph.D.

Then, suddenly, Professor Michael Middleton burst out of the seminar room door, his face smiling. "Congratulations, Clark," Middleton said. "You have passed your oral examination, and you are going to get your Ph.D." Clark was also congratulated, but not quite so warmly and happily, by Professor Carpman, the historian. As for Professor Brentwood, the expert on the U.S. Constitution, he came out the door of the seminar room, looked sternly at Clark, and then turned away and walked briskly down the hall back to his office.

Suddenly the three professors were gone and Clark was standing in the hall all by himself. He walked slowly back into the seminar room. As he looked around, he realized this was one of the last times he would be in this particular seminar room. He was going to get his Ph.D., and that meant he would be moving on and away from Johns Hopkins. This seminar room, where he had both learned and taught a great deal of political science, would no longer be part of his life.

Clark began picking up the three copies of his Ph.D. dissertation. The professors had left them sitting on the conference table. As he did so, Clark noticed that his Arch Of Racial Oppression was still on the chalkboard, exactly as he had drawn it. Clark took a minute to study his arch. It may have been a close call, but Clark's dissertation and its Arch Of Racial Oppression had qualified him to receive a Ph.D.

Clark Schooler then walked to the chalkboard. He picked up a chalkboard eraser. He very carefully and very thoroughly erased the Arch Of Racial Oppression.

As he did so, Clark realized something. It was one thing to wipe a chalk drawing of the Arch Of Racial Oppression off the chalkboard. It would be quite a different thing to wipe that arch away in reality.

In The Interim

The exact language of the United States Constitution can be changed by the amendment process. The first ten amendments, adopted shortly after the Constitution was first ratified by the states, constitute the Bill of Rights. Amendments have produced landmark changes in the Constitution and in life and government in the United States. The 13th Amendment, for example, abolished human slavery.

The meaning and application of the United States Constitution can be changed by decisions of the United States Supreme Court. Such decisions are said to set a precedent. The court thus can interpret, and reinterpret, the Constitution.

Perhaps the great fact about the U.S. Constitution is its durability and adaptability. The American people live happily and productively under the same basic document of democratic government that the Founders first proclaimed more than 200 years ago.

CHAPTER 5

CONGRESS AT WORK:
THE SENATE JUDICIARY COMMITTEE

With his Ph.D. degree in political science at last firmly in hand, Clark Schooler spent the summer of 1963 working at his old journalism job at the *Baltimore Banner*. Somewhat to Clark's dismay, the city editors at the *Banner* had come to regard Clark as a "rewrite man" rather than a "street reporter." He spent most of the summer working on the "rewrite desk," taking telephone calls from the various reporters and turning the facts they presented into written newspaper copy.

It started out as a dull summer where civil rights stories were concerned. Because President John F. Kennedy had sent a major civil rights bill to Congress and was pushing hard for its enactment, the various civil rights groups curtailed their protest marches and sit-in demonstrations. The new motto of the civil rights movement seemed to be: "We've shown them what we can do on the streets. Now lets see what they can do in Congress."

Periodically during the summer of 1963, Clark's services were commandeered by the Patriot Press newspapers, the national chain that owned the *Banner*. In the middle of July, Clark was temporarily assigned to a Patriot Press News Squadron that was covering the progress of President Kennedy's civil rights bill through the U.S. Congress.

Baltimore, Maryland, was close enough to Washington, D.C., that Clark could commute down to Capitol Hill in Washington each morning and drive back to his home in Baltimore in the evening. Baltimore and Washington were only 40 miles apart. Thanks to a new expressway, the Baltimore-Washington Parkway, the drive only took 40 minutes to 60 minutes each way, depending on traffic. On days when Clark did not feel like driving, he could go by train on the Pennsylvania Railroad, which ran passenger trains between Baltimore and Washington on an almost hourly basis.

The United States Congress is organized under the committee system. Legislative bills are introduced in the Senate or the House of Representatives and immediately routed to committee. The committees are small groups of senators or representatives, depending on which house of Congress the bill is in, that meet together and analyze the various provisions of the bill in detail.

Committees in the U.S. Congress are jurisdictional committees. Each committee has a specific type of legislation which the committee reviews and considers. Thus the House Agriculture Committee has jurisdiction over all bills that concern farming and agricultural production. The Senate Armed Services Committee looks over all bills on the subject of national defense and military preparedness.

The Patriot Press newspapers sent Clark down to Washington to cover Senate Judiciary Committee consideration of President Kennedy's brand-new civil rights bill. As soon as the bill was introduced in the Senate, one of the Senate clerks routinely sent the bill to the Senate Judiciary Committee. There the bill came under the control of the committee chairperson, Senator James Oliver Eastland, a Democrat from the Southern state of Mississippi.

Congressional committees do two main things. First, they hold committee hearings on a bill, inviting citizens and groups that are interested in the subject matter of the bill to come to Washington and testify for or against the bill. Second, committees hold mark-up sessions, where the committee members rewrite the bill before sending it on to the entire Senate or the entire House of Representatives. In the mark-up session, the committee can and usually does, by majority vote, make any changes it deems appropriate in the original bill.

The first thing Clark Schooler needed to do was to find out exactly what was in President Kennedy's proposed civil rights bill. That problem was quickly solved when the top Washington correspondent for the Patriot Press newspapers, Jim Senitall, telephoned Clark and invited him to go to lunch and discuss the bill's major provisions.

Personal time is at a premium on Capitol Hill. People have plenty of work to do. The more important the person, the more likely that person is to be short of time and hard-pressed to get all the day's necessary tasks completed. One of the best ways to expand the available working hours in the day is to turn meal times into meeting times. Capitol Hill thus is the land of the "working breakfast," the "luncheon meeting," and, on many days, the "evening banquet," where connections are made and particular points of view gently or forcefully pushed.

One of the most convenient places for a luncheon get-together on

Capitol Hill was the Carroll Arms Hotel. This stately brick building was located just a few blocks north of the Capitol building. The Carroll Arms actually was a hotel, but it was mainly famous for its dining room. Here, particularly during the weekday lunch hour, one could see a variety of well-connected and influential persons meeting and talking to each other.

The Carroll Arms was an exciting place to dine. Anyone could go and eat there. But, with a little luck, sitting at the next table would be a prominent member of Congress, or a famous newspaper columnist, or a well-known lobbyist for a powerful corporation or industry.

Clark Schooler and Jim Senitall sat down at a small table covered with a white tablecloth and ordered lunch. Clark looked around the room and then remarked to Jim Senitall that he did not see anyone famous eating at the Carroll Arms this particular noontime. Jim Senitall turned around, quickly surveyed the room, and brought Clark up-to-date on the various important people who were present and munching. There was a key chairperson of a House committee, the leading foreign policy correspondent for the *New York Times*, and so forth and so on for about eight of Clark's fellow lunch goers. As Jim Senitall obviously had intended, Clark was impressed with Senitall's ability to spot and name the great and near-great in Washington, D.C.

Jim Senitall was about 50 years old. In the traditional manner of newspaper reporters, he started out working on a small daily newspaper and, step by step, struggled his way up to become a leading national news reporter. He exuded a touch of that "been everywhere, seen everything" atmosphere characteristic of successful newspaper people. But Senitall kept his aura of journalistic superiority under control. He seemed to really want to help Clark get started on his newspaper assignment in the nation's capital.

Senitall was of medium height and medium build. He spoke quickly and forcefully in a no-nonsense manner. After exchanging the barest amount of pleasantries with Clark Schooler about where Clark was from and where Clark went to school, Jim Senitall got right down to business talking about President Kennedy's civil rights bill.

"A major battle has been raging at the White House," Senitall said. "The fur's been flying ever since the Birmingham demonstrations. President Kennedy promised the nation a strong civil rights bill, but a number of the insiders in the Kennedy administration are urging caution. They want the president to send Congress a relatively weak bill so as not to antagonize the Southern Democrats in Congress."

"The president has a lot of things he wants from Congress this year," Senitall continued. "President Kennedy wants to stimulate the national economy by cutting taxes. But that means getting a tax cut bill through the

Senate and the House of Representatives. The Southern Democrats aren't going to cooperate with the president on a tax cut if he's simultaneously pushing a strong civil rights bill. There is real fear among some of the president's closest advisers that the Southerners will hold the tax cut bill hostage for the civil rights bill."

"You mean," Clark interrupted politely, "that the Southern Democrats will refuse to support the tax cut unless President Kennedy either weakens or drops the civil rights bill."

"Precisely," Jim Senitall replied. The nationally-known newspaperman then gave Clark Schooler a critical look and said. "You really are a professor as well as a reporter, aren't you? You just clarified my statement for me. I'll bet you do that for all your students."

Clark was taken aback by Senitall's frank statement but quickly moved to defend himself. "I had a really good course on Congress in graduate school," Clark said. "I was taught to always look at the total legislative picture. Sometimes you cannot tell what is going on with one bill without being aware of what's happening with a completely different bill. It sounds like that's what's going on with the tax cut bill and the civil rights bill."

Senitall looked almost impressed that Clark had learned such a concept in graduate school. He asked: "Who taught you that course?"

"A guy named Ronald Pullman," Clark responded. "He was the legislative assistant to Senator Wallace Bennett of Utah. He came up to Baltimore on the train from Washington every Tuesday afternoon to teach Johns Hopkins students about his experiences on Capitol Hill. He was full-to-overflowing with little catch phrases for analyzing Congress."

"You were lucky to have that," Senitall said, and then went right back to discussing President Kennedy's civil rights bill.

"But there's another set of voices trying to get the president's ear," Senitall said. "These are the strong pro-civil rights people. They argue that the country is in flames over civil rights and that only a really tough civil rights bill will quiet the accelerated political activity in the black community. They argue the real threat to the president's political future is the prospect of more demonstrations and riots like Birmingham."

"No legislation originates in a vacuum," Clark interrupted again. "Bills are introduced in the United States Congress because somewhere 'out there' real people are upset with some aspect of the status quo and want to see things changed." Clark let that thought sink in. He then smiled at Jim Senitall and said: "That was another key piece of congressional lore from Ronald Pullman."

Jim Senitall laughed out loud. Apparently, it seemed to Clark, Senitall was enjoying hearing the academic version of how things happen on Capitol

Hill.

"As you might expect," Senitall continued, "the bill that President Kennedy presented to the Senate and the House of Representatives was somewhat in the middle of those two positions. But, in all fairness, I would characterize it as a strong bill. It's not tough enough to satisfy the more vocal civil rights supporters around the president. But it's a very practical and workable bill. It will be a real achievement for John Kennedy if he can somehow get Congress to enact this particular bill into law."

"There are eleven major provisions in the civil rights bill," Senitall continued, "but your readers will fall fast asleep if you try to describe and discuss all eleven of them. By unspoken agreement, the press is simplifying things for the American people by concentrating the discussion on just four provisions. Those four major provisions are important parts of the bill and relatively simple and easy to understand."

"Incidentally," Senitall pointed out, "up here on Capitol Hill, we refer to a major provision of a bill as a 'title.' The various titles of a bill are numbered in consecutive order, so you hear people talking about 'Title One,' and 'Title Five,' and so on. Did your intellectual pal, Ronald Patman, or whatever his name was, teach you about that?"

"Yes, Ronald Pullman," Clark replied, emphasizing the "Pull" in Pullman. "He also taught us that sometimes government programs become known by the title number in the bill in which the programs were enacted into law. For example, and I'm making this up, people might refer to a 'Title Five crop.' It would be 'Title Five' because the subsidy for that particular agricultural product was included in 'Title Five' of some long ago agricultural bill."

"That's right," said Jim Senitall, "and some of the title numbers of President Kennedy's civil rights bill are already well-known and being bandied about among the press and the congressional staff on Capitol Hill."

"The most important provision of the bill is Title Two," Senitall went on. "It outlaws racial discrimination in all public accommodations. Those are places such as restaurants, snack bars, motels, hotels, swimming pools, and so on. Those are private businesses, but the public is invited to come in and do business in them. Under Title Two, restaurants and hotels would have to serve all customers without regard to race, religion, or national origin."

"Title Two is the very heart of the civil rights bill," Senitall noted. "It is written in direct response to all the sit-in demonstrations across the country."

"Title Two is also the title that the Southerners will try the hardest to get chopped out of the bill," Senitall said. "If the Southerners succeed in that, the bill will be worthless. The nation will go back to sit-ins and Birmingham-style demonstrations and, possibly, riots."

"The next most important provision of the bill is Title Six," Jim Senitall continued. "It provides for the cut-off of U.S. Government funds to any state or local government program that practices racial discrimination. It means that colleges and universities in the South will not be able to get U.S. Government research funds if they discriminate against black students. It means that hospitals in the South will not get U.S. Government aid if they continue to refuse to treat blacks as well as whites in the emergency room."

Clark Schooler was impressed by Title Six. He knew enough about how widespread U.S. Government aid programs were in American society to know that the funds cut-off could have real impact. It would be a tough choice, financially, for a state or local government in the South to give up U.S. Government aid in order to maintain racial segregation. With the funds cut-off, remaining racially bigoted could start costing Southern governments real dollars.

"Title Three of the bill is very important but somewhat difficult to understand," Jim Senitall said. "You'll find it a challenge to explain it clearly to your readers. As proposed by the Kennedy administration, Title Three permits the attorney general of the United States to file suits to bring about the racial desegregation of public schools."

"The problem with present law," Senitall continued, "is that individual blacks have to file suits to get their schools desegregated. As you know, the right to school integration was guaranteed in 1954 by the Supreme Court in the *Brown v. Board of Education* decision. But often, when black people filed suits to desegregate their local schools, they became the victims of community persecution, some of it violent. Blacks who pressed for school integration often were fired from their jobs, or their kids were kicked out of public school for some trumped-up reason, or their license to operate their barber shop or beauty shop was taken away."

"Those were the more palatable types of punishments," Senitall went on. "In some cases, blacks who filed suits to desegregate their schools were beaten up on the street, or somebody would throw a dynamite bomb through their front window in the middle of the night."

"Title Three attempts to end all that by having the U.S. attorney general, rather than individual black persons, file the desegregation suit," Jim Senitall explained. "The local Southern whites will not be able to fire the attorney general, nor close his barber shop, nor will they be likely to try to throw a bomb in the front door of the Justice Department building here in Washington, D.C. Under Title Three, the United States Government takes on the full burden, and risks, of filing school desegregation suits."

As he was listening to Jim Senitall explain Title Three, Clark Schooler was reminded of his newspaper colleague, Bernard Martin, and Martin's viewpoint on "the willing suspension of law and order." It occurred to Clark that, if Title Three of the civil rights bill were enacted into law, African-Americans in Southern communities would be less subject to "the willing suspension of law and order." With the U.S. Government filing school desegregation suits on behalf of African-Americans, the African-Americans would, in effect, be protected from reprisals, possibly violent reprisals, from local whites.

"The last of the four major titles," Jim Senitall said, "is also probably the least likely to be enacted into law. It's Title Seven, which creates an Equal Employment Opportunity Commission. The commission will have the authority to limit job discrimination wherever work is being performed under U.S. Government contracts."

At that moment, two men at another table had finished their lunch together and were walking out of the Carroll Arms Hotel dining room. As they passed Clark's and Jim Senitall's table, one of the men stopped to talk with Senitall about some obscure piece of legislation that Clark had never heard of. Somewhere in the midst of the conversation, Jim Senitall introduced Clark Schooler to the two men. One was a Washington correspondent for the *Los Angeles Times*. The other was a reporter and commentator for Central Radio News, a small network of radio stations located mainly in the American Midwest.

The conversation quickly turned to President Kennedy's civil rights bill, and soon the two men pulled up empty chairs from adjoining tables and sat down with Clark and Jim Senitall. To Clark's pleased amazement, he was suddenly being briefed on the civil rights bill by three Washington correspondents, not just one.

Jim Senitall asked the man from the *Los Angeles Times*: "What do you think about Title Seven? Do you think equal employment opportunity is the legislative lamb being led to congressional slaughter that I think it is?"

The *Los Angeles Times* guy pondered the question for a few moments and then said: "It certainly would be the easiest part of the civil rights bill for the pro-civil rights forces to give up. The sit-in demonstrations were about getting served in restaurants, not about getting jobs in those restaurants. One way to lessen Southern opposition to the bill might be, at a strategic moment, to cut out equal employment opportunity. Then the Southerners could argue they had saved at least one part of the Southern segregation system."

The man from Central Radio News nodded his head in agreement. He said: "My sense is that President Kennedy put equal employment opporttu-

nity in the bill only because the civil rights lobbyists were screaming their
heads off for it. I think he will abandon that ship the minute the congressional waters get rough."

"And don't forget that the Democrats are going to need some Republican votes to get this bill passed," stated the *Los Angeles Times* reporter.
"Republicans are sensitive to anything that affects business, particularly
businesses that have U.S. Government contracts. After all, the Republicans
are the party of big business in this country. The pro-civil rights Democrats
might maneuver to pick up some Republican votes by jettisoning equal
employment. If nothing else, the business interests will be delighted to be
rid of all the paperwork to file with the government."

The conversation continued in this vein for a few more minutes. Then
the two men got up and went on their way.

The day after his lunch with Jim Senitall, Clark Schooler took his place
among the other news reporters covering the Senate Judiciary Committee
hearings on President Kennedy's civil rights bill. It was the 16th day of July
in the year 1963. The hearing room looked something like a court room. The
senators on the Judiciary Committee sat behind a high, horseshoe-shaped
bench at one end of the room. In front of the bench was a large table with
chairs. It was a witness table. Persons testifying before the committee sat
at the witness table so as to be facing the bench full of senators.

There also was a table for members of the press to sit at and take notes.
If the particular committee hearing was important enough, the hearing might
be televised. That would add the excitement of television lights and television cameras to the proceedings. In most cases, however, reporting on
committee hearings was the domain of the print press.

Occasionally the television networks set up their lights and cameras
in the hallway outside the committee hearing room. The television reporters
would try to grab important senators as they were leaving the hearing room
and then get them to answer questions about the hearing "on camera."

Behind the witness table and the press table were rows of seats for
spectators. Lobbyists and other persons interested in the work of the Judiciary Committee could come and sit in these seats on a first-come, first-
served basis. For most routine legislation, it was easy to get a seat and both
observe and listen to the committee hearing. If the bill was important and
getting lots of news media attention, however, interested persons often had
to get in line early in the morning to get a seat in the hearing room.

Clark noticed something about the high circular bench where the
senators sat. The height of the bench put the heads of the senators considerably above the heads of those who were testifying before the committee. The
senators thus looked down from a position of dominance on those giving

testimony. It occurred to Clark that it could be pretty intimidating to come before the Judiciary Committee and have to sit there and look up into the faces of questioning and cross-examining senators.

It was easy to keep track of which senators were Democrats and which were Republicans. The Democrats all sat on one side of the horseshoe and the Republicans sat on the other. At the head of the horseshoe sat the committee chairperson, who presided over the hearing and determined who would speak when. The committee chairperson was the senior member of the political party which had a majority in the Senate. In 1963 that was the Democratic Party.

Clark was impressed with the ornate character of the committee hearing room. The regal atmosphere was enhanced by the presence of a U.S. flag and, on the wall, the Great Seal of the United States. Well, why not? The United States was a powerful and wealthy country. A good bit of that wealth had been spent on decorating the committee hearing room with beautifully carved woodwork and paneled wooden walls. The horseshoe-shaped bench was a magnificent piece of furniture. And all the door handles, door hinges, and other metal fittings in the room were made of brass and kept immaculately polished.

It occurred to Clark that this was the way a king or an emperor would decorate a modern throne room. That is, if he had the money.

The chairperson of the Judiciary Committee was Senator James Oliver Eastland of Mississippi. To Clark Schooler, Senator Eastland was the epitome of the pro-segregation Southern Democratic senator. Clark gave himself a mental reminder that Senator Eastland represented the state where the riot at Ole Miss had taken place just about one year earlier.

Because he had taken that excellent course on Congress in graduate school, Clark Schooler was able to observe a number of things about the Judiciary Committee that the average person would have missed. In the first place, a number of the senators sitting at the far ends of the horseshoe-shaped bench were considerably younger in appearance than the senators sitting toward the middle. That was a result of the seniority system.

The more years a senator served on the Judiciary Committee, the more seniority he or she gained. Senators who were newly elected to the Judiciary Committee took the outermost seats on the horseshoe, the newest Democrats sitting on one side and the newest Republicans on the other. As older members of the committee retired from office, or departed to take seats on other Senate committees, the newer members would move progressively toward the center of the horseshoe.

This process of moving to the middle of the horseshoe could take years, sometimes even decades. That explained why the senators in the middle looked older than the senators on the far ends. Clark Schooler often said, jokingly, that an enterprising young member of Congress should take his or her vitamins, get plenty of exercise, avoid fatty foods, and give up drinking alcohol and smoking cigarettes. Such behavior would lead to a long life, and that would enable the Congress member to gain plenty of seniority on a congressional committee.

Seniority had its own set of rules. The concept was applied rigidly in both the Senate and the House of Representatives. When two members of Congress joined a committee on the same date, the person who had held high elective office, such as being governor of his home state, would have seniority over the other person. If neither of the two members had held high elective office, however, a coin would be flipped in the air. The winner of the coin toss would be the senior person of the two on that particular committee, and that would be true for the remainder of the time the two Congress members were on that committee.

Many aspects of daily life on Capitol Hill were controlled by seniority. Senior senators and representatives received the more desirable congressional office suites in the Senate and House office buildings. A desirable congressional office suite would be one that was close to the Capitol building or, better yet, had a spectacular view of the Capitol dome out the window. Clark had even been told, although he did not know if it was really true, that seniority could get a senator or representative a more convenient parking space for his or her automobile in the appropriate Capitol parking garage.

The chairperson of a congressional committee was the member of the majority party in that house of Congress who had served on the committee for the longest period of time. Committee chairpersons thus tended to be older, or in some cases almost superannuated. Committee chairpersons also were experienced, knew how to get things done in Congress, and tended to be conservative and cautious rather than liberal and aggressive.

The most important thing about congressional committee chairpersons, Clark knew, was the power they had to control the work of the committee. The chair of the committee set the committee agenda. If a younger member of the committee wanted to be recognized by the chairperson so he or she could speak and ask questions in committee hearings, well that younger member had better be nice and cooperative with the committee chair. If a younger member of the committee wanted his or her pet bill scheduled for hearings and passed by the committee, that young person had better be openly supportive of the committee chairperson.

In addition, the committee chair hired and assigned most of the committee staff, the paid employees who did research for the committee members and helped to write the actual legislation. If a younger member of a committee wanted to have any staff assigned to help him or her research and write bills, that young person needed to be on the best terms possible with the committee chairperson.

Putting so much power in the hands of the committee chairs resulted in the chairperson dominating the other committee members almost totally. The committee pretty much held the hearings and passed on the legislation that the committee chairperson wanted.

Clark Schooler zealously taught his students that the general working rule for younger members of Congress was: "To get along, go along." Cooperate with your committee chairperson, and you'll get some legislative goodies. And, if you live long enough, and get reelected enough, and your party is in the majority in your house of Congress, some day you, too, may get to be an all-powerful committee chair.

Senator James Eastland, chairperson of the Senate Judiciary Committee, convened the committee's hearings on President Kennedy's civil rights bill. After some brief formalities, Chairperson Eastland recognized one of his Southern Democratic colleagues on the committee, Senator Sam J. Ervin, Jr., of North Carolina. In a thick but pleasing Southern accent, Sam Ervin launched the Southern attack on this latest piece of civil rights legislation.

"I am emotionally opposed to this bill," Ervin began. "It attacks the very fiber, the very structure, of our unique Southern way of life. It empowers the national government, here in Washington, D.C., to come into our sacred and treasured Southland and invade the private lives and social arrangements of our citizens. This bill constitutes nothing more than a direct assault on the sacred constitutional freedoms of every Southern man and woman."

Clark noted that Senator Ervin was attacking the civil rights bill in military terms, flavoring his speech with words such as "invade" and "assault." This kind of flowery overstatement was often heard at congressional committee hearings. What Senator Ervin was hoping for was that one of his provocative phrases would catch the ear of one of the news reporters present. Then both the quote and Senator Ervin's name would be in the newspapers the next morning.

"But there will be no need for me to attack this bill on the emotional plane," Senator Ervin continued. "It is my intention to attack it on the intellectual plane. This bill violates almost every sacred principle of the United States Constitution. It violates our sacred state sovereignty. It violates our right to be free from the tyrannous hand of the power-grasping national government. This bill stands condemned by its manifest unconstitutionality. There is no clause or principle in the United States Constitution that can save it." [12]

Senator Ervin spoke for a considerable period of time, making complex arguments against the Kennedy civil rights bill based on narrow interpretations of the United States Constitution. Clark began to notice a considerable amount of boredom on the part of his fellow news reporters. "Tell me about it one more time," grumbled one reporter under his breath. "That's true, except for the supremacy clause," muttered another.

There was a lot of shuffling of reportorial feet and frequent trips to the rest room. In fact, Clark concluded, the reportorial trips to the rest room were more frequent than necessary. It was becoming clear to Clark that virtually all of his fellow reporters were convinced that nothing significant was going to happen at these particular committee hearings.

"It's always this way with the Senate Judiciary Committee," said an older reporter to Clark at the end of the first day of hearings. "This committee is famous as the burial ground of civil rights bills. In the past couple of decades, more than 120 civil rights bills have died before this committee."

"The hearings are just a sham," the man went on. "The Southern senators sit up there and amuse themselves by launching all these arcane constitutional arguments against the bill. When the Dixie boys finally get tired of that, Senator Eastland just puts the bill in his pocket and that's the last the Senate ever sees of that particular civil rights bill."

As Clark got to know them better, the news reporters began griping to Clark about having to cover these particular hearings. All those logical but subtly venomous Southern criticisms of civil rights had been lodged many times before. And the final outcome, which was the death of the bill at the hands of Senator Eastland, was preordained.

Clark began to figure something out. He had been given the so-called "opportunity" of covering the Senate Judiciary Committee hearings on the civil rights bill because none of the senior national reporters at the Patriot Press newspapers wanted the job. In reality, Clark concluded, he had been stuck with a boring assignment that none of the other reporters "in-the-know" wanted.

But Clark was not upset or disheartened by this fact. It was exciting to be covering a committee hearing, any committee hearing, on Capitol Hill. Clark had advanced, at least temporarily, from being a "Baltimore" reporter to becoming a "Washington" reporter. In addition, as a political scientist as well as a journalist, Clark Schooler was actually interested in the Southerner's arguments against President Kennedy's civil rights bill.

For one thing, Clark was impressed with Senator Sam Ervin's knowledge of the Constitution and his ability to make a very appealing defense of state's rights. "More than anything else," Ervin said, "the Founders of our great republic feared tyranny. They worried that the national government would become so powerful that it would begin to steal away the rights and freedoms of the individual. To guard against this threat of tyranny, the Founders preserved and enhanced the powers of the state governments as a needed check on national power. To weaken state government, as this civil rights bill proposes to do, will leave every American citizen at the mercy of an all-powerful, unchecked national power."

"Our Founders were logical," Ervin said, sounding more like a college professor than a U.S. senator. "They believed in an orderly universe in which one force was balanced by another. The best way to check national power, the Founders told us, was to balance state power against it. The Founders thus drew a delicate, finely balanced line between the powers of the national government and the state governments."

"This civil rights bill will move that line dangerously in the direction of the national government," Senator Ervin continued. "I tell you, with all my heart and mind, if we pass this civil rights bill, we will be moving that delicate line between nation and state to our peril. We will move that line toward national tyranny."

It occurred to Clark that this particular Senate hearing was really a sort of graduate student seminar. Weighty questions on the nature of the United States Government were being rigorously argued. But this particular graduate student seminar was not limited to a select few graduate students. Anyone who was interested could come in, take a seat, and observe the proceedings. Others could read about the committee hearing in considerable detail in the next morning's *New York Times* or *Washington Post*.

About every third day or so, Clark wrote a news story for the Patriot Press newspaper chain on the doings before the Senate Judiciary Committee. Of course Clark did not report everything that was taking place. That would have been boring and confusing for his readers across the nation. Clark did his journalistic duty and simplified the hearings, orienting his articles around only one theme or one really juicy quote that had been spoken that particular day. Clark called this journalistic process "imposing order where no order actually exists."

Clark also took a tip from Jim Senitall, his mentor in the Washington bureau of the Patriot Press newspapers. As Jim had advised, Clark limited his coverage of the Senate Judiciary hearings to only the four major provisions of the civil rights bill. Those provisions dealt with public accommodations, the U.S. Government funds cut-off, the attorney general suing in civil rights cases, and equal employment opportunity.

Interest in the Senate Judiciary Committee hearings picked up significantly when Attorney General Robert F. Kennedy, the president's younger brother, appeared before the committee to defend the civil rights bill. "Bobby" Kennedy, as almost everyone called him in everyday speech, was relatively young for a politician, both in years and in appearance. With his tousled hair and his boyish good looks, Robert Kennedy caused a ripple of excitement to run through the hearing room as he entered and took his seat at the witness table.

The attorney general appeared to be mainly interested in making the point that the civil rights bill was legally justified because it was based on the commerce clause of the U.S. Constitution. "There is hardly a broader grant of constitutional power than that embodied in the commerce clause," Robert Kennedy told the Senate Judiciary Committee. "That provision of the Constitution is unequivocal. The very words of the Constitution are: 'Congress shall have power . . . to regulate commerce with foreign nations, and among the several states.'"

Robert Kennedy continued his lavish praise of the commerce clause. "This grant of power is clear, specific, and unlimited in any way," the attorney general said. "Congress has the power, if it chooses to use it, to bar racial segregation in all hotels, motels, restaurants, and snack bars that are engaged in interstate commerce." [13]

Senator Ervin had begun the hearings by saying that no clause or provision of the Constitution could save President Kennedy's civil rights bill. Bobby Kennedy had come down to Capitol Hill to make the specific point that the commerce clause would, indeed, save the bill. And it would save it big time.

For the last two weeks of July of 1963, Clark Schooler sat and watched U.S. Senator Sam Ervin unceasingly grill Attorney General Robert Kennedy on virtually every last provision of President Kennedy's civil rights bill. And every argument Senator Ervin made was grounded in the U.S. Constitution. In a moment of disturbing academic enlightenment, Clark suddenly realized he was watching a rerun of his own Ph.D. oral examination. The Southerners were making the argument, just as Clark had, that the Constitution provided for and could be used to defend racial segregation.

But to Clark, this version of his doctoral oral examination was somehow weird and twisted. It was, perhaps, a reverse vision of his Ph.D. oral, one that was being seen in a dark mirror. Clark Schooler had condemned the fact that the Constitution had been used in such a way that racial segregation and oppression had grown and thrived in the United States. The Southern senators, on the other hand, were praising the Constitution for its many provisions which, in the hands of a skilled advocate such as Senator Ervin, could be used to justify the continuation of racial segregation.

It was as though Senator Ervin had become Clark Schooler's evil twin.

Senator Ervin possessed much the same factual knowledge that Clark did about the U.S. Constitution. But Senator Ervin was using that knowledge to justify racial segregation, not eradicate it.

Toward the end of July, Senator Sam Ervin's constant attacks on Robert Kennedy and the Kennedy administration civil rights bill produced an angry response from one of the Republican senators on the Senate Judiciary Committee. Senator Kenneth Keating, a pro-civil rights Republican from New York, lashed out mildly at Senator Ervin, accusing him of using stalling tactics and unnecessarily lengthening the discussion. Keating said in a sharp and critical tone: "With all these questions of the attorney general, which appear to be leading in no particular direction and to have no particular purpose, these hearings are rapidly approaching the appearance of a committee filibuster."

As the hearings dragged on into early August of 1963, Clark noted the interesting political party byplay where Robert Kennedy's appearance before the Senate Judiciary Committee was concerned. Robert Kennedy was a Democrat, simultaneously the brother and the attorney general of a Democratic Party president, John F. Kennedy. But the two men on the Senate Judiciary Committee who were Robert Kennedy's most vociferous critics also were Democrats. Sam Ervin of North Carolina and committee Chairperson James Eastland of Mississippi claimed the same loyalty and commitment to the Democratic Party that Robert and John Kennedy did. It was truly an intraparty squabble, with the members of the other political party, the Republicans, mainly relegated to the sidelines.

Something else interested Clark about these particular committee hearings. Although the subject matter of the civil rights bill was equal rights for black Americans, not one black face was to be seen on the Senate Judiciary Committee. And the principal person defending the civil rights bill, Attorney General Robert Kennedy, also was a white person. The fate of black civil rights in the United States was being debated exclusively by white people, with interested black citizens being relegated to sitting passively in the audience.

The day finally came when Chairperson James Oliver Eastland terminated the Senate Judiciary Committee hearings on the Kennedy administration civil rights bill. It was the 23rd day of August of 1963. The hearings were adjourned subject to the future call of the committee chair. Of course no such future call ever came. For all intents and purposes, the Senate version of President Kennedy's civil rights bill was tabled, killed, down the drain, dead and buried, dead as a doornail, dead and gone forever. Pick your favorite cliche, Clark thought, as he sat down at the typewriter to write his final story on these particular Senate hearings.

After Chairperson Eastland had personally assassinated the Senate version of the civil rights bill, Clark Schooler thought he would be returning to the rewrite desk at the *Baltimore Banner*. To Clark's surprise, the Patriot Press newspaper chain kept him in Washington, D.C., and assigned him to another Patriot Press News Squadron. This particular News Squadron was covering the upcoming 1963 March on Washington.

"Your job," Jim Senitall told Clark over the telephone, "will be to cover the transportation, feeding, and rest room arrangements for the march. You're to write about anything you can find that has to do with how they're going to get the marchers to Washington. You're also to write about what they're going to do with the marchers once they get them here. The Patriot Press wants everything we can possibly give them about the March on Washington. If they put out extra trash cans at the Lincoln Memorial, write about it. This story's red hot."

As so often happens in life, Clark had to force himself to be honest with himself. He was just a little bit disappointed that he was covering the rest room beat on this particular story. Jim Senitall got the plum assignment. He was to report on the speeches by the various civil rights leaders to be given from the front steps of the Lincoln Memorial. Another reporter, a woman whom Clark did not know, was assigned to make the actual march from the Washington Monument to the Lincoln Memorial. She would write the color story, a lively description of what the people looked like, what they shouted and sang, and what they said their feelings were as they demonstrated for civil rights on the green, grassy Mall in Washington.

Then Clark reminded himself that he was a newcomer to Washington news reporting. He comforted himself with the thought that Jim Senitall probably got some dull and mundane assignments when he was a younger and less experienced reporter. And Clark restored his optimism and positive good nature by remembering his belief that, with a little hard work and some creative imagination, a good reporter could turn almost any assignment, no matter how routine, into a good newspaper story.

United States civil rights leaders had long dreamed about a March on Washington. It was first proposed by A. Philip Randolph, a prominent African-American labor leader. The idea was that black Americans and their white allies from all over the nation would come to Washington and gather at the Lincoln Memorial to show their solid support for civil rights reform. With the Kennedy administration strongly pushing a major civil rights bill in Congress, August of 1963 seemed like the perfect time for such a March on Washington to take place.

Both the year and the place selected for the march were significant in African-American history. President Abraham Lincoln issued the Emancipation Proclamation, which freed the slaves in the rebellious Confederacy, exactly 100 years earlier in 1863. And when black soprano Marian Anderson had been excluded from singing in a segregated concert hall in Washington, D.C., she gave a free outdoor concert, to thousands of appreciative listeners, on the steps of the Lincoln Memorial instead.

President Kennedy himself was hostile to the idea of such a March on Washington but actually could do nothing to stop it. The "right of the people to peaceably assemble, and to petition the government for a redress of grievances," was specifically protected in the 1st Amendment of the U.S. Constitution.

The Kennedy administration was mainly fearful that the march might get out of control and turn violent. There was the possibility that pro-segregation counter-demonstrators would shout insults at the marchers, or even throw things at them, thereby provoking a violent response.

Clark did a good story on how the City of Washington provided 2,000 police officers as well as 2,000 volunteer marshals to direct and protect the marchers. In addition, more than 2,000 National Guard troops were on hand to help keep things orderly. Out of sight but definitely in the forefront of President Kennedy's mind, 7,000 U.S. Army soldiers and U.S. Marines were on alert and ready to go at the various military bases in the Washington area.

Transportation arrangements were massive and complex. Many of the marchers would be coming from New York, Philadelphia, and Baltimore by railroad train. Clark called a public relations officer at the Pennsylvania Railroad and learned that special extra trains would be operating the day of the march. "We are a common carrier," the railroad man told Clark, "required by U.S. law to haul any passenger that shows up at our train stations to ride a train in interstate commerce. We have people right now trying to estimate how many extra passengers we're going to have and how many extra passenger cars and locomotives we're going to need to haul them down to Washington and back."

A funny thing happened to Clark Schooler on his way to the march. The more information he gathered about the logistical arrangements, the more he liked this particular newspaper assignment. He wrote at length about how more than 1,500 chartered buses would be bringing marchers in from all over the country. He described in detail where the buses would unload their passengers and where the buses would be parked during the march and the speech making. He noted that some of the buses would be sleek new highway buses with comfortable seats and rest rooms. But other folks would be coming in school buses and church buses, some of them very old and very rickety in appearance.

Two of Clark's best stories were about people who chose unusual and colorful ways to get to Washington for the march. Twelve people decided to walk the more than 200 miles from Brooklyn, New York, to the nation's capital. One man came all the way from Chicago, a distance of more than 600 miles, on roller skates.

The more he worked the story, the more Clark began to catch the enthusiasm of the black Americans who were coming to Washington to demonstrate for civil rights. Clark talked with the spokesperson for a group of professionals from Harlem, the large black community in New York City that many persons regarded as the capital of black America. These doctors, lawyers, and successful businessmen were coming down to Washington on the train. And Clark talked to the ministers of African-American churches, all up and down the East Coast, who were recruiting their parishioners to make the trek, often in an old church bus, to the nation's capital.

Clark realized that he was beginning to feel the sheer depth of the commitment on the part of black Americans to publicly demonstrate their support for civil rights.

When August 28, 1963, finally arrived, Clark Schooler spent the first part of his day watching railroad trains full of marchers arrive, one after the other, at Washington's Union Station. Clark took notes as the marchers walked through the high-ceilinged and statuary-bedecked waiting room at the station and then boarded shuttle buses for the Washington Monument.

Among the marchers, Clark saw every possible type of human being and every conceivable style of dress. Many of the men were wearing coats and ties, and most of the women were in summer dresses. Some marchers were more casually dressed, but almost all were clean and neat in appearance. Instead of looking like a bunch of eccentric radical reformers, Clark later wrote, the marchers mainly resembled typical middle-class Americans.

Signs and banners often identified where a particular group of marchers came from. There were signs for Pittsburgh, Philadelphia, Richmond, Baltimore. The East Coast was particularly well represented. Clark estimated that roughly one-in-ten of the marchers were white supporters of African-American civil rights.

Clark then went up to the Washington Monument, the place where the march to the Lincoln Memorial was to begin. Beneath the gigantic marble obelisk that is the Washington Monument, Clark observed the preparation and distribution of literally hundreds of thousands of cheese sandwiches to those marchers who needed to eat. He observed from a distance the large platforms that were being assembled in front of the Lincoln Memorial to give the television cameras and the newspaper photographers a clear view of the proceedings. As he had been instructed to do, Clark studied the manner in which the marchers were being given water and soft drinks and provided with rest room facilities.

And then Clark got himself to a telephone and dictated his story to Patriot Press News Squadron headquarters in New York. As the actual march from the Washington Monument to the Lincoln Memorial began, Clark was busy describing all the pre-arrangements for the march to the millions of readers of all the Patriot Press newspapers.

As previously decided, Clark's story began the coverage in the Patriot Press newspapers. When the actual march was completed, the woman reporter telephoned in that part of the story. At the end of the day, Jim Senitall added the actual words of the various speech makers at the Lincoln Memorial.

Once Clark had phoned in his story, he was free for the remainder of the day. The marchers already had arrived at the Lincoln Memorial. The vast crowd filled and overflowed the space in front of the memorial. Clark was able to stand at the back edge of the crowd, at a spot that highlighted the scenic beauty of Washington, D.C. Clark had the image of the Lincoln Memorial, the speaker's stand, and the vast numbers of people clearly in view.

The Reverend Martin Luther King, Jr., was just beginning his speech. His voice sounded distant where Clark had positioned himself, but King's words, augmented by large outdoor loud speakers, carried clearly to Clark's ears.

Clark Schooler had heard enough speeches by Martin Luther King, Jr., to know that there would be a triple start statement. That was when King would start three sentences with the same phrase but then finish each sentence differently. It was a very effective speaking technique that Clark very much admired. A triple start statement went something like this:

"They put it down on paper, that all men and women in this nation are created equal."

"They put it down on paper, that all men and women in this nation are entitled to equal protection of the laws."

"They put it down on paper, that all men and women in this nation enjoy an equal right to liberty, freedom, and the pursuit of happiness."

Martin Luther King, Jr., would always put particular vocal emphasis on the third sentence in his triple start statement. It was a touch that always resulted in loud cheering, clapping, and shouts of "Amen, brother!" from the audience.

The triple start statement Clark was waiting and hoping for was not long in coming. Midway through his speech, Martin Luther King, Jr., hesitated for a moment, let the crowd get quiet and get its expectations up. Then the Reverend King said:

"One hundred years after emancipation, the lives of American blacks are still sadly crippled by the manacles and chains of discrimination."

"One hundred years after emancipation, too many black people live on a lonely island of poverty in a vast ocean of material prosperity."

"One hundred years after emancipation, blacks in the United States still languish in the corners of American society and find themselves exiles in their own land." [14]

As Clark knew it would, the crowd burst into strong applause at the end of the third sentence. The clapping and the shouting and the cheers came rolling to Clark's ears.

Clark pondered the words of Martin Luther King, Jr., on the oppression of African-Americans in the United States. Clark thought of some of the words of the 1st Amendment to the Constitution: "To petition the government for a redress of grievances." What other group in American history, Clark asked himself, had a list of "grievances" as great as those of black Americans?

The next day's newspapers were an absolute feast for Clark Schooler. The columnists and editorial writers of all the major newspapers and newspaper chains had been impressed with the March on Washington and with the speech by Martin Luther King, Jr. Despite all the fears of possible violence, the march had been peaceful, orderly, and almost totally without serious incident. And the Reverend King's speech was described as both "challenging" to the white majority in the United States and "inspiring" to every American, white or black. The general view of all the political writers was that the effects of the speech would be "permanent" and "enduring."

Unbeknownst to Clark Schooler, President John F. Kennedy had invited A. Philip Randolph, Martin Luther King, Jr., and other major civil rights leaders to come to visit at the White House once the march was over. The president declined to attend the march, but he exhibited a careful measure of public support for the march by welcoming the civil rights leaders into his official home. It was about 5 o'clock in the afternoon when President Kennedy greeted the leaders with a key phrase from Reverend King's speech: "I have a dream!" [15]

When he learned that many of the civil rights leaders had not eaten since breakfast, John F. Kennedy ordered them sandwiches and coffee from the White House kitchen. The newspapers reported that the civil rights leaders gently urged the president to strengthen the civil rights bill he had sent to Congress, particularly the section on equal employment opportunity. The president, the press said, was noncommittal. The chief executive emphasized instead that it now was time for all Americans interested in civil rights to begin lobbying Congress to pass the president's bill, in exactly the form the president had sent it to Capitol Hill.

In The Interim

Seniority still counts for a great deal on Capitol Hill in Washington, D.C., but it is no longer as important as it was in the 1960s. There was a wave of congressional reform in the early 1970s that weakened the ability of committee chairpersons to totally dominate the committee system.

In some instances since the 1970s, the senior member of the majority party on the committee has not been chosen committee chairperson. In addition, power has been passed downward to subcommittees. Members of the majority party without much seniority become subcommittee chairpersons and wield considerable power over the narrow area of the subcommittee's jurisdiction.

All the same, seniority is still important in Congress. By and large, it is those members who have served in Congress the longest who have the most power and influence.

Also on the disappearing list are the powerful Southern Democratic senators of the 1960s. The Southern United States has been shifting Republican over the past four decades, and many Southern seats in the U.S. Senate now are held by Republicans rather than Democrats.

In addition, a different kind of Southern Democrat is being elected to the Senate. These new Democrats from Dixie are more middle-of-the-road than their Southern Democratic predecessors. They tend to take more moderate stands on issues rather than highly conservative stands.

In other words, the South that was so heavily Democratic in the 1960s has become, by the early 2000s, a genuine two-party region. Democrats and Republicans now struggle hard against each other to win seats in Congress from the South. The old one-party Democratic Solid South is just a memory.

CHAPTER 6

CONGRESS AND STRATEGY:
HOW A BILL BECOMES A LAW

"We're not just offering this to you," Jim Senitall said with a great deal of seriousness. "We're strongly urging you to do it."

Clark Schooler should have known that something unusual was about to happen to him. Clark had been asked to stop by the Washington Bureau of the Patriot Press newspapers on the Monday morning following the March on Washington. When Clark walked into the office, he found Jim Senitall, the Patriot Press's top national political reporter, waiting to see him. To Clark's total surprise, someone else was there. It was Terry Songman, the city editor of the *Baltimore Banner*.

"I've come down from Baltimore to see you," Terry Songman said, "because the Patriot Press has an interesting proposal to make to you. We want you to become a Capitol Fellow. It's a program that puts you to work in a congressional office for a year."

"Capitol Fellows are a specially selected group of promising young professionals from across the nation," Jim Senitall chimed in. "They're newspaper people, college professors, up-and-coming young business executives, and talented state and local government employees. They meet together periodically for seminars on Washington politics, but most of the time they work in the offices of senators and representatives on Capitol Hill. And after their year in Washington is over, Capitol Fellows have a really interesting employment experience to highlight in their job resume."

"The Patriot Press is a strong supporter of the Capitol Fellows program," Terry Songman said. "One of our reporters was all set to be a Capitol Fellow, but another newspaper chain offered her their London Bureau. She decided to take that job instead. We're offering her fellowship to you."

"I apologize for the short notice," Jim Senitall said. Jim and Terry

Songman were alternating their speeches on this new job offer to Clark. "The program starts September 1. That's two days from now. It's this Wednesday. If you take the fellowship, and I sincerely hope you will, you can commute from Baltimore for the first few days. But, with a full-time job on Capitol Hill, you'll want to move from Baltimore and come live in Washington."

It was Terry Songman's turn to speak again. "Before she decided to go to London, the woman who was originally going to do this for us was appointed to work for Senator Thomas H. Kuchel of California. Senator Kuchel is a strong supporter of civil rights." Terry Songman hesitated for a second, then simultaneously smiled and winked at Clark Schooler. "Everyone at the *Banner* knows, Clark, that you're partial to civil rights. You'll find a real home in Senator Kuchel's office."

Clark knew who Senator Kuchel was. He was the assistant Republican leader in the U.S. Senate. That meant Kuchel was the Number Two man in the Republican Party in the Senate, serving under the Republican leader, Senator Everett M. Dirksen of Illinois. Clark also knew that Senator Kuchel pronounced his family name funny. It was pronounced "Keekle," as if the "u" were a long "e."

"You qualify for this job on two counts," said Jim Senitall. "You're both a beginning journalist and a young political scientist. You have the writing skills, and the research qualifications, that will prove really useful in a senator's office. And it will be a super experience for you. I know. I was a Capitol Fellow myself about fifteen years ago."

Terry Songman and Jim Senitall gave Clark exactly one hour to make up his mind about becoming a Capitol Fellow. Actually, Clark only needed about ten minutes. He had planned to work at the *Baltimore Banner* a year or so before looking for a job as a college professor. After spending six years of his life getting a Ph.D., Clark was ready to get away for a while from academic life. What better way to take a break than by spending a year in a senator's office on Capitol Hill? Terry Songman and Jim Senitall were very pleased with Clark's quick decision to accept their offer and become a Capitol Fellow.

Bright and early on Wednesday, September 1, 1963, Clark Schooler reported to the office of Senator Thomas H. Kuchel, Republican of California. The office was in the Old Senate Office Building, a large marble structure located on Constitution Avenue to the north of the Capitol building. A small electric subway train connected the Old Senate Office Building to the Senate wing of the Capitol.

Clark was greeted by Evan Harris, Senator Kuchel's chief of staff. Harris was an older man, probably in his late 50s or early 60s. He was distinguished looking, and he had a warm way of meeting and talking to people. Clark liked him instantly. Just as instantly, Clark realized that it was Evan Harris's likability that probably got him his position as Senator Kuchel's top executive assistant.

Senator Kuchel's office was actually a suite of offices, more than ten rooms filled with assistants, secretaries, interns, desks, telephones, dictating machines, and typewriters. There was a perpetual buzz of conversation in the office, as the various aides to the senator took telephone calls from California and then worked to solve whatever constituent problem had been presented to them. In the background was the persistent clacking noise of typewriters. Periodically the low drone of a human voice could be heard dictating a letter into a dictating machine.

Evan Harris explained to Clark exactly why all this activity was necessary. "California has 18 million people," Harris said, "and more people are moving into the state all the time. Senator Kuchel is one of only two California senators, so you can see why so many people are required just to answer the telephone and take care of whatever the callers have on their mind. But what's really staggering is the mail. Senator Kuchel receives thousands of letters a day. We try to answer every one of them with what appears to be a personal letter from the senator."

Clark was jolted by what Evan Harris was telling him. "I guess when the Founders created the U.S. Senate," Clark said, "they were not visualizing this situation. Equal representation in the Senate took the form of two senators per state. But I don't think the Founders ever visualized one state having 18 million people living in it, and the telephone and the U.S. Mail putting almost every one of those 18 million persons in direct contact with their U.S. senator if they want to be."

After Evan Harris had shown Clark every nook and cranny of Senator Kuchel's office suite, it was lunchtime. Harris walked Clark over to the New Senate Office Building (Senator Kuchel's office was in the Old Senate Office Building), and the two men had lunch in the Senate dining room.

This was very much to Clark Schooler's liking. The Senate dining room was lavishly appointed, with a very plush rug on the floor and a beautiful white linen table cloth on each table. The silverware was real silver, and an extremely well-trained and courteous staff of waiters served the meal. The entire west side of the dining room was plate glass windows, so the room had a bright and airy feel to it, even on cloudy and rainy days. On sunny days, delicate see-through curtains were used to keep the room from getting too bright.

"There are two Senate dining rooms," Evan Harris said to Clark as the two men took their seats at a table by the window. "The really prestigious one is in the Capitol building proper, right in the Senate wing. I'm afraid the Senate dining room in the Capitol is pretty much for senators only, but a number of the senators will eat over here in the New Senate Office Building. I actually prefer this dining room myself. It's easy to get a reservation over here, and it's quieter and less crowded while you're eating lunch."

Evan Harris saw Clark looking around the room, sensed what was going on in Clark's mind, and quickly looked around the room himself. "There's Senator Clifford Case of New Jersey over in the corner," Harris said to Clark, "and Senator J. Glenn Beall of Maryland is kind of in the center there."

As Clark was putting his napkin on his lap, Evan Harris gave Clark some important advice. "Be certain to order the Senate bean soup," Harris said with great seriousness. "The legend around here is that, years ago, a senator liked this particular bean soup so much that he ordered it placed on the menu every day. It's been on the menu ever since. Everyone agrees that it's one of the best tasting bean soups there ever was."

Clark took that advice and ordered the bean soup for his appetizer. For his main course, Clark had a large serving of chicken salad served in a half cantaloupe and garnished with pineapple chunks. The comfortable atmosphere in the dining room, coupled with the high quality of the food and the service, gave Clark a feeling of excitement and well-being that he thoroughly enjoyed.

Clark then asked Harris to tell him some things about Senator Kuchel, the man for whom Clark was going to be working but whom Clark had never met personally.

"Tom Kuchel comes out of the same liberal wing of the California Republican Party that produced Chief Justice Earl Warren," Evan Harris began. "As you know, Chief Justice Warren presided over and strongly supported the Supreme Court's *Brown v. Board of Education* decision that mandated racial integration in public schools."

"Back when Earl Warren was the Republican governor of California," Evan Harris continued, "Tom Kuchel was his leading political assistant. Governor Warren helped Kuchel get elected attorney general of California. Kuchel was so popular as attorney general that he was reelected by one of the largest majorities ever piled up in a California statewide election."

"Tom Kuchel's big break into national politics came in 1952," Evan Harris went on. "At that time Richard Nixon was a U.S. senator from California. Dwight Eisenhower picked Nixon to be his running mate in the 1952 presidential election. That fall, Ike was elected president and Dick Nixon was elected with him as vice-president. That left a vacancy for California in the U.S. Senate. State governors fill vacancies in the U.S.

Senate, so Governor Warren filled that California vacancy with his most trusted lieutenant, Tommy Kuchel."

"So the senator came to Washington in January of 1953," Harris said. "It's now 1963, so he has represented California in the U.S. Senate for just over ten years. He definitely is a liberal Republican. You can tell that from his issue positions. In the Senate, he is a strong supporter of civil rights. He also favors a national health care plan for taking care of the elderly people over 65 years of age. The senator supports the business community as much as any other Republican, but he also believes in using government to improve social and economic life in the United States. A lot of conservative Republicans disagree with Senator Kuchel on that particular point. The real conservatives don't want government to do anything."

Evan Harris suddenly lowered his voice, as if he were letting Clark Schooler in on a big secret. "Here in the Senate," Harris said, "Kuchel is the informal leader of a small but very important group of five liberal Republican senators. The other four are John Sherman Cooper of Kentucky, Jacob Javits of New York, Kenneth Keating of New York, and Clifford Case of New Jersey. Senator Case is the guy I pointed out to you earlier sitting over in the corner of the dining room."

"That's how Senator Kuchel got himself elected assistant Republican leader in the Senate," Harris whispered on. "To please the conservative Republicans, they elected Everett Dirksen of Illinois, a conservative, the Republican leader. To please the liberal Republicans, and thus keep everybody happy, they elected Tom Kuchel, a liberal, the assistant Republican leader.

"Kuchel gets along really well with Senator Dirksen," Harris continued. Harris let the sound level of his voice rise back to normal. "Even though Dirksen's a conservative and Kuchel's a liberal, the two men work hard to keep all the Republicans in the Senate working together in a harmonious fashion. But on a lot of roll call votes, Dirksen and the conservative Republican senators will vote one way, and Kuchel and his little band of liberal Republican senators will vote completely differently."

Then the tone of Evan Harris's voice suddenly changed from serious to playful. "Hey, Clark," Harris said, "be certain to order the raspberry sherbet for dessert. The sherbet, and it has to be the raspberry, is almost as famous in the Senate dining room as the Senate bean soup."

Clark Schooler enjoyed his raspberry sherbet. It was indeed very tasty. It came with a wafer-thin graham cracker on the side.

As the two men were finishing their meal, Evan Harris gave Clark some additional advice about his new job as an assistant to Senator Kuchel. "Don't spend all day working in the office," Harris said. "We want you to get out some of the time. We want you to move around Capitol Hill, seeing people, being seen, and going to meetings. There's a group of Capitol Hill staffers working on President Kennedy's civil rights bill. I'll get you in touch with them. They meet one afternoon a week, just to keep themselves up to date on what is going on. You can represent the senator at those meetings. You'll learn a lot about civil rights and the Senate in the process."

Evan Harris and Clark Schooler walked back to Clark's new office in the Old Senate Office Building. As they parted company, Evan Harris made what Clark considered to be a wonderful offer. "Anytime you want to go to lunch in the Senate dining room," Harris said, "please do so. I can't get you into the one in the Capitol, but you can eat at the one in the New Senate Office Building anytime you want to. Take important people you meet on Capitol Hill to lunch there. Above all, take important people who come in from California to lunch there. And you can take your friends to lunch there. It's a lot of fun."

In a moment of rare social courage, Clark asked Even Harris: "Can I take a date, a girlfriend, to lunch there?"

"Yes, you can," Harris replied. "The senators and their staffers take their wives and children to lunch there, so you can certainly take a date there. Enjoy it."

Then Evan Harris gave Clark Schooler a look that was both serious and knowing. "Above all, Clark," Harris said, "use the Senate dining room to advance yourself, and the senator, politically."

Clark was given a desk and a telephone in the Kuchel office suite. He was assigned a secretary and an electric typewriter. Clark sat quietly in his new office for a moment. Then, for inspiration, Clark walked over to the window of his new office and looked out.

His window was on the east side of the Old Senate Office Building and looked across North East 1st Street to the west wall of the New Senate Office Building. As Clark's gaze rose up the marble wall of the New building, he saw a saying carved into the wall. By this time it was mid-afternoon, and a warm late-summer sun was lighting up the marble wall. The saying on the wall of the New Senate Office Building read: The Senate Is The Living Symbol Of Our Union Of States.

Clark stared at the saying and thought about it for a moment. He finally decided he agreed with the saying. With equal representation for each state, in the form of two U.S. senators per state, the Senate was, indeed, the "living" symbol of American national unity.

The next six weeks were very important ones in Clark Schooler's intellectual development. Clark found helping to answer Senator Kuchel's legislative mail to be a unique educational experience. Clark quickly learned to use the telephone to get the information he needed to answer each letter or group of letters.

The word around Capitol Hill was that answering the mail was boring and tedious. It was a job fit only for high school and college interns. Clark did not find it that way. Each letter was another opportunity to learn something new about American government. Each letter was an official excuse to make another personal contact. Each letter gave Clark a chance to telephone his way into one more office and find out what they were doing there and what kind of information they had there.

Clark learned something else during his first six weeks working in Senator Kuchel's office. He learned how to use borrowed power. He saw how the simple phrase, "I'm Clark Schooler from Senator Kuchel's office," opened doors for him and got his telephone calls returned promptly. It fascinated Clark that he, Clark Schooler, was essentially no one. But identifying himself as being from Senator Kuchel's office made him someone of instant importance. It made him someone who other people wanted to talk to and get to know. It made other people willing to listen to him and to try to fulfill his requests, whether those requests were for information or some form of government action.

Clark Schooler worked hard at keeping a sense of reality about his newfound abilities. He constantly reminded himself that his power was, indeed, only borrowed. It was Senator Kuchel who was the V.I.P., the Very Important Person. Without the phrase "from Senator Kuchel's office" trailing his own name, Clark was just another face in the crowd.

As the weeks went by and the mail got answered, Clark began to regard Washington, D.C., as a sort of giant governmental research university. All over the city, people who worked for the U.S. Government were gathering information and then using that information to try to make government policy and improve government services. Working for Senator Kuchel, and learning how to use the telephone, gave Clark Schooler the opportunity to wander through this great governmental research university, learning all he could and, occasionally, getting a chance to apply what he had learned.

Slowly, without his half realizing it was happening, Clark was beginning to change. With each additional telephone call, with each new personal contact made, Clark was becoming familiar with, knowledgeable about, and intellectually comfortable in Washington, D.C. To use a popular expression, Clark Schooler was becoming "Washington savvy."

Although Clark had a busy first day on the job with Senator Kuchel, his first day of work did not end early. At six o'clock Clark made his way up Massachusetts Avenue North West to the headquarters of the Capitol Fellows program. There Clark joined the other 1963-1964 Capitol Fellows for a sit-down dinner and an introductory, get-acquainted meeting.

The dinner was impressive. A combination plate, including both sirloin steak and lobster tail, was served along with a variety of vegetables and a salad. During that dinner, the Capitol Fellows began the process of meeting each other, getting to know each other, and sharing their various work experiences prior to coming to Washington.

As impressive as the dinner were the accomplishments of Clark's fellow Capitol Fellows. One political scientist had just written and published a book on the work of the House Ways And Means Committee, the committee in the House of Representatives that worked on tax policy. One of the young business types was already the vice-president of an upstart business computing systems company in New England. And the journalists were all from very well-known big city newspapers, such as the *Chicago Tribune*, the *Atlanta Constitution*, and the *Cleveland Plain Dealer*. The *Baltimore Banner*, where Clark had worked and trained, was definitely bush league compared to the newspapers for which the other journalists had worked.

There were both men and women in the Capitol Fellows program for 1963-1964. Almost all of the Capitol Fellows were married and had brought spouses and children to Washington with them. But a number of the Fellows, men and women alike, were unmarried.

Clark quickly made contact with two of the unmarried male Fellows who were journalists. The three young men decided to make common cause, and save money, by finding an apartment and rooming together.

The next two or three evenings were spent in avid apartment hunting. Clark Schooler and his two new friends looked at and rejected what seemed like every conceivable type of living space. There were third floor walkup apartments in small apartment buildings, bare bones accommodations in converted garages, basement apartments with sidewalk level windows, etc. Finally, the three young men struck apartment gold when they found a reasonably-priced small row house in the residential area east of the Capitol building known as Capitol Hill.

The house was two stories high, with a living room, dining room, and kitchen on the first floor. There were multiple bedrooms and a bathroom on the second floor. The house was furnished in Salvation Army eclectic, but the living room chairs and sofa were surprisingly comfortable, and the beds and mattresses were in good shape. Typical of downtown Washington housing, the home had no front yard. The front wall rose up right at the back edge of the front sidewalk.

One of Clark's new house mates had brought a television set with him to Washington. The television was placed in the downstairs living room for all three to enjoy. The TV set helped to keep the three Capitol Fellows plugged in to national television news and analysis.

The house was located in the 100 block of Sixth Street South East. It was only six blocks to the Capitol complex, so all three young men could walk to their jobs and not have to hassle with trying to park a car each day close to the Capitol building.

And so it was, by the second week in September of 1963, that Clark Schooler found himself with a promising assignment in Senator Kuchel's office. He had a more-than-acceptable place to live on Capitol Hill, and he had two friendly and compatible fellow-journalist housemates with whom to pal around Washington. Things, Clark thought to himself, were looking good.

But the positive progress in Clark Schooler's personal life was not reflected on the national scene. The Sixteenth Street Baptist Church was an African-American church in Birmingham, Alabama. This particular church was well-known to those Americans who had been closely following the civil rights struggle in the United States.

It was from the Sixteenth Street Baptist Church that Martin Luther King, Jr., and the Southern Christian Leadership Conference had orchestrated the protests and demonstrations against racial segregation in Birmingham in the spring of 1963. Those were the protests and demonstrations that had moved President Kennedy to begin forcefully pushing a major civil rights bill in Congress.

On September 15, 1963, the church building was a busy place. Religion classes were in session, and classrooms and hallways were filled with boys and girls dressed in their church-going best. Four young girls, three of them young teenagers and one an 11-year-old, stopped to chat, primp, and just hack around in a basement lounge. The girls were Addie Mae Collins, 14; Carol Robertson, 14; Cynthia Wesley, 14; and Denise McNair, 11.

In the dark of the previous night, unknown persons had placed a homemade bomb under the back steps of the Sixteenth Street Baptist Church. The bomb detonated with a powerful blast. The four closest persons to the explosion were the four little girls. Their innocent and unknowing decision to comb their hair and goof around a little had put them in exactly the wrong place at precisely the wrong time. All four were killed instantly. Their bodies had to be dug out from under the piles of shattered debris left in the bomb's wake.

Twenty other Sunday school children were injured by the blast. Angry blacks took to the streets of Birmingham to express their frustration and outrage. The Birmingham Police responded with military-style countermeasures. Two more black youngsters died.

The national news media went into high gear and high dudgeon over what came to be known as "the Sunday school bombing." Individual photographs of all four of the dead girls were printed on page one of most major newspapers. At the time the pictures were taken, the four girls were all clothed in white dresses. Looking at the photographs, Clark Schooler theorized that those were the girls' first communion dresses, or their Sunday school graduation dresses, or something like that.

In the sharp contrast provided by black-and-white newspaper photography, Clark was impressed by the way the white dresses highlighted the dark skin of the girls' faces. The white dresses emphasized the girls' youth and innocence. Their dark skin clearly identified them as members of an oppressed minority.

Along with much of the rest of the United States, Clark Schooler and his two new house mates sat and watched events develop in Birmingham on the television set in their living room. It was mid-September, and the three Capitol Fellows had only been at their new jobs on Capitol Hill for about two weeks.

The television scenes and newspaper stories from Birmingham were enraging. One particularly poignant photograph showed a black man on his knees praying in the midst of the rubble created by the explosion. There was television film of each girl's casket being carried from the church following the funeral service. There were television interviews with the parents of the dead girls. These interviews included tearful accounts of the parents' hopes and dreams for their daughters. Those hopes and dreams had been blown to smithereens by a racist bomb.

The news media augmented the coverage of the Sunday school bombing with interviews with prominent civil rights leaders. Clark and his two house mates watched and heard Martin Luther King, Jr., relate the bombing to the need for action from Washington, D.C. "Unless some immediate steps are taken by the U.S. Government," King said, "my pleas for nonviolence will fall on deaf ears and we shall see in Birmingham and Alabama the worst racial holocaust the nation has ever seen."

Martin Luther King, Jr., also accused Alabama's pro-segregation governor, George Wallace, of using racist rhetoric that helped contribute to the bombing. "The blood of our little children is on your hands," King charged.

When Martin Luther King, Jr., had finished his attack on Governor Wallace, one of Clark's housemates said to no one in particular: "Hey! The civil rightsers are working this one for every last bit of political mileage they can get."

The young man speaking was Greg Netherton. He was born and grew up in northern Louisiana. "I'm from one of the poorest parts of one of the poorest states in the nation," Netherton told Clark when the two first met. It was obvious to Clark, however, that Greg Netherton had adeptly escaped the grinding poverty so often found in the rural South. Greg was a graduate of Vanderbilt University, a prestigious private university in the Southern state of Tennessee. He had gone from Vanderbilt to a good job as a newspaper reporter on the *New Orleans Times-Picayune*.

"You really can't blame the civil rights leaders for taking advantage of this," Clark answered back. "After all, it isn't as though they were the one's who planted the bomb. Some rabid segregationist, or segregationists, did that."

It had not taken Clark very long to figure out that Greg Netherton was another living, breathing example of a "rational Southerner." If not outspokenly supporting full and immediate integration of the races, Greg was willing to admit that the time had come for the South to back away from its traditional application of rigid rules of racial segregation.

In just a few days of acquaintance, Clark had concluded that Greg Netherton was a slightly less intellectual version of Clark's fellow Johns Hopkins graduate student, Beau Stevens. It was while debating Beau Stevens in graduate school seminars that Clark had first come in contact with the unique thought and behavior patterns of the "rational Southerner."

One way in which Greg Netherton was reflecting his "rationality" was the congressional office to which he had been assigned as a Capitol Fellow. Greg was working for U.S. Representative Charles Weltner, a young Democrat from Georgia. Weltner was known as one of the most progressive Southern voices in the House of Representatives. The Northern press seemed to admire Representative Weltner, always describing him as a spokesman for the more liberal "New South" rather than the more conservative "Old South."

The television was continuing to carry comments by Martin Luther King, Jr. "The brutal murder of these four girls," King said, "shows the immediate need for legislation empowering the attorney general of the United States to file suits on behalf of citizens whose civil rights have been violated." [16]

Clark sat up abruptly in his chair. "Why, those words are straight out of President Kennedy's civil rights bill," Clark sputtered. "That's Title Three. The attorney general files the suit so that local black persons won't have to run the lethal, and sometimes fatal, risk of filing the suit themselves."

The television then switched to Roy Wilkins, a prominent civil rights leader with the National Association for the Advancement of Colored People (NAACP). "In light of this most recent bombing," Wilkins harangued into the camera, "President Kennedy should cut off every nickel of U.S. Government funds being spent in Alabama. The president can begin by closing Maxwell Air Force Base near Montgomery. And, while he's at it, the president should push harder for equal employment opportunity." [17]

Clark was really agitated. "It's like they're reading us the provisions of the civil rights bill and urging us to pass it in the little girls' memory," Clark exclaimed. "The U.S. funds cut-off to government programs that racially discriminate is one of the most important parts of the civil rights bill. And so is equal employment opportunity."

Clark's other house mate stared at the TV set and then grumbled loudly: "This is so exploitive! They really don't care about the girls. All they really care about is their civil rights bill. I mean, sure, the bill's important. But do they have to be pushing it so hard at this sad moment in American history?"

Clark's second house mate was named Carl Brimmer. A native of Washington state, he was a graduate of Reed College in Oregon. After college, Carl had knocked around in a variety of writing jobs before settling down for a few years as an editorial writer on a newspaper in Anchorage, Alaska. Undoubtedly a thoughtful person to begin with, Carl Brimmer had gained real intellectual depth while sitting at his typewriter everyday and fashioning editorial policy for an Alaskan newspaper. He had a wide-ranging knowledge of the major political issues facing the United States. And he had decidedly liberal Democratic views about what policies should be adopted to deal with those issues.

"It's all manipulated," Carl expounded. "It can't just be left the sorrowful tale of four girls being blown up at their Sunday school. For some unknown reason, people think it has to be turned into some positive good, some great cause. It has to be twisted to someone else's useful purpose."

As a Capitol Fellow, Carl Brimmer had been assigned to Senator Frank Church of Idaho. Senator Church, like Brimmer, was a dedicated liberal Democrat and a longtime friend and supporter of President Kennedy. Frank Church was a relatively young man for a politician, in his 40s, and was considered "a man with a future" on Capitol Hill.

It had been interesting for Clark Schooler and Carl Brimmer to compare notes on their early experiences as senatorial aides. Clark was amazed to learn that Senator Church of Idaho, a state with a very small population, received around only 25 or 30 letters per day. It was a stunning comparison with the thousands of letters a day that Senator Kuchel of California routinely received. Carl Brimmer was helping Senator Church answer his mail, but Senator Church took the time every day to read each incoming letter and the letter that his staff had written in return. "Senator Church supervises all his mail very closely," Carl explained to a somewhat envious Clark, "and participates actively in the preparation and writing of his letters back to his constituents."

During the following days, while Clark was at work, he struck up a brief conversation with Evan Harris, Senator Kuchel's chief of staff. Clark explained the reaction of his two house mates to the Birmingham Sunday school bombing, noting that his Southern friend, Greg Netherton, had thought the civil rights forces had overplayed the tragedy in behalf of the civil rights bill. Clark went on to say that his more liberal Democratic friend, Carl Brimmer, had agreed that political exploitation was taking place.

Evan Harris hesitated not one second in giving his reply. "American politics is not a pillow fight," Evan Harris said. "It's an all-out battle in which you throw every punch you can, just as hard as you can."

"You have to learn to use your resources, and I mean all your resources," Evan Harris went on. "American politics is a highly-competitive process. Your opponents will be using every weapon at their disposal. That means you have to use every weapon, every conceivable weapon, at your disposal. You exploit every contact you've got, every connection you can make, and every event that takes place. You've got to use all of it if you want to succeed."

"In my opinion," Evan Harris concluded, "the civil rights leaders would have been derelict in their duty if they had not used the deaths of the four Sunday school girls to advance the civil rights bill."

The political and news media reaction to the Sunday school bombing continued at a fever pitch. A leading newspaper columnist wrote that the central black neighborhood in Birmingham should be labeled "Dynamite Hill" because of all the racial bombings that had taken place there.[18] Hubert H. Humphrey, U.S. senator from Minnesota and the assistant Democratic leader in the Senate, publicly asked President Kennedy to declare a "National Day of Mourning" for the four black girls.[19] Throughout the country, both North and South, memorial services and memorial marches were held in remembrance of the young victims.

It was about this time, shortly after the Sunday school bombing, that Clark Schooler first met Senator Kuchel in person. Evan Harris came to Clark's office one morning and said the senator had a few spare minutes and wanted to meet Clark. Evan Harris and Clark rode the electric subway car from the Old Senate Office Building to the Senate wing of the Capitol.

As they were riding along, they passed a distinguished older man walking toward the Capitol rather than riding on the subway car. "That's Senator Proxmire of Wisconsin," Evan Harris said, somewhat enviously. "He always hikes along the cement walk next to the subway tracks rather than ride the subway. He says we're all ruining our health by sitting on the subway car instead of walking."

Senator Kuchel turned out to be, in Clark's view, a very typical United States senator. He was 48-years-old but looked slightly older. He was not a tall man, but he was not noticeably short in stature. Kuchel tended on the heavy side, but Clark decided it would be going too far to call him fat. Bulky might be a better word, or perhaps roly-poly. He had dark hair and wore glasses most of the time. Similar to most politicians, Kuchel had a deep, clear voice that could easily be heard in the back row of any auditorium or assembly hall.

The discussion was brief, only about ten minutes. It centered mainly around Clark's experiences working as a newspaper reporter and covering civil rights events in Baltimore. It turned out that Senator Kuchel had never actually visited Baltimore. But he had passed through the city by automobile when going to Philadelphia and New York.

Kuchel had been appalled by the conditions he had observed through his car windows while driving past the old, red-brick row houses of center-city Baltimore. From what Kuchel had seen, Baltimore was block after block of rundown row houses, each one filled to the brim with African-American men, women, and children.

Senator Kuchel asked Clark a question: "Is it really as bad for black people in Baltimore as it looks?" [20]

Clark was somewhat surprised by that question. Kuchel was one of the leading supporters of black civil rights in the U.S. Senate. Surely this senator should know, Clark thought, of the desperate economic hardships and difficult living conditions faced by many center-city minority groups in the United States.

Clark answered Senator Kuchel's inquiry this way: "What you saw in Baltimore was real. Much of the area surrounding downtown Baltimore is filled with obsolete and poorly maintained housing which is sold and rented to black people. And there is high unemployment, large numbers of illegitimate births, and lots of crime in these areas. But it's not the whole story. What you did not see is that there also is block after block of middle-class black housing in Baltimore, with the houses well-painted and the lawns nicely trimmed."

"There is a thriving and varied black community in Baltimore," Clark concluded, "but the less well-off portions of that community are readily visible from the major highway routes passing through Baltimore. And, for many of those people, things are as bad as they look."

Senator Kuchel seemed to be listening carefully to Clark's observations. The senator acted as though he appreciated hearing them. At the conclusion of their meeting, Clark and Senator Kuchel agreed on one point. Whether the black people living in Baltimore were poor, or middle-class, or even wealthy, all of them had been the victims of legal racial segregation.

In the midst of all the hullabaloo over the Sunday school bombing, Clark Schooler's telephone rang. The man on the other end of the line identified himself as Joseph L. Rauh, Jr., representing the Leadership Conference on Civil Rights. "I'd like us to get together some afternoon," Joseph Rauh said to Clark. "Senator Kuchel is going to be a big part of the civil rights bill, which means you're going to be a big part of the civil rights bill. I want to make sure you're up to date on what the bill's about and all the things that have been going on."

Clark did not know who Joseph L. Rauh, Jr., was. But Clark had heard of the Leadership Conference on Civil Rights. That was the major lobby group backing the civil rights bill. Because Clark was always anxious to go new places and see different offices in Washington, Clark readily agreed to find his way to Joseph Rauh's office up on "Eye" Street Northwest.

"Eye" Street was a popular street for lobbyists' offices. The street was named for the letter "I" in the alphabet, but the street name often was spelled out as "Eye" to avoid confusion with the Roman numeral one, also designated with an "I."

Joseph Rauh turned out to be an affable and talkative middle-aged man in his early fifties. He was tall, and he was lively and agile as he moved about his office. His last name was pronounced as if it rhymed with "brow" or "scow" or "meow." He greeted Clark warmly and then offered Clark a chair opposite his desk. Joseph Rauh sat at his desk and pontificated to Clark, much as a senior professor might talk to and lecture a graduate student.

As so often happens with politically active people, the walls of Joseph Rauh's office were filled with photographs of Rauh with a variety of famous United States politicians, almost all of them well-known Democrats. Prominently displayed were photographs of Rauh with former presidents Franklin Delano Roosevelt and Harry S. Truman.

Joseph Rauh politely began the afternoon's conversation by inquiring about Clark's family background, education, and professional experience as a journalist. Once those niceties were out of the way, Rauh launched into a brief oration on his own life story. "I was born and grew up in Cincinnati, Ohio," Rauh began, "where both my grandfather and my father were in the shirt manufacturing business. Thanks to the shirt factory, I was able to go to Harvard University in Massachusetts for both my undergraduate degree and my law degree. I majored in economics, and I also played center on the basketball team."

"After law school," Rauh went on, "I came right to Washington to be a law clerk at the Supreme Court. The year was 1935, and the country was in the middle of the Great Depression. I threw myself into the New Deal, President Roosevelt's all-out program for using United States Government aid programs to end the Depression. In 1941, just prior to World War II, I helped to write the executive order that President Roosevelt issued to racially integrate all the defense plants during the war. Then I provided legal counsel to lend-lease, President Roosevelt's program for sending military supplies to Great Britain prior to the United States coming into World War II."

"I was in the Army during World War II," Rauh continued, "serving as an officer in the Philippine Islands under General Douglas MacArthur. When the war was over, I set up a private law practice here in Washington, but I've elected to spend much of my time lobbying for a variety of liberal causes."

"In one sense," Rauh noted, "you could say I went to work for New Deal liberalism in the mid-1930s and then never stopped. In 1947, I was one of a small group of people who founded Americans for Democratic Action, better known by its initials as the ADA. That's an organization that raises money and uses it to lobby Congress on behalf of a variety of liberal causes. But right now, Clark, as you already know, I'm lobbying for the civil rights bill that President Kennedy sent up to Congress last June."

"I do this kind of lobbying for little or no pay," Joseph Rauh said without even a hint of embarrassment. "A lot of people have made a lot more money than I have in Washington, but you'd be hard-pressed to find anyone who's had more fun." [21]

"Like most economic liberals," Rauh explained, "I believe in using the United States Government to solve the nation's economic and social problems. In the final analysis, it's the U.S. Government's job to put people to work, and it's the U.S. Government's job to see that people have enough to eat and a safe place to live. Right now, I believe it's the job of the U.S. Government to end the racial discrimination that has marred this nation's history ever since the slaves were freed at the end of the Civil War."

By this time it was clear to Clark Schooler that Joseph Rauh wanted Clark to know that Joseph Rauh was a bona fide New Deal liberal. Rauh was succeeding at this. Clark was duly impressed with Rauh's long career in Washington and the variety of liberal causes, most of them successful, with which Rauh had associated himself.

Clark then moved the conversation on to what he thought was the next logical subject. Clark asked: "Can you tell me something about the Leadership Conference on Civil Rights? I know the organization is a super lobby, a coalition of various lobby groups working for a piece of major legislation. But I don't know much about the Leadership Conference specifically."

"The Leadership Conference is probably one of the largest and best organized lobbies in U.S. political history," Joseph Rauh answered. "One key part of it is the big labor unions, such as the Teamster's Union and the AFL-CIO."

Clark knew that the AFL-CIO was a combination of the two largest labor unions in the United States, the American Federation of Labor and the Congress of Industrial Organizations.

"There are a number of national church groups that belong to the Leadership Conference," Joseph Rauh went on, "such as the National Catholic Welfare Conference, the Synagogue Council of America, and the National Council of Churches. All the major civil rights groups are in it, including CORE, the Urban League, and the NAACP."

"This is too big a country," Rauh went on, "and the Congress is too much of a labyrinthine maze, for one lobby group alone to be able to get a major bill enacted into law. You have to build giant combinations of lobby groups to get really big and important bills through the Congress. Building such a combination of lobby groups to support civil rights is what the Leadership Conference does."

"Our efforts are much greater than just sending a lobbyist or two up to Capitol Hill," Joseph Rauh lectured. "We grind out a constant stream of press releases, fact sheets, and newsletters about the current status of the civil rights bill. At key moments in the legislative process, we bring important members of our various organizations to Washington. By important members, I mean labor union presidents, well-known bishops and ministers, and the top civil rights leaders. We sic 'em on key members of Congress, just when the bill is before an important committee, or coming up for a vote on the House or Senate floor."

"Believe me," Rauh continued, "we are relentless about this. We work at 'matching,' putting a cardinal of the Catholic Church to work on a senator who is a Catholic. Or we send a bishop of the Episcopal Church to try to persuade an Episcopalian in the House of Representatives. We're particularly influential with legislators who have a large number of labor union members in their constituency. If they're from Michigan, they tend to fall right into line when a high mucky-muck from the United Automobile Workers shows up at their office door. If they're from West Virginia, they start jumping through hoops when the president of the United Mine Workers comes to call."

At this point, Clark Schooler interjected a question: "Do you ever worry, Mr. Rauh, about overplaying your hand? Are you ever fearful of getting too abrasive and pushy?"

"Never," Joseph Rauh replied with sincerity and finality. "You know the old saw: 'The best defense is a good offense.' Well, in the halls of Congress, the best defense against weakening amendments to your pet bill is the strongest possible offense you can put up. The Leadership Conference is backing President Kennedy's civil rights bill, sure enough. But we're demanding more. We're pressing for equal employment opportunity in all private industry, not just U.S. Government contractual employment. We want the attorney general to sue in all civil rights cases, not just school cases. Clearly stating what you want, and going for it as hard as you can, is the only way to play the legislative ball game." [22]

Joseph Rauh's telephone rang. He picked up the phone, listened for a moment, and then said: "Of course. Send him right in." Seconds later, the door opened and in walked a tall and distinguished looking African-American man. He was dressed in a dark blue suit with a white shirt and a colorful necktie. In his dress and his manner, he was indistinguishable from every other middle-aged lawyer in Washington.

Clark Schooler recognized the man right off. He was Clarence Mitchell, Jr., director of the Washington Office of the National Association for the Advancement of Colored People (NAACP). Similar to Clark, Clarence Mitchell was a resident of Baltimore, Maryland. It was well-known in the national capital that, bright and early every business day, Clarence Mitchell rode the commuter train from Baltimore to Washington. He then spent his working time lobbying Congress on behalf of African-American civil rights. Clarence Mitchell was such a familiar presence on Capitol Hill that he was often referred to in print as "the 101st senator."

"Clarence! It's good to see you again," Clark blurted out. Clarence Mitchell and Clark Schooler had met before. Clark had taken a group of his women students from Goucher College on a field trip to the NAACP headquarters in Baltimore. Clark and his students had been treated to a virtuoso performance by three generations of the Mitchell family, including Clarence Mitchell, Jr., each generation representing a different phase of the quest for black civil rights.

On that field trip, Clarence Mitchell's mother-in-law, Nellie Jackson, had begun the presentation. She took a religious approach, pointing out that all people, no matter what their skin color or station in life, were equal in the eyes of God. She noted how "faith" and "prayer" had sustained African-Americans through more than two centuries of slavery and almost one century of racial discrimination. "God will open their eyes," Nellie Jackson said of those white people who were racial segregationists. She convincingly projected her abiding faith that "God would lead black people to freedom."

The second speaker was Clarence Mitchell, Jr. Just as Clark expected a national spokesman for the NAACP to do, Mitchell referred frequently to the Declaration of Independence and the United States Constitution. He noted that those stirring documents contained the legal guarantees of liberty and equality that would eventually free African-Americans from the bonds of racial segregation.

"The best place for black men and women to fight for their rights," Clarence Mitchell, Jr., said, "is in the court room and in the halls of Congress." He cited *Brown v. Board of Education* as the kind of Supreme Court decision that, in the end, would help to free American blacks. He called on Congress to pass all-encompassing civil rights legislation.

Last on the speaking agenda at the Baltimore NAACP was Clarence Mitchell, III, the son of Clarence Mitchell, Jr., and the grandson of Nellie Jackson. Clarence Mitchell, III, was a young African-American man in his early twenties. He had participated in a number of civil rights demonstrations, some in Maryland and some outside the state. He had developed something of a reputation as a confrontational, outspoken young fighter for immediate civil rights reform. "White society, particularly in the South, will never voluntarily integrate with the black race," Clarence Mitchell, III, told the students, at one point clenching and waving his right fist. "It's only by taking to the streets, and by making forceful nonnegotiable demands, that blacks can get what's due them from the white oppressors." [23]

Later, while mentally reviewing this field trip experience, Clark realized that he had witnessed personal expressions, by three generations of the Mitchell family, of the three major techniques being used by African-Americans to try to racially integrate America. Nellie Jackson represented the moral suasion that can be applied through religious belief. Clarence Mitchell, Jr., a true spokesman for the NAACP, stood for the justice and equality of the American legal system as accomplished through suits filed in U.S. Courts and laws passed by Congress. Clarence Mitchell, III, manifested the youthful idea that only confrontation in the streets could change anything as firmly established in the United States psyche as racial segregation.

Clark Schooler and Joseph Rauh, Jr., had both stood up as Clarence Mitchell, Jr., walked into Rauh's office. Clarence Mitchell acknowledged Clark's greeting and, whether he actually did or not, acted as though he remembered Clark bringing his class on a field trip to the Baltimore NAACP. After some pleasant chitchat, some of it about race relations in Baltimore, Clarence Mitchell pulled up a chair of his own. The three men sat down. Clark's indoctrination in the work of the Leadership Conference on Civil Rights continued.

Clarence Mitchell, Jr., rubbed his chin, looked at Clark carefully for a few seconds, and then asked a question: "Clark, I know you taught political science at both Johns Hopkins and Goucher College, but how much do you really know about the way a congressional bill becomes a United States law?"

Clark laughed softly as he began his answer: "In most government text books, Clarence, they have a drawing of a little rolled up piece of paper with eyes, a nose, and a mouth. The little guy is labeled, 'A Bill,' and he has little feet on which he makes his way through Congress. Usually 'A Bill' starts by being introduced in the House of Representatives, goes to committee in the House, then goes to the House Rules Committee, and then gets adopted in a vote on the House floor. Then 'A Bill' walks over to the Senate, goes into Senate committee, is passed on the Senate floor, and heads off to the White House for the president's signature."

Clarence Mitchell and Joseph Rauh were both smiling along with Clark as he gave this mechanical and orderly description of legislative procedure in Congress. Mitchell and Rauh both were well aware of the simplified versions of "How A Bill Becomes A Law" that tended to appear in college and high school civics texts.

"But I know different," Clark continued. "I know that many bills are introduced on any given legislative subject. Sometimes hundreds of bills are introduced on a subject like civil rights, or medical care for the aged, where there's great public interest. The real question is, of all the bills introduced on any given subject, which one is going to be selected by the appropriate committee chairperson to move forward."

"And you always want to keep this in mind," Clark added. "Bills are changed, often radically, as they move through the House of Representatives and the Senate. Sometimes, only a small part of the bill that is introduced remains in the law that is finally passed. There's an old Capitol Hill joke, somewhat overstated, that goes like this: Any similarity between the original bill introduced and the law finally passed is purely coincidental."

Clark found himself warming to the task of demonstrating his knowledge of Congress to two of the more important men in Washington. "I also know," Clark said, "that often two bills on the same subject will be going through Congress at the same time, one bill working its way through the House of Representatives and the other bill going through the Senate. Of course, the House bill will usually have different language, or wording, from the Senate bill."

"Often," Clark rambled on, "when there are two different versions of the same bill passed by each house, the bill will be sent to a House-Senate conference committee. That's because exactly similar versions of the bill must pass both the House and the Senate. Key members of Congress from the relevant committees in the House and the Senate will be the conferees. They will make compromises and work out common language between the Senate and the House bill. Then a conference report will go back to both the Senate and the House to be adopted without amendment. If both houses pass the conference report, that's what goes up to the White House for the president's signature."

At that moment in Clark's legislative pontifications, Clarence Mitchell interrupted. "Clark, I know you know what a Senate filibuster is," Mitchell said in a flattering manner. "I also know you know that it takes a 2/3 cloture vote to end a filibuster and get the bill passed in the Senate. But what happens when a bill that has successfully survived a cloture vote in the Senate goes to conference committee?"

Clark's eyes widened, and he unintentionally put his hand to his forehead. No one had ever asked him that particular question before. "Uh," Clark replied, "the bill goes back to the Senate and, uh, faces a second filibuster?" Clark's tone of voice indicated that what had started out as a statement of fact had ended up as a question.

"Precisely," said Joseph Rauh. "Clark, my good friend Clarence Mitchell has just taught you the first lesson in 'How A Civil Rights Bill Becomes A Law.' You have to put the civil rights bill through Congress in such a way that it doesn't go to conference committee. If you can avoid going to conference, the bill doesn't go back to the Senate for a second filibuster and a second cloture vote."

Clark now was fully aware that he still had a great deal to learn about legislative strategy making. Suddenly, Clark found himself back in college and graduate school, playing the role of student rather than teacher. "How do you keep a major bill from going to conference committee?" Clark blurted out the question with an intellectual enthusiasm customarily displayed only by a first year college student.

"You begin in the House of Representatives," Clarence Mitchell said slowly and clearly, "and get the bill passed there. Then the House bill comes over to the Senate, where it is, of course, amended. That's what bicameralism is all about. After the bill has survived the filibuster and been successfully clotured, the bill goes back to the House of Representatives."

"Then," Mitchell continued, "and this is critical, the House agrees to the Senate changes without amendment. That eliminates the need for a conference committee. Exactly the same bill has passed in the House that passed in the Senate. That has the effect of sending the bill right to the president's desk without having to go back to the Senate for another filibuster and another cloture vote."

Clark shook his head up and down in agreement and wonder. It was the obvious way to get a civil rights bill passed into law. If you could get the House to agree to all the Senate amendments, then there would be only one filibuster and one cloture vote in the Senate. But Clark had never thought of the technique himself, nor had he ever heard anyone else discuss it.

"But there's one thing you have to be very careful to do when your civil rights bill is in the Senate," Joseph Rauh said. "You have to check your Senate amendments with key House members to make certain the amendments are acceptable to the House. Remember! The key step in the process is the House of Representatives agreeing to all the Senate amendments without even one little change allowed."

Similar to the "Red Rubber Ball" of the popular song, the morning sun of understanding was starting to shine in Clark's brain. He now knew the reason that Clarence Mitchell and Joseph Rauh were wasting an afternoon on a Senate aide. It was important to them that everyone working in the Senate, even a legislative assistant such as Clark, know that all Senate amendments to the civil rights bill, when it got to the Senate, had to be acceptable to the House leadership. That was the best way to head off a second filibuster, and the need for a second cloture vote, both of which would be required if the civil rights bill went to conference committee.

Clark also had begun to figure something else out. "Based on this legislative logic," he said, "you guys were just as happy that, this past summer, Senator James Oliver Eastland killed the Senate version of the civil rights bill in the Senate Judiciary Committee. I mean, you two wanted to start the process in the House of Representatives anyway."

"That's right," said Clarence Mitchell. His voice indicated his relief that Clark had seen the light and now was able to grasp some of the key steps in getting a civil rights bill passed. "I know you covered those hearings for the Patriot Press newspapers. Those Senate hearings were a great showcase for Senator Eastland and Senator Ervin. It also was nice for Bobby Kennedy to be able to present President Kennedy's civil rights bill to the news media and the public, although very few reporters or average citizens were paying attention. But Senator Eastland snuffing out the Senate version of the civil rights bill made no difference to us. For the strategic reasons we've been discussing, we always start a civil rights bill in the House of Representatives."

Joseph Rauh then gave Clark Schooler a more detailed view of how to get a civil rights bill through Congress. "We start the bill in the House of Representatives," Rauh said. "It goes to the House Judiciary Committee, where committee Chairperson Emanuel Celler, a New Yorker, always gives it favorable hearings. Then we hit our first roadblock. Before the bill can go to the House floor for a vote, it goes to the House Rules Committee. The chair of the Rules Committee is a Southerner from Virginia, and he'll do everything in his power to slow the bill down."

"Eventually," Rauh continued, "the Rules Committee chairperson will let the bill out of the House Rules Committee. The bill should pass easily on the House floor, because there's no filibuster in the House, and the vast majority of House members are from the North and the West. Once the bill is passed in the House, of course, it goes over to the Senate. That's when the real fun begins." [24]

Joseph Rauh gestured by opening his hands in the direction of Clarence Mitchell. The gesture meant it was Clarence Mitchell's turn to carry on the lecture.

"The first problem in the Senate," Mitchell said, "is your old friend from last summer, Senator Eastland. Under ordinary circumstances, the House-passed bill goes directly to the Senate Judiciary Committee. But if we ever let the civil rights bill into Senator Eastland's hands, we will never see it again. Similar to all civil rights bills, it will go into the Judiciary Committee and never come out. We therefore have to bypass the Senate Judiciary Committee. We do that by sending the civil rights bill directly to the Senate floor for debate."

"Then," Mitchell said with a heavy sigh, "it's time for the Southerners to filibuster. It's also time for us to come up with a 2/3 vote for cloture. That's 67 out of 100 votes in the Senate. While all that's going on, we have to make certain all Senate amendments are acceptable to the House." [25]

Clarence Mitchell looked over at Joseph Rauh, who took the conversational ball right back from him. "If we get cloture," Rauh said, "it's a relatively easy process from there on in. The civil rights bill, now as amended by the Senate, goes back to the House. The House agrees to all the Senate amendments, because all those amendments have been pre-approved by the House leadership. Then the bill heads right up Pennsylvania Avenue to the White House for a signing ceremony with President Kennedy."

There was a sudden silence. Clark was sitting there working at absorbing all the information Mitchell and Rauh had just given him. Joseph Rauh seemed to sense that Clark's mind was reeling somewhat from all the facts it had just been fed.

"Last July," Rauh said, "we held a meeting for the top officers of the Leadership Conference to brief them on all the obstacles to getting a civil rights bill passed in Congress. Martin Luther King, Jr., was there. After Clarence Mitchell and I had described the various obstacles and the various ways to overcome those obstacles, Martin Luther King whispered out loud: 'Mighty complicated, isn't it?'" [26]

Clark's meeting with Joseph Rauh and Clarence Mitchell ended at that point. When Clark stood up to leave, he thanked both men for taking the time to fill him in so fully on civil rights strategy making.

In an attempt to have the meeting end on a light note, Joseph Rauh said with a smile: "You know, we're the Gold Dust Twins. A Southern Democrat, Senator Harry Byrd of Virginia, gave us that name. Senator Byrd was referring to a picture of a white child and a black child that appeared on the label of cans of Old Dutch Cleanser. That was a cleaning and scouring powder that your mother and grandmother used to use." [27]

"Yes," said Clarence Mitchell, also smiling with both pride and amusement. "The Gold Dust Twins were on cans of Old Dutch Cleanser in almost every bathroom and kitchen closet in America. They were one of the earliest examples of voluntary and beneficial racial integration."

In The Interim

Lobbyists such as Joseph Rauh, Jr., and Clarence Mitchell, Jr., remain an integral and influential part of the legislative process in Congress. In fact, lobbyists are so important that many observers refer to them as an informal Third House of Congress.

The years from the 1960s to the 2000s have seen the rise of a number of lobby groups that represent social and environmental causes rather than economic interests. The Sierra Club is an excellent example of a lobby that works to advance a social good, an improved outdoor environment, rather than to enrich a private corporation or further the interests of labor union members.

Lobby organizations work to influence who gets elected to Congress as well as support particular legislative bills. In the 1970s Congress passed legislation allowing lobby groups to form Political Action Committees, also known by their initials as PACs. These organizations raise funds and contribute them to candidates for public office. A lobby group has much greater access to and influence over a member of Congress when the lobby group's PAC has made a large contribution to the Congress member's election or reelection campaign.

And super lobbies such as the Leadership Conference on Civil Rights are still very important on Capitol Hill. For example, more than 60 organizations engaged in the production and marketing of food have formed a cooperative lobbying effort known as the Food Group.

CHAPTER 7

PRESIDENT AND CONGRESS:
AT NIGHT AT THE WHITE HOUSE

Exactly as he had promised, Evan Harris put Clark Schooler in touch with a group of Capitol Hill staffers who were working in support of President Kennedy's civil rights bill. The group met once a week, usually on Thursday afternoons at 4 o'clock. The meeting place moved around Capitol Hill, but most of the time the meeting was held in a conference room in the Old Senate Office Building.

From time to time some of the more important persons working on behalf of civil rights would come to the meeting and give a briefing on their particular job or responsibility. Sometimes even a senator or a representative, or a key personage in the Kennedy administration, would stop by to speak and, not-so-coincidentally, lobby for their particular part of the civil rights cause.

The first meeting Clark attended was held in early October of 1963. The conference room had a large table in the center with a number of chairs around it. The outer rim of the room, however, was completely lined with chairs. The chairs extended around all four walls. As a result, when necessary, the room could comfortably contain a large number of persons.

Important visitors gave their talks and briefings while sitting at the conference table. Most of the staffers, Clark Schooler included, sat on the chairs lining the walls. Very few formal lectures or lengthy talks were ever presented at these meetings. The style was that of a conversation or a chat, with the civil rights staffers frequently interrupting the guest speakers with questions and comments.

On the day Clark first attended one of these meetings, the guest speaker was Francis Charles O'Brien, a deputy assistant something-or-other at the Department of Justice. Clark could never quite remember his exact job title.

Known to everyone as Frank O'Brien, he was a relatively young lawyer, in his 30s or 40s, from Massachusetts. As one would expect of an Irish-American lawyer from Massachusetts, O'Brien had a thick New England accent.

Frank O'Brien had been given his civil rights assignment by Attorney General Robert Kennedy, the member of President Kennedy's cabinet who headed the Justice Department. O'Brien's specific job was to watch over and become expert in the exact language of the Kennedy civil rights bill as it made its way through the House and the Senate.

"President Kennedy's civil rights bill was introduced in the House of Representatives on June 20, 1963," O'Brien began. "It was introduced by Emanuel Celler, the chairperson of the House Judiciary Committee. The House clerk gave the bill the number H.R. 7152."

Thanks to his graduate studies, Clark already knew that "H.R. 7152" stood for "House of Representatives 7152." The bill took the initials "H.R." because it had been first introduced in the House of Representatives. If it has been first introduced in the Senate, the bill would have been numbered "S. 7152," for "Senate 7152."

"When H.R. 7152 arrived in the Judiciary Committee," Frank O'Brien went on, "Chairperson Celler assigned the bill to Subcommittee No. 5. Emanuel Celler chaired that subcommittee as well as the full committee. For years, Celler had been carefully constructing Subcommittee No. 5 to be strongly favorable to civil rights. In fact . . ."

Someone in the room interrupted Frank O'Brien with a question: "I thought Subcommittee No. 5 was the anti-trust subcommittee, not the civil rights subcommittee. How could Celler send a civil rights bill to an anti-trust subcommittee?"

"Committee chairs such as Emanuel Celler are all-powerful," Frank O'Brien replied, "and everyone knows it. Nobody bothered to complain when he assigned the civil rights bill to the anti-trust subcommittee."

"And Celler had a good reason for doing that," O'Brien said. "Whenever a Democratic vacancy occurred on Subcommittee No. 5, Celler filled it with a liberal supporter of civil rights. There are no senior Southerners on the subcommittee. The subcommittee consists of Celler, five other Northern liberals, and a Texan."

A murmur of surprise and discomfort rippled through the conference room at the mention of the word "Texan." After all, Texas was a Southern state that had seceded from the Union during the Civil War. Frank O'Brien quieted the group by pointing out that this particular Texan was "favorable to civil rights"

"As you know all too well," O'Brien continued, "the Senate version of President Kennedy's civil rights bill met an early death last August at the hands of Senator Eastland, the chair of the Senate Judiciary Committee. Well, the water's all running in a different direction in Subcommittee No. 5. It would be hard to imagine a more favorable forum for a civil rights bill."

The committee system is not neutral. This concept from graduate school played across Clark Schooler's brain. A committee chairperson can shape both the committee hearings and the committee bill writing session, the mark-up of the bill, to favor the committee chairperson's point of view.

It was true, Clark remembered, that committee hearings often looked like a court trial. Witnesses before the committee raised their right hand and swore on the Bible to tell the truth. Committee members questioned those witnesses with the same gusto that aggressive prosecuting attorneys displayed when cross-examining court defendants. But there was no "judge" at a committee hearing to guarantee that both sides of an issue were presented equally and fairly. Committee chairs used committee hearings to build a strong case either for or against the bill under consideration, depending on the political goals of the particular committee chair.

"Chairperson Celler held hearings on the civil rights bill while it was before Subcommittee No. 5," Frank O'Brien said. "It was as though a heavenly choir of civil rights supporters had gathered to unstintingly sing the praises of the bill. The Reverend Walter E. Fauntroy spoke on behalf of Martin Luther King, Jr., and the Southern Christian Leadership Conference. George Meany, the president of the AFL-CIO, testified on behalf of the labor movement. They even trotted out old Norman Thomas to talk for the U.S. Socialist Party."

"By and large," O'Brien went on, "the various speakers were walking down the left side of the street. The National Council of Churches made a presentation, as did Americans for Democratic Action. Just about every lefty, liberal lobby group in the United States testified before Subcommittee No. 5."

"When the bomb blew up in Birmingham and killed the four black Sunday school girls," O'Brien said, "it was too much for Emanuel Celler and Subcommittee No. 5. Under heavy pressure from Clarence Mitchell and Joe Rauh from the Leadership Conference on Civil Rights, the subcommittee began to strengthen the civil rights bill. The subcommittee went into mark-up session and put everything in the bill the liberals wanted."

"The subcommittee members voted to give the attorney general the power to sue in all civil rights cases, not just school cases," O'Brien noted. "The subcommittee voted in an equal employment opportunity section that applied to all private industry, not just to private employers working on U.S. Government contracts. It soon became clear that Subcommittee No. 5 had gone out of control for civil rights."

At that moment an intense-looking young woman spoke up from one of the chairs along the wall of the room. She identified herself as an aide to Representative Arch Moore, a liberal Republican from West Virginia. "That's not true," the young woman said. "The subcommittee was not out of control. They had a good strategy, and they were sticking to it. In order to beat the filibuster in the Senate, this bill will be watered down with a series of compromises. The best way to minimize the damage from those Senate compromises is to pass as strong a bill as possible in the House of Representatives. Subcommittee No. 5 should be praised for passing out a liberal bill." [28]

Frank O'Brien of the Department of Justice countered that argument quickly.

"I respectfully disagree," O'Brien said in a firm but not-unfriendly manner. "We're going to need the votes of moderate Republicans to pass this bill in the House of Representatives. Remember, all the Southern Democrats will vote against the bill in the House, and there are not enough liberal Democrats to produce a majority vote in the House. We need a moderate bill that will unite liberal Democrats with moderate Republicans, not drive those two groups apart. The Subcommittee No. 5 bill is much too liberal. It will drive the moderate Republicans right out of the civil rights coalition and into the arms of the Southerners."

Frank O'Brien's call for a moderate bill rather than an ultra-liberal bill was supported by an older man who identified himself as working for Representative William McCulloch, a Republican from western Ohio.

"It's called 'walking the plank,'" the older man said. "You liberal Democrats try to force moderate Republicans in the House to vote for a strong civil rights bill. Then the bill goes over to the Senate. The Southern Democrats in the Senate either filibuster the bill to death or water it down into uselessness. That leaves the moderate Republicans in the House in the position of having voted for a strong civil rights bill that didn't get enacted into law. Then the moderate Republicans get criticized by their moderate and conservative constituents for voting for a liberal civil rights bill. That's why we call it 'walking the plank.' The difficult vote, and all the criticism for it, will accomplish nothing, because the too-liberal civil rights bill is killed in the Senate."

"My boss is Representative William McCulloch," the older man went on. "He has always pressed for passing a moderate civil rights bill in the House of Representatives that, when the bill gets over to the Senate, will attract the moderate Republican votes required to cloture the filibuster and produce a civil rights bill." [29]

Someone piped up: "That's giving in too early. If you start with a compromised bill in the House, you'll end up with a twice compromised bill after its been through a Senate filibuster and all the moderating deals necessary to get a successful cloture vote in the Senate. The members of Subcommittee No. 5 were right to mark up as strong and liberal a bill as possible."

For the remainder of the meeting, the arguments flew back and forth over whether the House of Representatives should pass a liberal civil rights bill, as reported by Subcommittee No. 5, or a more moderate bill, as recommended by Representative William McCulloch.

Clark Schooler was shocked by the direction taken by the meeting. Supposedly all the congressional staff people at the meeting were strong supporters of civil rights. Despite that, there were strong differences of opinion over what was the best strategy to pass the bill. And the civil rights supporters, Clark observed, were split along both political party and ideological lines. Liberal Democrats and liberal Republicans wanted a very strong, very liberal bill. Moderate Democrats and moderate Republicans wanted a more compromised version of the bill.

One question was dominant in Clark Schooler's mind as the meeting broke up. How were the civil rights forces going to defeat the Southern Democrats and the Senate filibuster if the civil rights forces could not even agree among themselves on the correct legislative strategy?

Clark made it a point after the meeting to go up and talk personally for a few minutes with Frank O'Brien of the U.S. Department of Justice. Clark did have some minor questions he wanted answered, but his real reason for initiating the conversation was to let Frank O'Brien know that Clark Schooler was working for Senator Kuchel and was a strong supporter of President Kennedy's civil rights bill. Clark extended the conversation as long as possible, which Frank O'Brien seemed more than willing to do, so that Clark's name and opinions would become familiar to Frank O'Brien.

Making an impression, and making certain people remember you, was an important technique that Clark had learned to use to increase his influence in Washington.

It was a happy day for the Leadership Conference on Civil Rights when Emanuel Celler called a press conference and released to the news media the text of the civil rights bill voted out by Subcommittee No. 5. The immediate result was a wave of quotes and commentary in the media either supporting or condemning the subcommittee report. Clarence Mitchell and Joseph Rauh immediately called for this strengthened civil rights bill to move forward "without dilution or delay." [30]

But Representative William McCulloch of Ohio, the senior Republican on the House Judiciary Committee, expressed to the press his grave reservations about the work of Subcommittee No. 5. He said the new version of the bill was "too far-reaching." McCulloch worried that applying equal employment opportunity to all of American industry "went too far." Conservative members of Congress and conservative newspaper columnists lined up in support of McCulloch's position. Some conservatives began calling the subcommittee bill "extreme." [31]

As soon as the newly-strengthened civil rights bill was reported out by Subcommittee No. 5, it moved to the full Judiciary Committee of the House of Representatives. The political environment changed completely. Whereas Subcommittee No. 5 was packed with liberal Democrats, the full Judiciary Committee was somewhat evenly split three ways. There were conservative Southern Democrats, liberal Northern Democrats, and moderate Midwestern Republicans.

Clark Schooler, along with every other civil rights supporter in Washington, was jolted when the Southern Democrats on the full Judiciary Committee announced that they would vote for the Subcommittee No. 5 version of the bill. The Southerners were not stupid, Clark quickly learned. They knew that an overly-liberal civil rights bill might not even pass the House of Representatives, let alone survive a determined Southern filibuster in the Senate. The strong subcommittee bill was scaring away moderate supporters of civil rights at a mile-a-minute, both in the House and in the Senate.

The Southerners were applying, Clark came to realize, one of the oldest of legislative strategies. You strengthen a bill you oppose in order to defeat it. The Southern Democrats were strengthening the civil rights bill in the Judiciary Committee with the confident assumption that such a strong bill would have less of a chance of passing on the House floor.

Then Clark thought of another legendary political science cliché. "Politics makes strange bedfellows." The liberal Democrats on the Judiciary Committee, some of them the strongest civil rights supporters in Congress, were happily joining hands with the Southern Democrats, all of whom strongly opposed civil rights, to pass out a ferociously liberal civil rights bill.

In mid-October of 1963, the attorney general of the United States, Robert Kennedy, requested that he be allowed to come up to Capitol Hill and meet in executive session with the members of the House Judiciary Committee. Executive session meant that the meeting would be closed to both the public and the news media. That meant that civil rights lobbyists such as Clarence Mitchell and Joe Rauh could not go to the meeting, sit in the audience, and put visual pressure on Robert Kennedy.

Visual pressure consisted of frowning hard and looking pained if the attorney general tried to get the Judiciary Committee to report out a weakened civil rights bill. Such non-verbal messages would remind Robert Kennedy that he risked losing the favor and support of major civil rights groups if he tried to water down the legislative handiwork of Subcommittee No. 5.

But the meeting was closed, and that meant Mitchell and Rauh could not go to it. The morning that Attorney General Kennedy was testifying before the House Judiciary Committee, Clark Schooler's telephone rang. On the line was a woman who identified herself as a volunteer at the Leadership Conference on Civil Rights. Her voice sounded somewhat familiar to Clark, but he could not identify who it might be and thus did not think very much about it.

"Clarence Mitchell asked me to call you," the woman said. "He is convinced that Robert Kennedy is going to urge the Judiciary Committee to weaken the civil rights bill. Mr. Mitchell's going to hold a press conference in the hall outside the meeting room to criticize the actions of the attorney general. He would be very pleased if you would come to the press conference and provide audience support."

Evan Harris, Senator Kuchel's chief of staff, had told Clark to get out and get around on Capitol Hill. What better way to accomplish that purpose, Clark thought, than attending a Clarence Mitchell press conference on a civil rights bill? Then, thinking that his two house mates also would enjoy the show, Clark telephoned Carl Brimmer and Greg Netherton and invited them to meet him at the press conference. Both agreed to do so, even Greg Netherton, who was working for a Southern Democratic member of the House of Representatives.

The three young men met in front of the meeting room where the House Judiciary Committee was gathered behind closed doors with Attorney General Robert Kennedy. Clark was disappointed by the low level of activity. Only two television cameras had been set up for Clarence Mitchell's press conference. There were only four or five print reporters present. And only about twenty or so people had taken the necessary time off to provide Clarence Mitchell with an appreciative, supportive, and enthusiastic audience.

Clark did a double take when he saw the young black woman who was orchestrating the press conference for the Leadership Conference on Civil Rights. It suddenly dawned on Clark why he had somewhat recognized the voice of the woman who had called him to come to the press conference. Clark was looking at Vonda Belle Carter, the black woman student from Morgan State College in Baltimore who had been one of the leaders of the civil rights protest at the Montebello Theater.

As so often happens when providing audience support, there was some waiting to do before Clarence Mitchell arrived on the scene. During this period, Clark and his two house mates engaged Vonda Belle Carter in a brief conversation. Clark reminded Vonda Belle of where they had met before, and then Clark identified himself as working for Senator Kuchel. Vonda Belle acknowledged that she had recognized Clark's name when she called him that morning from the Leadership Conference offices, but admitted she had been too shy to remind Clark of where they had met before.

Clarence Mitchell appeared on the scene and the press conference was about to get started. Vonda Belle Carter grabbed Clark Schooler's arm and, in a whisper, asked if he and Greg Netherton and Carl Brimmer would go stand behind Clarence Mitchell during the press conference.

Clark looked at the group of people standing behind Clarence Mitchell and knew instantly what Vonda Belle was attempting to accomplish. There were only black people providing the human background for the press conference. If the three young white men would go and stand behind Clarence Mitchell, the human background would be racially integrated. That way, in the newspaper photographs and the television coverage, the people standing behind Clarence Mitchell would be both black and white.

Human background was considered very important when sending out visual images of important people into the mass media. Human background was much preferable to a blank wall or an outdoor landscape for a backdrop. The sea of human faces behind the person being interviewed gave the audience something to look at when the audience became tired of looking at the one talking head. Also, if the main person talking was middle-aged or elderly, putting more youthful and more attractive faces in the human background made the main speaker seem younger and more energetic.

Clark Schooler told Vonda Belle Carter that he and his friends would gladly provide human background for Clarence Mitchell. Clark and Greg and Carl sort of moseyed over and, separating themselves from each other, integrated themselves into the small crowd of people assembled behind Clarence Mitchell. The black people already there seemed to understand what was going on, made room for the three young white men, and even gave forth with murmured greetings such as "Hi" and "How are you doing?" The black people appeared pleased that some white people had shown up for this particular press conference.

As he took his place in the assembled multitude, Greg Netherton said to no one in particular: "Is this a good place for me to stand?"

A young black man looked up at Greg, smiled, and said brightly: "Yes. You're to stand there. And you're to stand there and look white."

There was general laughter all around to this glib remark.

Clarence Mitchell, Jr., was the very picture of a distinguished, successful, American black middle-aged male. But his press conference was highly confrontive and abrasive. Mitchell lambasted Robert Kennedy up one side and down the other for meeting with the Judiciary Committee in an attempt to weaken the civil rights bill.

"There is no reason for this kind of sellout," Clarence Mitchell said in a loud and accusatory voice. "Robert Kennedy should be in there fighting for the subcommittee bill, not trying to weaken it." Clarence Mitchell clenched his fist. He did not wave his fist in the air, but he raised it up in front of his chin, more to show how mad he was rather than look like he was ready to start a fight.

"Every person in that room," Mitchell ranted and raved on, "is a white man. There's not one black person in there to represent the interests of black Americans. But what those white men are doing will greatly affect the 10 percent of the population that is black. I don't know if black people are being protected." [32]

Clark was struck by the obvious truth of what Clarence Mitchell was saying. Capitol Hill was essentially a whites-only world. And about one out of every four white persons you met on the Hill had a strong Southern accent. Clark knew there was one African-American in the House of Representatives. He was Adam Clayton Powell of New York. Perhaps there were others. But virtually all the senators and representatives, and their key aides and committee staffers, were white. Clarence Mitchell was absolutely right. The legislative fate of black America was almost totally in the hands of white Americans.

When the press conference was over, Greg Netherton said with a self-effacing smile: "Well, I guess I can't ever go home again." Vonda Belle Carter heard him say it. She turned and looked at Greg with a mystified and slightly angry expression on her face.

"Don't worry," Clark said to Vonda Belle. "It's a joke. Greg comes from Louisiana. The home folks down South won't appreciate Greg appearing on national television with a leading spokesman for the NAACP."

Vonda Belle got the joke. Everyone parted smiling.

The next day's newspapers were filled with what Robert Kennedy had said in the supposedly "closed session" of the House Judiciary Committee. Apparently almost every member of the Judiciary Committee had walked out of the meeting and then tried to get his or her name in the newspapers by telling the press every last word of Robert Kennedy's testimony.

"What I want is a bill, not an issue," the attorney general told the committee members. Robert Kennedy lambasted the liberals for trying to look good to their own liberal constituents in their home districts but for doing nothing to actually advance the civil rights bill.[33]

Kennedy suggested the Judiciary Committee drop the equal employment opportunity provisions from the bill completely. The attorney general said the employment provisions were too controversial. Those job-opportunity provisions, he argued, just might prevent the equal accommodations and the funds cut-off provisions from being enacted into law.

But Robert Kennedy's pleadings were to no avail. The liberal Democrats and the Southern Democrats on the Judiciary Committee stuck by their guns and prepared to vote out the Subcommittee No. 5 version of President Kennedy's civil rights bill.

Mike Palm's Restaurant was the nightly dining spot for Clark Schooler, Greg Netherton, and Carl Brimmer. Although there was a kitchen in their house on Sixth Street Southeast, none of the three young men liked to cook or, actually, knew how to cook a decent meal. They would eat breakfast at home, which was always dry cereal and cold milk. They would eat lunch in one of the restaurants or cafeterias located in the Capitol complex. But the favorite place to go for dinner, night in and night out, was Mike Palm's.

The restaurant was located in a small commercial area just to the east of the Capitol on Pennsylvania Avenue South East. There was a formal dining room upstairs and a more informal area, with red checked table cloths and a constantly-on television set, downstairs. The three young men preferred the downstairs area because of its more casual atmosphere and because they could watch political news and analysis programs on the TV set while eating.

The restaurant's owner also was its namesake. Mike Palm, who appeared to be in his early 60s, was present in his restaurant every night, greeting customers as they came in the door and often going from table to table and striking up brief conversations. He projected an atmosphere of warmth and generosity. Mike Palm was one of the things the three young men liked best about Mike Palm's restaurant.

Dinner could be late in the evening for Clark, Greg, and Carl. There was a lot of work to be done on Capitol Hill, and late hours at the office routinely postponed the evening meal. It was often 8 or 9 P.M. before the young men would finish eating dinner and then make the short, two-blocks or so walk back to their house on Sixth Street South East.

It was several days after Attorney General Robert Kennedy had held his executive session with the House Judiciary Committee. Clark and Greg and Carl were eating dinner in the downstairs dining room at Mike Palm's Restaurant when, suddenly, Frank O'Brien from the Justice Department was standing at their table. O'Brien had been eating upstairs and had recognized Clark when he came in the door of Mike Palm's with his two house mates and headed for the downstairs dining area.

Clark introduced Frank O'Brien to Greg and Carl. After the usual pleasantries, O'Brien got down to business.

"Something big is going to pop tonight," O'Brien told Clark in a voice that Greg and Carl could easily hear. "President Kennedy has called a meeting at the White House on the civil rights bill. I'm about to head up there myself to staff the meeting for the Justice Department. The president told Emanuel Celler to be there to represent the liberal Democrats on the Judiciary Committee. President Kennedy also invited William McCulloch to come and speak for the moderate Republicans."

"But here's the really big news," O'Brien went on in an excited voice. "The president has also asked the House Republican leader, Charles Halleck of Indiana, to come to this little after-hours gathering. The word is that John Kennedy and Robert Kennedy are furious that the House Judiciary Committee is going to pass out such a liberal and far-reaching bill. The purpose of the late-hour meeting tonight is to stop the Subcommittee No. 5 version of the bill dead in its tracks."

"Now here's the reason I'm telling you this," Frank O'Brien said to Clark. "I need a Republican congressional aide to come along to staff the meeting for the Republicans. None of Halleck's or McCulloch's people can make it. When I saw you here having dinner, I thought I'd see if you could go to the White House in their place. Can you?"

"Let's see," Clark said sarcastically. "Do I want to go up to the White House and attend a meeting with President Kennedy?"

Clark then looked at Frank O'Brien and said enthusiastically: "You bet I do!"

The Cadillac limousine was the officially approved way for important personages in the United States Government to move from place to place in the city of Washington. In fact, one measure of big success in American politics was having access to a chauffeur-driven limousine. The president, of course, had a limousine, but so did all the major leaders of Congress. But the real measure of success in the early 1960s was to have one of those expensive new automobile telephones in your limo so that you could talk politics and cut deals while riding around town.

Most government limousines were shiny black, Clark had observed, but some of the newer ones were painted a dark metallic gray. It was an automobile color that almost exactly matched the dark gray-flannel suits that well-dressed businessmen and male college students were wearing. Clark always referred to that particular color of government limousine as "Big-Shot Gray."

Clark and Frank O'Brien rode from Capitol Hill to the White House in the limousine of Charles Halleck, the top Republican in the House of Representatives, who was officially called the minority leader. Charles Halleck sat in the big back seat of the limo and worked on some papers and made some telephone calls. Frank O'Brien and Clark rode on jump seats that folded down out of the front seat of the limo.

Clark thoroughly enjoyed his ride in a big, dark, and official U.S. Government limousine. It was a feeling he had come to call "pseudo-big shot." He luxuriated in his newly-gained importance as the familiar sites of Washington went by out the limousine windows. The giant automobile glided quickly and smoothly up Pennsylvania Avenue. On the left side of the street they drove by the National Archives, where the original copies of the Declaration of Independence and the United States Constitution were stored and displayed. Then, still on the left, came the Department of Commerce, the Department of Justice, which was where Frank O'Brien worked, and the old Post Office. On the right side of Pennsylvania Avenue, they drove past such Washington landmarks as the National Theater and the historic Willard Hotel.

The House Republican leader's Cadillac limousine pulled up at the Diplomatic Entrance to the White House. "The president wants to keep the press from knowing about this meeting," Frank O'Brien explained to Clark. "The participants are to use the Diplomatic Entrance to the White House rather than the main entrance in front."

After exiting the limo, the three men made their way to the Oval Office, which is the president's office and small reception room. President Kennedy was already seated for the meeting, along with Emanuel Celler, chair of the House Judiciary Committee, and William McCulloch, the top Republican on the Judiciary Committee. Charles Halleck confidently joined the group by sitting down on one of the comfortable upholstered chairs close to the president. Frank O'Brien and Clark sat at the outer edge of the group on surprisingly comfortable wooden chairs with arm rests and padded seats.

Clark looked around. He was, indeed, in the Oval Office, the ultimate control center of the U.S. Government. There were the three glass windows, looking out toward the Washington Monument, with the president's giant wooden desk sitting in front of them. Clark particularly noted the television sets, turned off at the moment, that kept the president in immediate touch with what television news was saying about him and his administration.

Frank O'Brien took out two paper pads and handed one to Clark. "You and I are to take notes," O'Brien whispered to Clark. "The reason you are here is that I like to have both a Democratic and a Republican set of notes on a meeting as important as this one. That way, if any Republican political types question what I say happened, I can send them to you for the Republican version of what happened."

The White House meeting began with a comment from Emanuel Celler, chair of the House Judiciary Committee. The first thing Clark noticed about the meeting was that Emanuel Celler was called "Manny," Charles Halleck was called "Charley," and William McCulloch was called "Bill." But President Kennedy always was addressed respectfully as "Mr. President."

Clark's notes on the meeting read like this:

CELLER: Mr. President. Can I say that the Judiciary Committee has been working on your civil rights bill since last May? We have a lot of effort invested in it. That's why I think the Subcommittee No. 5 bill is the one that should move forward at this time. I think . . .

HALLECK: Well, wait a minute, Manny. As House Republican leader, I want a good, meaningful civil rights bill, just like you do. But there are Southerners on the committee who want to report out the worst possible bill. Manny, all the deep South guys are going to vote for your subcommittee bill in the Judiciary Committee. That's how bad that bill is. It's way too strong.

PRESIDENT KENNEDY (trying to referee between the two of them): That subcommittee bill is not what I want either, Charley. I'm willing to get the liberal Democrats on the subcommittee together and tell them I think they're crazy to support such a liberal bill. I think I can pull enough of those liberals Democrats off the bill that, if you'll deliver some Republican votes, we can put together a majority on the Judiciary Committee for a moderate bill.

HALLECK: I want to vote for a civil rights bill. I don't think I could ever vote for the one Manny's subcommittee dreamed up.

MCCULLOCH: As the ranking Republican on the Judiciary Committee, I'm interested in civil rights as a cause. I'm not interested in it as a political issue to gain an advantage over the Democrats. So when the subcommittee reported such a liberal version, it was like the roof fell in on our heads. The Democrats are playing partisan politics instead of really supporting civil rights.

PRESIDENT KENNEDY (still playing referee): Now I think, if we'll all work together on this thing, there's a chance for everybody to come out in pretty good shape.

HALLECK: We've got to pass a bill, Mr. President. I have struggled with my conscience. Clearly a black man and his family have a right to go get something to eat and a place to sleep. In a department store, black people have a right to sit down and buy a sandwich and eat it at the table if they want to. If a black goes in and buys a pair of overalls, he should be able to buy and eat a sandwich, too.

CELLER: Now look, look. Forgive me for being the devil's advocate. It's one thing to get me and Bill McCulloch here to agree on a more moderate bill. It's quite another thing to get the liberal Democrats on the Judiciary Committee to vote for it. I can get some of the Democrats to go along with you, Mr. President. I try to whip my committee into line. But I can't get some of the others.

PRESIDENT KENNEDY: Manny! The liberal Democrats and the moderate Republicans are not very far apart. We can do this thing!

HALLECK: Mr. President. The liberal Democrats on the subcommittee loaded this bill up. They loaded it way beyond anything you asked and way beyond anything we ought to do. And then the feeling got around that the Republicans are supposed to be the goats. The Republicans are being forced to slit their political throats by being the bad guys who have to vote down the subcommittee bill and replace it with something more sensible.

PRESIDENT KENNEDY: Charley. What if we get a reasonable number of Democrats to support a moderate bill? We can't deliver all the Democrats, but we can deliver a reasonable number. Will you and the Republicans be prepared to go for that bill? Will you make it a bipartisan bill?

HALLECK: Reaching compromise between liberal Democrats and moderate Republicans is not going to be that easy. You said, very correctly, Mr. President, when this all began, that some people will think we've gone too far and others will think we have not gone far enough.

PRESIDENT KENNEDY (putting his hand on Halleck's shoulder in a joshing way): Come on, Charley, you're a very shrewd politician. You can deliver the votes for a compromise bill. Besides, we're better off if we get together. We can bear the heat for the compromise together.

HALLECK: Manny Cellar's subcommittee blew this thing up in our faces. The whole purpose was to put the Republicans in the position of weakening the bill.

MCCULLOCH: Can I interrupt here, Charlie? The moderate Republicans were being taken for a ride, Mr. President. It's not fair to . . .

PRESIDENT KENNEDY: Don't worry about Manny Celler and the subcommittee bill. That's over with. (The president gives a murderous look at Emanuel Cellar to convince him to abandon the subcommittee bill.)

HALLECK: I'm with you, Mr. President. I've gotten to the point where I want to vote for a civil rights bill. I've been saying that all up and down the Republican side of the aisle in the House of Representatives. If Manny Celler will get together with Bill McCulloch and negotiate in good faith, I'll support a bipartisan compromise. Like you, I don't really see a big problem here.

CELLER (forced to capitulate now that President Kennedy and House Republican Leader Halleck have reached an agreement to agree): Let me see. Do I have things clear in my mind? I'm to negotiate a compromise version of the bill with Representative McCulloch here. Then the Judiciary Committee majority is to vote down the Subcommittee No. 5 version. Then the committee is to replace it with the new bipartisan compromise McCulloch and I are going to agree on.

PRESIDENT KENNEDY (glad that the light has finally dawned): Right, Manny! You and Representative McCulloch should get together tomorrow morning, let's say at 9 or 9:30.

HALLECK (starting to leave the meeting): Mr. President, you and I both have some pretty tough people to convince to vote for this new compromise bill of ours. But, as president of the United States, you're in a much better position to work your guys over than I am to work mine over.[34]

Clark stopped taking notes at that point in the conversation. House Republican Leader Halleck's parting remark produced a hearty round of laughter as the meeting broke up.

Charles Halleck's limousine took the House Republican leader directly home, then dropped off Frank O'Brien and Clark Schooler at their respective residences. Once again, Clark thoroughly enjoyed riding around Washington in a government limousine.

When Clark entered his home on Capitol Hill, he discovered his two house mates waiting to hear his tale of the night meeting at the White House. Clark read them his notes. When he finished, Clark blurted out:

"What ever happened to separation of powers?"

Clark asked the question in a loud voice. But he was asking it to himself as well as Greg and Carl. "The presidency and the Congress are supposed to be co-equal branches of government," Clark said in a wondering voice. "The theoretical model, found in every American Government text book, calls for the president and the Congress to exactly check and balance each other."

"But look what happened," Clark said with an air of criticism in his voice. "The president summoned top congressional leaders up to the White House like a king demanding an audience with his lowliest subjects. President Kennedy had both those guys, the Democratic chair of the House Judiciary Committee and the Republican House leader, on the carpet. The president was calling the tune. The House of Representatives leadership was forced to dance to the presidential jig."

Carl Brimmer gave a very practical response. "A telephone call from the White House is a telephone call from the White House," he opined.

"Everyone responds the same way when the president beckons. They are thrilled! Excited! And anxious to do the president's bidding, because they associate it with the good of the country. President Kennedy has a big stake in this bill, and he's not going to let Congress mess it up for him. Anyone would come out in the night if the president called them to the White House. The president is the biggest 'Big Cheese' there is."

Clark protested: "But the civil rights bill is only in committee in the House of Representatives. It's not as though the bill was being voted upon in the full House of Representatives. John F. Kennedy is sticking in his presidential nose at the very beginning of the process."

Greg Netherton, from the state of Louisiana, made his comment on the events of the night. "There was not a white Southerner in there," Greg said, skillfully satirizing Clarence Mitchell's remarks at the press conference outside the House Judiciary Committee meeting with Robert Kennedy. "I don't know that the white South was being protected."

Clark Schooler and Carl Brimmer both looked at Greg Netherton and smiled. But Greg's point was an apt one. President Kennedy had not invited even one Southern Democrat to his night meeting at the White House.

Forgetting that he was not in a classroom, Clark said in his most professorial voice:

"The president's ability to lead Congress is more subtle, and more powerful, than it first appears. A wise president does not sit around the White House and simply wait to veto legislation after it is passed by Congress. Tonight, President John F. Kennedy directly shaped the pending civil rights bill, even though the bill is only at the committee level in the House of Representatives. These are presidential powers and activities which the Constitution does not mention. These are presidential powers and activities which our Founders never envisioned."

It became known as the "night meeting" at the White House. The way the press covered the story, thanks to ample numbers of intentional leaks from the White House, President Kennedy had read the riot act to the House leaders. The president virtually ordered House Judiciary Committee Chair Emanuel Celler, a Democrat, to sit down with William McCulloch, the ranking Republican on the House Judiciary Committee, and work out a bill that both men could support. Then the Republican leader in the House, Charles Halleck, was told to deliver the votes for Celler's and McCulloch's mutually-agreed-upon bill when it came up on the House floor.

It took about five days of heavy bipartisan negotiating, but soon the night meeting at the White House bore the intended fruit. Celler and McCulloch did what President Kennedy told them to do and wrote a new, compromised version of the bill. House Republican Leader Halleck signed off verbally on the new civil rights bill, even though the bill was still in committee.

The new bill gave the president much of what he demanded, but not all of it. Equal employment opportunity remained in the bill, even though the president wanted it dropped, but it survived in a weakened form that would be enforced by the courts rather than Labor Department administrators. As for Title Three, the attorney general was authorized only to join racial desegregation suits already filed by black citizens. The attorney general could not file such suits on his or her own volition.

At the end of October, Chairperson Emanuel Celler called the House Judiciary Committee into a final mark-up session. The liberal Democrats and the moderate Republicans on the committee were working solidly together. Thanks to the night meeting at the White House, the overly-liberal Subcommittee No. 5 version of the bill was voted into the trash can by a tally of 19 to 15. Then the bipartisan compromise bill, prepared at the behest of President Kennedy, was reported out by a vote of 23 to 11. Mainly only the Southern Democrats, now isolated and alone, voted against the new version of the bill.

Upon being passed by the House Judiciary Committee, H.R. 7152 went automatically to the Committee on Rules of the House of Representatives. The news media, well aware of the results of the night meeting at the White House, began referring to the legislation as the "bipartisan" civil rights bill.

Once at the House Rules Committee, the bill was lodged solidly in the hands of Rules Committee Chair Howard W. Smith of Virginia. Smith was well-known on Capitol Hill as an arch foe of racial desegregation and African-American civil rights.

In The Interim

The power of the U.S. president to influence the Congress has grown stronger since the 1960s. Presidents are expected to initiate an entire panoply of programs in Congress. In the early 2000s, there were calls for the president to recommend legislation that would "save" Social Security by preventing that program from running out of money at some future date. The president also was importuned to initiate legislation that would provide aid to senior citizens to help pay for expensive prescription drugs.

But there are occasions when presidents follow the lead of Congress rather than the other way around. That happened in 1996, when a Republican Congress passed a major welfare reform bill. The president at the time, William Clinton, a Democrat, signed the bill into law, despite the fact the bill required most welfare recipients to find a job or be forced off of welfare.

Up to that time, Democrats generally had opposed making people work when they were on welfare.

It is simple reality that the president and his administration are expected to play a major role in crafting and advancing major legislation in Congress. As a result, one of the most frequently asked questions on Capitol Hill is: "Does the president support or oppose this bill?"

CHAPTER 8

THE PRESIDENT:
TAKING COMMAND AND CONTROL

Clark Schooler and his two house mates, Greg Netherton and Carl Brimmer, had just attended a learning session for the Capitol Fellows at the Department of Agriculture on 14th Street in Washington, D.C. The Capitol Fellows often gathered together to be briefed on the policies and activities of the various departments and agencies of the U.S. Government. The three young men walked out of the building together. It was well after the noon hour, and getting a good lunch was the foremost thought on all three minds.

As usual, it was Greg Netherton, Clark's house mate from the Southern state of Louisiana, who had a good suggestion to make. "Let's walk up 14th street, cross the Mall, and head into downtown," Greg said with his usual enthusiasm for all things Washington. "We can find a nice place to eat lunch on Pennsylvania Avenue."

It was a cool but sunny and pleasant late fall day, so the three young men agreed to make the walk. Clark marveled at the beauty of the scene as they hiked up 14th Street across the Mall. To Clark's left, he could see the gleaming white marble of the Washington Monument and the Lincoln Memorial. To the right, his gaze encountered the equally beautiful white marble of the Capitol building.

As the three young men approached Constitution Avenue and the National Museum of Science and Technology, they noticed a taxicab parked on 14th Street with a small group of men gathered around it. Taxicabs were always in demand in Washington, particularly at lunchtime, so it was unusual to see a taxi parked and not out on the street making money.

Greg Netherton, ever friendly and inquisitive, called over to one of the men gathered around the taxicab. Greg yelled: "What's going on?"

One of the men, probably the cab driver, yelled back: "President

Kennedy has been shot at in Dallas!"

The three young men raced over to the taxicab. The cab driver had a portable radio which he had placed on the roof of his cab. The cabby had turned up the volume on the radio so that everyone nearby could hear the news reports coming in from Texas.

There was not much detailed news. There was just a series of isolated and seemingly unrelated facts. "President Kennedy was riding in his open-top limousine through downtown Dallas." "Crowds of people cheered and waved to the president from the sidewalk as his limousine drove through the city." "The shots were fired just as the presidential car was driving down a hill before going under a railroad bridge." "First Lady Jacqueline Kennedy was riding in the limousine with the president, as was Texas Governor John Connally and Mrs. Connally." "After the shots were fired, the presidential limousine raced to the accident room at nearby Parkland Hospital in Dallas."

The three young men milled around on the sidewalk next to the taxicab. They really did not know how to react to this jarring news, mainly because there were so few definite facts. Once again, it was Greg Netherton who came up with a good idea of what to do next. "Let's go up and stand outside the White House," Greg said. "Whatever happens, there should be plenty of action up there."

Clark Schooler, Greg Netherton, and Carl Brimmer took off for the White House as fast as they could go. That was not overly fast, because all three were dressed in full length winter overcoats on top of their suit coats and neckties. Clark later thought it must have been funny to see three young men running as quickly as they could through downtown Washington with such heavy clothing on.

Soon the three of them were running alongside the tall iron fence surrounding the White House grounds. Without anyone saying to do so, the three young men stopped at the West Gate opposite the front of the White House.

The West Gate was an opening in the iron fence that permitted vehicular access to the circular driveway that led to the main entrance to the White House. That was the entrance with the large covered porch held up by towering white pillars. The West Gate also permitted vehicular access to the West Wing of the White House, which contained the president's Oval Office and the nearby Cabinet Room.

As with all White House gates, there was a small guard house. Clark, Greg, and Carl were not the only persons in Washington who had thought to gather outside the White House as this particular moment in American history. About 10 to 15 people were standing on the sidewalk next to the guard house. The uniformed White House guard on duty had turned up the volume on his Secret Service two-way radio so that everyone could hear what was going on.

As Clark stood on the sidewalk outside the West Gate and listened to the Secret Service radio, it suddenly dawned on him that he was hearing the actual communications of Secret Service agents in Dallas. Most of the messages were incomprehensible or insignificant, dealing with minor issues such as where to park the presidential limousine outside Parkland Hospital. But, periodically, there were reports about President Kennedy.

Apparently the president had been seriously injured. Clark heard that he was being wheeled into an operating room at the hospital. In the meantime, Vice-President Lyndon Johnson and his wife, Lady Bird Johnson, had been placed in a small, private waiting room at the hospital. In another small, private waiting room nearby was the president's wife, Jacqueline Kennedy.

The Secret Service radio buzzed along in this manner for about 15 minutes. Clark and his friends picked up what stray bits of information they could. One Secret Service agent back at the scene of the shooting reported that the shots had been fired from an upper floor of the Texas School Book Depository Building, a multi-story structure in which text books for public schools in Texas were stored. In another message, an agent referred to the fact that Mrs. Kennedy's dress was bloodstained. Another communique mentioned that Texas Governor John Connally, who was riding in the open car with President Kennedy, also had been wounded and was undergoing examination at Parkland Hospital.

By this time it was nearing two o'clock in the afternoon. But all thoughts of hunger and lunch had been shoved aside. The three young men continued their wait outside the West Gate of the White House. In his mind, Clark contrasted the mood with that from three weeks earlier. On that late October night, he had actually been inside the White House sitting in the presence of President Kennedy. Clark had been witness to the young and glamorous president negotiating a compromise civil rights bill with Democratic and Republican congressional leaders. That night, Clark's mood had been upbeat and optimistic. But now, on a sunny afternoon in late November, Clark's feelings standing outside the White House were ones of worry and fear.

Clark was jarred out of his thoughts by the crisp voice of an agent speaking on the Secret Service radio. "Shortly after 1 P.M. Central Time," the voice said with definiteness, "President John F. Kennedy was pronounced dead by physicians at Parkland Hospital. The cause of death was a gunshot wound to the brain." There was a brief pause, as if to let the gravity of that message sink in deeply. Then the voice said matter-of-factly:

"All units proceed to the protection of President Lyndon Baines Johnson."

Unable to believe what he had just heard, Clark turned to the uniformed White House guard in the guard house at the West Gate and asked: "Does that mean he's dead?"

"That's the Secret Service two-way radio," the White House guard replied in a kind but firm manner. "President Kennedy is definitely dead and gone." [35]

It later occurred to Clark that he and Greg Netherton and Carl Brimmer must have been among the first human beings on the entire planet Earth to learn of President Kennedy's assassination. He later read, in the countless newspaper accounts of that fateful day, that President Kennedy's staff had waited to inform Mrs. Kennedy and Vice-President Johnson of the death before releasing the news to the press and public. The Kennedy staff also delayed the news that Texas Governor John Connally had been seriously wounded but was going to recover. These courtesies to Jacqueline Kennedy and Lyndon Johnson had taken some time. Only afterward did a White House staff member go and tell the frantic group of reporters gathered at the hospital that the president was dead.

That meant that Clark and his two house mates, standing in front of the White House in Washington, D.C., had learned of the assassination well ahead of the working press and the general public. Clark figured that probably only a hundred people or so were able to hear the Secret Service two-way radio network that first carried the grim news. And he and his two friends had been among those one hundred or so persons. The point was only of passing interest, however. Within the next two hours, the news was spread by underground television cables and trans-oceanic radio to the far corners of the world.

Clark and Greg and Carl remained on the sidewalk outside the West Gate of the White House listening to the Secret Service radio. By piecing various scattered reports together, they learned that President Johnson and Mrs. Johnson were flying back to Washington on Air Force One. On the plane with them was President Kennedy's widow, Jacqueline Kennedy, and the casket containing the deceased president's body. Before the airplane took off for the nation's capital, a Texas judge came aboard and Lyndon Johnson was sworn in as president of the United States.

Upon hearing the news of the swearing in, Clark marveled at the efficacy of the United States Constitution and the enduring wisdom of its authors. The Founders had created the vice-presidency so that, if the president should die in office, power would be transferred in a swift and orderly manner to a constitutionally-designated successor. There was no lengthy period of transition during which the nation was leaderless and in a possible state of turmoil. As the Constitution commanded him to do, Lyndon Baines Johnson took the oath of office and promptly grabbed the reins of national government that had just fallen from the hands of the slain John F. Kennedy.

The show at the West Gate of the White House was far from over. In fact, it was just beginning. The uniformed guard told the three young men that the National Security Council, the president's top foreign policy and defense advisers, had been called to a meeting at the White House. In addition, the bipartisan leaders of Congress had been summoned to the president's official home. Both groups were to meet with President Johnson as soon as Air Force One had returned him to Washington and a U.S. Marines helicopter had brought him to the White House.

Clark and Greg and Carl watched with a mixture of fascination, awe, and respect as the black and grey limousines, bearing the top leaders of the United State of America, drove through the West Gate of the White House and unloaded their influential cargo at the main entrance. It became a game among the three young men to see who could say the name of the important person, or persons, as each limousine went by. In some instances, none of the three could recognize and identify the important personage. Greg Netherton scored extra points in the game, although no one was keeping score, because of his ability to recognize important Southern political and governmental leaders as they rode in their limousines through the West Gate.

A big moment was when Hubert H. Humphrey, the assistant majority leader in the United States Senate, arrived by limousine at the White House. Humphrey was a Democrat from Minnesota. During the 1960 presidential primaries, Humphrey had been John F. Kennedy's principal competitor for the Democratic nomination for president. Many observers believed that John Kennedy had nailed down the nomination when he defeated Humphrey in both the Wisconsin and West Virginia presidential primaries.

Because he had been a candidate for the Democratic nomination for president in 1960, Humphrey had one of the best known faces in American politics. The three young men said his name simultaneously the minute his face came into view in the back seat of his official limousine.

Clark was somewhat overwhelmed by the irony of the situation. Kennedy had defeated Humphrey in the 1960 Democratic presidential nomination sweepstakes. But now it was reality that the victory had led indirectly to John F. Kennedy losing his life.

A long afternoon and evening began to end for the three young men when the guard at the West Gate told them that President Johnson's helicopter was on its way in from the airport. It was routine, for security reasons, for Air Force One to take off and land at nearby Andrews Air Force Base.

Using a military air base instead of a public airport, such as Washington National, kept the president and his traveling party away from the crowds of people and the huge numbers of airplanes using the public airport. The guard said the new president's helicopter had just left Andrews Air Force Base and was beginning to make its way over the modest homes and crowded streets of southeast Washington.

That tip gave Clark and Greg and Carl just enough time to walk around the White House and take up an observatory position on 15th Street Northwest. They could easily see the rear of the White House, with its distinctive circular back porch, as well as the large grassy area where the helicopter would land. They soon heard the choppy whirling sounds of the helicopter's rotor blades as the big metal bird approached the White House and prepared to come down. There was the customary flurry of light and noise and draft from the helicopter blades as the craft settled softly onto the back lawn at the White House.

The three young men were too far away to be able to identify the various persons getting out of the helicopter and hurrying into the White House. But they knew that one of them was the new president, Lyndon Baines Johnson, a Democrat from Texas. On President Johnson's shoulders now rested the major responsibility for governing the United States. In President Johnson's hands, Clark suddenly realized, now rested the fate of the late President Kennedy's civil rights bill.

Lyndon Johnson took up the responsibilities of the American presidency with a determined attitude and a skilled hand at making government work. His first task was to restore calm and rebuild the confidence of the American people. The new president began the process of restabilizing the national psyche on the evening of the day President Kennedy was assassinated. When Air Force One returned from Dallas and landed at Andrews Air Force Base, Lyndon Johnson walked off the airplane and, standing before a battery of television cameras and microphones, made his first statement, as president, to the American people.

"This is a sad time for all people," President Johnson said. "We have suffered a loss that cannot be weighed. For me, it is a deep personal tragedy. I know that the world shares the sorrow that Mrs. Kennedy and her family bear. I will do my best. That is all I can do. I ask for your help. And I ask for God's help." [36]

President Johnson felt a particular need to reach out to African-Americans and African-American political leaders. In the weeks immediately following the assassination, Johnson invited all of the major black civil rights leaders to come and visit with him in the Oval Office at the White House. Each visit concluded with Lyndon Johnson and the particular civil rights leader appearing before the television cameras. The two would report to the nation on their meeting. They would comment on the high level of concern for civil rights that would characterize the forthcoming Johnson presidency.

Thus Clark and his two house mates looked at their television and saw Lyndon Johnson meeting with Roy Wilkins, the national president of the NAACP. Another White House visitor was Whitney Young, Jr., executive director of the National Urban League. Then it was Clarence Mitchell, Jr., the top Washington lobbyist for the NAACP, walking out of the Oval Office with Lyndon Johnson's arm around his shoulder. The major purpose of these meetings was to show black Americans, and white Americans as well, that Lyndon Johnson was not going to be a segregation-tolerating white man from Texas. Lyndon Johnson was going to be a president who fully supported the integrationist civil rights policies of the Kennedy Administration.

Perhaps no president was better prepared to push a civil right bill through Congress than Lyndon Johnson. Before agreeing to run as John F. Kennedy's ticket-mate for vice-president, Johnson had been the Senate majority leader, the most important political leader in the United States Senate. It was Johnson's job, as majority leader, to round up the votes to get major bills passed by the Senate.

Lyndon Johnson had become famous for his persuasive powers as Senate majority leader. A tall man, with a clearly-discernable Texas accent, Johnson made it a point to know every member of the Senate and what their political desires and political problems were. He believed strongly, and said frequently, that thinking human beings could adjust their goals to the needs of others and work out compromise solutions. One of Lyndon Johnson's favorite phrases, stated with almost biblical sincerity, was: "Come, let us reason together."

Clark Schooler, similar to most Americans, had one enduring picture in his mind of Lyndon Johnson at work as an accomplished legislative leader. This enduring portrait of Johnson was often repeated in the press and in personal conversations about the man.

The enduring picture was that of a hapless senator, not Lyndon Johnson, who had become the latest target of the legendary "Johnson treatment." The senator had his back to a wall of the Capitol building. Lyndon Johnson was standing in front of the senator, close up, with his arms extended straight out on both sides of the senator's head. The palms of Lyndon Johnson's hands were pressed against the wall, his forearms creating a trap around the senator's head and shoulders from which the senator could not easily escape.

The poor senator was going to have to listen to what Lyndon Johnson had to say. And the senator might not be able to slip away from Lyndon's forceful physical and mental presence until he had agreed to support Majority Leader Johnson's latest legislative endeavor.

There was a strong contrast between President Johnson and President John F. Kennedy in terms of working with Congress. Although John Kennedy served in the Senate prior to his election as president in 1960, Kennedy was never a Senate leader, as Johnson was. And John Kennedy was not particularly famous for turning out legislation. Lyndon Johnson, on the other hand, came to the presidency with one of the most distinguished legislative records ever compiled by a Senate majority leader.

Another statement about Lyndon Johnson that Clark Schooler heard and read all the time was: "Lyndon knows Capitol Hill so well he knows where all the bodies are buried." The expression meant that Lyndon Johnson knew who the powerful people were on Capitol Hill and what kind of arguments would move them to support particular bills. Lyndon Johnson knew about past legislative victories, and he knew who had benefitted from those victories. He also knew about past legislative defeats, and he knew who had suffered because of those defeats. And it was all information that could be used to make Lyndon Johnson, who had just ascended to the presidency, a more effective presidential leader of Congress.

Five days after President Kennedy was assassinated, the new president, Lyndon Johnson, was scheduled to give a speech to a joint session of the House of Representatives and the Senate. The joint session was held in the House chamber, which was designed to accommodate a larger number of persons than the Senate chamber.

The president came down the aisle of the House, quietly greeting his many political friends gathered for this auspicious occasion. Lyndon Johnson climbed the stairs to the speaker's rostrum. He looked around the House chamber. He seemed to be drawing consolation and strength from the people gathered before him.

There was a moment of quiet. Then the next sound was the voice of President Lyndon Johnson:

"All I have, I would have given gladly, not to be standing here today."

That comment set the tone for the remainder of the speech. The new president lavished unending praise on the life and accomplishments of John Fitzgerald Kennedy, his slain predecessor. President Johnson reminded Congress, and the American people, that President Kennedy had proposed many adventurous governmental ideas and bold legislative programs with the words: "Let us begin." Johnson pledged to work with Congress to complete the job of enacting those adventurous ideas and bold programs into law. Johnson's new words were: "Let us continue."

And President Johnson made the centerpiece of this new legislative initiative the civil rights bill then pending in the House of Representatives. He urged Congress to pass the bill as a "memorial" to President Kennedy. Johnson said:

"No oration or eulogy could more eloquently honor President Kennedy's memory than the earliest passage of the civil rights bill for which he fought so long. We have talked long enough in this country about equal rights. We have talked for one hundred years or more. It is time now to write the next chapter, and to write it in the books of law." [37]

The new president's words received sustained applause from the immediate audience. In the days after it was given, the speech received high praise from the press corps and the commentators, almost all of whom had a pro-Northern bias. Clark Schooler, a loyal Republican, and Carl Brimmer, a dedicated Northern Democrat, both were swept away by the speech and became instant admirers of Lyndon Johnson. Greg Netherton, ever the rational Southerner, was not so easily swayed.

"I thought Lyndon Johnson was from Tex-us," Greg Netherton complained after the three young men had watched the president's speech on television. Greg pronounced it "Tex-us" in a weak attempt to sound like a native Texan with a heavy Texas-style Southern accent.

"Those people are not liberals down in Tex-us," Greg Netherton grumbled. "They've lived racially segregated all their lives. They're as biased against minorities as you can get. Who'd have ever thought Lyndon Johnson would go all-out for a civil rights bill? He used to be a Southerner. He should be torpedoing the civil rights bill, not pledging to pass it in John F. Kennedy's memory."

"Unlike most Southerners," Carl Brimmer replied, "Lyndon Johnson has learned to do political addition. He added all the Northern whites who are liberals to all the Northern minority groups that believe in civil rights. That came out to be a much larger figure than the number of segregationist Southern whites."

Carl Brimmer made the comment in a sarcastic tone but with a sardonic smile on his face. Greg Netherton took it in the factual but lighthearted spirit in which it was intended.

"It's more like this," Clark Schooler chimed into the conversation. "Lyndon Johnson's already got solid support in the South. He's one of their down-home boys no matter what bills he supports. But he badly needs to establish his credentials with Northern and Western white liberals, and Jewish voters, and black voters, and labor union members. I think he's decided the best way to do that is go overboard for Kennedy's civil rights bill."

"What a hypocrite Johnson is," Greg Netherton answered back. "From segregationist white Southerner to integrationist left-winger in one easy step. Why do we let him do that?"

"It was a bit more than one easy step," Carl Brimmer said without answering Greg's question. "It's true that Lyndon Johnson was a typical segregationist Southerner when he was a representative and a senator from Texas, although not a very outspoken one. But when Lyndon Johnson became Senate majority leader in the 1950s, he became a great compromiser on civil rights. As majority leader, he pressed both the Northern senators and the Southern senators to search for common ground and at least take a few steps forward on civil rights. So Lyndon didn't really become a flag-waving, minority-loving, Northern liberal all at once."

"I think it's time for me to acquaint you gentlemen with Clark Schooler's First Law Of Changing Constituencies," Clark Schooler said with mock professorial solemnity. "That law is: As politicians change their constituencies, politicians change their politics. The idea here is that, as a politician rises from serving a congressional district as a representative, to serving a whole state as a senator, and then serving the entire nation as president, that politician alters his political positions to match the changed character of each new constituency."

That was quite an extended statement, even for Clark Schooler, and it left his two house mates silent. They both looked at Clark as if they expected to hear more, so Clark gave them more.

"Lyndon Johnson is a perfect example. He's specimen number one of this particular law of political behavior," Clark lectured. "When he was a U.S. representative from a segregationist part of Texas, you did not hear a word about racial integration from him. And that only changed slightly when he became a U.S. senator from the entire state of Texas. But when Lyndon Johnson became Senate majority leader, his constituency was suddenly the Senate of the United States, and he had to 'represent' both Northern and Southern points of view. That's when a second Lyndon Johnson, the 'great compromiser' that Carl described earlier, first emerged."

"Now an assassin's bullets have made Lyndon Johnson the president of the United States," Clark continued. "Now his constituency is the entire nation, and the part of that constituency that knows him the least and distrusts him the most is the Northern and Western liberals in the Democratic Party. What better way to win this doubting and wavering new constituency to his side than by giving all-out support to the civil rights bill?"

On a Thursday afternoon in mid-December of 1963, Clark Schooler attended his second meeting of the Capitol Hill staff members who were supporting the civil rights bill. Once again the guest speaker was Frank

O'Brien. He was the Justice Department lawyer specifically charged with shepherding the civil rights bill, now occasionally referred to as President Johnson's civil rights bill, through Congress.

"There's a big problem with President Johnson's 'memorial' to John F. Kennedy," Frank O'Brien began. "The civil rights bill is presently mired in the House Rules Committee. The committee chair, Howard Smith of Virginia, has a firm grip on the bill and doesn't look as if he's ever going to let go."

Someone raised their hand and asked a nuts-and-bolts question: "The civil rights bill was reported out favorably by the House Judiciary Committee shortly before President Kennedy was assassinated. Why didn't the bill just go directly to the House floor for a vote?"

"Because the House of Representatives has 435 members," Frank O'Brien replied. "That means debate is limited in the House. The people who make the rules under which bills are debated are the House Rules Committee. They decide the manner of the debate, how much time will be allotted for the debate, and all kinds of stuff like that."

Another hand went up followed by another question: "Is it true that the House Rules Committee can kill a bill by simply refusing to send it to the House floor?"

"That particular rumor is true," Frank O'Brien replied, "but that's something that doesn't happen very often. Most of the time the Rules Committee simply delays bills it doesn't like rather than killing them outright. If the Rules Committee can delay a bill long enough, though, that can have the effect of killing the bill. That's because there may not be enough time left in that particular Congress to get the bill passed in both the House and the Senate."

No one bothered to ask how long a "Congress" was. But Clark Schooler knew the answer to that question. A session of Congress is just one-year long. Two sessions, a first session and a second session, make up one "Congress," which is two-years long. A "Congress" lasts from one congressional election to another. But the important thing to remember, Clark reminded himself, was that all bills die at the end of each two-year Congress. If a bill does not pass in two years, in a particular Congress, it must start all over again at the beginning of the next Congress.

Frank O'Brien went on with his discourse: "The House Rules Committee has traditionally been dominated by Southern Democrats and conservative Republicans. Those two groups have been delighted to use the Rules Committee to delay bills favored by liberal Democrats, and often the lengthy delay results in a slow death for the bill."

"The Rules Committee chairperson is Howard Smith of Virginia,"

Frank O'Brien went on. "He's as conservative a Southern Democrat as you would ever want to find. And he's a crafty one, too. Chairperson Smith has a curious way of vanishing from Capitol Hill for considerable periods of time whenever a bill he doesn't like comes before the Rules Committee."

"Howard Smith owns a dairy farm back in his congressional district in Virginia," Frank O'Brien explained. "One time in 1957, just when a major bill supported by Democratic liberals was before the Rules Committee, Chairperson Smith disappeared from Washington and headed for his dairy farm. According to Smith, his dairy barn had burned down and he was needed at home. Then, in 1959, when another bill Smith disliked was before the House Rules Committee, Smith left for Virginia because, he said, his dairy cattle were sick and required his full attention."

This description of House Rules Committee reality provoked a lot of knowing smiles and even a few guffaws from the assembled congressional aides. But there was little genuine happiness in the laughter, because everyone knew that the pending civil rights bill was certain to get somewhat similar treatment from Howard Smith.

There was a noise outside the meeting room door and then a knock on the door. In walked Joseph Rauh, one of the principal lobbyists for the Leadership Conference on Civil Rights. Rauh apparently was working alone this particular day and did not have his usual partner, Clarence Mitchell, working with him.

In a gesture of respect from a somewhat younger man to an older one, Frank O'Brien introduced Joseph Rauh to the group and yielded the floor. Joseph Rauh immediately launched into a tirade against Chairperson Smith and the House Rules Committee.

"There's only one way we'll ever get the civil rights bill away from old Howard Smith," Rauh said with considerable fervor. "That's to blast the bill out of his and the Rules Committee's hands. The best way to do that is with a discharge petition."

"Emanuel Celler, the chair of the House Judiciary Committee, filed a discharge petition on HR 7152 on December 9, 1963," Rauh continued. "If a majority of the members of the House will sign that petition, the civil rights bill will move directly from the Rules Committee to the House floor. And there won't be one thing Howard Smith can do to stop it."

Someone interrupted with a question: "How many signatures are required to force a bill out of the Rules Committee with a discharge petition?"

"Just 218 signatures," Joseph Rauh replied. "That's a simple majority of the total House membership of 435. I'm proud to report that more than 100 representatives signed the discharge petition on the first day it was available. If we can get the 218 signatures quickly enough, we can have the civil rights bill up for debate on the House floor before Christmas. If that happens, there will have been no delay because of the House Rules Committee." [38]

"Furthermore," Rauh continued, "President Johnson is supporting the discharge petition. He's being briefed every day on which members of the House have signed the petition. Johnson is making personal telephone calls to those representatives who are holdouts and are slow to sign. The president said at a meeting with the nation's governors that he wants the civil rights bill passed in the House and over in the Senate by January 1, 1964." [39]

At this moment an older man sitting at the back of the room virtually shouted at Joseph Rauh: "My boss isn't going to sign that discharge petition no matter who calls him."

There was an embarassing pause in the discussion. Every head in the room turned and looked at the man who had spoken so loudly and forcefully. Clark Schooler recognized him instantly as the top congressional aide to Representative William McCulloch of Ohio. McCulloch was the informal leader of the sizeable group of House Republicans who now were supporting the bipartisan civil rights bill.

"How many times are we going to have to tell you, Joe," the man said crisply and coolly. "The House Republican leadership has agreed to support the civil rights bill and get it voted out of the Rules Committee without needing a discharge petition. If the Republicans on the Rules Committee side with the liberal Democrats, as they've promised to do, then the votes are there to use the regular procedures. There won't be a need to resort to the high jinx of a discharge petition."

Joseph Rauh fired back instantly: "If we wait for the Rules Committee to vote, it will be next summer before the bill gets to the House floor. You and your boss are not showing enough respect for all the tricks Howard Smith can pull to slow the bill down and possibly knock it out."

Representative McCulloch's aide was undeterred. "You're not showing enough respect for the deal President Kennedy negotiated at the White House with the Republican House leadership," the older man countered. "At that now famous 'night meeting,' which took place shortly before the president was killed, the Republican leaders agreed to support the bill. If Lyndon Johnson continues to support your foolhardy discharge petition, the Republicans are going to get their feelings hurt and begin thinking that Lyndon Johnson doesn't trust their word of honor. If that happens, and the House Republicans stop supporting the president's civil rights bill, the bill is dead for sure." [40]

Joseph Rauh and William McCulloch's congressional aide were glaring hard at each other. Frank O'Brien adroitly maneuvered the discussion in a more peaceful direction. "The latest word in the Justice Department," O'Brien said, "is that President Johnson is no longer pressing members of the House to sign the discharge petition. Furthermore, the top Democratic leaders in the House, such as House Speaker John W. McCormack, of Massachusetts, and House Democratic Leader Carl Albert, of Oklahoma, have not signed the petition. Similar to the House Republican leaders, the Democratic leaders want to uphold the agreement negotiated by President Kennedy. They want to get the bill out of the Rules Committee in the normal manner. That means by a majority vote of the committee."

Joseph Rauh refused to be silenced. "They will be betraying the memory of John F. Kennedy, not honoring it," Rauh exploded. "Chairperson Smith will never move that civil rights bill unless there is a genuine threat of a discharge petition."

Clark Schooler detected a slight change in Joseph Rauh's position with that particular statement. Rauh was no longer insisting that the discharge petition was the only way to get the bill out of the Rules Committee. Rauh now was saying the "threat" of a discharge petition was what was required.

Clark was well aware that certain proposed actions have threat-value. Sometimes important and powerful players on Capitol Hill will take action, or not take action, in order to head off a threatened action by someone else.

Once again it was Frank O'Brien who stepped in with a soothing and quieting statement. "Chairperson Smith has publicly announced that he will hold Rules Committee hearings on the civil rights bill in January of 1964," O'Brien said. "The exact words that Howard Smith used were 'reasonably soon in January.' I think President Johnson is now ready to uphold conventional House procedures. He wants to let the Rules Committee meet and vote in January, just like Howard Smith says he's going to have the committee do." [41]

The meeting ended at that point. For the next month, Joseph Rauh continued to insist that the discharge petition was a necessary tool for getting the civil rights bill out of the Rules Committee. But an insufficient number of members of the House of Representatives were willing to sign the discharge petition. Suddenly it was Christmas of 1963 and New Years Day 1964, and the civil rights bill remained firmly in the grip of Chairperson Howard Smith of the House Rules Committee.

Clark Schooler found himself a little put-off by Joseph Rauh's outspoken insistence on using the discharge petition to blast the civil rights bill out of the House Rules Committee. And Clark's newly-discovered critical attitude toward Joseph Rauh upset Clark. Above everything else, Clark wanted to be personally all-out in support of Rauh and the Leadership

Conference on Civil Rights. But it was obvious to Clark that it would be better to vote the bill out of the Rules Committee under normal procedures than to use the unusual and highly-suspect instrument of the discharge petition.

Clark mentioned his now-ambivalent feelings about Joseph Rauh to Evan Harris, Senator Kuchel's Chief of Staff. Evan listened patiently to Clark's complaints, then gave an answer shaped by Evan Harris's long years of experience on Capitol Hill.

"I question whether the lobbyists for the Leadership Conference should be criticized for being so outspoken and vociferous in behalf of their cause," Evan Harris said. "Joseph Rauh might very well be praised for putting relentless pressure behind the discharge petition. Capitol Hill is a busy place. It can be easy to let things go, and sort of slide by, if someone isn't perpetually calling for action."

"Joe Rauh knows what he's doing," Evan Harris continued. "He's putting the screws to everybody involved with that discharge petition. And, make no mistake about it, the guy he's putting the screws to most directly and painfully with that petition is Lyndon Johnson. The president now knows he has to get the civil rights bill out of the Rules Committee or he's going to get all kinds of noisy and pointed criticism from Joe Rauh."

Evan Harris then gave Clark a smile. "You know," Evan concluded, "just because you like and admire Joe Rauh doesn't mean you have to agree with him on every issue."

The United States Constitution provides that the president "shall from time to time give to the Congress information of the State of the Union, and recommend to their consideration such measures as he shall judge necessary and expedient." On Wednesday, January 8, 1964, Lyndon Baines Johnson gave the first State of the Union address of his still new presidency.

"Let this session of Congress be known as the session that did more for civil rights than the last hundred sessions combined," Lyndon Johnson said to both the House and the Senate and the cameras of all three major television networks. "As far as the writ of federal law will run, we must abolish not some but all racial discrimination." [42]

To Clark Schooler, this was an amazing, almost incredible, statement for a U.S. president to make. It was the first time in all of American history that a president had called for eliminating "all racial discrimination." And it was the first presidential request that discrimination be eliminated "as far as the writ of federal law will run."

One way or another, by hook or by crook, Clark Schooler succeeded in getting into a number of the House Rules Committee hearings on the civil rights bill. Some days the lines of people waiting to get into the hearings were relatively short, and Clark could get in exactly like any other member of the general public. On other days, when the lines were long and every public seat in the hearing room was taken, Clark exercised his prerogative as a former journalist and pulled up a chair at the end of the press table.

Exactly as he had promised, Chairperson Howard Smith opened the Rules Committee hearings early in January of 1964. But starting the hearings was the only concession Howard Smith made to the civil rights forces. It soon became clear to Clark Schooler, and anyone else in Washington who was paying attention, that Chairperson Smith intended to have the hearings drag on for weeks and perhaps even months. Under Smith's skilled command, the House Rules Committee hearings were going to delay action on the civil rights bill almost as effectively as if no hearings were held at all.

A long list of Southern Democrats opposed to civil rights showed up at the Rules Committee hearings to testify against the bill. Leading the list was none other than Chairperson Howard Smith himself, who charged that the bill had been "railroaded" through the House Judiciary Committee by Judiciary Chair Emanuel Celler and his liberal supporters on the Judiciary Committee.

"This nefarious bill is as full of booby traps as a dog is of fleas," Howard Smith charged. He particularly attacked the provisions of the bill that forced restaurants, snack bars, and movie theaters to serve people of any race, religion, or national origin. "The commerce clause of the United States Constitution," Smith argued with reasonable-sounding logic, "was never intended by the Founders to apply to small businesses such as neighborhood eating places and local movie theaters." [43]

Representative Edwin E. Willis of Louisiana labeled the civil rights bill "the most drastic and far-reaching proposal and grab for power ever to be reported out of a committee of the Congress in the history of our republic." Representative Willis then joined Chairperson Smith in attacking the constitutionality of the bill. "The 14th Amendment was designed to restrict only state action," Representative Willis fumed. "This bill allows the U.S. Government to regulate areas of individual discrimination, not state discrimination, and that is a power never mentioned in the 14th Amendment." [44]

But these Southern arguments were strenuously challenged. Judiciary Chair Emanuel Celler requested to speak and devoted his remarks to the necessity for immediate action on civil rights issues. Clark Schooler had developed something of a liking for Emanuel Celler. The man was aged, well past his sixties, but he was still active, almost brisk, and could testify before a congressional committee in an argumentative and feisty manner. Clark found himself intellectually grooving with Emanuel Celler.

"The campaign by black Americans for equal rights cannot be halted,"

Celler said, almost shaking with emotion. "You can no more stop it than you can stop the tide. Black people in the United States still wear some of the badges of slavery. It is small wonder that, for so many black persons, patience is at an end. I know this bill is painful medicine for the South to have to swallow. It means changing patterns of life that have existed for a century or more. I wish it could be otherwise, but it cannot. The die is cast. The movement cannot be stayed." [45]

Emanuel Celler was joined in speaking for the bill by Representative William McCulloch of Ohio, the ranking Republican on the House Judiciary Committee. McCulloch repeated his oft-stated position that House members should not be forced to cast unpopular votes to pass a strong civil rights bill and then see the bill watered down in the Senate to escape a filibuster. "I would never be a party to such a course of action," McCulloch said. "My head is still bloody from casting strong votes for civil rights that were given away or bargained away in the Senate. I feel very strongly about this." [46]

On the day Emanuel Celler and William McCulloch were speaking at the House Rules Committee hearings, Clark Schooler was sitting at the press table. Next to Clark was Jim Senitall, the Washington correspondent for the Patriot Press who had been one of Clark's journalistic mentors. Jim Senitall leaned over to Clark and whispered: "This is just like going to the movie theater and watching the previews of coming attractions."

That was all Jim Senitall said to Clark, but it was all that he needed to say. It was suddenly clear to Clark that both the Southerners and the Northerners were using the Rules Committee hearings to test out and practice their various arguments for and against the bill. Later they would use perfected versions of these arguments when the civil rights bill was being debated on the floor of the House of Representatives. Just as the previews at the movie theater gave a quick look at a future film attraction, the hearings of the House Rules Committee gave a quick look at what the future House debate was going to be like.

Clark Schooler turned Jim Senitall's casual and confidential whisper into one of Schooler's Laws of Political Behavior: House Rules Committee hearings provide previews of upcoming debates in the House of Representatives.

Toward the end of January, Clark Schooler had become convinced that the hearings before the House Rules Committee would go on forever. As a result, Clark worried, the civil rights bill would never be reported to the House floor. But, just when Clark least suspected it would happen, Chairperson Howard Smith announced that the Rules Committee would vote out the civil rights bill on January 30, 1964. That would permit debate in the full House of Representatives to take place during early February.

When asked by the news media as to why he had agreed to release the civil rights bill from his strangling grasp, Smith simply scowled and made the sour comment: "I know the facts of life around here." [47]

Although it was well-known that Smith opposed the civil rights bill with every fiber of his being, no one questioned that the representative from Virginia would move the bill out of the Rules Committee on the date promised. It was, Clark reminded himself, one of the best known rules of congressional behavior: Politicians often break promises to the press and the public, but they seldom if ever fail to keep pledges to each other.

The following afternoon there was a hastily-called meeting of the congressional aides supporting the civil rights bill. This ad hoc group on Capitol Hill was starting to take up a considerable amount of Clark Schooler's time, but Clark was finding it time unusually well spent. The meeting quickly turned into a lively debate over exactly why Chairperson Howard Smith had agreed to allow the civil rights bill to escape the House Rules Committee.

Joseph Rauh of the Leadership Conference on Civil Rights attended the meeting from beginning to end. "Chairperson Smith released the bill because he could feel the hot fire of the discharge petition breathing down his neck," Rauh said with his usual air of assuredness. "When most of the representatives went home for Christmas vacation and talked with their constituents, they found real support in their home districts for the civil rights bill. Additional signatures on the discharge petition were virtually certain. There soon would have been enough signers to discharge the bill from the Rules Committee and thereby embarrass the gee-willikers out of old Howard Smith." [48]

But there was another view of why Howard Smith had agreed to release the bill. "From the very beginning," said Frank O'Brien of the Justice Department, "we've had bipartisan agreement on the Rules Committee. The liberal Democrats and the moderate Republicans on the committee have been ready to vote the bill out. It's all part of the compromise negotiated by President Kennedy at that now-famous night meeting at the White House."

"The committee majority has been patiently waiting," O'Brien continued, "for Howard Smith to have his big day in the sun. They've given Smith and his Confederate buddies plenty of time to make their tired old arguments against civil rights. But even Howard Smith now realizes his time is up. Smith knows that, if he doesn't move the bill out, the committee majority will rebel against his leadership and move it out for him."

That sounded like a pretty reasonable explanation to Clark Schooler, more plausible than Joseph Rauh's emphasis on the discharge petition. But just at that moment that wise older man, Representative McCulloch's congressional aide, spoke up.

"Let me tell you what really happened here," the man said, sounding a great deal like Clark Schooler lecturing a classroom full of political science students. "The ranking Republican on the House Rules Committee is Representative Clarence Brown of Ohio. Although they belong to two different political parties, Democrat Howard Smith and Republican Clarence Brown are probably two of the closest friends on Capitol Hill. They're both conservatives. And on most legislation, Smith and Brown are in general agreement on what the Rules Committee should do, and when it should do it."

"This was one time," the older man continued, "when Howard Smith and Clarence Brown were on different sides of an important issue. Brown simply reminded Smith that he had the moderate Republican votes and the liberal Democratic votes to override Smith anytime he wanted to do so. Brown made it clear that the Republican House leadership had promised President Kennedy to move the bill. In the end, Clarence Brown was going to have to support his Republican leaders rather than his longtime friend Howard Smith."

"It was just this simple," the older man concluded. "Clarence Brown personally asked Howard Smith, as an old friend, to end his obstructionism. It's easy to deny your opponents on Capitol Hill. It's very difficult to deny your friends. Smith gave in, not to the discharge petition or the committee majority, but to an old friend of his named Clarence Brown." [49]

The meeting room was absolutely quiet when the older man finished speaking. After a few seconds, someone asked some sort of technical question, and the discussion haltingly got going again. But the meeting broke up shortly thereafter. The older man had reemphasized a point that everyone present knew was true: Personal friendships can be powerful motivators in American life and politics.

It was, Clark Schooler later concluded in his own mind, an excellent example of what he called multi-factor analysis. There probably was no one specific reason that Chairperson Smith moved the civil rights bill out of the Rules Committee. Surely the discharge petition had some effect, even if it wasn't the all-powerful factor that Joseph Rauh contended it was. And that now legendary bipartisan agreement was certainly a factor, because that had produced more than enough pro-civil rights votes on the Rules Committee to outvote the Southerners. And yet, what Representative McCulloch's aide said about Smith's and Brown's friendship also was certainly true.

Most people, even great scholars, try to implement single-factor analysis, Clark thought. They want there to be just one reason why this or that happened, or why this or that fact is true. But life, particularly political life, is more complicated than that. There often are many reasons, not just one reason, for why things turn out the way they do.

On January 30, 1964, exactly as he had promised, Chairperson Howard Smith called the House Rules Committee into session. By a vote of 11 to 4, the civil rights bill was reported out. Six Northern Democrats and five Republicans on the committee voted for the bill. Only the four Southern Democrats, including Howard Smith, voted against it.

The bipartisan agreement negotiated by President Kennedy at the night meeting at the White House had worked perfectly. The Kennedy civil rights bill, now the Kennedy-Johnson civil rights bill, had advanced to the floor of the U.S. House of Representatives.

In The Interim

A wave of reform which swept Congress in the 1970s greatly weakened the power of the chairperson of the House Rules Committee. In the early 2000s, the Rules Committee continues to review legislation and set the conditions under which bills are to be debated in the House of Representatives. But the committee and its chair no longer have the ability to tie up legislation completely, particularly if it is legislation that the speaker of the House wants advanced to the floor of the House.

In the 2000s, the House Rules Committee continues to provide previews of upcoming legislative debates on the floor of the House of Representatives. Both those "for" and those "against" the bill under discussion try out and perfect their arguments for future use in the House debate proper.

The discharge petition continues to be a viable part of House of Representatives procedure. But the discharge petition still is rarely used. The vast majority of bills in the House are voted up or down in committee, including the Rules Committee, and the results are accepted by winners and losers alike.

CHAPTER 9

THE HOUSE OF REPRESENTATIVES:
"VULTURES IN THE GALLERIES"

By early February of 1964, Clark Schooler had gained a measure of prestige and position in Senator Kuchel's office. Clark was completely in charge of answering the senator's legislative mail. Only the most sensitive reply letters needed to be checked by Senator Kuchel himself. Best of all, when Clark's secretary answered the telephone, she would always say: "Good morning. Mr. Schooler's office."

Clark loved the sound of that.

One morning the telephone rang. The secretary answered and gave the customary greeting. She listened to the caller for a few seconds, then put the call on hold and said to Clark: "It's Vonda Belle Carter from the NAACP."

"Wow," said Vonda Belle when Clark took the call. "Now it's 'Mr. Schooler's office.' You've really come up in the world. I'm worried you won't have any more time for me and the civil rights movement."

"Senator Kuchel and 'Mr. Schooler' are completely committed to the civil rights movement," Clark replied with a smile in his voice. "What can I do for you?"

Vonda Belle's joking tone of voice turned to one of complete seriousness. "Clarence Mitchell is calling a meeting this afternoon of all the staff people on Capitol Hill who are supporting the civil rights bill," she said. "He wants to lay out a somewhat revolutionary strategy for getting the bill through the House of Representatives without the Southerners passing a whole bunch of weakening amendments."

"I thought you and your liberal house mate from Idaho might be willing to participate in this," Vonda Belle continued. "You can bring your progressive Southern house mate from Louisiana, too, but I doubt that he'll do it.

Anyway, the meeting is at 4 P.M. at the AFL-CIO building."

Vonda Belle Carter was right about one thing. Greg Netherton of the Southern state of Louisiana declined the invitation to help Clarence Mitchell and the NAACP get the civil rights bill through the House of Representatives. "The spirits of my Confederate ancestors will haunt me forever if I do that," Greg said.

Clark Schooler and Carl Brimmer hopped into a taxicab to ride up to the headquarters building of the American Federation of Labor-Congress of Industrial Organizations. The AFL-CIO was providing meeting space for the Leadership Conference on Civil Rights. The AFL-CIO building was located north of the White House, nestled among an entire cluster of buildings containing lobbyists' offices.

More than 100 persons were gathered in a large meeting room in the AFL-CIO building. Most of them were African-Americans, but there were a number of white persons other than Clark and Carl. Vonda Belle Carter called the meeting to order, then turned things over to Clarence Mitchell.

The middle-aged black man stood up and took a few seconds to look around at the audience. Then he launched into a detailed discussion of the rules and procedures of the United States House of Representatives.

"When the House of Representatives considers major legislation," Clarence Mitchell began, "it resolves into the Committee of the Whole. This simply means that the entire House membership is meeting in committee rather than in regular session. What it really means is that the House is operating under a completely different set of rules."

"There are only two visible changes when the House becomes the Committee of the Whole," Mitchell continued. "First, the mace is taken down from its mounting. Second, instead of the speaker of the House serving as the presiding officer, the speaker chooses some other member of the House to preside for him."

Vonda Belle interrupted Clarence Mitchell and, in a low voice, suggested that he tell the group what the mace was. Mitchell responded: "The mace is a medieval club. It is topped with a metal head and often decorated with fine carvings, jewels, and precious metals. It has been used since the Middle Ages to symbolize the power and authority of parliaments, universities, and city governments. The mace is mounted next to the speaker's rostrum whenever the House is in regular session."

"But in the Committee of the Whole," Mitchell went on, "the mace is removed. And the speaker saddles some other poor representative with the somewhat tedious job of presiding over the debate."

"But that's not all that changes," Mitchell said. "In the Committee of the Whole, there is a very lenient quorum rule. In regular session a majority of the House, 218 representatives, is required to be present to conduct business. That's called having a quorum. But, in the Committee of the Whole, only 100 members need to be present to have a quorum and conduct business."

"And that's only the first of our problems," Mitchell explained. "With such a small quorum requirement, just 100 members, a lot of representatives do not bother to attend the debate. That means they're not there when you need them to vote down weakening Southern amendments. We have to have a way of making sure that all the liberal Northern representatives are present on the House floor when the civil rights bill is considered in the Committee of the Whole."

Someone had a question. "You mean," the questioner asked, "that the House of Representatives will amend a major piece of legislation, such as the civil rights bill, with only a small number of representatives present on the House floor."

"That's precisely what happens in the Committee of the Whole," Mitchell answered. "With a civil rights bill, the Southerners all show up religiously and support weakening amendments. If you don't have all your Northern supporters on the floor, some of those amendments can slip through and become the law of the land."

"There's a second problem in the Committee of the Whole," Clarence Mitchell pointed out. "There are no roll call votes. No written record is kept of who votes for and against amendments to the bill. There are only teller votes. The representatives just walk down the aisle past a teller, a House clerk, to show whether they are supporting or opposing a particular amendment."

"Then," Mitchell went on, "when the Committee of the Whole has finished amending the bill, the House resolves itself into regular session. The mace is put back on its stand. The speaker of the House returns to the rostrum. The bill is accepted or rejected by a roll call vote. And that's the only roll call vote, with the yeas and neas publicly recorded, that is held."

"The Committee of the Whole leads to a whole lot of deception," Clarence Mitchell said. "Because there are no roll call votes, a representative can vote for all kinds of weakening amendments to the bill and not be held accountable. Then, when the House is back in regular session, the representative can cast a recorded vote in favor of the bill. Although he's done everything he can in the Committee of the Whole to weaken the bill, the representative can pass himself off as a strong supporter of the bill because he voted for it in regular session."

That was a mouthful of legislative information, and a hand went up in the audience. "Does this mean," a young African-American woman asked, "that major amendments can be added to bills in the House of Representatives and we have no way of knowing who voted for or against the amendments?"

"Amendments can be passed that gut the legislation," Mitchell said vehemently. "Amendments can pass that tear the heart out of your bill. And in the Committee of the Whole, there is no written record of how each member of the House voted."

"There's a third problem," Clarence Mitchell said. "Under ordinary conditions in the House of Representatives, the Democratic and Republican whip systems get members to come to the floor and vote on key amendments to major bills. The whip systems are working whether the bill is being considered in the Committee of the Whole or in regular session. A whip is a representative designated to get himself and a specific group of his party colleagues on to the House floor and voting the party line on major amendments."

"But, when it's a civil rights bill," Mitchell said, "the Democratic Party whip system in the House of Representatives breaks down completely. Why? Because the Democratic whip in the House is Representative Hale Boggs of the Southern state of Louisiana. Boggs would be severely punished at the polls by white voters in his home state if, as Democratic whip, he lifted one little finger in behalf of the civil rights bill. The final result is there is no whip system to get Northern Democratic liberals to the House floor to vote down weakening Southern amendments to a civil rights bill."

"Don't be fooled by the large number of representatives who have publicly announced their support for this bill," Mitchell explained. "It's true that over 220 Democrats and Republicans in the House have committed themselves to the civil rights bill. And they've promised to oppose all Southern attempts to dilute the bill. But these commitments are of little value unless the representatives are physically present on the House floor at all times and voting our way."

By this time Mitchell's audience, including Clark Schooler and Carl Brimmer, was almost completely dismayed by the hidden tactical problems that needed to be overcome to get the civil rights bill through the House of Representatives unscathed. But there was even more.

"A fourth problem," Clarence Mitchell said in a weary tone of voice, "is that no writing or note taking is permitted in the House visitor galleries during the Committee of the Whole. If you want to keep track of whether a particular member is present, and how he or she is voting on particular amendments, you have to do it all by memory."

Having thus articulated the problem clearly, Clarence Mitchell then proceeded to present a solution.

"We're going to pack the visitor galleries of the House of Representatives," Mitchell said. "Before each session of the Committee of the Whole, civil rights supporters are going to get in line early and, when the visitor galleries open, go in and get good seats. Each gallery watcher is going to be assigned to watch four or five pro-civil rights representatives to make certain they are present on the House floor. The gallery watcher also is going to memorize whether a particular member is voting with us on amendments or not. In effect, we are going to set up a whip system in the galleries."

"If a gallery watcher sees that a particular representative is not present for a key vote, the watcher will leave the gallery." As Clarence Mitchell further explained his plan, his psychological enthusiasm became more evident and his voice rose in volume and clarity. "The watcher then will telephone the Leadership Conference offices, where there will be a master chart of office locations in all of the House office buildings. On each floor in each House office building, we'll have office visitors stationed at telephones in the offices of representatives friendly to our cause."

"When word comes from the Leadership Conference that this-or-that representative is not present on the floor," Mitchell went on, "the office visitor will hurry to the representative's office, ask to see him or her, and encourage the truant to get down to the House floor as soon as possible."

"This way," Clarence Mitchell triumphantly concluded, "there will be no playing hookey. Pro-civil rights representatives are either going to be present for the debate, or they're going to get all kinds of hassle and grief from our office visitors."

A young black man dressed in a suit coat and tie stood up and spoke out strongly. "That's a good plan for getting absent representatives who support us to the House floor," he said in a somewhat challenging manner, "but what about if the representative is voting for Southern amendments that cripple the bill?"

"Whenever we can arrange it," Mitchell replied, "the gallery watcher will be a civil rights supporter from the representative's home district, perhaps someone who knows the representative personally. If the representative starts to vote for weakening amendments, the gallery watcher will go down and have a House page call the representative off the House floor. The gallery watcher will then ask the errant representative to begin to loyally support the civil rights bill."

At this point, Vonda Belle Carter spoke up, "We won't just be asking for these misbehaving representatives to vote pro-civil rights on amendments," Vonda Belle said sagaciously. "We'll be subtly, but not too subtly, letting them know that their votes on civil rights amendments are being memorized and recorded and will be made known to civil rights types in their home districts."

"Their pro-Southern votes will particularly be made known," Clarence Mitchell said with a smile, "when the representatives come up for reelection." [50]

The discussion went on for a while, as Clarence Mitchell and Vonda Belle Carter explained the details of Mitchell's plan and answered questions. It became clear that most of the gallery watchers and office visitors were going to be activist civil rights types, brought in by bus, train, and airplane from around the nation. The longer the meeting went on, the more mystified Clark Schooler and Carl Brimmer became over just what they were doing there.

When the meeting finally ended, Vonda Belle Carter called Clark and Carl over for a private briefing. "We want to have some white middle-class faces in the House galleries to go along with the civil rights types," Vonda Belle explained. "So Carl, if you're willing to do it, you're a gallery watcher. As for you Clark, there are a number of representatives who have virtually no black persons for constituents. They are mainly from upper New England and the Rocky Mountain West. If you would, we'd like you to be, when needed, their office visitor."

Both young men signed on for the duration of the time the bill would be debated and amendments voted in the House of Representatives.

That evening the Capitol Fellows gathered at the Rotunda restaurant near the Capitol for one of their periodic dinners together. Clark Schooler found himself seated next to one of the female Fellows, a young woman whom Clark had seen around at Fellows meetings but had not yet met.

As was his usual habit, Clark looked directly at the young woman and said: "Hi. I'm Clark Schooler from Senator Kuchel's office."

Without missing a beat or batting an eye, the young woman looked back at Clark and said: "It's always interesting to meet a man who has no identity of his own."

That response, Clark later realized, was the perfect summation of the personality and verbal skills of a woman whose name, he soon learned, was Bonnie Kanecton. She was possessed of the sharpest wit and the quickest comeback lines of any woman he had ever met. Best of all, Bonnie knew how to be humorously sarcastic without hurting other people's feelings. In the coming months, Clark frequently found himself being intellectually demolished by Bonnie Kanecton. And he found himself enjoying every minute of it.

Bonnie was that rare breed known as the native Washingtonian. Her mother and father were originally from Chicago, Illinois, but Bonnie's father had worked for years as the administrative assistant to a Republican member of the House of Representatives from the Chicago area. Bonnie had left Washington to go to Vassar College in New York, but she had returned to the nation's capital to get her law degree at Georgetown University.

When Clark asked Bonnie what her assignment was as a Capitol Fellow, she replied simply: "I'm an attorney with the Senate Subcommittee on Constitutional Amendments."

Bonnie and Clark spent most of the meal chatting with each other. The conversation revealed that Bonnie, similar to Clark, was unmarried and available to meet new people and make new friends.

Clark liked Bonnie. In the instinctive manner in which young people relate and respond to one another, Clark said all the right things and displayed all the proper body language to let Bonnie know he was interested in her. And Bonnie responded to Clark's somewhat obvious early infatuation with her. She invited Clark to come up to her apartment in Georgetown the following Friday night for dinner with her and her two women roommates, who were also Capitol Fellows.

The following Friday evening, Clark Schooler jumped in his 1951 Ford Victoria hardtop convertible and headed from Capitol Hill toward Georgetown. There were many routes by which to make the drive, but Clark chose to drive up Pennsylvania Avenue past the National Theater and the front of the White House. Going that way, he thought, he could see the automobiles of the great and near-great of Washington as they started about their weekend business.

The emphasis was on the word "business." The talking and persuading and contact-making that characterized political life in Washington did not end on the weekend. In many ways, it just became more intense.

Clark would think to himself: Who's in that shiny black Cadillac over there? Perhaps it's the Senate majority leader heading to a state dinner at the White House. And that olive drab sedan with military markings painted on it? Maybe that's one of the country's top generals and his wife going to an important dinner at the Russian embassy. And that couple in a green Oldsmobile? Possibly it could be a reporter for the *New York Times* taking the spouse to a dinner and a speech by a visiting dignitary at the National Press Club.

Clark had come to call these kind of Friday and Saturday night social events the weekend hustle. He regarded them as an important, perhaps even vital, part of the governmental process. Of course, many of the automobiles, like his own, only contained people going on a Friday or Saturday night date. But in Washington, D.C., one never could tell when, at what appeared to be a purely social event, a beneficial political contact might be made, or a vitally important political conversation held, or a crucial deal cut.

Clark found pleasure and excitement in driving around Washington through the weekend hustle. Hey! What about that car with diplomatic plates over there? It could be the ambassador from France on his way to a very exclusive dinner party at a Cabinet member's home in Alexandria, Virginia.

As Clark's 1951 Ford rolled past the White House, Clark noted that the large front porch light was on and a long line of limousines were unloading their passengers. Just like Clark Schooler, the president of the United States had an important dinner to go to this Friday night.

With a little jog left-turn, Pennsylvania Avenue turned into M Street Northwest. Clark Schooler and his automobile were in Georgetown. This collection of late 19th and early 20th Century homes clustered around the intersection of M Street and Wisconsin Avenue. The area was dripping with Victorian atmosphere. The streets were narrow, some of them still paved with rough cobblestones. The red brick row houses, most of them two or three stories tall, were trimmed with attractive woodwork, mainly painted white. The backyards of these homes were small, but many sported an attractive rear patio with plenty of plants and flowers and wrought-iron patio furniture.

Some very important people in Washington opted to live in Georgetown, mainly because of its relative closeness to the White House and the Capitol. In this particular row house, one might find a former secretary of state. Down the street might live a senior member of the House of Representatives. When they were young and newly married, Senator John F. Kennedy and his wife, Jacqueline, made their home in Georgetown.

But, more than anything else, Georgetown was filled with young men and women, many of them single, sharing apartments and, sometimes, entire houses. These young people had heard the siren song of the nation's capital. They had come from all over the United States, hoping to get jobs in government and politics. Their collective dream was to begin professional lives of significance and relevance. And those who could afford the rent liked to live, and socialize, and play together in Georgetown.

Bonnie Kanecton's apartment was on Congress Street, a narrow residential street just west of Wisconsin Avenue. She and her two Capitol Fellow roommates lived in a second floor walk-up. The apartment had a wonderfully spacious living room with two large windows facing on Congress Street. Unlike many apartments inhabited by young people in their 20s and early 30s, this apartment was tastefully furnished. It had Oriental rugs on the floor and comfortable upholstered furniture in the living room.

When Clark walked in, he was immediately introduced to Bonnie's two roommates. One of the young women was named Molly McClusky. She was from Atlanta, Georgia, where she had worked as an assistant feature pages editor for the *Atlanta Constitution*. Her assignment as a Capitol Fellow was working in the U.S. Navy's public relations office at the Pentagon.

Bonnie's other roommate was Mary Samuels. She was from Tennessee. She worked for the Central Intelligence Agency, and that was all that Clark ever learned about her job. Because the CIA gathered information about foreign nations, some of it by cloak-and-dagger spying, CIA employees were notoriously closed-mouthed about themselves and their place of employment. As a Capitol Fellow, Mary Samuels worked on Capitol Hill with the staff of the House Foreign Affairs Committee.

Both Molly McClusky and Mary Samuels had dates that evening. Soon the living room was filled with six young people talking and chatting and munching hors d'oeuvres that one of the women had, seemingly effortlessly, whipped up. At some point one of the young women suggested they all go to dinner and go ice skating at the Chevy Chase Country Club. To Clark's complete surprise and wonderment, he soon found himself and Bonnie Kanecton in the front seat of Clark's car, driving north on Connecticut Avenue toward Chevy Chase, one of Washington's most upscale and best-known suburbs.

The Chevy Chase Country Club perhaps was one of the most exclusive and influential private club in the entire United States. It was certainly a leading club in Washington, D.C. Among its members were prominent members of Congress, both present and past. The financially successful of Washington were to be found there, particularly if they were old money rather than nouveau riche. One could add tons of tone to a wedding reception, or a dinner meeting, or an awards ceremony, by holding it at the Chevy Chase Country Club.

The "Ch" in "Chevy" was pronounced with a "ch" sound, as in chocolate. It was not pronounced with a "sh" sound, as in Chevrolet. Longtime members often referred to it just as Chevy. "I'm running out to Chevy for a swim," they would say casually. Or: "Let's meet for lunch at Chevy tomorrow."

The Chevy Chase Country Club had all the same things any good private club has, but often with just a little more size and a little more luxury. There was a golf course, which stretched all the way from Connecticut Avenue to Wisconsin Avenue, covering a considerable piece of ground. There was a swimming pool, and even some bowling alleys. And, of course, there was the main dining room, where the power elite of Washington could be found eating dinner any night of the week, but particularly on weekends.

Chevy was also the hangout of that venerable national treasure, the Washington hostess. These were the women, all of them wealthy and well-connected, who threw the parties that really mattered in the nation's capital. These women and their husbands mainly entertained in their grand homes, often found on Massachusetts Avenue or out on River Road. But occasionally they would throw their parties at the Chevy Chase Country Club.

These were the elegant events that brought together the leaders of Congress, members of the president's Cabinet, ambassadors from the most populous and influential nations, and sometimes even the president himself. And, as Clark well knew, such parties were anything but just social occasions. Many a key deal, or even an international treaty, was worked out in the living room of a Washington hostess, or in a private dining room at Chevy.

For young people, the place to be at the Chevy Chase Country Club was the grill. This casual restaurant did not require a suit coat and necktie the way the main dining room did. And the grill was noisy, filled with young people having lively conversations and occasionally dancing to out-of-date records in an old juke box. There was none of the quiet and reserve and propriety that was so overwhelming in the main dining room.

Clark Schooler and Bonnie Kanecton met Bonnie's two roommates and their dates in the grill. The entire entourage had a casual but filling dinner. The grill was located on the second floor of the main building at the country club, above the bowling alley. The grill overlooked the outdoor ice skating rink. Large plate glass windows permitted party types in the grill, while eating their meal, to watch the skaters zoom and pirouette around the ice.

In the traditional manner of a private club, no one was ever seen paying a bill at Chevy. At one point during the evening, Clark pretended not to notice that Bonnie signed a piece of paper with the number 61 on it. Clark never found out who the real human being was who had to pay account number 61 each month, but he assumed it was Bonnie's father.

Dinner was followed by ice skating, with rental skates available for those who did not own their own. Clark was a reasonably decent ice skater, having played intramural fraternity hockey at Williams College. He could readily skate around the rink side-by-side with a young woman. And, because Clark could skate backward, he could take a woman in his arms and, with her skating forward, waltz her around the ice in the manner of ballroom dancing.

When the young women discovered this, Clark became a very popular skating partner. Clark dutifully split his duet skating time equally between Bonnie and her two roommates.

In the ensuing weeks, Bonnie Kanecton and the Chevy Chase Country Club became an important part of Clark Schooler's social life. At least once a week, and sometimes twice, Clark would be invited to join Bonnie and her roommates for dinner in the grill and skating on the ice rink at Chevy.

But Bonnie Kanecton introduced Clark Schooler to much more than the Chevy Chase Country Club. She knew her way very well around the Washington social scene. She and Clark went to the Cellar Door, a night club on M Street in Georgetown that featured folk singing as its principal form of entertainment. Bonnie and Clark sat together and listened to baleful anti-war and anti-segregation folk songs whined to the accompaniment of a conventional guitar. They enjoyed hearing emerging folk singing stars such as Judy Collins and the duo Ian and Sylvia.

And Bonnie knew where to find a good meal in the nation's capital. Clark and she had dinner at Maxim's, a French restaurant on Connecticut Avenue that really did seem as if it were tucked away in a little corner of the Rive Gauche in Paris rather than in Washington, D.C. And Bonnie steered Clark to Paul Young's, a downtown restaurant which was particularly popular among the leading politicians and elected office-holders in Washington. One went to Paul Young's to be seen as well as to get a good meal.

And then there were the parties. If there was a party going on anywhere among the upwardly mobile youth in Washington, Bonnie Kanecton seemed to know about it and have an invitation to it. Clark found himself socializing with Bonnie and her friends at the F-Street Club, a private, in-town, dining and entertaining club located a few blocks west of the White House. Or Clark and Bonnie would gather with other young people at someone's house or apartment in Georgetown. It seemed that at least one night each weekend, Bonnie had a party somewhere in Washington for the two of them to go to.

At many of those parties, Clark would run into Bernard Martin, the African-American newspaper reporter who covered the riot at Ole Miss with Clark. Bernard would come with his wife, Loretta, who was a strikingly beautiful black woman. It seemed to Clark that Bernard and Loretta had sort of established themselves as the token, but highly acceptable, young black couple to invite to a "with it" party in Washington. Clark noticed, somewhat sheepishly, that he always felt better at a gathering if Bernard and Loretta were there too. That meant that Clark was leading an "integrated" rather than a "segregated" social life.

One Saturday night Clark Schooler escorted Bonnie Kanecton to the annual ball of the Merrie Maids and Noble Knights of Georgetown. This was an organization of unmarried men and women living in Georgetown that existed for no other purpose than to host a sensational dinner and dance each year. Clark found the event to be a Victorian delight, a charming throwback to an age when everyone dressed up in formal clothes and behaved with great dignity and respect for one another.

The band hired for the evening played traditional dance tunes, so called "standards." But every once in a while the band would belt out one of those noisy new rock-and-roll songs. Amazingly to Clark, women in long gowns and men in tuxedos would step out on the dance floor and, despite their fine and elaborate clothing, go through the accentuated physical gyrations of rock-and-roll dancing.

Bonnie Kanecton was a social leader as well as a socialite. She was a member of the Board of Directors of the Merrie Maids and Noble Knights of Georgetown. There was no question about it. Bonnie knew social Washington like a book. And she was letting Clark read that book over her shoulder. Clark was enjoying, and profiting, from every word of the book.

Meanwhile, Clark Schooler and Carl Brimmer were spending their daytime hours helping Clarence Mitchell and the NAACP get the civil rights bill through the House of Representatives. Carl Brimmer kept tabs from the House galleries on four members from Idaho and Montana, two of whom he had met personally. It turned out to be dull work. All four representatives were unusually faithful about staying on the House floor and voting solidly to reject all weakening Southern amendments.

But Carl Brimmer enjoyed getting a bird's-eye view of the debate. With a coalition of liberal Northern Democrats and moderate Midwestern Republicans supporting the bill, most of the action consisted of weakening Southern amendments being voted down by substantial majorities.

Carl quickly divined how the system worked. The liberal Northern Democrats were taking their cues from Emanuel Celler, the chair of the House Judiciary Committee. The moderate Midwestern Republicans were getting their signals from William McCulloch, the ranking Republican on the Judiciary Committee. If a Southern amendment was a weakening one unacceptable to the civil rights forces, Representative Celler and Representative McCulloch both would speak briefly against it. Civil rights supporters on the House floor would get the message, no matter how arcane or complex the language of the amendment might be. The Southern amendment would be quickly voted down.

Carl Brimmer also noticed something else going on as the civil rights bill was under consideration in the House of Representatives. Nicholas Katzenbach, the deputy attorney general in the Civil Rights Division at the Justice Department, also was in the gallery during most of the debate. When problems arose on the floor for the civil rights forces, Nicholas Katzenbach left the gallery and went down and met with Emanuel Celler and William McCulloch just off the House floor. Sometimes these impromptu strategy sessions were held in the office of John McCormack of Massachusetts, the speaker of the House.

One time Carl Brimmer saw Clarence Mitchell and Joseph Rauh, the lobbyists for the Leadership Conference, join Nicholas Katzenbach in one of his meetings with representatives Celler and McCulloch. It was obvious that Katzenbach, an employee of the executive branch, and Mitchell and Rauh, two lobbyists, were directly involved in making legislative strategy for getting the civil rights bill passed in the U.S. House of Representatives.

Carl Brimmer encountered some real excitement the day the funds cut-off was being debated. Representative Oren Harris, a Democrat from Arkansas, offered an amendment that would have made the funds cut-off optional. Under the terms of the amendment, U.S. Government officials would have been given a great deal of latitude in cutting off funds to state government programs that practiced racial discrimination. Under the original bill, the cut-off of funds was mandatory.

This amendment, a typical Southern attempt to weaken the bill, ordinarily would have attracted no attention and been routinely voted down. But, in a complete surprise to the civil rights forces, Representative Hale Boggs, the House Democratic whip, gave a stirring speech in support of Representative Harris's amendment. Because Boggs was the Democratic whip and therefore part of the House Democratic leadership, civil rights supporters immediately became suspicious. They feared that, behind their backs, the Democratic leaders in the House were about to give in to the Southerners and intentionally weaken the bill.

Republican Representative John Lindsay of New York, a committed civil rights supporter, quickly organized a strong counterattack against the Harris amendment.

"This amendment will gut the funds cut-off provision," Lindsay told the House, shaking his fist in anger as he said the word "gut." Lindsay railed on: "This is the biggest mousetrap that has been offered since the debate on this bill began. I am appalled that this is being supported in the well of the House by the Democratic whip. Does this mean there is a cave-in by the Democratic leadership on this important title." [51]

As this mini-crisis deepened on the House floor, the word spread among the Leadership Conference gallery watchers to get every pro-civil rights representative on to the House floor. The vote could be close when the Harris amendment came up for a vote. Although a Southerner, Hale Boggs was a popular and powerful leader in the Democratic Party. He just might have enough influence to get the Harris amendment through, particularly since all the Southerners were lined up solidly behind it.

One of the gallery watchers, a black woman from Boston, Massachusetts, noticed that one of the representatives she was watching for, a man from Vermont, was not present on the House floor. She rose instantly from her seat and hurried out of the House gallery. Moments later she was telephoning the Leadership Conference offices, dutifully reporting the Vermont representative's absence at this key moment in the floor debate on the civil rights bill.

Clark Schooler had been sitting at a desk with a telephone deep in the depths of the Longworth House Office Building. He had brought along a stack of work, mainly copies of *Congressional Quarterly Weekly Report*. He was reading them in order to keep up with what was going on in both houses of Congress. He was deeply engrossed in an article about a bill providing for a new dam and recreational lake in northern California when the telephone rang. Clark virtually jumped when the phone's bell sounded. Up to this point in time, he had found his duties as an office visitor to be less than demanding.

"Things are exploding on the House floor," Vonda Belle Carter said. "We need every last pro-civil rights vote, and we need those votes on the House floor right now." She then gave Clark Schooler the name and the office number of the absent representative from Vermont. "Do whatever you can to get him present and voting," Vonda Belle said as she ended the telephone call. "And do it pronto!"

Clark always enjoyed visiting the offices of the various senators and representatives. Typically, these offices were decorated with photographs and paintings of the state or the district from which the senator or representative came. One time, when Clark had been in the office of a senator from North Carolina, he had been transfixed by a set of marvelous photographs of the Atlantic beaches of eastern North Carolina. The surf was rolling in, the sandy beaches appeared to stretch for miles, and the beautiful red and orange colors of a glorious sunrise were reflected in the fluffy clouds hanging above the ocean.

Another time, Clark had stopped by the office of a representative from western Colorado. There was a large painting of the Rocky Mountains. It filled almost an entire wall and completely dominated the entrance room to the office suite. The colorful evergreen forest of the lower slopes of the Rocky Mountains contrasted magnificently with the soaring grey granite mountain peaks, some still covered with the white of spring snows. Clark often said that visiting a senator's or representative's office was like taking a mini-tour of the part of America the senator or representative represented in Congress.

With such a mini-tour in mind, Clark was not disappointed when he walked into the office of his assigned representative from Vermont. Apparently the representative's part of Vermont was apple country, because there were beautiful photographs of apple trees and apple orchards tastefully distributed around the walls. There also were photos of classic white-painted New England churches and sleepy New England villages nestled at the foot of verdant New England foothills. There even was a painting of a classic New England covered bridge.

"The representative can see you in just a few minutes," the receptionist said. She was a strikingly attractive and well-dressed young woman with an unmistakable New England accent. She asked sweetly: "Would you like to have a mug of apple cider while you're waiting?"

"No thank you," said Clark. "I'm not thirsty. I'll just sit here and enjoy all these photographs of your representative's home district."

The receptionist busied herself at her desk, but after about two minutes she looked up at Clark and said, a little more pointedly but still very nicely: "Are you certain you wouldn't like to have a mug of our delicious apple cider?"

The light bulb of realization finally blazed on in Clark Schooler's brain. No one, he suddenly understood, ever went in to see this particular representative without having a tall mug of Vermont apple cider in his or her hand. It was so obvious that Clark was literally embarrassed. Apple cider was the main product and principal employment producer in this representative's home district. Anyone who visited his office was going to drink a mug full of Vermont apple cider, whether the person wanted it or not.

"You want everyone who comes here to have some apple cider, don't you?" The words were barely out of Clark's mouth when the young woman stepped to a close-by mini-refrigerator and poured Clark his apple cider. It was served in a glass mug with a nice handle on it. The mug was large and had a picture of an apple orchard, an apple tree, and a wooden barrel of apple cider engraved on it. "You can keep the mug as a souvenir of your visit," the receptionist said. She escorted Clark in to see the representative.

He was a relatively young man in his early 40s. He was good looking, as many politicians are, and had something of a no-nonsense air about him that Clark found typical of most members of Congress. There was a large jug of apple cider sitting on one corner of his desk. Close to his right hand was a mug of apple cider, which he drank from periodically while he and Clark were talking. His mug was the same engraved glass mug that Clark had been given to drink from and take with him as a memento of the encounter.

"Your presence is badly needed on the House floor," Clark began the conversation. "The Southerners are trying to weaken the civil rights bill with an amendment that makes the funds cut-off discretionary rather than required. Hale Boggs, the House Democratic whip, is backing the amendment, so we need every last vote we can find to kill this amendment dead in its tracks."

Clark decided to emphasize his message by taking a long drink from his mug of apple cider.

"We don't have very many black persons in Vermont," the representative said. "In fact, we have hardly any at all. As a result, the funds cut-off is going to have virtually no effect in Vermont. I thought I would leave the voting on funds cut-off amendments to representatives from states that would be affected by them. Besides, I had some letters to write and telephone calls to make back to my home district."

Clark framed his response with an appeal to national responsibility. "It's true that there are very few blacks in northern New England," Clark said. "I know that's true, because I went to Williams College in western Massachusetts, and there were hardly any black persons around there, either. But civil rights is an issue of national significance. The Leadership Conference on Civil Rights is urging you to support the black people's quest for freedom all over America, not just in Vermont."

"Your responsibilities to your district are important," Clark continued, interspersing almost every sentence with a sip of apple cider. "But equally important are your responsibilities to all of the American people. After all, you sit in the United States House of Representatives, not the Vermont House of Representatives."

Clark hoped he had not sounded too much like a college professor in making such a statement to a member of Congress. To Clark's great relief, the representative began looking somewhat embarrassed rather than angry.

"I thought I'd try to steal a few minutes and get some of this junk off my desk," the representative said with something of a sense of resolve coming into his voice. "But I can see that was a mistake. The civil rights bill is important. I need to be down on the House floor."

The representative then smiled at Clark. "I promise you this. You won't ever have to come and summon me to the House floor again on this civil rights bill. And, by the way, it's nice to see that your ad hoc whip system, which I've been reading about in the newspaper, really does work. If nothing else, I gave you a chance to test it out."

The representative from Vermont escorted Clark out of his office. Then the two men walked briskly from the Longworth House Office Building to the House of Representatives and the door to the House floor. Along the way, it turned out that the representative was interested in a bill that Senator Kuchel was supporting, a bill providing U.S. Government subsidized health care for citizens over the age of 65. Clark briefed the representative on some of the provisions of the bill. Clark promised to send over some printed information on the bill from Senator Kuchel's office.

Clark returned to his post in the Longworth House Office Building. He telephoned Vonda Belle Carter and left a message for her with the volunteer who answered the telephone. The errant representative from Vermont, Clark reported, was now "present and voting" on the floor of the House.

Thinking of this incident with the representative from Vermont, Clark reminded himself that members of Congress are required to serve both immediate constituent interests and somewhat broader and more general national interests. In this case, Clark opined to himself, the representative from Vermont had needed a little direct encouragement to make national interests as important as constituent interests.

Carl Brimmer had been keeping tabs on all the action from the House galleries. The Harris amendment making the funds cut-off optional was moving rapidly toward a vote. Additional representatives were coming through the doors on to the House floor. They had been stirred to action by telephone calls and office visits that had been generated by Clarence Mitchell's gallery watchers.

The situation clarified somewhat when Republican William McCulloch of Ohio, the senior Republican on the House Judiciary Committee and a strong civil rights supporter, proceeded to a microphone. "If the Harris amendment is adopted," McCulloch intoned with great gravity in his voice, "my individual support of this legislation will come to an end." [52]

William McCulloch's statement turned the tide on the Harris amendment. To keep McCulloch and his Republican allies supporting the civil rights bill, the Northern Democrats in the House had no choice but to stick with the Republicans and vote down the proposal to make the funds cut-off optional. When the members of the House finished walking past the "yea" teller and the "nay" teller, the amendment had been easily rejected.

The defeat of the Harris amendment in no way slowed down the commitment of Southern representatives to try to weaken the civil rights bill. A few days later, in early February of 1964, Representative Howard Smith of Virginia introduced an amendment to prohibit discrimination in employment on the basis of sex as well as race, religion, and national origin.

At first glance, one might think such an amendment would strengthen the civil rights bill. But there was method in Representative Smith's madness. He knew many members of the House of Representatives were strongly opposed to requiring equal treatment of the sexes by law. If Smith succeeded in getting his amendment added to the bill, these representatives might vote against the civil rights bill when it came up for final passage in the House.

"Howard Smith is using one of the oldest of legislative devices," Clark Schooler pontificated to no one in particular when he learned about Smith's sex amendment. "It's called divide the opposition. Smith isn't really interested in promoting women's rights. What he wants to do is get the civil rights supporters who are for women's rights fighting with the civil rights supporters who are against them."

Because Howard Smith was chair of the House Rules Committee, and thus considered part of the House Democratic leadership, his sex amendment attracted a great deal of attention from the press and the public. Smith used the occasion to make enthusiastic speeches in favor of women's rights. "It is indisputable fact that, all throughout industry, women are discriminated against," Smith said. "Generally speaking, they do not get as high compensation for their work as the male sex gets."

Smith then made a statement that summed up his true feelings about the civil rights bill and his sex discrimination amendment: "This bill is so imperfect, what harm will this little sex amendment do?" [53]

Representative Edith Green, a Democrat from Oregon, saw through Howard Smith's plan to complicate the issue of racial discrimination with the quite separate and considerably different issue of sex discrimination. She told her House colleagues: "At the risk of being called an Aunt Jane, if not an Uncle Tom, let us not add any amendment to the civil rights bill that will get in the way of our primary objective. I support the equal treatment of women in employment, but I do not believe this is the time or the place for this amendment." [54]

Clarence Mitchell and his gallery watchers and office visitors began routinely rounding up both Democratic and Republican members of the House to vote down Howard Smith's sex discrimination amendment. And Vonda Belle Carter, as she had been doing all along, was helping to coordinate the battle from Leadership Conference headquarters. But then something went terribly wrong for the civil rights forces. A group of women members in the House of Representatives, including both Democrats and Republicans, began a concerted drive to pass the Smith amendment and add a prohibition on sex discrimination in employment to the civil rights bill.

Leading the fight was Representative Martha W. Griffiths, a Democrat from Michigan and a white woman. She went to a microphone on the House floor and pointed out that the civil rights bill would protect the employment rights of black women but would leave white women with no protection at all.

"If this bill passes the way it is now," Representative Griffiths said, "white men will continue to have tremendous advantages over white women in employment. But this bill is going to take black men and black women and give them equal employment rights. Down at the bottom of the list is going to be a white woman with no rights at all. White women are going to be last in line at the hiring gate. A vote against this amendment today by a white man is a vote against his wife, or his widow, or his daughter, or his sister." [55]

Next at the microphone was Representative Katharine St. George, a Republican from New York. "This amendment will simply correct something that goes back, frankly, to the Dark Ages," she said, sounding like a school marm lecturing a classroom full of unruly students. "The addition of that little, terrifying word, s-e-x, will not hurt this legislation in any way." She then spoke directly to her men colleagues in the House: "We outlast you. We outlive you. We nag you to death. We are entitled to this little crumb of equality." [56]

Clark Schooler realized some form of trouble was brewing when he got an office visitor assignment on the sex discrimination amendment from Vonda Belle Carter. She gave Clark the name and office location of the missing representative that Clark was to corral and try to drive down to the House floor to vote against Howard Smith's sex amendment. Then, as sort of an afterthought, Vonda Belle said: "I really do feel like I'm working against my white sisters on this one."

"Well," Clark huffed into the telephone. "You aren't going to join forces with Howard Smith and the Southern Democrats are you? That makes as much sense as all the chickens deciding to go into business with Colonel Sanders."

Clark's reference was to a newly emerging chain of fried chicken restaurants, Kentucky Fried Chicken, which was owned by a man named Colonel Sanders. The colonel appeared in the advertising for the restaurants, wearing a white Palm Beach suit and sporting a pointed mustache and having a heavy Southern accent and looking every bit the part of a "Southern colonel."

"I know," Vonda Belle replied. "I feel terribly guilty about this. I don't want to help the Southern Democrats in any way whatsoever. But white women are almost as badly discriminated against on the job as black men and women are. Why can't we have this in the bill? It would really change things."

"You can say that again," Clark said. "There are only about 20 million black men and women in this nation. But there are over 100 million white women. It won't be a civil rights bill any more. It mainly will be a women's rights bill."

But the forces of legislative history turned out to be with Vonda Belle Carter rather than Clark Schooler. As a result of near instantaneous but skillful legislative engineering by Representative Martha Griffiths, the civil rights majority in the House of Representatives broke apart over the issue of non-discrimination against women in employment. When the vote was taken, Howard Smith's sex amendment passed by a vote of 168 to 133.

"I saw a unique opportunity when Representative Smith introduced the amendment," Martha Griffiths later told the press. "Smith had just given us 100 Southern Democratic votes in support of women's employment rights. Using those Southern votes as a base, I figured I could split off enough pro-women's rights votes from the civil rights coalition to get the amendment passed. And that's exactly what happened." [57]

It was a reminder to Clark Schooler that real surprises can take place when legislation is being debated in the U.S. House of Representatives and the U.S. Senate. Neither President Johnson, nor the Justice Department, nor the Leadership Conference on Civil Rights, nor the NAACP had wanted women's employment rights added to the civil rights bill. But an unlikely coalition of Southern Democrats and women's rights supporters put the provision in the bill all the same.

"I'll bet," Clark Schooler later said to Vonda Belle Carter and Carl Brimmer, "that Howard Smith never remotely suspected that the women members of the House would take his sex amendment so seriously. If old Howard had any inkling his amendment would actually be added to the bill, well, I'm sure old Howard would have never introduced it."

Clarence Mitchell's gallery watcher and office visitor system was proving very effective at maintaining high levels of attendance and voting on the House floor. This was true even for the Tuesday-to-Thursday set. These were representatives from the East Coast who lived close enough to Washington to go home to their districts for extra-long Friday-through-Monday weekends. But suddenly these representatives were showing up for Monday, Friday, and even Saturday sessions.

Joseph Rauh of the Leadership Conference was particularly impressed with this sudden break with long-standing congressional tradition. "When the Tuesday-to-Thursday eastern congressmen answered present to a quorum call on a Saturday," Rauh said, "old timers began talking about miracles." [58]

But was the Leadership Conference on Civil Rights over-organized in its efforts to pass the civil rights bill? Was the gallery watcher and office visitor system proving too effective? That suddenly became the case. The Southerners, unable to get any of their weakening amendments passed in the House, began attacking the gallery watcher and office visitor system rather than the civil rights bill itself. "This monstrous bill," fumed Southern Democratic Representative James A. Haley of Florida, "would not be winning were it not for those vultures in the galleries." [59]

Faced with such criticism, Clarence Mitchell reluctantly sent his gallery watchers and office visitors back to where they had been recruited from. Carl Brimmer abandoned his post in the House gallery. Clark Schooler left his borrowed desk and telephone in the Longworth House Office Building. The excitement ended for both young men as they reluctantly returned to their more routine assignments as Senate aides.

One reason Clarence Mitchell withdrew his gallery watchers and office visitors was that the vast majority of the non-Southern members of the House of Representatives had been totally sensitized to the importance of quashing all weakening amendments to the bill. The momentum behind the civil rights bill had become so great that even the equal employment opportunity provisions, the provisions that many pundits and prognosticators said would be removed in the House of Representatives, were adopted virtually unchanged.

By Monday evening, February 10, 1964, the Committee of the Whole had finished its work. The House of Representatives convened in regular session. The mace, that ornate Medieval club, was placed back in its mounting. And the speaker of the House, John W. McCormack of Massachusetts, took charge of the proceedings.

The House passed the civil rights bill by a record vote of 290 to 130. Clark Schooler, Carl Brimmer, and Vonda Belle Carter watched this sweet moment of victory from the House gallery. The three young people were elated with the results. The coalition of liberal Northern Democrats and moderate Republicans, first assembled at President Kennedy's now-legendary night meeting at the White House, had held together and prevailed completely over the Southern Democrats.

As Clark, Carl, and Vonda Belle were leaving the House gallery after final passage of the bill, they encountered Clarence Mitchell and Joseph Rauh in the hallway. They all stopped to chat with one another and enjoy this moment of legislative triumph. About this time, a Leadership Conference intern came up to Clarence Mitchell and Joseph Rauh with a message to call President Johnson at the White House.

The two men left the group and went to a nearby telephone booth. They returned a few moments later with weary but rejoiceful looks on their faces. "Despite all our hard work getting the civil rights bill through the House," one of them said, "there will be no rest for the legislatively weary."

Lyndon Johnson had worked hard from the White House to get the civil rights bill passed in the House of Representatives. He had made many telephone calls and squeezed lots of elbows in the bill's behalf. Now, the president had virtually shouted his instructions to Mitchell and Rauh into the telephone. He said:

"What are you fellows doing about the Senate? We've got the bill through the House. Now we've got the big job of getting it through the Senate!" [60]

In The Interim

The House of Representatives is considerably more partisan in the 2000s than it was in the 1960s. But many observers, particularly older scholars, argue that the House of Representatives was a better legislative body when it was less party oriented and passed most legislation on a bipartisan basis.

Public opinion polls in the early 2000s reported that the American public wanted less partisanship in Congress and more cooperation between the two major parties when enacting legislation.

CHAPTER 10

THE SENATE:
THE FILIBUSTER AT FULL FORCE

The Capitol Hill staff members supporting the civil rights bill gathered for a meeting in a conference room in the Old Senate Office Building. The mood at the start of the meeting was exceptionally upbeat. The civil rights bill had passed the House of Representatives without suffering any major setbacks in the form of damaging or weakening amendments. The bill now was in a sort of legislative limbo. It had passed the House, but it had not yet come over to the Senate for action in the upper house.

The speaker at this particular meeting was Ralph Shepard. He was the special assistant on civil rights to Senator Hubert H. Humphrey, the Democratic whip in the Senate. It was well known that Senator Humphrey was a longtime supporter of civil rights and would be playing a major role in guiding the civil rights bill through the Senate.

"Almost everybody in the United States has heard the word filibuster," Ralph Shepard began. "But very few people know how the filibuster really works. The word conjures up the image of Southern senators with leather lungs giving bombastic speeches on irrelevant subjects. A lot of people regard the filibuster as a sort of comic opera rather than a serious impediment to important legislation. They think of Southern senators reading obscure passages from the Bible, or conducting arcane discussions on names found in the New Orleans telephone directory, or telling jokes with one another, some of the jokes having a racist tinge."

"But those kind of ridiculous filibusters no longer exist," Shepard continued. "The Southerners have learned how to stay on the subject of civil rights and only discuss topics that are relevant to the debate. They want to look wise and thoughtful to the folks back home. They no longer are willing to run the risk of looking and sounding like fools and buffoons."

Ralph Shepard's well organized presentation was interrupted by an early question: "Can just one senator, talking by himself, conduct a filibuster and defeat an important bill?"

"Single-senator filibusters are well-known in Senate lore," Shepard replied, "but they constitute no long range problem to the Senate. These one-person filibusters attract a lot of attention in the press but rarely last more than 24 hours. That's about as long as one human being can hold out without getting some rest."

Clark Schooler had been looking for an opportunity to make a contribution at these pro-civil rights staff meetings. Up to this point, he had played the proper role of a newcomer and had only been a passive listener at these meetings. But the subject of the single-senator filibuster was one which Clark knew something about.

"There are two claimants to the title of having delivered the longest speech in the history of the Senate," Clark chimed in with a somewhat weak and wavering voice. "The first is Senator Strom Thurmond, a South Carolina Democrat. He gave a 24-hour speech against a civil rights bill in 1957. That's been the longest speech ever recorded in the Senate. But Senator Thurmond's Southern pals helped him out by periodically requesting quorum calls. That enabled Strom to leave the Senate chamber from time to time to answer periodic calls of nature."

"The second claimant is Senator Wayne Morse of Oregon," Clark continued. As Clark's little lecture went on, his voice and confidence gained strength. "Senator Morse gave a 23-hour speech against an offshore oil drilling bill. He strenuously opposed drilling for oil in oceans and bays because he feared it would lead to environmental pollution. But during this marathon speech, lasting almost a full day and night, Senator Morse never once left his desk on the Senate floor. He had somehow solved the major problem of uninterrupted single-senator filibusters. That problem was the need to visit the rest room."

Clark's historical contribution to the discussion was well received by the group of Capitol Hill staffers. There were a few smiles when he mentioned Senator Morse's unique achievements, and no one looked or acted as if Clark's comments were out of place or otherwise inappropriate.

"The type of filibuster that totally shuts down the Senate," Ralph Shepard said, "occurs when a sizable group of senators get together and proceed to talk the bill to death. They refuse to stop debating until the bill is either withdrawn or seriously weakened by amendments. The filibustering senators divide up into teams in order to make the work lighter. Often all they do is hold casual little discussions that are no more trouble to carry on than a pleasant conversation."

"They talk on endlessly," Ralph Shepard said, a tone of vexation beginning to come into his voice. "They know that the bill they are trying to kill will be enacted into law if it ever comes to a vote in the Senate. So they continue to blather to one another, oblivious to the passage of precious legislative time. The usual outcome of a filibuster is that the other senators give up, withdraw the bill in question, and allow the Senate to move on to other business."

The discussion then turned technical in nature. "The filibuster is found in the Senate rules," Ralph Shepard explained, "and the rules state all too clearly: 'No senator shall interrupt another senator in debate without his consent.'"

"You have to interrupt a speaking senator in order to hold a vote on a bill," Shepard concluded. "But under the rules, no senator can be interrupted when speaking on the Senate floor. That's what makes the filibuster possible, and 100 percent legal."

At that moment, a middle-aged woman stood up at the back of the room. She was a legislative aide to Senator Clifford Case of New Jersey. Senator Case was a liberal Republican and a strong supporter of civil rights. The woman was smartly dressed in a woman's dark business suit with a white blouse. She spoke with the smoothness and assurance that comes from longtime service in a staff capacity on Capitol Hill.

"The Senate rules and the filibuster exist," the woman said, "because a majority of senators believe in them. You will not be able to get the civil rights bill passed by changing the Senate rules. The only way to get the bill passed will be to end the debate with a cloture vote, a vote of 2/3 of the senators to stop debate and vote on the bill."

Apparently the woman was just getting warmed up to the topic. "The Founders of this nation did not intend the Senate to be a popular body," she said. "They did not want the Senate responding to the temporary majority that won the most recent election. When writing the United States Constitution, the Founders took care to insulate the Senate from the popular will in two ways."

"The first way," the woman continued, "was to have equal representation in the Senate. There are two senators for each state, regardless of a state's population. The traditional role of the Senate is to protect the states with small populations from the states with large populations. The filibuster fits nicely with this traditional role of the Senate. Senators from small states can band together and filibuster what they consider to be oppressive legislation favored by large states."

"The second way," the woman went on, "was to have senators serve a six-year term, with only 1/3 of the Senate elected every two years. That makes the Senate a continuing body. The Senate cannot be completely changed by the results of just one election. Elections to the Senate are held every two years, but only one out of every three senators is up for reelection at any one time. Two out of three senators are held over without having to undergo judgement by the voters. The Senate thus is designed to respond mainly to long-term shifts in the political winds and is somewhat insulated from the short-term effects of the latest political breeze."

"Senators are very proud of the unique character of the Senate," the woman concluded. "And most senators believe the filibuster is a logical extension of the Senate's role of checking the mad passions of popular democratic government. The Founders of our nation did not create the filibuster, but most senators believe the Founders would view the filibuster with favor. It adds to the image of the Senate as the more thoughtful and prudent of the two houses of Congress."

Clark Schooler took it upon himself to respond to the woman's well-thought out and historically accurate statements. "I agree with everything you just said," Clark stated in a discussional rather than a confrontive tone. "But there is a grim irony here for those concerned with civil rights. The filibuster has not been used very much to protect the small states from the large states. It's mainly been used by Southern senators, some of them from fairly large states such as Virginia and Georgia, to oppress the minority group known as Southern blacks. The filibuster has enabled Southern senators to stop Northern and Western senators from passing national laws designed to protect the civil rights of black persons in the South."

"The situation is almost laughable," Clark said with emphasis. "The filibuster is proclaimed by the Southerners as an instrument for protecting the minority rights of small states. But in reality, the filibuster is mostly used to deny the minority rights of black Americans."

Ralph Shepard directed the discussion to the actual day-to-day mechanics of the filibuster. "There will be 18 Southern senators participating in the blabathon," Shepard pointed out. "They will divide into 3 teams of 6 senators each. Each team will take charge of the filibuster for one entire day. That means each Southern senator gets two days off between assignments on the Senate floor."

"But, even working only every third day, the Southern senators have an easy time of it," Shepard continued. "Only 3 of the 6 senators need to be present in the Senate at any given time. That means each member of that day's team gets half the day off. As for the 3 senators on the Senate floor, only one has to be speaking at any particular moment. The other two help out by asking lengthy, detailed questions. Or they give forth with the spontaneous thoughts that pop into their minds as the first senator is talking."

"It's strange," Ralph Shepard ruminated. "People think of the filibuster as exhausting for the Southerners. But the truth is the Southerners have an easy time of it. In reality, the filibuster is more physically challenging for those trying to end the filibuster than for those conducting it."

"The reason is another Senate rule," Shepard continued. "It's the quorum rule. To be officially in session, the Senate has to have 51 senators present and answering to a quorum call. The Southerners keep their eyes on the clock, and every two hours one of them will suggest the absence of a quorum. That means the civil rights forces have to contact and rush to the Senate floor at least 51 senators."

"The Southerners just love it," Shepard went on, "when the civil rights forces fail to round up a quorum of 51 senators. That means the Senate stops work for the rest of that day. The filibusterers can put their speeches away. They'll use those speeches sometime in the future. But most important is the embarrassment. When the Northern and Western senators fail on a quorum call during a filibuster, and the Senate quits and goes home, civil rights supporters across the country accuse the Senate majority of not really wanting to pass a civil rights bill."

"The regimen required to beat a filibuster is physically and mentally taxing," Ralph Shepard said. He seemed to be warning his fellow Senate aides about very difficult days ahead. "The pro-civil rights senators have to be on Capitol Hill every day and ready to meet a quorum call every two hours. That makes it hard to go back to your home state and spend time giving speeches and mending fences. The liberals and moderates fighting the filibuster, on duty every day, thus become ever more harried and frustrated. The Southerners, on the other hand, work only half a day every third day. They become ever more casual and relaxed."

"The filibuster disrupts the work of the Senate in every way," Ralph Shepard concluded. "The Southern senators will not allow committees to meet while the Senate is in session. The result is that badly needed legislation gets stalled and jammed up in committee. So, as weeks and sometimes months go by, the Senate produces no legislation. The pro-civil rights senators are working very hard, but as the drone and drawl of the filibuster drag on, these senators have nothing to show for their efforts."

Once again the middle-aged woman who worked for Senator Clifford Case of New Jersey stood up and took over the discussion. "There are three ways to end a filibuster," she said with confidence and finality, "but only one of them works."

"The first way," she continued, "is to surrender to the Southerners and amend the bill in such a way that the Southerners no longer object to it. In the past, this has been the usual outcome of virtually all civil rights filibusters. The pro-civil rights senators from the North and West just wear out, give up, and let the Southerners have their way. The result is a defanged civil rights bill, a piece of legislation that does next to nothing to end racial segregation in the Southern United States."

"The second way," she said, "is to try to exhaust the Southerners and make them give up. But that way never works. As Ralph Shepard just pointed out, the filibuster exhausts those trying to stop it, not those who are conducting it. 'Hold the Southerners feet to the fire,' people say. 'Hold round-the-clock sessions to tire the Southerners out.' But it's actually the civil rights forces that end up with their feet in the fire, and the Southerners stay as cool as a cucumber."

"Round-the-clock, 24-hours a day sessions have been tried in the past," the woman noted. "Back in 1960, when Lyndon Johnson was the Senate Democratic leader, he brought in U.S. Army cots so pro-civil rights senators could have a place to nap during all-day and all-night sessions of the Senate. It actually was quite comical. My boss, Senator Case, woke up from a deep sleep. He raced down to the Senate chamber to answer a quorum call he had only dreamed about."

"The third way to end a filibuster," the woman said, "is to garner the 2/3 vote needed to invoke cloture. That's 67 out of 100 senators." Then the woman delivered a stern warning. "The truth is, cloture is rarely applied in the Senate, and it has never been successfully applied to a civil rights bill. In fact, cloture has only been successfully used once. That was in 1962 on a communications satellite bill. This dreary historical record suggests that it will be extremely difficult to mount a successful cloture vote for the civil rights bill that is just now coming to the Senate."

The meeting ended at that point. Clark Schooler left the room in a state of deep political dejection. Things had gone so perfectly for the civil rights bill in the House of Representatives. Clark had been hopeful that the same sort of quick success might be possible in the Senate. But the meeting had made it very clear to Clark that the filibuster was an unusually powerful, and successful, legislative weapon.

The Senate of the United States, Clark thought to himself, was about to face one of the greatest struggles in its history. And, at this point, no one could say with any real certainty how that struggle was going to turn out.

Clark was shaken out of his depression over the filibuster by a telephone call from Bonnie Kanecton. "You're invited to tea and crumpets this Sunday afternoon at 2 P.M.," Bonnie said cheerfully.

"I've never seen a crumpet, let alone eaten one," Clark responded. "What happens when I embarrass you by not knowing how to eat a crumpet?"

"Don't worry," Bonnie said. "I've never seen or eaten a crumpet either. It's actually going to be coffee and coffeecake."

"Dress to kill," Bonnie added. "A *Washington Post* reporter and photographer are coming by the apartment to interview us and get some photographs. They're doing a story for the society section of the paper on young people living in Georgetown. But bring a change of casual clothes and your ice skates. After the newspaper interview, we're all going to run out to Chevy for an early dinner and ice skating."

When the telephone call was over, Clark thought about it for a minute. Bonnie Kanecton had never given Clark a specific opportunity to respond "yes" or "no" to her invitation to come over for coffee on Sunday afternoon. She had assumed, and rightly so, that Clark was free that Sunday and ready and waiting to go along with any social project Bonnie concocted. It was clear that Bonnie Kanecton had spent enough time with Clark Schooler to gauge, all too correctly, that Clark had no other girlfriend at the time but Bonnie.

The appointed day and hour arrived. Clark appeared at Bonnie's apartment dressed in a brand new blue-and-grey tweed business suit. Bonnie and her two roommates also were dressed in their Sunday best, as were their two escorts. The six young people sat with the reporter from the *Washington Post* in the apartment's posh living room and had a long, informal chat about lives and careers in Georgetown. Following the discussion, a *Washington Post* photographer stopped by and posed the young people for a series of photographs.

The reporter from the *Washington Post* turned out to be the assistant editor of the society section. She was a slightly older woman, in her late 30s or early 40s, but was very professional. Like most newspaper people, she had decided the theme, or angle, of her story before ever arriving at Bonnie's apartment. She shaped her discussion with the young people to support that theme, carefully discarding information that disagreed with her theme.

The theme was that Georgetown was a sort of youthful mirror of political life in Washington, D.C. Georgetown was filled with young men and young women working to be the political leaders of the American tomorrow. At the same time, these young men and young women were learning the political arts and social graces that would make some of them the great Washington hosts and hostesses of the future. Georgetown was thus a juvenile micro world that mimicked the larger world of high powered politicians and manipulative political spouses who were the shakers and movers of the nation's capital.

In framing her story, the reporter was delighted to learn that Clark Schooler worked for a U.S. senator. That was exciting! She was not interested that Clark had a Ph.D. in political science and previously worked as a college professor. That was much too stuffy! The reporter was really snowed by the fact that Bonnie Kanecton was on the Board of Directors of the Merrie Maids and Noble Knights of Georgetown. That social connection fit the Washington hostess-in-training theme perfectly.

As the underlying theme of the newspaper article became clear, Clark could see Bonnie Kanecton begin to bristle at being cast in the role of a prospective Washington hostess. "Actually, I'm thinking about going into politics myself," Bonnie said pointedly, "and perhaps even running for office. My future husband can host all the parties."

Two Sunday's later, the newspaper article ran as the lead story on page one of the society section of the *Washington Post*. The headline blared out: "Upwardly Mobile Lads And Lasses Move In And Move Up In George-town." The story was accompanied by a photograph that almost completely filled the top half of the front page of the society section.

The photograph was too much. It was in full color, not just black and white. It showed the comfortable and ornate furnishings of the living room at their very best. A painting was visible on one wall, giving an aura of intellectual class to the setting. The three young men and the three young women were arranged as individual couples, standing and chatting infor-mally with one another with coffee cups in their hands. The coffeecake, with dessert plates of fine china, was visible on a cocktail table. There was a window in the center of the photograph. Out the window could be seen part of the beautiful tree-lined street scape that typified Georgetown.

It was a photograph, Clark later concluded, that produced a melancholy longing in people when they looked at it. You wanted to be in that picture. You wanted your life and circumstances to change so that you could be one of those six young people in Georgetown. You wanted to be, as they were, dressed in stylish clothing, chatting in a luxurious apartment, and enjoying what appeared to be a sophisticated and urbane social life. And, of course, you wanted to be quietly preparing to take your future place among Washing-ton's political and social elite.

The newspaper article and photograph made Clark Schooler something of an overnight celebrity around Senator Kuchel's office. "My wife and I have lived in this town for 12 years," Evan Harris, the Chief of Staff, said to Clark the following Monday morning. "My wife's lifelong dream has been to be mentioned in the society section of the *Washington Post*. You, Clark, are in town for less than a year and get a front page story and a photograph. Rose can't get over it. She says it's just not fair."

It was a lesson to Clark as to why politicians value good press coverage so highly. Almost everyone he worked with or ran into over the next few weeks mentioned to Clark that they had seen his photograph in the newspaper. And every once in a while, a store clerk or a restaurant waitress would look at Clark quizzically and ask: "Wasn't that your picture I saw in the *Washington Post* last week?"

Shortly after the article appeared in the *Washington Post*, Clark invited Bonnie Kanecton to have lunch with him in the Senate dining room in the New Senate Office Building. Clark was struck by the way in which Bonnie seemed to be not the least bit awed or impressed by the occasion. She listened politely while Clark pointed out to her the various high-powered politicians, most of them senators but some of them lobbyists and Cabinet members, who were dining with her that day. Unlike other guests Clark had brought to the Senate dining room, Bonnie made it a point not to look at the great political persons while Clark was identifying and describing them.

The lunch turned out to be what Clark liked to call a "credentials" date. When a college-educated man and a college-educated woman start to get serious about one another, they sooner or later go on a date where they demonstrate their budding intellectuality to each other. Clark often derisively mimicked such dates by saying: "Mumble-mumble-Faulkner; mumble-mumble-Hemingway; mumble-mumble-des Cartes; mumble-mumble-de Tocqueville; and so on." Clark often compared such an intellectual display on the part of a man and woman to the elaborate courtship rituals, such as a male peacock spreading his feathers, that characterize other animals.

It turned out that Bonnie Kanecton did not know very much political science, but she was the font of all knowledge when it came to civil rights law. In addition, she had majored in English literature and classical philosophy at Vassar and could discuss those subjects with great facility. Bonnie proved to Clark that she was intellectually adept. Only in Bonnie's case, Clark was happy to note, the intellectualism was considerably brightened by Bonnie's sharp wit and biting sarcasm.

Toward the end of their meal together, Bonnie looked at Clark and said matter-of-factly: "Clark. Before our dating each other goes any further, I think you owe me an apology."

Clark was simultaneously confused and amused. "Tell me," he said somewhat mockingly, "what did I do?"

"What you did," Bonnie said slowly and carefully, "was fail to remember me."

"Fail to remember you," Clark repeated back, still showing a less than serious attitude toward what Bonnie was trying to tell him. "Believe me, Bonnie, I could never forget a social and intellectual lioness such as you."

"You forgot me soon enough when you met me six years ago at the

CORE demonstration at the Monarch Shopping Center in Baltimore," Bonnie said to Clark. "I wasted two good hours of my life talking to a man I thought was a responsible and capable newspaper reporter. But not one word of what I said there in front of the White Dinner Plate appeared in the next day's *Baltimore Banner*. You done me dirt, Clark. You took me for a ride. And you owe me a super-big apology."

Clark was mortified. He stammered helplessly: "That was you?"

"You bet it was me," Bonnie replied, and then flashed Clark a great big smile. "I could have killed you that Sunday morning when the newspaper came out without a word about our protest. And I really could have killed you when we sat together practically all evening at the Capitol Fellows dinner and you didn't recognize me at all. Only the fact that you're a reasonably good ice skater saved your life."

Clark said softly but with great sincerity: "Bonnie. I apologize."

"Good," Bonnie said with a note of finality. "That settles that. By the way, Clark, I had another reason for bringing this up."

Bonnie hesitated a moment to give added importance to what she was going to say. She concluded:

"I don't want you to think I spend all of my spare time at the Chevy Chase Club."

It took Clark Schooler almost two weeks to get used to the idea that Bonnie Kanecton, the Georgetown socialite, had led civil rights demonstrations for CORE long before such an activity was at all socially fashionable.

In his capacity as a legislative aide to Senator Thomas H. Kuchel of California, Clark Schooler enjoyed the privilege of the Senate floor. That meant that Clark could go on the Senate floor to meet with Senator Kuchel while the Senate was in session. Senator Kuchel liked to save precious time by going over routine paperwork with Clark while simultaneously listening to the debate in the Senate.

Fortunately for Clark, he could go on the Senate floor even when he did not have work to do with Senator Kuchel. That Senate aides could do this was officially acknowledged by the fact that chairs and sofas had been placed along the walls of the Senate chamber for aides to sit on and witness the proceedings. When interesting action was scheduled on the Senate floor, Clark Schooler made it a point to go to the Senate, find himself a comfy place to sit, and watch the legislative drama in the upper house of Congress unfold.

Thus Clark was present in the Senate chamber on the first day the Senate took up the civil rights bill. Mike Mansfield of Montana, the Democratic leader in the Senate, was patiently waiting at his desk on the Senate floor. The ornate door at the head of the center aisle of the Senate opened.

Through the door and down the center aisle came a clerk from the United States House of Representatives. The clerk was carrying the bundle of printed paper that was the actual civil rights bill, the same bill that earlier had passed in the House by a comfortable majority.

If the situation had been ordinary, the House clerk would have quietly handed the bill to the Senate clerk, who would have routinely routed the bill to the Senate Judiciary Committee. But the situation was not ordinary. Senator Mansfield was preparing to step outside the bounds of normal Senate procedure.

"I request that House Bill 7152 be read the first time," Mansfield said matter-of-factly. The Senate clerk read the name and number of the bill. Then Mansfield said: "I object to the second reading of the bill today." [61]

With this little piece of arcane parliamentary procedure, Democratic Leader Mansfield stopped the civil rights bill from being forwarded to the Senate Judiciary Committee. In effect, the Democratic leader took the bill under his own control. Mansfield then made a motion that the bill be brought directly up for debate on the Senate floor. Senator Mansfield, using the somewhat stilted formal language of the Senate, carefully explained his procedural motion to his Senate colleagues:

"The Senate leadership proposes to the Senate that this measure be placed on the calendar without referral to committee, and that the Senate as a body proceed immediately to its consideration."

Senators work hard at always being polite and civil with one another. In fact, civility is one of the most highly admired norms of Senate behavior. In justifying these unusual procedures to the Senate, Mike Mansfield never mentioned the name of the Senate Judiciary Committee or its chair, Senator James Oliver Eastland of Mississippi. Mansfield simply said:

"The procedures which the leadership is following are not the Senate's usual procedures. However, the reasons for these unusual procedures are too well-known to require elaboration." [62]

But Democratic Leader Mansfield's sensitive treatment of the Senate Judiciary Committee and Senator Eastland was not copied by the Senate's more liberal supporters of civil rights. These senators made it crystal clear why the civil rights bill could not be allowed to go anywhere near the Senate Judiciary Committee.

"Over 121 consecutive civil rights bills died in the Senate Judiciary Committee from 1953 to 1963," said Hubert H. Humphrey of Minnesota, the Democratic whip in the Senate.[63] Then Senator Kenneth Keating, a Republican from New York, stated his opinion: "Giving the bill to Senator Eastland will result in a bore-athon. The senator from Mississippi has decided that the filibuster rules of the Senate also apply to his committee.

There will be lots of talk, but no bill will ever come back to the Senate. That's why the Judiciary Committee is the traditional graveyard of civil rights legislation." [64]

And criticism of Senator Eastland and the Judiciary Committee came from off the Senate floor as well. Clarence Mitchell, of the NAACP, made public a telegram he sent on the subject. The telegram read:

"Sending the civil rights bill to the Senate Judiciary Committee will be regarded as betrayal. If there is one thing that strains the faith of citizens, it is a persistent effort to give an aura of respectability to committee hearings on civil rights run by Senator Eastland. To the man in the street, such hearings are the equivalent of the stacked deck, the hanging judge, and the executioner who enjoys his work." [65]

Clark Schooler, of course, did not need to be told what would happen to the House-passed civil rights bill if it went to the Senate Judiciary Committee. Clark, after all, had begun his career as a Washington newspaper reporter the previous summer by witnessing the Judiciary Committee hearings on the Senate version of the civil rights bill. Clark had watched Senator Eastland and his Southern colleagues condemn the bill verbally for a few weeks and then summarily kill it.

With the civil rights bill now the first order of business before the Senate, Democratic Leader Mansfield addressed his fellow senators. He rose from his desk on the Democratic side of the front row of desks in the Senate. Mansfield stepped slowly into the well of the Senate, then he turned and faced his colleagues.

Clark Schooler was impressed with Mike Mansfield's ability to choose meaningful and moving words when speaking to the Senate. Clark realized that some of Mansfield's comments were probably scripted by the senator's aides, men and women like Clark himself. But much of the time Mansfield seemed to be speaking without notes and saying what were genuinely heartfelt sentiments.

"Let me say at the outset," Mansfield began, "that I should have preferred that the civil rights issue be resolved before my time as a senator. This senator from Montana has no lust for conflict in connection with this matter. It is an issue which divides deeply. But the time is now. The crossroads for civil rights in the United States of America is here in the Senate."

Senator Mansfield then pledged to his colleagues that he would not try to use obscure legislative rules or sharp parliamentary tricks to head off the anticipated filibuster of the civil rights bill. He referred to himself in the third person as he said:

"Your Democratic leader has no suave parliamentary tactics by which to bring this legislation to a swift vote. Even if there were parliamentary tricks or tactics, the Democratic leader would not be inclined to employ them. I can think of nothing better designed to bring this institution into public disrepute and derision than a test of this profound and tragic issue by an exercise in parliamentary fireworks."

Clark Schooler listened with rapt attention as Senator Mansfield concluded his oration by urging the Southerners to stop hiding behind the Senate rule book and to forthrightly deal with civil rights as an issue. Mansfield concluded:

"For the truth is that we will not find in the Senate Rule Book even the semblance of an answer to the burning questions which now confront the nation and, hence, this Senate. We senators would be well advised to search, not in the Senate Rule Book, but in the Golden Rule, for the semblance of an adequate answer!" [66]

Under ordinary conditions in the United States Senate, legislation is sent to the relevant committee and marked up by that committee before coming to the Senate floor. Under those circumstances, the chairperson of the relevant Senate committee becomes the floor leader for the bill when it is debated in the Senate. It is the floor leader's job to arrange for the presentation of a strong case for the bill during the Senate debate and to round up the votes needed to get the bill passed.

In the case of the civil rights bill, it was well-known that Senate Democratic Leader Mike Mansfield was not going to allow the bill to go to the Senate Judiciary Committee. As a result, there was no floor leader for the bill when Mansfield moved to place the bill directly on the Senate calendar.

That was just as well, of course. Imagine it, Clark Schooler thought to himself. James Oliver Eastland of Mississippi, the chair of the Senate Judiciary Committee and an ardent foe of civil rights, serving as the floor leader for the civil rights bill. Clarence Mitchell and Joseph Rauh of the Leadership Conference would have gone apoplectic at just the thought of such a development.

But the civil rights bill needed a floor leader, and Democratic Leader Mansfield did not want to take on the job himself. As the titular leader of all the Democrats in the Senate, Mansfield wanted to remain above the civil rights debate. That was so that, if things went a certain way, Mansfield could negotiate a compromise between the Southerners and the civil rights forces to amicably end the filibuster. Such a compromise would, of course, involve removing some of the stronger provisions from the bill, such as the U.S. Government funds cut-off or the equal employment opportunity provision.

Mike Mansfield therefore named Hubert Humphrey, the Democratic whip in the Senate, the Democratic floor leader for the civil rights bill. To help secure vitally needed Republican votes for the bill, Senator Thomas H. Kuchel of California was named the Republican floor leader.

Suddenly, Clark Schooler found himself to be a legislative aide to the man, Senator Kuchel, who was mainly responsible for rounding up the Republican votes needed to cloture the civil rights bill. Now added to Clark's working day were an intense round of strategy meetings to determine the best way to accomplish what often appeared to be an impossible task. That was to get 67 out of 100 senators to vote to end a filibuster.

Clark was particularly struck by the bipartisan nature of the task. He was working with Democratic staff as intensely as with Republican staff to try to get the job done. Party lines blurred almost completely as passing the civil rights bill, rather than advancing the Republican cause, became Clark Schooler's main professional purpose in life.

The filibuster had been going on for about a month when, on Saturday, April 4, 1964, Clark was awakened by an early morning telephone call.

"Get over to the Capitol right away," said Ralph Shepard from Senator Humphrey's office. "There's a real possibility we're not going to get a quorum on the floor for today's session of the Senate. I'm calling all the missing Democratic senators. Please come over and help me by calling some of the missing Republicans."

Clark got up, dressed, ate a hurried breakfast of cereal and toast, and raced over to his office. He sat down at his telephone with a list of the missing Republicans and their home telephone numbers. The news was all bad. Republican senators who had promised to be on the Senate floor that morning had played hookey and gone back to their home states to "meet with the voters."

Senator Wallace Bennett, a Republican from Utah, had run away to Salt Lake City to make a politically obligatory appearance at the annual conference of the Church of Latter Day Saints, the Mormon Church. Given the fact that the Mormon Church was the dominant religion in Utah, and that the state had been founded as a haven for Mormons, Clark understood perfectly why Senator Bennett had left town. But a collateral result was difficulty making quorum that morning.

It was the same story with Republican Senator Roman Hruska of Nebraska. How could he possibly pass up Founders' Day ceremonies in Omaha celebrating the birth of the Republican Party? But there went another badly needed body to meet the quorum call.

Ralph Shepard was not having any more luck with truant Democrats. Senator Henry Jackson had flown the coop to dedicate a new Forest Service laboratory in Washington state. Senator Clinton Anderson, from New Mexico, was in Albuquerque holding a pow-wow with some of the state's

Pueblo Indian tribes.

And thus it was. Every senator who should have been in Washington that morning to help the civil rights forces had a good excuse as to why he or she was out of town. "Campaigning for reelection." "Meeting with a key lobby group back home." One exasperated Senate aide quietly complained to the press: "When the siren song of politics calls, senators just can't resist." [67]

There was a grim hour on the Senate floor during which the Southerners stood quietly at their desks, waiting to see if the civil rights senators could muster a quorum. But it was no use. All the telephoning by Senate aides was simply revealing that all the needed senators had skipped out of town that day.

Hubert Humphrey, the Democratic floor leader for the civil rights bill, threw in the towel. He called a press conference. Humphrey gathered together Clark Schooler, Ralph Shepard, and all the Senate aides who had feverishly made telephone calls that morning. Humphrey invited them to stand behind him to form the requisite human background for the press conference.

Senator Humphrey stood in front of the television cameras, the microphones, and the print reporters with their paper note pads at the ready. He intentionally projected a look of total exasperation. Slowly and systematically, Humphrey read aloud the names of the absent civil rights senators and their excuses for not being in Washington that morning.[68] He then announced that the Senate would not be going into session that day. The press quickly nicknamed the event the Saturday debacle.

Democratic Leader Mike Mansfield made the same announcement on the Senate floor . There would be no meeting of the Senate that day. The Southern senators smiled and laughed, saved their speeches for another time, and let everyone know they had scored a major victory. Senator Mansfield agreed with them. He labeled the lack of a quorum "a sham and an indignity upon this great legislative institution." [69] Senator Humphrey seconded the thought. "The only way we can lose the civil rights fight," Humphrey asserted, "is not to have a quorum when we need it." [70]

Clark Schooler was feeling badly about the Saturday debacle. The story played very big in the next day's Sunday newspapers. And there were a number of newspaper editorials and television commentaries that were highly critical of the civil rights forces in the Senate.

"Don't feel so bad," Evan Harris, Senator Kuchel's chief of staff, said to Clark a few days later. "Whip counts taken by Humphrey and Kuchel themselves told us the previous Thursday that we weren't going to make quorum. For a while, Hubert and Tom debated canceling the Saturday session of the Senate. But it was decided to make an example of the errant civil rights senators instead. We knew there would be adverse press reports. We decided to let those press reports shape up our wandering senators so there would be no failed quorum calls in the future."

"You mean," Clark said, "that was a staged failure."

"Yes, it was," Evan Harris said with a smile. "Best of all, the press covered it exactly the way we wanted them to cover it. The guys who didn't show up for the quorum call really got burned." [71]

Clark noticed over the next weeks and months that the staged failure strategy worked perfectly. Senators Humphrey and Kuchel never again had a problem mustering a quorum during the Southern filibuster of the civil rights bill.

On a beautiful Wednesday afternoon later in April, Clark Schooler found himself at D.C. Stadium, the home field of Washington's "baseball" Senators. President Lyndon Johnson had come out to this "Opening Day" game with a group of his leading Cabinet members. As tradition demanded, the president threw out the "first ball" of the 1964 major league professional baseball season.

On hand to witness this event were a considerable number of "real" U.S. senators. They were seated throughout the stadium, watching Lyndon Johnson's athletic antics and simultaneously enjoying the baseball game.

The baseball Senators were the butt of many jokes, mainly because of their uncanny ability over the years to lose baseball games. One joke mixed George Washington's reputation with that of his namesake city's baseball team. The joke went: "Washington: First in the hearts of his countrymen. Last in the American League."

True to form, by the end of the third inning, the baseball Senators were well on their way to losing their first game of the 1964 season. Suddenly, over the public address system at D.C. Stadium, an urgent message blared out: "Attention, please, there has been a quorum call in the United States Senate. All U.S. senators are requested to return to the Senate chamber immediately." [72]

Clark sprang into action. Senators began getting up from their seats and walking toward the back of the stadium. Clark and a number of other Senate aides had the job of herding the senators to one particular entrance to the stadium. At that entrance, a group of shiny black limousines waited to whisk the senators down East Capitol Street to the Capitol building.

Clark Schooler had worked as a Senate staffer for a long enough time that almost all of the senators recognized him as a Senate aide and were willing to follow his directions. Once in their limousines, the senators had a police motorcycle escort, with sirens blaring and lights flashing, to clear the way for them on their mad dash to the Senate chamber.

All the time Clark was rounding up senators and helping to guide them to their limousines, Clark could hear the sound of flashbulbs popping and television cameras grinding. The press had been tipped that there was going to be lots of live action to photograph and film that afternoon.

Among the senators who left the baseball game to meet the quorum call were the top leaders of the Senate. Democratic Leader Mike Mansfield, Democratic Whip Hubert Humphrey, and Republican Leader Everett Dirksen all got out of their seats to go and do their quorumly duties. But one senator did not move a muscle. That was Democrat Richard Russell of Georgia, the leader of the filibustering Southerners in the Senate.

It was a wonderful day for Clark. He watched with pride as, loaded with their senatorial cargo, the shiny limousines with their police escort disappeared up the street. Then Clark and a group of the other Senate aides went back into D.C. Stadium and watched the rest of the baseball game. Hopes for a late-innings rally and a Washington Senators victory did not materialize, however.

The "Opening Day" for the baseball Senators was a big success for the civil rights forces. A quorum of 51 senators was assembled within less than 20 minutes of the announcement going out over the public address system at D.C. Stadium. The civil rights forces had been well prepared, with the limousines and police motorcycles ready to go at the very minute they were needed.

And best of all was the press coverage, both written and visual. Print stories oozed with praise for the efficiency of the civil rights forces. There were excellent and exciting photographs of well-known Senate leaders getting up and leaving the stadium. And tremendous television footage of limousines and motorcycles, delivering U.S. senators for a quorum call, zooming down East Capitol Street.

It was all great publicity for the civil rights forces. But it did nothing to stop the Southern filibuster. Suddenly it was early May of 1964. The filibuster had been going on for two solid months. And there was no sign whatsoever that the Southerners would ever give in and let the Senate majority pass a civil rights bill.

In The Interim

Procedures in the U.S. Senate have changed very little in the past 40 years. Senators continue to be very independent in their statements and their actions. Senators still can speak on the Senate floor anytime they want to, simply by rising at their desks and waiting to be recognized in turn. The result is that the Senate leadership has very little direct control over what senators say and how senators vote. Senate leaders, in both the Democratic and Republican parties, have to lead by persuading rather than by issuing orders or making threats.

The situation contrasts strongly with the House of Representatives. Over on the House side of the Capitol, debate is limited and carefully controlled. In the House, party leaders have some leverage to control the statements and votes of House members.

There has been one major change in the Senate Rules. In the early 1970s, the number of votes required to invoke cloture was reduced from a 2/3 majority (67 or more votes) to a 3/5 majority (60 or more votes). This has made it somewhat easier to stop a filibuster with a cloture vote.

CHAPTER 11

CAMPAIGNS AND ELECTIONS:
GEORGE WALLACE FOR PRESIDENT

By early May of 1964, the filibuster of the civil rights bill had degenerated into a stalemate. As the Southerners talked on and on, the Senate floor became a place of monumental inaction and stupefying boredom. The attention of the nation, and the national press, slowly began to turn elsewhere.

So Clark Schooler was not surprised one morning when he heard a voice say to him: "Get up to Baltimore and get up there fast! George Wallace is getting hotter than a firecracker on the Fourth of July."

President Lyndon Johnson looked directly into Clark Schooler's eyes as he gave him that order. The two men were in the Oval Office at the White House. Johnson was sitting behind his large wooden office desk. Clark was seated on a chair in front of the desk.

"Wallace almost beat me in Wisconsin and Indiana," Lyndon Johnson roared on. "Now he's running for president in Maryland and the polls show he just might win there. It's up to you, Clark Schooler, to stop George Wallace in Maryland and save the civil rights bill."

At that moment, Clark turned in his chair to watch the three television sets that lined one side of the Oval Office. Each set was tuned to one of the three major TV networks. Alabama Governor George Wallace was pictured on all three TV screens. It was the same George Wallace who had threatened to "bar the school house door" rather than racially integrate the University of Alabama.[73]

Governor Wallace was standing behind a portable wooden podium set up on the front steps of the Maryland state capitol in Annapolis, Maryland. Wallace was announcing his candidacy in the upcoming Democratic presidential primary in Maryland. He was challenging President Johnson, the

Democratic incumbent. Wallace shook his fist in the air as he spoke.

"I stand here in the great Border State of Maryland," Wallace orated. "I speak for every white Marylander who believes in the right to associate with whomever you please. I call on every white Marylander to join me in opposing President Johnson's civil rights bill. I call on white Marylanders to vote for George Wallace for president and send Lyndon Johnson a message he'll never forget." [74]

"And," Wallace added with a grin on his face, "I don't care if they do send Clark Schooler up to Baltimore to help out. I'm still going to win Maryland!"

At that moment, Clark Schooler awoke with a start. He was not in the Oval Office with President Johnson. He was alone in his own bed in his house on Sixth Street Southeast on Capitol Hill. It had all been a dream.

But George Wallace running for president was not a dream. Early in 1964, the Alabama governor had announced his candidacy for the Democratic nomination for president of the United States. Wallace said he would run against President Johnson and campaign on the issue of all-out opposition to racial integration.

Clark Schooler knew George Wallace from having reported on Wallace's famous attempt to prevent racial desegregation at the University of Alabama. Wallace had been forced to back down, and the university had been integrated by a U.S. court order. But Wallace had emerged from the confrontation as the hero of Southern segregation. He had successfully turned himself into a national symbol of opposition to black civil rights.

Wallace's strategy was to try to win presidential primary elections outside the old South. He therefore filed in the Democratic presidential primaries in Wisconsin, Indiana, and Maryland.

What would happen if Wallace won one of those three primaries? Civil rights leaders feared that their plans for beating the filibuster would be seriously damaged. Word leaked out of the White House that President Johnson himself told close associates that a Wallace victory would "stiffen the Southerners and their will to keep on fighting the civil rights bill." [75]

Lyndon Johnson thought that, after a Wallace primary victory or two, the pro-civil rights forces in the Senate might begin to fall apart.

President Johnson refused to permit open season on his presidential administration by campaigning against George Wallace himself. Johnson quickly recruited "favorite son" candidates to run in his place in each of the three states. In Wisconsin, the Johnson stand-in was Democratic Governor John W. Reynolds. In Indiana, Johnson was replaced on the ballot by Democratic Governor Matthew Welsh. In Maryland, the man chosen to run in President Johnson's stead was Democratic U.S. Senator Daniel Brewster.

Things had gone well enough for the Johnson forces in Wisconsin. Governor Reynolds won the primary and guaranteed all of Wisconsin's delegate votes at the upcoming Democratic National Convention for President Johnson. But George Wallace polled more than 264,000 votes in Wisconsin, many more than the news media had predicted he would get in a Northern state. Suddenly George Wallace was winning the "expectations game." Wallace had lost the primary, but he did better than expected. In the eyes of the press, that made him a "winner." Clark Schooler read a typical report in *Time* magazine:

"The real issue in the primary was civil rights. Wallace had entered the Wisconsin primary to demonstrate that many Northern, as well as Southern, whites are unhappy about current civil rights trends. And he demonstrated that dramatically." [76]

The outcome was much the same in Indiana. Governor Welsh defeated George Wallace by a margin of more than two-to-one, but the newspaper and television commentators focused all their attention on the 170,146 votes that George Wallace polled. Skillfully exploiting the advantage created by the news media's playing of the expectations game, Wallace claimed his second place finish in Indiana was a victory.

"Our campaign for states' rights won," Wallace told the press on primary night in Indiana. "We began by shaking the eyeteeth of all those Northern liberals in Wisconsin. The noises you hear tonight are the eyeteeth falling out of all the Northern liberals in Indiana." [77]

Suddenly, national press attention shifted to Maryland's Democratic presidential primary scheduled for mid-May of 1964. It would be George Wallace's last chance to try to win a presidential primary held in the North or a Border State.

And the civil rights forces were genuinely frightened that Wallace just might win Maryland. Here was a state that had not seceded from the Union during the Civil War, but it was a former slave state and located south of the Mason-Dixon line, the traditional boundary between Northern freedom and Southern slavery. George Wallace had polled more than 30 percent of the vote in Wisconsin and Indiana, both of them Northern states that were steadfastly loyal to the Union during the Civil War. It was not inconceivable that Wallace could poll 50 percent or more in a former slave state such as Maryland.

Clark Schooler's unnerving dream about George Wallace and Lyndon Johnson had been accurate in one respect. He had been asked to go up to Baltimore and help out in the campaign to defeat George Wallace in Maryland. Only the order had not come directly from President Johnson. It was Evan Harris, Senator Kuchel's chief of staff, who sat Clark down and told him the best thing he could do for the civil rights bill was to go back to his home state and work against Wallace.

"With the Senate tied in knots by the filibuster," Evan Harris explained, "we can do without you here in Washington for two weeks or so. Don't ask me, Clark, how the White House found out you know a lot about Maryland politics? But they did find out. They've been after me all week to get you up there as quickly as possible. Please leave for Baltimore first thing tomorrow morning. The rest of the staff can keep up with the legislative mail while you're gone."

Clark shook off his dream about President Johnson and Governor Wallace and ate breakfast. He grabbed his bags, which he had packed the night before, and said a temporary goodbye to his two house mates, Greg Netherton and Carl Brimmer. He got into his 1951 Ford hardtop convertible and pointed the hood ornament toward Baltimore.

Less than an hour later, Clark and his 1951 Ford were rolling down Redwood Street in downtown Baltimore. Clark found a place to park his car close to the Emerson Hotel. U.S. Senator Daniel Brewster placed the headquarters for his 1964 campaign against Alabama Governor George Wallace in a suite of rooms at the Emerson.

"Brewster for President," blared the sign above the marquee at the Emerson Hotel. But no one was fooled. Everyone knew that a vote for "Brewster for President" was in reality a vote for "Lyndon Johnson for President."

But Clark did not immediately go into the Emerson Hotel. Instead, he stepped into Bickford's, a small and inexpensive restaurant across the street from the Emerson.

Bickford's was only a block or so from Baltimore City Hall and just a few blocks from the Maryland court building and the U.S. court building. Bickford's thus was the unofficial hangout of Democratic politicians in Baltimore city. Because so many important decisions in Maryland politics were made over a chicken salad sandwich in a booth at Bickford's, the place was nicknamed "10 Downing Street," the address of the residence of the British prime minister in London.

Clark had arranged to meet with Albert Kurdle, a childhood friend. Al Kurdle had lived over the back fence from Clark Schooler when the two of them were growing up in Baltimore. Clark always referred to Albert as "the friend of my youth." The two boys had struggled through puberty together, often going on double dates and, at different times of course, often dating the same girls.

Al Kurdle's family owned a major share of Quality Meats, a well-known local meat packing plant in Baltimore. It was traditional that young scions in the Kurdle family work their way up in the business before assuming executive positions in middle age. Al Kurdle thus was working at Quality Meats as a route salesman, calling and visiting store owners and store managers and taking their orders for a wide range of Quality meat products. Clark Schooler thus often kidded Albert by calling him a "hot dog salesman."

But there was a serious side to Albert Kurdle's profession that made him unusually valuable to Clark. Al Kurdle had a job in which he met the public and traveled around the city of Baltimore. Al Kurdle always knew the latest jokes that were being told. He also knew "the word on the street" about the latest goings-on in Maryland politics.

And Albert was not just sociable with white people. He had a real knack for talking to and gaining the friendship of black people. In the early 1960s, it was fashionable for youthful whites to go out dancing and listen to jazz music at the various African-American night clubs in Baltimore. But there was a grossly unfair double standard in effect. Young white couples could go on a date to a black night club and be properly, if not warmly, received. But black couples were not permitted to go to white night clubs. Black couples would be turned away firmly, and sometimes impolitely, at the outside doorway to a white night club.

Clark Schooler and Albert Kurdle often went to black night clubs when on a double date. Young white women found it exciting, almost sort of dangerous, to go to a black night club in Baltimore in the early 1960s. Adding to the thrill was the almost certain fact that the parents of the young white women would strongly disapprove of such behavior if the parents ever found out about it.

It was while at black night clubs that Clark Schooler discovered he was almost jealous of Al Kurdle's ability to get along with black people. Albert always seemed to know exactly what to say and how to say it. It appeared to Clark that, with no more than an "I'm hip" here and an "I'm cool, daddy" there, Al Kurdle could wipe away the subtle, unpleasant tension that often characterized relationships between white people and black people.

As Clark had arranged to do, he met Albert in Bickford's. The two young men sat down in a booth and ordered an early lunch. Clark began the conversation. "Can you believe," Clark said, "that the poor voters of Maryland are going to have to suffer through a Democratic presidential primary involving George Wallace and his fierce anti-black rhetoric?"

"Too bad," Albert replied. "It's further proof that there are infinite varieties of the human experience."

The "infinite varieties" saying was one that Clark had heard from Albert many times before. Clark had no idea where his friend had gotten it.

But whenever Clark told Albert a sad story in which something really bad happened to someone, Albert would inevitably turn to his "infinite varieties of the human experience" line.

"Human beings have lived every conceivable type of life and existed under every conceivable circumstance," Al Kurdle told Clark. "Now it's our turn to undergo that peculiar variety of the human experience known as 'George Wallace for President.'"

Clark decided to get right down to business. He asked: "What's the word on Wallace and Brewster?"

"The word is that Wallace will probably win the primary," Al Kurdle said matter-of-factly. "The thinking starts with the Eastern Shore of Maryland, on the east side of the Chesapeake Bay, and with Southern Maryland, south of Baltimore city. Those are rural farming areas which, prior to the Civil War, had large numbers of plantations and large numbers of black slaves to work those plantations. That's going to be Wallace country for sure."

Clark decided to launch a counter argument. "But those votes will be offset by Western Maryland," Clark said. "That's Appalachian mountain country up there. They never had any plantations or very many slaves. Senator Brewster should win up there. A big Brewster vote in Western Maryland will offset the Wallace vote on the Eastern Shore and in Southern Maryland."

"Good thinking," Albert replied. "But the real problem for Senator Brewster is going to be Baltimore city. The Democratic political bosses are all officially supporting Brewster. But in private, those same bosses are telling everyone that the white working-class voters of Baltimore are going to vote for Wallace. There's a real possibility that, this time out, the Democratic faithful in Baltimore are not going to follow the instructions of their Democratic leaders."

Clark pondered that disturbing thought for a moment. "We call it white backlash," Clark said. "In the central city, it's the white working class that works and lives close to the black neighborhoods. These lower middle-class white voters think black gains are going to cost them personally. Above all, they are frightened that equal employment opportunity will take away their jobs and give those jobs to black workers. George Wallace proved particularly adept at winning white backlash votes in Wisconsin and Indiana."

Depressed over the thought of Baltimore city's white voters going for Wallace, Clark decided to change the subject. He asked Albert: "What's the situation out in the suburbs?"

"Nobody talks about them very much," Albert said. "I think most people assume that the suburbs are filled with white people and therefore

Wallace will do reasonably well out there. That's why the word is that Wallace will win this election. Everywhere you go in Baltimore city, everyone is saying that Wallace has it won!"

Clark's lunch with Al Kurdle had been both disturbing and valuable. No wonder, Clark thought, that Lyndon Johnson was recruiting anyone who knew anything about Maryland politics to go to the aid of Senator Brewster. The situation was looking dire for Brewster. That meant the situation was looking dire for Lyndon Johnson. And for the civil rights bill.

Once inside the Emerson Hotel, Clark found his way to the set of meeting rooms that had been turned into "Brewster For President" headquarters. The people there were expecting Clark. Early that afternoon, Clark was invited to attend a campaign staff meeting presided over by Senator Daniel Brewster himself. The purpose of the meeting was to whip up the staff for a major "Brewster for President" rally that was to be held that evening in Baltimore city.

Danny Brewster, as he was called by those who knew him well, was the first speaker at the meeting. He began his talk by taking his listeners into his confidence.

"Let's be honest about it," Brewster said. "I was not Lyndon Johnson's first choice to be his stand-in candidate to run against George Wallace here in Maryland. President Johnson's first choice was my good friend, J. Millard Tawes, the Democratic governor of Maryland."

"Tawes is probably the most popular and most successful Democrat in Maryland politics," Brewster went on, "but Tawes turned the president down. Turned him down flat. And then Tawes let it be known that he didn't think that maybe Wallace could be beaten in Maryland. 'Beating Wallace is not a cinch,' Tawes said. 'And it's not our fight,' Tawes said. Tawes thought Lyndon Johnson should run against Wallace himself and not make some poor Maryland politician take the heat in Johnson's behalf."

"But I saw that the eyes of the nation were on Maryland," Brewster said, his voice gaining a tone of commitment and enthusiasm. "I saw that there had to be a political leader who would step forward to save Maryland from the disgrace of being the only state outside the secessionist South to give its convention delegate votes to George Wallace. I knew that there had to be a man from Maryland who would have the courage to stand up and turn back Wallace in his final drive for votes in the North."

"When no one else would do it," Brewster said, "I decided to do it. Because the job of beating George Wallace in Maryland is a job that must be done." [78]

It was a great pep talk. Brewster and his staff set out for that evening's "Brewster for President" rally with spirits high and all flags flying.

Clark Schooler had watched, with a political scientist's trained eye, the swift development of Daniel Brewster's political career in Maryland. Danny grew up in Baltimore County. That was the populous county to the north of Baltimore city that contained some of Baltimore's most upwardly mobile suburbs.

Danny Brewster was a member of the so-called horsey set, a group of people with large homes with a stable for the family horses. For amusement, these people often ran steeplechase races, galloping over the countryside on horseback and jumping wooden fences and low stone walls. Because of the resemblance of these horse races to English fox hunting, Danny Brewster's part of Baltimore County often was referred to as "Hunt Country."

In the manner of English nobility, Danny Brewster was "born" to a career as a Maryland politician. Due to his family's prominence in Baltimore County affairs, Brewster was elected to the Maryland state legislature in his late twenties. It was Clark Schooler's opinion that Danny Brewster had been sent to the state legislature the way other people's children were sent to summer camp. Before anyone knew it, Danny Brewster had been elected to the U.S. House of Representatives and, shortly thereafter, to the United States Senate. To most observers, Clark included, Danny Brewster was the "Golden Boy" of Democratic politics in Maryland.

The Fifth Regiment Armory was a favorite location for Democratic Party political rallies in Baltimore city. Located just to the north of downtown Baltimore off Howard Street, the building could hold the large crowds of people that turned out for Democratic rallies in such a Democratic city. More important, the Fifth Regiment Armory was reasonably handy to the urban, white, working-class neighborhoods that housed the most loyal members of Baltimore's Democratic Party political machines.

Clark Schooler arrived at the Fifth Regiment Armory early for the "Brewster for President" rally. He watched the individual attendees as they poured into the building and took their seats. Clark noticed two things that disturbed him. The first was that the crowd was composed almost entirely of white people. A number of African-Americans had come to show their support for Brewster, but they were few and far between. Given the large African-American population in Baltimore city, and given George Wallace's pro-segregation viewpoint, Clark thought that many more black people should have shown up at the rally.

The second thing that disturbed Clark was that many of the people were bringing signs to wave at the rally but were keeping what was painted on the signs hidden from view. In some cases the text of the sign was covered with brown paper, which could be ripped off once the rally began. In other cases, the entire sign was hidden in a large paper bag with just the handle sticking out.

The rally began with a band playing and the crowd singing the Star Spangled Banner. The words to the national anthem had been written in Baltimore, by Francis Scott Key, during the shelling of Fort McHenry in the War of 1812. Clark was extra emotional about the Star Spangled Banner just because of its direct relationship to his hometown.

The Fifth Regiment Armory contained a raised stage from which speakers could address the audience. A microphone and a podium were placed at the center of the stage. A bank of footlights illuminated the speakers as they came on to the stage to participate in the ceremonies.

The opening speaker at the rally was U.S. Senator William Proxmire of Wisconsin, a prominent liberal in the Senate and a strong supporter of civil rights. Proxmire was one of a number of U.S. senators who had agreed to come over to Maryland and help draw crowds to "Brewster For President" rallies. Clark was looking forward to hearing what Senator Proxmire would have to say.

The senator from Wisconsin was about five minutes into his speech when a man in the audience stood up on his chair and yelled "Cadillac pink!" That particular slur implied that Senator Proxmire, and by implication Senator Brewster, was a wealthy Communist sympathizer. Opponents of racial integration often accused strong supporters of civil rights of being Communist revolutionaries in disguise.

Whether it was purposefully intended or not, the words "Cadillac Pink" set off a round of boos and catcalls from the audience. Another man jumped up on his chair and shouted "Race-mixing socialist!" Suddenly, almost the entire audience was on its feet, raising a ruckus and screaming racial epithets at Senator Proxmire.

And then the signs came out. Brown paper coverings were ripped away. Signs were pulled out of their paper bags. Some of the signs were "Wallace For President" banners. Others were homemade affairs emblazoned with the famous racist slogan: "Two-Four-Six-Eight; We Ain't Going To Integrate!" One sign close to Clark read: "Senator Proxmire: Maryland Does Not Want Or Need Advice From Wisconsin."

A member of Senator Brewster's campaign staff came to Clark Schooler and asked him to help get the few African-American attendees safely out of the rally. The almost all-white audience had not turned on the few blacks in its midst, at least not yet. Some of the more militant blacks did not want to leave, but the Brewster staffers prevailed on them "to get out while the getting was good." The Brewster forces had completely lost control of the rally and did not know what was going to happen next.

One section of the audience seemed to be particularly noisy and yelling very offensive racial slurs. Clark later learned that this was an official George Wallace "jeering squad." These people made it a point to go to Brewster rallies, sit together in one section, and jeer rather than cheer for Danny Brewster. On this particular night, however, the entire hall seemed to have turned into a pro-Wallace jeering squad.

Senator Proxmire of Wisconsin was absolutely dwarfed by the pro-Wallace roar. His efforts to quiet the audience proved completely futile. He slowly drifted off the stage.

By this time, Clark Schooler was standing out of sight of the audience at the left side of the stage. He was watching in amazement. He had never in his life heard or felt the deep hatred that was coming across the footlights from this particular group of people.

Senator Brewster also was standing at the left side of the stage. He was furious at what was happening. Over the din, he shouted to a group of his campaign advisers standing near by:

"What's happened to my popularity? Just two years ago, in 1962, I was elected to the U.S. Senate by one of the largest vote margins in Maryland political history. Where has all that support gone?"

Brewster was bewildered as well as angry. "I've never been booed or razzed before in my entire political career," he raged. "Until tonight, people have always treated me with respect." [79]

Clark Schooler shouted back:

"This is a racial fight. All the rules are changed."

In a last ditch effort to save the rally, the band was ordered to play some patriotic march music as loudly as possible. After a few minutes of "Stars and Stripes Forever," Daniel Brewster himself stepped on to the stage to try to quiet the crowd. But it was no use. The catcalls and jeering and insults and racial slurs were even louder than when Senator Proxmire had tried to speak.

As Senator Brewster and Senator Proxmire hurried away from the rally, which had been a total failure, all Clark could think of were the words he had spontaneously yelled at Senator Brewster:

"This is a racial fight. All the rules are changed."

Clark Schooler and Al Kurdle were enjoying another lunch at 10 Downing Street, also known as Bickford's.

"It was incredible," Clark said as he described the "Brewster For President" rally the previous Saturday night. "The audience absolutely refused to let Senator Brewster or Senator Proxmire speak."

"There's no accounting for taste," Albert replied. "Some people even like Schultz's!"

Here was another favorite Al Kurdle line. It referred to the fact that different people liked different things. In some cases, people preferred inferior products to what most other people thought were superior products. As for Schultz's, that was a rival meat packing plant in Baltimore which was the principal local competitor with Quality Meats. Al Kurdle and all the rest of the people at Quality Meats had to face the fact that some people actually liked Schultz's meats better that Quality meats.

"George Wallace has his supporters in Maryland," Albert said with an air of finality, "and there's not much you and Danny Brewster can do to stop them from voting for Wallace."

Later that day, Clark attended an emergency meeting of the "Brewster for President" campaign staff. Most of the staffers were in a quandary, not knowing what to do to stop Governor Wallace's growing momentum in the Maryland presidential primary. The one person who did have some advice was Clark Schooler.

"You have to forget the traditional Democratic technique in Maryland of lining up political machine support in Baltimore city," Clark said. "The white working class is going to ignore the political bosses and vote for Wallace. That vote is gone. The sooner you forget about it the better."

"And stop having Senator Brewster give speeches in Baltimore city," Clark lectured on. "They're all going to end the way Saturday night ended. Everyone will be cheering for Wallace and jeering Danny Brewster."

"The way to win this election," Clark said, "is to unite the black vote in Baltimore city with the upper middle class white suburban vote in the Baltimore suburbs and the Washington, D.C., suburbs in Maryland. The best source of Brewster votes will be in Montgomery County, the most affluent part of Maryland's piece of the Washington suburbs."

Clark's mini-oration was stopped at that point. One of the older campaign staff members said: "Black voters in Baltimore city are famous for not bothering to vote. It is political legend that blacks are apathetic voters, particularly in presidential primaries. There are no black political machines to deliver black voters to the polls."

Clark had a ready response. "Have Senator Brewster campaign in the black churches in Baltimore," Clark said. "Those are the same churches where they have been holding civil rights meetings and organizing sit-in demonstrations. Put the black ministers of Baltimore to work on it. They can turn out a record black vote for Daniel Brewster."

"As for the Baltimore suburbs and the Washington suburbs in Maryland," Clark continued, "the best way to go after them is with advertising."

Clark was amazed at what he was saying and how forcefully he was saying it.

The Lyndon Johnson White House had arranged for a top Washington campaign consultant to come up to Baltimore, just as Clark Schooler had, to write press releases and advertising materials for the Brewster campaign. The man composed what Clark thought was a pretty good advertising slogan: "Reject George Wallace's Invitation To Be Irresponsible." The slogan implied that anyone who voted for Wallace was not taking seriously the great civil rights crisis currently facing the United States.

"That slogan will not work in downtown Baltimore," Clark said when he first heard the slogan proposed. "But, effectively written into radio and television spot ads, it will go like gangbusters in the Baltimore suburbs and the Maryland suburbs north of Washington."

It was another lunchtime and Clark Schooler and Al Kurdle were once again at 10 Downing Street. "I keep pushing the 'black vote plus suburban white vote equals victory' line everywhere I go," Clark said to Albert. "I push it with every newspaper reporter and television reporter that interviews me. They've let me push it particularly hard on WJZ-TV, Channel 13, the ABC outlet here in Baltimore. Yesterday I told them: 'We're playing both ends against the middle. Low income blacks in Baltimore and high income whites in the suburbs against working-class whites.'"

Clark thought about the Wallace-Brewster race for a moment and then said with a touch of wonder in his voice: "A lot of people have praised me for identifying this potential 'blacks plus upscale suburban whites' voting combination. To me, it's the most obvious thing in the world."

Al Kurdle gave Clark one of his all-knowing looks. "In the land of the blind," Albert said, "the one-eyed man is King!"

A few days later, Clark Schooler was standing on Race Street in Cambridge, Maryland. This waterfront city on Maryland's Eastern Shore was famous for the fleet of large sail boats, the "last commercial sailing fleet in the world," which plied the Chesapeake Bay dredging for oysters. To preserve a dwindling supply of oysters, Maryland law required that oyster dredging be done only from slow moving sailing ships, not from high-speed power boats.

Ironically, the dividing line between the white community and the black community in Cambridge ran right down Race Street. On this particular occasion, more than 50 Maryland state police officers and 400 National Guard troops were posted on Race Street. They were facing toward the African-American section of town, with billy clubs, rifles, and tear gas at the ready.

Several blocks away, in the center of the white part of town, Alabama Governor George Wallace was giving a campaign speech in a volunteer firemen's hall. It was well known that Wallace was intentionally campaigning in cities like Cambridge, where there was a strong tradition of racial segregation and bitter white resistance to racial integration. Wallace had come to Cambridge, Clark opined, in hopes of tempting the racially sensitive black population there to do something about Wallace's visit, preferably something violent.

Clark had attended the first part of Governor Wallace's speech. Wallace described how some civil rights demonstrators had recently protested by lying down in the street and stopping automobile traffic in front of restaurants and snack bars that refused to serve African-Americans. "If any of those civil rights protesters try to lie down in front of my car," Wallace told a wildly cheering white audience, "you can believe that will be the last thing those protesters ever do." [80]

Clark had drawn opposition duty for this particular event. The Brewster forces sent campaign staffers to Wallace speeches and rallies in Maryland, just to keep an eye on what was going on and to quickly report important developments back to campaign headquarters. Suspecting that the more interesting action was going to be on the streets of Cambridge that night, Clark left the Wallace speech early and proceeded to Race Street. Clark took up a position from which to watch the action at the corner of Race Street and the main street of the city.

"Here they come," one of the state troopers yelled. Clark looked into the distance. Several blocks away he could see a band of civil rights demonstrators coming down the street. They were singing the anthem of the civil rights movement, "We Shall Overcome." The group was mostly black, but there were some white faces visible. Block by block, the group advanced on the state police and the National Guard.

Clark felt his heart start to beat faster and his body perspire, even though it was a cool spring evening. It was much the same feeling he had two years earlier, in 1962, when he was a newspaper reporter covering the riot at Ole Miss.

When the civil rights marchers were one block away, they broke ranks. A few voices were heard yelling: "Keep it nonviolent!" "Don't hurt anyone!" But those voices were quickly drowned out by more animalistic yells, screams, threats, and epithets. The black crowd threw rocks, bottles, and anything else it could find at the police officers and soldiers who stood between them and the Wallace rally.

The state police and the National Guard responded with tear gas and billy clubs. Anyone who made the mistake of trying to cross Race Street into the white part of town was either gassed or whacked over the head with a billy club. Suddenly paddy wagons were pulling up and carrying off to jail those demonstrators who were captured and arrested.

At the height of the riot, which was quite bitter and violent, Clark realized he was at Ole Miss in reverse. At the University of Mississippi, white segregationists had gone out of control and attacked the immediate authority symbol of U.S. marshals. At Cambridge, Maryland, it was black civil rights protesters who were defying the law in the form of the state police and the National Guard.

Clark moved far enough back from Race Street to watch the bricks flying and the tear gas blowing without being in any danger himself. The police and National Guard line held tight. The demonstrators were thrown back. But it was a long night for the authorities. Random attacks, with a brick thrown here and a firebomb tossed there, continued long after Governor Wallace had finished his speech and left town.

But Wallace got what he wanted. As election day neared, Maryland voters and the rest of the nation watched saturation television coverage of the African-American rioting in Cambridge. The Brewster campaign responded with more Get-Out-The-Vote meetings in African-American churches in Baltimore city, and more radio and television ads beamed at the Baltimore suburbs and the Maryland suburbs of Washington.

Maryland was quiet by election day in mid-May of 1964. When all the votes were counted, Senator Daniel Brewster defeated Governor George Wallace by 57 percent to 43 percent. But Wallace did much better in Maryland than he did in Indiana and Wisconsin, where he received 30 percent and 34 percent of the vote respectively.

George Wallace immediately claimed his 43 percent of the vote was a victory. Speaking to his supporters at an election night rally, Wallace looked at the crowd and the television cameras and said:

"Everyone knows we won tonight. We had against us the national Democratic Party. We had against us the Democratic organization here in Maryland. Yet, in spite of all that opposition, Maryland voters have given me a vote that represents the philosophy of state's rights, local government, and individual liberty."

Later, talking to individual reporters, Wallace gave a more frank analysis:

"Look here. If it hadn't been for the black bloc vote, I'd have won it all. I got a majority of the white vote." [81]

Wallace was right when he claimed that he had won the white vote in Maryland, Clark realized. But, when giving election night interviews as a spokesman for the Brewster campaign, Clark hammered away on a familiar theme. "A winning combo of black votes in Baltimore city," Clark said, "was added to upper income white votes in the Maryland suburbs. That combination produced a clear majority for civil rights."

Clark made that statement to any reporter who would listen and during a number of television interviews. Clark would add: "This election proved that, in Northern and Border States where large numbers of black Americans have the right to vote, being against civil rights is a losing proposition."

Senator Brewster was jubilant. "There is no substitute for victory," he told the news media on primary election night. "We will go to the Democratic National Convention, and Maryland will stand up and cast its convention votes for President Johnson." [82]

The next morning, Clark Schooler and Albert Kurdle met for a late breakfast at Bickford's. Clark was exultant and almost giddy over the big election victory from the day before. "This is significant," Clark said with great enthusiasm. "The civil rights forces in the U.S. Senate would be absolutely blasted this morning if George Wallace had won Maryland."

"I have to give you guys credit," Al Kurdle replied. "I wouldn't have bet two cents on your chances of beating Wallace two weeks ago. And almost all the guys I talk to around town would have agreed with me on that point. You really turned it around."

"I think," Clark said, "that working in the Brewster campaign against George Wallace may end up being one of the most significant and important things I ever do in my life."

Albert Kurdle looked at Clark with that all-knowing look that Albert saved for those times when he made major pronouncements on the nature of humanity and the universe in which humans dwell.

"You have a right to say that," Albert pontificated. "After all, your life means what you say it means."

All the shouting and vote counting was over. Clark Schooler got into his 1951 Ford hardtop convertible and headed back to Washington, D.C. Clark was enthusiastic. Governor Wallace had been defeated in Maryland. That ended once and for all the dream of the Southern filibusterers in the Senate that Wallace would win Maryland and unleash a national groundswell of opposition to the civil rights bill.

When Clark Schooler returned to Senator Kuchel's office following the Democratic presidential primary in Maryland, Evan Harris, Kuchel's chief of staff, had some instructions for Clark. "If anyone from the press calls you about the Maryland presidential primary," Harris said, "I want you to do some shaping of the news. I want you to offer an explanation for why Wallace got such a high percentage of the vote, 43 percent, in Maryland. The explanation I want you to give is that Senator Brewster was not a very strong candidate and proved to be a poor campaigner."

"That's not true," Clark answered vehemently. "Senator Brewster busted his . . . uh . . . tail to win that election. He was willing to run when no one else in Maryland would take the risk and make the fight. In my opinion, he was a true champion. He was a lion in the fight. As we used to say at the campaign headquarters in Baltimore, Dan Brewster was the only Saint George willing to draw his sword and take on the segregation-breathing dragon of Alabama Governor George Wallace."

Evan Harris spoke in such a way as to quiet Clark down. "You know that's true, and I know that's true," Harris said. "But we can't have the general public thinking that 43 percent of the voters in a Border State like Maryland really wanted George Wallace and his anti-segregation viewpoint for president. We've got to have another explanation for Wallace's strong showing. And the one we're using is that Dan Brewster wasn't as strong a candidate as he might have been."

Clark remained agitated. "That's not shaping the news," Clark said. "That's changing history."

"Nonetheless," Evan Harris replied, "we can't let Governor Wallace continue to portray his vote in Maryland as a victory. If we let Wallace get away with that, the Southerners filibustering the civil rights bill will build on that point. The filibuster will last all summer and into the fall. We can't let that happen."

"Who is this 'we' that wants me to take this 'trash Brewster' line," Clark said, starting to get himself under control.

"It's the White House," Evan Harris said. "They believe they have to totally discredit George Wallace if we're ever going to get cloture on the civil rights bill."

Again, Clark thought, it was the total political picture. He had to downplay Brewster's abilities as a candidate in order to weaken Governor Wallace. And Clark had to do that in order to help the civil rights bill.

Clark did as he was told. Three different reporters called him who were doing postmortem stories on the Maryland presidential primary. Clark said that Danny Brewster was not as powerful a speaker as he might have been, particularly when facing a bombastic demagogue such as George Wallace. And Clark hinted that Brewster's aristocratic upbringing among the "horsey set" limited his ability to appeal to working-class white voters.

Clark believed that both points had some truth to them. He was not outright lying to the press. But he believed it was grossly unfair to Senator Brewster to emphasize only those two points.

So Clark tried to divert the reporters by offering the Basement Playroom Theory of presidential primaries. "Presidential primaries don't elect anyone to office," Clark volunteered to the reporters who called him. "Presidential primaries offer a safe environment in which disgruntled voters can cast a negative vote and not have to worry that the person they are voting for will necessarily be elected president of the United States."

"A lot of Maryland voters went down into the basement playroom and had a wonderful romp with George Wallace," Clark explained. "Those voters had a great time supporting Wallace and voting for him. But when the general election rolls around in November, those same voters will come out of the basement playroom and go up to the living room. Once there, in an election that actually chooses the president, they will cast a serious and sensible vote for either the Democratic or Republican candidate."

Clark's diverting stratagem was moderately successful. Two of the three reporters picked up on the Basement Playroom Theory. Their stories attributed Wallace's strong showing to Maryland voters casting a meaningless protest vote rather than Senator Brewster's weaknesses as a candidate.

One way to manipulate the press, Clark thought, is to overload inquisitive reporters with lots of extraneous facts. Doing it that way, the reporters just might overlook and fail to write about the one or two facts you would rather not see in the newspapers or on television news.

In The Interim

The presidential nominating system is the most rapidly changing part of the electoral process in the United States. In the 1960s, barely ten states held Democratic and Republican presidential primaries. At that time, most of the delegates to the national conventions were selected in state party caucuses and conventions. This caucuses/conventions nominating system was dominated by powerful political bosses or influential state governors.

In the early 1970s, in an effort to increase voter participation in the presidential selection process, a large number of states adopted presidential primaries. By the 1976 presidential election, about 3/4 of the states were holding presidential primaries. Winning a major party nomination for president thus became a matter of winning presidential primaries rather than electing delegates at state party caucuses and conventions.

This led to the phenomenon of momentum, often referred to as the "Big Mo." Presidential candidates who won the early presidential primaries tended to win subsequent presidential primaries. This was due to all the national publicity and news coverage that was showered on candidates who were victorious in early primaries.

Throughout the last half of the Twentieth Century, the state of New Hampshire jealously guarded its favored position of hosting the first presidential primary for both the Democratic and Republican parties. The New Hampshire primary emerged as both the first stop, and the most important stop, on the presidential primary trail. Candidates campaigned early and hard in New Hampshire in hopes of jump starting their presidential cam-

paigns with a big New Hampshire victory.

As more and more states realized the importance of holding an early presidential primary, a process known as front-loading came to be. States began scheduling their presidential primaries at earlier and earlier dates, thereby hoping to have a more significant impact on the presidential primary race. The final result was large numbers of states holding early primaries, many of the primaries held on the same day. These big early presidential primary election days, with many states voting at the same time, became known as mega-Tuesdays.

Front-loading and mega-Tuesdays quickly led to early closure. This was the fact that, if a presidential candidate won a small number of early primaries, about eight or ten or so, the race was "closed." The early front runner was declared the presumptive party nominee for president. As for those states that held presidential primaries after early closure occurred, their primaries were irrelevant to the presidential nominating process.

The schedule of presidential primaries continues to change in the 2000s. Every four years, the states jockey with one another to be among the first to vote and thus hold a relevant presidential primary.

Many observers argue that the presidential nominating process in the United States needs to be reformed. One suggestion is to hold national presidential primaries, one for the Democrats and one for the Republicans, in which voters throughout the nation vote for their choice on a national primary election day.

A variation of this plan calls for two presidential primary election days in each political party. In the first primary, all the party candidates for president would run against each other. On the second primary day, about two weeks later, the top two vote-getters in the first primary would run off against each other. The winner would be that political party's nominee for president.

Another suggested reform is called Small States First, Large States Last. Under this plan, there would be five presidential primary election days. The primary days would be scheduled two weeks apart. Only states with small populations would be allowed to vote on the early primary days. States with large populations would vote on the later primary days. The assumption of this plan is that, with the states with large populations voting last, no single candidate would win enough support to be declared the winner until the final presidential primary day.

Despite all the changes in recent years, one thing is still definitely true about presidential primaries, such as the Lyndon Johnson-George Wallace contest of 1964. Presidential primaries provide some of the most colorful, hard fought, and exciting elections in the American political process.

CHAPTER 12

THE SENATE:
THE GREAT AMENDER

Throughout the spring of 1964, President Lyndon Johnson used the news making powers of the presidency to call on the Southerners to stop the filibuster and let the Senate majority pass a civil rights bill. Johnson literally turned the White House into an electronic soapbox, speaking to his fellow Americans over the television waves the way an old time politician would stand on a real soapbox when giving a political speech.

Clark Schooler, Carl Brimmer, and Greg Netherton were eating most of their meals in the basement of Mike Palm's Restaurant on Capitol Hill. It was while eating a late dinner and watching the late news on television that the three young men were able to witness and appreciate President Johnson's many virtuoso performances on the tube.

Practically any situation where Johnson gave a speech or met with the press was turned into a presidential lecture on ending the filibuster and getting the civil rights bill enacted into law. At a special press interview on the occasion of President Johnson's first hundred days in office, Lyndon Johnson sat casually on a sofa in the Oval Office and literally boiled over with executive enthusiasm. He said:

"I don't want to predict how long the Senate will be discussing this bill. I am hopeful and I am an optimist and I believe they can pass it and I believe they will pass it and I believe it is their duty to pass it. And I am going to do everything I can to get it passed." [83]

Whenever Lyndon Johnson met with a distinguished visitor in the White House Rose Garden, or if he was dedicating a new national park far from the nation's capital, there was always a mini-oration on the civil rights bill. "Those senators have been debating the civil rights bill for a good many days," Johnson said, "and obviously there will be much debate yet in the offing. But I believe, after a reasonable time, the majority of the senators will be ready to vote. And I hope that a vote can be worked out." [84]

Clark, Carl, and Greg were impressed by the president's electronic handiwork. "This constant presidential electronic barrage must be having an effect," Carl Brimmer said one night at a late dinner. "Can there be any question in anyone's mind that Lyndon Johnson is supporting the civil rights bill?"

"There's an even more important point," Clark Schooler added. "Lyndon Johnson is putting up a good argument, whether he really believes it or not, that 67 votes can be found for cloture and the bill actually will be passed into law."

But by the month of May, even President Johnson appeared to be getting exasperated with the way the filibuster seemed to be dragging on forever. In a prepared speech to the American Society of Newspaper Editors, Johnson spoke with something of a whine in his voice. He said:

"Our nation will live in tormented ease until the civil rights bill now being considered in the Senate is written into law. The question is no longer: 'Shall it be passed?' The question is: 'When? When? When will it be passed?'" [85]

Greg Netherton, the voice of the rational South, listened to this particular Johnson statement and answered the question directly. "Maybe it will never pass," Greg said somewhat confrontively to the presidential image on the TV set. "Maybe the filibuster will succeed! Or maybe the bill will pass heavily amended, in a form that you, President Johnson, and my civil rights house mates, won't like very much!"

Neither Clark Schooler nor Clark Brimmer were upset by Greg Netherton's comments to a two-dimensional television image of Lyndon Johnson. Clark and Carl both regarded Greg's words as a precise statement of the current situation.

One day Clark found himself in the Senate dining room. But it was not the subsidiary Senate dining room in the New Senate Office Building. This was the real Senate dining room. It was the one in the Capitol building proper. Clark Schooler and the Senate aides supporting the civil rights bill were enjoying a working breakfast discussing strategy for getting 67 votes for cloture.

As often happened, the discussion was being led by Ralph Shepard, Senator Hubert Humphrey's special assistant for civil rights. "The key to a successful cloture vote is Senator Everett Dirksen of Illinois," Shepard began. "Dirksen is the Republican leader in the Senate. Dirksen has gotten eight to ten Midwestern Republicans to give him their votes on the civil rights bill. That means those senators won't vote for cloture until Dirksen tells them to. The end result is we have to win Dirksen over to our side to get those last few votes for cloture."

It was about that moment that a waiter presented Clark Schooler with the most appetizing plate of scrambled eggs and bacon he had ever seen. The serving was garnished with buttered toast and orange slices and chopped pineapple. Continuing to listen to Ralph Shepard, Clark began to eat his breakfast with enthusiasm.

"President Johnson is doing his part," Shepard said. "Lyndon is using a technique he calls the hero in history approach. He's hanging back and letting Everett Dirksen take the lead in the final struggle over the civil rights bill. That way a hero's niche is being carved out for Senator Dirksen. And the prospect of being a hero will help coax Dirksen into going our way on civil rights."

"President Johnson has been burning poor Senator Humphrey's ear off," Shepard continued. "The president calls Hubert Humphrey almost every day with more instructions."

Ralph Shepard then effectuated an exaggerated Texas drawl and pretended to be Lyndon Johnson speaking:

"Now you know this bill can't be clotured unless you get Ev Dirksen," Ralph Shepard mimicked the president. "You and I are goin' to git 'im. You make up your mind right now to spend time with Ev Dirksen. You've got to let ol' Ev have a big piece of the action. Ol' Ev's got to look good all the time." [86]

There was a generous round of laughter when Ralph Shepard finished his imitation of President Johnson. Clark took advantage of the gap in the conversation to signal one of the waiters and ask him to bring Clark a second helping of scrambled eggs.

The discussion of the civil rights bill resumed. The middle-aged woman who was a civil rights adviser to Senator Clifford Case of New Jersey made an observation. "I saw Senator Humphrey on television on 'Meet The Press' this past Sunday morning," she said. "Humphrey gave soaring personal praise to Dirksen. Humphrey said Dirksen would put the well-being of the United States above the narrower interests of the Republican Party. Humphrey said Dirksen would see the civil rights bill as a moral issue and not a partisan Republican issue." [87]

While waiting for his second helping of scrambled eggs, Clark Schooler decided to join in the discussion. "Not too many people across the country watch Sunday morning politics shows like 'Meet The Press,'" Clark said with an aura of great knowledge. "I doubt that very many average viewers saw and heard Humphrey trying to butter up Dirksen."

"That's not the point," the adviser to Senator Case replied tartly.

"Everyone in official Washington watches 'Meet The Press.' You can bet good green money that Senator Dirksen watches it religiously. Humphrey really laid it on thick. He called Dirksen a 'great senator' and a 'great American.' Humphrey said that, when the civil rights bill passes the Senate, Everett Dirksen of Illinois will be its champion." [88]

About this time, the waiter brought Clark his second helping of scrambled eggs. The waiter deftly placed the plate, a piece of fine china decorated with the great seal of the United States, right in front of Clark. As the waiter put the plate down, Clark noticed something interesting about the waiter's hand.

It was a rich shade of dark chocolate brown.

Ralph Shepard resumed the discussion at this particular Capitol Hill working breakfast.

"What you saw on 'Meet The Press,'" Shepard said, "was typical of what's happening every day in the hallways, and the inner offices, and the meeting rooms of the Senate. Humphrey will run into Dirksen and say to him: 'We can't pass this bill without you, Everett.' The next time Humphrey sees Dirksen, Humphrey will croon: 'We need your leadership in this fight, Everett.' Then Humphrey will ride next to Dirksen on the Senate subway and wax majestic: 'The successful passage of this civil rights bill will go down in history, Everett!'"

"Which means," Ralph Shepard opined, "that Everett Dirksen will go down in history. That's an idea that interests Senator Dirksen a lot." [89]

Clark was barely listening. His eyes moved from the waiter's hand to the waiter's face. The face was black like the hand was. Clark's gaze then wandered over all the other waiters in the room. They were lined up against one wall of the dining room, attentively waiting to fulfill any request from the diners they were serving. There were about eight waiters serving about 25 breakfasters, roughly one waiter for every three persons eating.

All of the waiters were males. All of the waiters were African-American.

Clark Schooler was suddenly jolted by the realization that, in the Senate dining room in the U.S.Capitol building, the staff of waiters was completely racially segregated.

Ralph Shepard was winding up the breakfast meeting.

"Senator Humphrey is peddling one particular line to Ev Dirksen," Shepard said conclusively. "It is the line that this is the opportunity for Dirksen to be the great man of the hour, the great man of the United States, the great man who saves the civil rights bill. And now, it appears that Dirksen is beginning to swallow the great man hook. When that hook is firmly caught in Everett Dirksen's gullet, we will wind him in along with

8 or 9 additional Republican senators and have ourselves a clotured civil rights bill." [90]

Clark Schooler was struck by his own adult naivete. He had been working on Capitol Hill and eating in the two Senate dining rooms for almost a year. It had taken him that long to specifically perceive and bring to the forefront of his mind something that was perfectly obvious. Racial segregation was being practiced daily in the dining rooms of the U.S.Capitol, the very heart and symbol of the American democracy.

How many other white persons, Clark anguished, lived their daily lives in a racially segregated world and never even noticed that this particular form of human separation was taking place?

Then Clark was overwhelmed by a sense of great irony. All of the people eating at this particular working breakfast were white. They were working on a legislative bill that would vitally effect every black person in the United States. But no black person had been invited to come and dine and participate in the discussion. Blacks were present only to serve the food and clear away the dirty dishes when the white folks were finished dirtying them.

It was some weird form of intellectual segregation, Clark thought, in which blacks were not allowed to join in the "brainy" work of passing legislation. That was true even for legislation that greatly affected black people.

Clark's tortured brain was suddenly asking him a series of questions: Were the black waiters listening to and following the breakfast table conversation about the civil rights bill? Were they aware that, as blacks, their future rights were being thought about and argued over by a breakfast table full of white persons? Did any of the black waiters wonder why they were not asked their opinion about what needed to be done? Or were the waiters so accustomed to their role as second class citizens that they never heard any of the conversation, concentrating their minds only on their assigned task of serving a morning meal?

How did it feel, Clark thought, to hear white people planning a struggle for civil rights legislation and, because you were black, not being allowed to participate in that legislative struggle?

That thought gave Clark the creeps.

The meeting was over. Clark hastily finished his second helping of scrambled eggs. As Clark got up to leave the table, he thanked the waiter for the extra attention.

"Glad to do it, sir," the African-American waiter replied cheerily. "I hope you enjoyed your meal, sir."

Clark could not detect even a hint of resentment or sarcasm in the waiter's voice.

Meetings on what do about the filibuster of the civil rights bill were coming thick and fast. One afternoon Clark Schooler walked into yet another gathering of the Capitol Hill aides and assistants supporting the civil rights bill. But Clark discovered things were going to be different when he walked into the meeting room in the Old Senate Office Building and saw both Joseph Rauh, Jr., and Clarence Mitchell, Jr., sitting at the table. If the two lobbyists for the Leadership Conference on Civil Rights were present, there probably were going to be some fireworks.

Things became even more intense when Senator Hubert H. Humphrey, the Democratic floor leader for the civil rights bill, walked in and sat down. He was closely followed by Senator Thomas H. Kuchel, the Republican floor leader, who pulled up a chair next to Humphrey. Clark could not tell whether it was intentional or not, but senators Humphrey and Kuchel had seated themselves in such a way that they were directly across the table from Rauh and Mitchell.

Ralph Shepard of Humphrey's staff, who generally presided at such meetings, never had a chance to formally open the meeting. At the precise moment that both Humphrey and Kuchel were seated at the conference table, Joseph Rauh launched an all-out verbal assault. Given that the four men were all supposed to be friends and political allies, at least on civil rights issues, Clark Schooler was fascinated and somewhat shocked by the obvious bitterness of the exchange:

RAUH: "The word is all over the Senate. The great senators Humphrey and Kuchel are beginning to negotiate a compromise version of the civil rights bill with Senator Dirksen. Are the rumors true? Are the great senators Humphrey and Kuchel really going to sell the civil rights bill down the river?"

HUMPHREY: "Sooner or later, we have to talk with Senator Dirksen. It's simple mathematics. He has in his back pocket, tucked up real tight against his backside, the eight or nine Republican votes we need to make a 2/3 vote for cloture."

KUCHEL: "Face the facts, guys! No Dirksen! No deal!"

MITCHELL: "This is an incredible reversal of our agreement. We all said all along that there would be no compromises to the House bill when it came over to the Senate. Are you two caving in to Dirksen? If you do cave in, you are putting the Leadership Conference in a box and nailing down the cover. We'll be powerless to pass a strong civil rights bill."

RAUH: "The Leadership Conference is united in thinking that dealing with Dirksen is unwise. Dirksen means compromise and a weak bill. There should be no dealing with Dirksen until all other avenues of gaining cloture have been exhausted. We had that pledge from you, Hubert Humphrey. Right from you! We need to hold Dirksen off with his weakening amendments."

HUMPHREY: "We are going to talk about cloture. We have to think ahead. We have to plan exactly how we are going to cloture the filibuster. If we can't pass the bill as it is, we have to think about passing the bill as it might be. We have to plan . . ."

MITCHELL: "You are shooting your friends in the civil rights movement if you trade with Dirksen."

HUMPHREY: "We don't have the necessary 67 votes for cloture."

KUCHEL: "Get real, Clarence! We need to be talking votes here. That means no more talk about 'no compromises.'"

MITCHELL: "Black Americans will never understand or tolerate the weakening of the civil rights bill. Black people feel very deeply about this piece of legislation. Violence in the streets will inevitable flow from any weakening of this bill."

HUMPHREY (trying to calm things down): "Clarence, don't get so excited. You rose three feet out of your chair when you said that."

RAUH: "Senators Humphrey and Kuchel talking publicly about compromising with Senator Dirksen means that some of the amendments to the bill proposed by Senator Dirksen will be adopted. What a disaster! Some of those Dirksen amendments are as bad as those proposed by the Southerners."

HUMPHREY: "So far, we have made no definitive deal with Senator Dirksen. But we have to talk out loud. Right now, we're having enough trouble getting 51 senators on the Senate floor to meet every Southern quorum call. All those brave fighters for civil rights want to be elsewhere, usually back in their home states electioneering. Democratic senators have actually said to me: 'If the survival of the nation depends on my being here, then let's just forget about the survival of the nation.'"

RAUH: "I'm worried that you guys aren't trying hard enough. If you'd really put the pressure on, we could get 67 votes for cloture. And we wouldn't have to kneel down and genuflect to Senator Dirksen."

HUMPHREY: "You're starting to sound like Lyndon Johnson. He grabbed me by my shoulder the other day and almost broke my arm. The president said: 'You've got to get those 67 votes for cloture.' I told Lyndon he was grabbing the wrong arm. He should have been grabbing Ev Dirksen by the arm and telling him to get the votes."

MITCHELL: "This is starting to have 'sell out' and 'let down' and 'back to the old plantation' written all over it."

HUMPHREY: "Give a little, Clarence! I have the Senate wives calling me right now and asking: 'Why can't the senator be home now?' The wives add: 'The Senate isn't being run intelligently.' Then President Johnson calls and says, 'What about my military appropriations bill? What about my poverty bill? What about my food stamps bill?'"

RAUH: "What's more important? Those pet bills of Lyndon's, or the civil rights of millions of American blacks?"

HUMPHREY: "Joe! Clarence! We aren't going to sell you out. And if we do, it will be for a whale of a price!" [91]

At that precise moment, bells began ringing in the halls of the Old Senate Office Building to signal a quorum call on the Senate floor. Literally saved by the bell from the wrath of Joe Rauh and Clarence Mitchell, senators Humphrey and Kuchel jumped up out of their chairs, shot out the door, and hurried down the hallway in the general direction of the subway over to the Capitol and the quorum call on the Senate floor.

Clarence Mitchell was left sitting with something of a dazed look on his face. "Sell us out," Mitchell said softly, almost to himself. "And for a whale of a price. You've got to wonder. Just how bad is that going to be?"

The meeting was over. The remaining participants stood around for awhile, engaged in separate conversations. One by one, they began drifting out the door. Suddenly, unintentionally, there were only two persons left in the room. They were Clark Schooler and Clarence Mitchell.

"It was nice to have a fellow citizen of Baltimore in the room with me during such a heated discussion," Clarence Mitchell said.

Clark replied: "These are very exciting moments in the Senate, Clarence." Clark tried to shape his words so as not to reveal his growing worry that some sort of deal probably had to be worked out with Senator Dirksen. "The filibuster is dragging on for what seems like forever," Clark went on. "There's a growing feeling that we have to hold a cloture vote and be done with it, even if we don't have the 67 votes for cloture."

"I know that feeling is there," Mitchell replied wearily. "And I know Hubert Humphrey has his problems, as he just told us. But I have my problems, too. I want a strong bill."

"You know, Clarence," Clark said, going back to the subject of his and Clarence Mitchell's hometown. "I have a theory about Baltimore. Because Maryland is a Border State, black people have had it better in Baltimore than in most big Southern cities in the United States. Sure, Baltimore is racially segregated. But blacks are allowed to work as policemen in Baltimore. They're allowed to drive buses and taxicabs. And blacks have been given the right to vote in Maryland. We have black persons serving on the Baltimore City Council and in the Maryland state legislature. So, Clarence, those things make Baltimore quite different from almost all of the big, racially segregated cities further South."

"I think you may be right about that," Mitchell responded.

At that moment, Clarence Mitchell walked over to Clark Schooler and put both his hands on Clark's shoulders. He held Clark at arm's length as he talked. Mitchell spoke in a low but very firm voice.

"Clark Schooler," Mitchell said. "You are a truly good white person. I'm aware that you were one of the first white newspaper reporters in Baltimore to write stories about black people that did not involve crime. I know you covered early civil rights demonstrations in Baltimore in a way that was objective but also very fair to the civil rights cause. You're a Capitol Fellow, and you've been working hard for Senator Kuchel, and that means working hard for the civil rights bill. And you've even come over and stood behind me when I have been holding important press conferences and releasing important statements for the NAACP."

Clark really didn't know what to make of what Mitchell was suddenly saying. "Clarence," Clark said softly, "I was very pleased to do all that."

"Then why," Mitchell said, "do you repeatedly call me 'Clarence' to my face?"

Clark was completely startled and caught totally off guard by Mitchell's question. Clark's eyes widened. He suddenly felt as though all the strength was draining out of his body.

"I'm more than 25 years older than you are," Mitchell continued. "I'm certain you don't repeatedly address white men who are 25 years older than you are by their first names. And yet, just because I'm black, you take the liberty of calling me 'Clarence,' almost as though I was a delivery man or an apartment janitor."

Clark was barely able to speak. "Claren . . . uh . . . Mr. Mitchell. I really don't know what to say."

"I'll bet you don't call Senator Humphrey 'Hubert' when you talk to him," Mitchell went on. "I'll bet you don't address Senator Kuchel as 'Tom.'"

Clarence Mitchell was, of course, absolutely right. Without ever realizing it or thinking about it, Clark had developed a life habit of addressing African-Americans of any age or importance by their first names. It suddenly dawned on Clark that, if he had spent any time with Martin Luther King, Jr., he probably would have started addressing him to his face as "Martin."

Mitchell ended this part of the conversation as quickly as he had begun it. He let go of Clark's shoulders and stepped back. He changed the subject by telling Clark he really did agree with Clark's view that things were not "all that bad" in Baltimore for the city's black population.[92]

Clark Schooler realized there was no point in his trying to go back to work for the rest of that particular day. Clarence Mitchell had completely altered Clark's view of himself and the world he had been living in. Clark told his secretary in Senator Kuchel's office that he had a meeting to go to some distance away from Washington. He would not be back in the office for the remainder of the afternoon.

It is one of the great historical and literary traditions of American life. It has been portrayed in countless history books, novels, theatrical plays, and even musical compositions. When things go wrong for Americans, they get on their horse, or in their covered wagon, or in their 1951 Ford Victoria hardtop convertible, and head west.

For Clark, heading west from Washington, D.C., meant driving the interstate highway toward Frederick, Maryland, and the Appalachian Mountains. Clark had no idea where he was going. It was as though he simultaneously wanted to drive away from Washington and much of his past life.

After about an hour and a half of driving, Clark and his 1951 Ford were well past the town of Frederick when Clark saw a sign for Antietam Battlefield. Clark had heard about Antietam all of his life but had never visited there. Rather than come to his senses in Ohio, or perhaps even Kansas or Colorado, Clark decided to end his westward trek and pay a long overdue visit to the Civil War battleground on the banks of Antietam Creek.

It was the middle of a late spring afternoon when Clark arrived at the battlefield. Antietam, Clark learned, had been the bloodiest single day of the Civil War. More soldiers, Northerners and Southerners alike, had died there in 24 hours than on any other battleground in the War Between The States. True, more men had died overall at the Battle of Gettysburg, but it had taken three days to get the killing done there. The one-day battle at Antietam had killed many more soldiers, from both sides, than any single day at Gettysburg or any other Civil War battle.

Clark suddenly realized why, subconsciously, he had stopped his westward excursion at Antietam. The issue at stake at Antietam, as in the entire Civil War, was human slavery for millions of African-Americans in the United States. On that one day of incredible pain and slaughter, the North had sacrificed wave after wave of soldiers in a continuing, but at that point fruitless, effort to defeat the South and end human bondage in America.

It occurred to Clark that this was what was happening in the Senate with the civil rights bill in 1964. Northern forces, Democrats and Republicans alike, were giving all they had to defeat the Southern filibuster and drive racial discrimination from the field. But, as at Antietam, these great sacrifices on the part of the North were meeting only with frustration. The South, by dint of great struggle and commitment, was continuing to hold its ground and maintain the status quo.

Clark found his way to Burnside's Bridge, the site of the key battle at Antietam. He found a spot on the banks of Antietam Creek where he could sit and gaze upon Burnside's Bridge and watch the afternoon sun go down. As he did so, Clark's thoughts went back to his encounter with Clarence Mitchell and what it said about Clark himself. In virtually a state of reverie, Clark reviewed some of the major events of his past life in a world of racial segregation.

Racial awareness had begun for him, Clark decided, in 1951 when he was 16 years old. His mother and father were taking him and his brother to Ford's Theater, the only "legitimate theater" in Baltimore where one could see a touring Broadway play. The family was going to see the Jerome Kern and Oscar Hammerstein musical "Show Boat" to celebrate Clark's older brother's birthday.

To get into the theater, the family had to dodge a picket line of whites and blacks protesting racial discrimination at Ford's Theater. The pickets, Clark later read in the newspaper, were claiming that a "white's only" Ford's Theater violated the "separate but equal" doctrine promulgated by the Supreme Court in 1896. Since there was no separate theater where blacks could see a touring Broadway play, the picketers argued, even the antiquated separate but equal principle required that black people be allowed to buy a ticket and watch the show at Ford's Theater.

"Pay no attention to those pickets. They're just causing trouble."

Clark's mother had said that to Clark and his brother as she maneuvered her family through the picket line. Clark later learned that was the same thing African-American mothers often said to their children, teaching and encouraging them not to make the mistake of making trouble for white folks.

A point of irony, Clark recalled. Half the cast of the musical "Show Boat" was African-American. The most famous song in the production, "Old Man River," was sung by a black man. The lyrics of that song lamented the unfair treatment of black men and women working at menial jobs on the boats and docks along the Mississippi River.

Clark and Harry, a friend from Clark's private high school, were going through the process of choosing a college or university. They were in

Princeton, New Jersey, getting a look at the campus and interviewing at Princeton University.

After a long day of talking to admission officers and wandering the Princeton campus, Clark and his friend decided to take the night off by going to a local movie theater. They were slightly late arriving at the theater. They entered the auditorium and took their seats when the theater was dark and the movie had already started playing.

When the film was over, and the lights brightened in the theater auditorium, Clark looked around. He saw that, for the first time in his life, he was attending a motion picture with black people. "Look, Harry," Clark blurted out to his friend. "there are some . . ." Clark had realized the inappropriateness of what he was saying in time to at least not complete the sentence.

Harry leaned over to Clark and whispered softly in Clark's ear. "Get with it," Harry intoned with pointed disdain for Clark's naivete. "We're in New Jersey. They let black people into movie theaters up here."

Attending Williams College in Massachusetts was a turning point in Clark Schooler's journey toward racial awareness. Or at least Clark Schooler always thought so. Abhorrence of racial segregation and support for racial integration were routinely expressed in the classroom at Williams, by both faculty and students alike. But Clark later realized there were few if any palpable actions to back up these strongly held views.

In the entire four years that Clark Schooler was at Williams College, from 1953 to 1957, only one African-American was in attendance. He was the son of a United States Government Foreign Service officer. The young man was a graduate of Phillips Exeter Academy, one of the most upscale private preparatory schools in the United States. As a child, this particular African-American had lived in a number of the foreign countries where his father had been posted by the State Department.

This black college student was fluent in both French and German. He virtually oozed international sophistication. He in no way resembled the black persons that Clark occasionally saw and dealt with while growing up in Baltimore, Maryland. Welcome or not, the Baltimore version of an authentic American black person was not present at Williams College in the 1950s.

His senior year at Williams, Clark lived in a small dormitory. It was a somewhat grand three story brick building with a two story front porch comprised of four tall white wooden pillars capped by a triangular pediment. Inside the dormitory, a grand staircase led upstairs between a wood paneled living room and a wood paneled dining room and opened out into an interior hallway leading to a series of three-person, three-room bedroom suites. It was in one of these bedroom suites that Clark first noticed the picture.

The picture was a black and white photograph of a meeting of the Ku Klux Klan, the secret Southern society devoted to maintaining racial segregation in the American South, by force if necessary. The Klansmen were portrayed in their white robes with hoods over their heads. This particular group was lined up on horseback facing the camera, the exposed heads of the horses contrasting with the covered faces of the Ku Klux Klan members. If one studied the photograph for a while, one could see that one of the equestrian Klansmen had a looped up rope, perfect for a hanging, attached to his horse's saddle.

But the picture was not just a small photograph sitting in a frame on a table or something relatively obscure like that. The picture was an enlargement, blown up to poster size, and covering the better part of one interior wall. Furthermore, the room in which the picture was displayed had been set aside by the suite's occupants as a sort of little living room, with a sofa, a cocktail table, and a couple of comfortable chairs. This was a room in which people were entertained socially, but with the eye holes of the Klansmen's hoods gazing down on the room's occupants from the wall.

College students are expected to have school spirit and be supportive of one another, so Clark never complained or criticized the picture or the fact that it was displayed in a relatively prominent place in his dormitory. So far as Clark knew, none of his dorm mates ever complained either. The picture remained on the wall, a permanent part of their daily lives.

Also during Clark's senior year at Williams, he and two other political science majors joined together to write a senior research paper. Such a paper was required of all graduating seniors and could be undertaken as a group project. The subject chosen by the three young men was the National Association for the Advancement of Colored People (NAACP).

The final paper that was turned in was exactly what was expected of respectable Williams students of the 1950s. The history of the NAACP was carefully reviewed with an emphasis on the organization's many court suits on behalf of African-American civil rights. The traditional legalistic approach of the NAACP was highlighted, and the paper concluded with a ringing description of the NAACP's most recent achievement. That was successfully arguing the case for the Supreme Court's school desegregation decision of 1954, cited as *Brown v. Board of Education*.

The paper earned all three students an A grade and many favorable written comments from James MacGregor Burns, the supervising political science professor.

Respect for the NAACP and racial integration ended at that point. In researching the paper, Clark had written to the NAACP's national headquarters for information. The NAACP had responded in a most helpful manner, mailing back several publications, one of them a history of the organization that became the major research source for the paper. The NAACP also sent back a separate letter asking Clark and his two fellow political science majors if they wanted to found a chapter of the NAACP among the student body at Williams College.

Unbeknownst to Clark, and definitely without his approval, the letter calling for the founding of an NAACP chapter at Williams College was posted in a prominent spot on a bulletin board in Clark's dormitory. One of Clark's dorm mates with some artistic talent had drawn some decidedly African-American faces, in caricature style, around the outer margins of the letter. Someone else had decorated the letter with little sarcastic phrases, such as "Yes, indeedy!" and "Let's do it!" Both those who posted the letter on the bulletin board and most of those who read it considered founding an NAACP chapter at Williams College a big joke.

Remembering the concept of college students as supportive of one another, Clark again said and did nothing.

Chapin Hall was a large building containing a major auditorium at Williams College. It was the preferred site for college assemblies, major lectures, Dixieland jazz concerts, and visiting musical groups. The music presented ranged from piano recitals and classical string quartets to more popular forms such as dance bands and individual singers.

One of the most popular solo acts to play Chapin Hall during the 1950s was William Sarkaster, a chemistry professor at Yale University who, in his spare time, composed popular songs that made ironic comments on contemporary American society and college life. Professor Sarkaster was a popular attraction on the New England college entertainment circuit, playing his own compositions on the accordion and singing his lyrics in a slightly flat but wonderfully animated voice.

Sarkaster's repertoire included a song entitled, "In My Bad Old Dixie Home Down South." The song humorously recited all the wonderful things the singer would get to do once he left the cold and unfriendly North and returned to the town he grew up in back in good old Dixie. The lyrics were filled with traditional Southern slang references such as "corn pone" and "grits" and "you all."

Toward the end of the song, Professor Sarkaster would intone the lines:

I want to take off these shoes, which are really pinchin'
Put on my white sheet, and go to one more lynchin'

At this point Sarkaster would stop, wait for the audience to get the joke, and leave time for the waves of laughter which he knew were surely coming. And, even in abolitionist New England, the waves of laughter always came.

When the laughter subsided, Professor Sarkaster, of Yale University, would finish the song with a flourish:

In my bad old Dixie home down South!

Thinking about the professor and his song at a later time in his life, Clark realized that, when hearing the line about a lynching, Clark never visualized in his mind the black person who was going to be tortured, hanged, and mutilated. He only visualized a bunch of good old Southern white boys out having a good time.

Was it only at Williams College that this sort of thing was going on in the 1950s? Clark's boyhood friend, Albert Kurdle, had gone to Cornell University in Ithaca, New York. One weekend Albert drove over from Cornell to Williams. Albert picked up Clark, and the two young men then drove to Princeton University in New Jersey. They went down to Princeton to visit a mutual friend attending college there.

The mutual friend belonged to an "eating club." The Princeton student body was broken up in to small groups that ate their meals together. This particular eating club was popular with Southern students attending Princeton, with a number of the members being from Louisiana and Mississippi. After dinner on Saturday night, the eating club held an impromptu get-together. At some point during the evening, the traditional, jovial, collegiate song singing began.

One song, which the members of this particular Princeton eating club sang with great gusto, had new words applied to a current popular song. The current song was entitled "Davey Crockett" and had an opening line that went:

Dav-e-y, Dav-e-y Crockett, king of the wild frontier

But the Princeton version of the song was somewhat different. The opening lines were:

Autherine, Autherine Lucy, black as you can be,
Autherine, Autherine Lucy, you're not goin' to school with
    me!

The song, Clark knew, referred to Autherine Lucy, a young black woman who had tried in the mid-1950s to get admitted to the racially segregated University of Alabama. A U.S.Court had ordered her admitted under the *Brown v. Board of Education* decision that desegregated public schools. But the Board of Trustees at the University of Alabama had succeeded in keeping Autherine from registering for classes on a technicality. The entire Autherine Lucy affair had been taken as a big victory for pro-segregation forces in the South.

The next day, Sunday, driving back from Princeton to Williams, Clark mentioned to Al Kurdle his discomfort with the Autherine Lucy song and other racist songs similar to it. Al Kurdle listen to Clark's sentiment and then responded loudly, as if talking to the world as well as Clark Schooler. Albert shouted: "Everybody but cave 12 can get lost!"

Al Kurdle offered no further analysis of what he had just said. Al gave a smug look to suggest he had just summed up a vitally important aspect of human life in a single sentence.

Clark took the phrase to mean that people are naturally clannish. Ever since the days of the cave dwellers, people have instinctively formed social groups and come to regard other groups as alien and inferior.

Clark Schooler graduated from Williams College and left college life behind him. But something stayed with him, much to his regret. It was the hidden attitudes of racism, which he found could be just as big a problem at Williams College in New England as at his childhood home in Baltimore. These attitudes were ingrained in a person, Clark concluded, hiding deeply inside, waiting to pop out at the most inopportune times.

And good old Clarence Mitchell had popped one of those hidden attitudes out of Clark just that previous morning. Clark wondered: How many such hidden attitudes were still within Clark Schooler? And how many such hidden attitudes were still within the American people?

The sun was setting along the Appalachian Mountain ridge line to the west of Burnside's Bridge at Antietam Battlefield. Clark realized it was time for his reminiscences to end. He walked back to his car, got in, and began driving back toward Washington, D.C.

As he rolled down the highway back to the nation's capital, Clark Schooler labeled himself "Unseeing Man." It was a play on a famous novel, "Invisible Man," which was written by an African-American author named Ralph Ellison. The point of Ellison's novel was that blacks were "invisible" to most white people and treated as such.

If Ralph Ellison is the invisible man, Clark thought to himself, I am the unseeing man. I am quite unable to really see black people as they are and understand the things black people experience and feel.

As the filibuster rolled endlessly on, Clark Schooler was spending much of his time watching the action on the Senate floor. One day he was sitting on one of the sofas provided for Senate aides when, to his amazement, Clark found himself sitting next to Beau Stevens, the "rational Southerner" who had been Clark's friend and fellow student in graduate school at Johns Hopkins.

Clark looked at Beau, did a double take, and then whispered: "Beau, what are you doing here in the Senate?"

Beau Stevens was enjoying the noticeable fact that Clark was both surprised and mystified by Beau's presence. "I heard you were working for Senator Kuchel and for the civil rights bill," Beau said with a smile and a wink. "So I decided to come down and work for the Southern filibusterers and against the civil rights bill."

Clark promptly invited Beau Stevens to have lunch with him the following day in the Senate dining room in the New Senate Office Building. After the two young men had ordered lunch, Clark began the conversation.

"Beau," Clark said. "I always regarded you as my 'rational Southerner,' the man who saw that the South was wrong about racial segregation and could discuss the topic in an enlightened and reasonable manner. What are you doing working for Senator Richard Russell, the leader of the Southern Democrats opposing the civil rights bill?"

"I guess hometown and home state roots go deeper than we think," Beau replied. "After all, I'm from Georgia, just like Senator Russell. I have decided to fight for Southern honor if not for white supremacy and racial segregation."

Clark looked at Beau with amazement and said: "You're kidding, right?"

"No, I'm not," Beau replied. "It's the thing to do when you're from Down South. We Southerners realized long ago that we cannot defend our brave Confederate soldiers for fighting to preserve slavery during the Civil War. Slavery is completely discredited now. So we defend our soldiers for fighting for honor and the integrity of the Southern homeland."

Clark asked: "And exactly what are you fighting for with Senator Russell and the Southern filibusterers?"

"State's rights and the integrity of the United States Constitution," Beau replied with a high degree of confidence and certitude. "The national government in Washington must not be allowed to destroy our federal system by forcing racial integration on sovereign state governments. The states themselves should end racial segregation in the South. As Senator Russell has said on the Senate floor, racial desegregation should not be enforced with a U.S. Government blackjack." [93]

"But desegregation will never happen if we leave it to the individual Southern states," Clark said, working hard to quell the testy and confrontational tone that was trying to creep into his voice.

That statement by Clark seemed to be Beau Stevens's cue to launch into a major lecture on Senator Russell and the Southern mind set. Clark did not mind. Similar to Beau, he was a political scientist, and he liked to both give and listen to lectures himself.

"Richard Brevard Russell, Jr.," Beau began, "is from the small farming village of Winder, Georgia, some 40 miles northeast of Atlanta. He grew up in the black belt country of the Deep South. Winder is located in a string of counties where blacks were in the majority and whites were in the minority. But all the land in the black belt is owned by wealthy white people, like Senator Russell, and farmed by black tenants and sharecroppers. It just seemed natural to Richard Russell that the white people should be running things and the black people should be doing all the heavy work."

"You have to realize," Beau continued, "the strength of mutual reinforcement in the South. Everybody a young white person ever meets or talks to believes in white supremacy and racial segregation. All of a young person's role models are segregationists. And anyone who doesn't support this existing Southern way of life immediately becomes very unpopular with most of their white friends, neighbors, and fellow workers down at the office or the factory."

"For a politician," Beau went on, "supporting racial segregation is an absolute requirement for keeping your elected office, whether you're the local dogcatcher or a U.S. senator. If you don't come out loud and strong for white supremacy, your opponent will, and your opponent will soon replace you in office. And remember, thanks to literacy tests and other Southern white stratagems, most blacks aren't allowed to vote in the Deep South."

"Richard Russell is a lifelong bachelor," Beau Stevens lectured on. "When he was first elected to the Senate in 1932, the legend is that Russell promptly memorized the Senate rulebook. It is also rumored that Richard Russell reads every word of the *Congressional Record* in bed each night before going to sleep. Well, why not? He doesn't have a wife or children to worry about."

"Russell has now served more than 30 years in the Senate," Beau rambled on. "He has used every one of those years to build his skills and qualify himself to be the Southern leader in the Senate. As a true son of the South, Dick Russell considers being Southern leader, and fighting for racial segregation and the integrity of the U.S. Constitution, as being more important than being Senate majority leader."

"We know that's true," Beau said, starting to wind his lecture down, "because in 1951 Richard Russell had the chance to run for and probably get elected Senate majority leader. The Democrats were in control, then as now, and the previous majority leader had been defeated for reelection. But Russell elected to stay on as Southern leader, even though that's not an official Senate leadership position. He threw his support for majority leader to a young and ambitious Democratic senator from Texas, who won the post. His name, incidentally, was Lyndon Johnson."

"I found I couldn't abandon Richard Russell and my Southern home-land in their hour of need," Beau Stevens concluded with great seriousness. "Remember, it was Richard Russell who made the filibuster respectable. He's the guy who stopped talking about upholding racial discrimination when filibustering a civil rights bill. He now talks mainly in terms of de-fending state's rights from U.S.Government intrusion."

Clark's and Beau's food was served and the conversation lightened up while they were eating. Mainly they reminisced about their graduate school days at Johns Hopkins and brought each other up-to-date on what all of their former graduate school pals were currently doing.

After dessert, Clark returned the conversation briefly to Senator Rus-sell. "Have you ever heard the story," Clark said, "about Lyndon Johnson and Richard Russell and the time the Senate was meeting 24-hours-a-day in an effort to break a filibuster and pass a civil rights bill?"

"No, I haven't," Beau replied. "Tell it to me."

"It was about 2 o'clock in the morning," Clark began. "They had put Army cots in the senator's offices so the senators could snooze between quorum calls. Lyndon Johnson was Senate majority leader and orchestrating the attempt to stop the filibuster. Johnson was in his pajamas and about to lie down on his cot, but he got worried that Richard Russell might try to pull a surprise legislative maneuver sometime in the middle of the night. Johnson put on his bathrobe and slippers and hot footed to the Senate chamber. He stood just inside the doorway where he could look things over."

"As Johnson was standing there," Clark continued, "he saw Richard Russell, the Southern leader, walk in one of the other doorways to the Senate chamber. Russell, like Johnson, was dressed in his pajamas, slippers, and bathrobe. Russell had come down to make certain Lyndon Johnson didn't try to pull any surprises."

The two young men laughed warmly together over Clark's story.

"You've picked one of the great grey lions of the Senate to work for," Clark said, being the good Senate aide and working to end the luncheon on a friendly and upbeat note. "Richard Russell has succeeded in defeating or weakening, with the filibuster, every civil rights bill that's made it to the Senate floor in the past 30 years. That's why those of us working for the civil rights bill call him, with fear and trembling, 'The Defending Champion.'"

"I know," Beau said, agreeing with Clark. "He's one of the Senate greats. But the civil rights forces are more organized and determined than ever before. It's going to be a terrific fight. You and I are going to see a lot of legislative bloodletting as the battle goes forward."

On a Tuesday in May of 1964, U.S.Senator Hubert Humphrey made his way though the Capitol to the office of Everett Dirksen, the Republican leader. Humphrey and Dirksen sat down, opposite each other, around a big mahogany table and began to negotiate a mutually acceptable version of the civil rights bill. Above their heads, a large tinkling glass chandelier gave an aura of luxury and sumptuousness to the proceedings below.

Other persons of importance were present at this symbolic first formal meeting between Humphrey and Dirksen. Mike Mansfield, the Democratic leader in the Senate, was on hand. Attorney General Robert Kennedy stopped by to represent the Justice Department and President Johnson. With Bobby Kennedy was his top civil rights legislation sidekick, Deputy Attorney General Nicholas Katzenbach.

By this time, Clark Schooler was an astute enough observer of Washington folkways to note the significance of the meeting being held in Senator Dirksen's office. It sent a clear signal to the political cognoscenti that Dirksen was in control in this particular situation and was the most important person involved in the negotiations. Hubert Humphrey, Mike Mansfield, Robert Kennedy, and Nicholas Katzenbach would not have obediently come to Dirksen's home turf if they had not regarded Dirksen's support as a key element in gaining a 2/3 vote for cloture.

The meeting began with a severe jolt for Senator Humphrey and the civil rights forces. Senator Dirksen handed Humphrey a sheaf of more than 70 amendments that he wanted added to the civil rights bill. Humphrey was appalled by this action on Dirksen's part. But Humphrey needed Dirksen's vote for cloture and the votes of Dirksen's fellow Republicans in the Senate. Humphrey had no choice but to begin negotiating over Dirksen's giant pile of amendments.

Clark Schooler promptly decided in his own mind that Everett Dirksen, the Republican leader in the U.S. Senate, should be nicknamed "The Great Amender."

There was yet another meeting of the Senate aides supporting the civil rights bill. As usual, the first speaker was Ralph Shepard, who spoke with a great deal of discomfort in his voice. "Those 70 or so amendments were prepared by Dirksen's demons," Shepard said. "The demons are a group of young men and women lawyers on Dirksen's staff who specialize in going through Democratic bills and finding Republican-style amendments for Dirksen to introduce and push on the Senate floor. Apparently Dirksen's demons went over the House-passed civil rights bill with a fine toothed comb and came up with 70 or more ways to weaken the bill."

Clark Schooler jumped into the discussion. "It seems to be happening just the way Clarence Mitchell and Joseph Rauh said it would," Clark opined. "We've started talking with Senator Dirksen, and the bill is getting more diluted and compromised by the minute."

"Sometimes you have to abandon your friends in a tough legislative struggle," Ralph Shepard replied. "It is harsh to have to turn our backs on strong supporters such as Clarence Mitchell and Joe Rauh over at the Leadership Conference on Civil Rights. It is easy to offend your enemies. It takes far more courage to disagree with and work against your friends. But, as in this case, turning on your pals can be the precise action which brings legislative victory." [94]

At exactly that moment, two young men dressed in grey flannel suits and carrying bulging valises walked into the meeting. Clark had never laid eyes on the two men before. As they walked into the room, all conversation came to an immediate halt. The sudden quiet was both noticeable and somewhat disturbing. The two young men looked around the room, and all the pro-civil rights aides looked back at them. The stillness was broken when one of the young men said:

"We're from Senator Dirksen's office. Now that Dirksen and Humphrey are negotiating on the civil rights bill, we thought we should begin attending these civil rights bill meetings that you have been holding. We have some ideas that you might find helpful in writing a better bill and getting that bill to a successful cloture vote."

Clark Schooler was disconsolate. He had always thought that it would be pro-civil rights aides like Ralph Shepard who would write the detailed language of the civil rights bill. Among Senate aides the process was called "dotting the i's and crossing the t's." U.S. senators did not bother themselves with that kind of detail work. Senate aides did it. But suddenly it dawned on Clark that these two young men from Senator Dirksen's staff, and not Clark's pro-civil rights friends, were the one's who would do the detail work on the civil rights bill.

The two young men were, of course, two of those famous Dirksen's demons. They began introducing themselves to everyone in the room. There suddenly was a great deal of activity and conversation in the room as everyone stood up to formally meet each other and shake hands.

Dimly, in all the commotion, Clark heard a woman's heels coming down the marble floor of the hallway outside the room. He was only dimly aware that a person wearing a dress had entered the meeting room and was introducing herself to everyone along with the two young men. Clark did not really pay any attention to what the woman was doing and saying until she was standing right in front of him.

"Hello, Clark," the woman said, extending her hand for Clark to shake it. "It's nice to see you again."

The woman was young, and attractive, and suddenly very familiar to Clark. She was Bonnie Kanecton.

Yes. It was the same Bonnie Kanecton who was, like Clark, a Capitol Fellow. It was the same Bonnie Kanecton who took Clark skating at the Chevy Chase Club. It was the same Bonnie Kanecton who Clark had come to think of as his new girlfriend.

Bonnie Kanecton was a Dirksen demon.

No, Clark thought, correcting himself in his own mind.

Bonnie Kanecton was a Dirksen demonette.

In The Interim

The political party that has the majority of the members of the U.S. Senate is called the majority party. The party that has the minority of the members is called the minority party. But, due to the open and fluid nature of the U.S. Senate, the minority party often plays a key role in determining legislative outcomes in the Senate.

As was the case in the 1960s, there are very few straight party line votes in the U.S. Senate in the 2000s. The majority party in the Senate almost always needs the votes of a number of key members of the minority party to get major bills passed in the Senate. The result is to put pressure on the majority leader in the Senate to work with the minority leader rather than against him or her. And the phenomenon of the majority leader and the minority leader working together fits nicely with the idea that the Senate is a place of comity and cooperation rather than conflict and confrontation.

One well-documented theory holds that almost all the major bills that have passed the Senate throughout American history have been the result of bipartisan cooperation rather than straight party line voting.

CHAPTER 13

THE SENATE:
"AN IDEA WHOSE TIME HAS COME"

"You really surprised me," Clark said to Bonnie as they were having dinner that evening at the Carriage House in Georgetown. "I must have looked as if someone hit me over the head with the Capitol dome."

"You were stunned," Bonnie replied with a smile, unable to suppress her great amusement over the situation. "But it's not my fault. You're the one who wasn't swift enough to figure out that someone who works for the Subcommittee on Constitutional Amendments is also on Senator Dirksen's staff."

"I never put the two together," Clark replied, now also smiling. "You didn't play fair. You never said you were on the Republican staff of the subcommittee. If you had, I'll bet I would have connected you to Dirksen."

"I wasn't required to tell you everything about where I worked and who I was," Bonnie replied. "We lawyers are trained to just answer the specific question and not to volunteer any additional, potentially damaging information. You asked me where I worked and I answered the question honestly. I said, 'the Subcommittee on Constitutional Amendments,' which was an absolutely correct answer."

"You had a moral obligation to tell me more," Clark argued.

"My answer will stand up in court as complete and sufficient," Bonnie shot back.

"It was one of the worst moments of my life," Clark said. "I can't believe that you and your fellow Dirksen's demons are going to have such a powerful say over the final language of the civil rights bill."

"Clark," Bonnie replied. "Where's the problem? Dirksen is a Republican. Supposedly you and Senator Kuchel are also both Republicans. We're not going to destroy your civil rights bill. And Dirksen's demons are not really demons. We're actually a group of very good lawyers who know how to write enforceable legislation."

"Enforceable legislation," Clark said with a questioning look on his face. "What's the Dirksen version of that?"

"Legislation that actually works when it's applied to the real world," Bonnie answered. "Democrats like to fill congressional bills with flowery phrases about lofty intentions and grandiose plans for the future. Senator Dirksen likes to take those bills and amend them so that the resulting laws will actually work in a practical way. That's what we mean by enforceable legislation."

By this time Bonnie Kanecton was totally committed to her defense of Senator Dirksen. She launched into a major dinnertime oration on the topic.

"Everett McKinley Dirksen is from Pekin, Illinois," Bonnie began. "Pekin is a small town on the Illinois River near Peoria, but don't make the mistake of thinking Dirksen is a small town kind of person. Because it is a lively river town, Pekin is a very diverse community in terms of the local economy and social life. True, Dirksen is from the Midwestern heartland of America, but he's anything but a country bumpkin."

"The country around Pekin was in Abraham Lincoln's congressional district when Lincoln served in the House of Representatives in the late 1840s," Bonnie continued. "Dirksen always reminds people he's from 'Abraham Lincoln's home district.' And Dirksen loves to quote Lincoln in his speeches. You can rely on Ev Dirksen, with his great admiration for Abraham Lincoln, to help crank out a reasonable and workable civil rights bill."

"Dirksen had already distinguished himself as an orator when he was in high school in Pekin," Bonnie rattled on. "He served as a soldier in France in World War I. After the war was over, Dirksen returned to Illinois and went right into politics. During the 1930s and 1940s, he served in the U.S. House of Representatives. Dirksen was elected to the U.S. Senate in 1950. He became Republican leader in the Senate in 1958. Technically speaking, Dirksen is the Senate minority leader, because the Republicans were in the minority in 1958, just as they are now in 1964."

Clark jumped into the conversation at this point, mainly so Bonnie could start eating her dinner, which had just been served.

"I have to give Dirksen credit," Clark said. "He's one of the most colorful characters in American politics. The seedy clothes and the rumpled hair are his political trademarks. Reporters write at length about his 'wavy pompadour' and his 'heavy lidded eyes' and his 'loose full orator's lips.' One writer described his hair as 'the kelp of the Sargasso Sea.' Another said he had 'the melancholy mien of a homeless basset hound.'" [95]

"I love to go down on the Senate floor and just sit there and listen to Dirksen debate," Clark went on. "Everyone says he has a mellifluous voice, and he's very persuasive in what he has to say. The newspaper reporters and Senate aides all have their favorite nicknames for him. 'Old Silver Throat.' 'Old Honey Tonsils.' 'The Rumpled Magician of Metaphor.' My favorite is 'The Wizard of Ooze.'" [96]

By this time, Bonnie had made a good start on her evening meal. In good lawyer style, she resumed control of the conversation.

"For almost all of Dirksen's career in Congress," Bonnie said, "Everett Dirksen and the Republicans have been in the minority. Dirksen quickly learned that the best way for the minority to influence legislation is through the amendment process. Dirksen specializes in drawing up Republican amendments that improve bills that are working their way through a majority Democratic Congress. Then he goes looking for Democrats, usually conservative Democrats, to support his Republican amendments."

"As a result," Bonnie explained, "the term 'Dirksen amendment' has a special meaning in the Senate. Whenever the Democrats introduce a major bill or propose a gigantic new government program, Dirksen begins by expressing his 'grave doubts' and 'sincere reservations' about the new legislation. Then Dirksen introduces carefully crafted amendments to the bill, always letting it be known he is available for 'negotiation' and 'compromise.' Then, when the Democratic leadership needs some Republican votes to pass the bill, Dirksen negotiates the final compromise and receives much of the credit for getting the bill through the Senate."

"Truth be known," Bonnie concluded, "Dirksen works harder than most senators at studying the details of legislation. He's a skilled lawyer, and he takes pride in being an adept legal draftsman. He thinks of himself as a professional legislator whose full time business is writing good laws. Dirksen can be counted on to do his legislative homework. And a lot of Democratic senators, some of whom don't want to work that hard, are pleased with and heartily approve of most of the changes that Dirksen makes to Democratic bills."

Clark was getting worried that Bonnie Kanecton would sing the praises of her boss, Everett McKinley Dirksen, all night long. Clark was spared that fate when two people leaving the Carriage House after dinner stopped by Clark's and Bonnie's table for a brief chat. The two people were Carl Brimmer, one of Clark's house mates, and Vonda Belle Carter, of Morgan State College and, more lately, the NAACP.

Carl Brimmer and Vonda Belle Carter said they had been to a late meeting that afternoon at the NAACP and decided to have dinner together. They said they had spent the dinner discussing Senator Dirksen's recent dramatic entry on to the civil rights bill scene. Clark quickly introduced Bonnie Kanecton to Vonda Belle Carter. Looking straight at Vonda Belle, Clark made the added comment: "Bonnie works for the Subcommittee on Constitutional Amendments. She's Senator Dirksen's patronage."

Vonda Belle reacted just the way Clark hoped she would. "Breaking bread with the enemy," Vonda Belle said with mock surprise in her voice. "Clark, I'm shocked by this treacherous act."

Vonda Belle had been diplomatic and played the situation for laughs, but Clark could not help but feel she was genuinely amazed and a little let down. Clark was having what obviously looked like a romantic dinner with one of those Dirksen's demons.

The two couples exchanged further pleasantries. Then Carl and Vonda Belle went on their way out the restaurant door.

The table where Clark and Bonnie were sitting was by a front window at the Carriage House. Clark could look out and see people walking past on the sidewalk on Wisconsin Avenue. As he and Bonnie were ordering dessert, Clark happen to glance out the window and see Carl Brimmer and Vonda Belle Carter walking away from the restaurant. Carl's white-skinned hand was tightly gripping Vonda Belle's dark-skinned hand. They were walking shoulder to shoulder and talking very excitedly with each other.

Every one of Carl's and Vonda Belle's body movements and facial expressions suggested to Clark that the two persons were deeply involved with each other.

During the month of May of 1964, all the action on the civil rights bill took place in Senator Dirksen's office. The negotiations went on long enough that the process became somewhat ritualized. In the afternoon, Dirksen's demons would negotiate with members of Humphrey's staff and civil rights lawyers from the Justice Department. The following morning, senators Dirksen, Humphrey, and Kuchel would meet and approve the language adopted the previous day by the staff. Deputy Attorney General Nicholas Katzenbach would sit in on behalf of the Justice Department. The senators and Nick Katzenbach would work to resolve the few thorny issues on which the staff members could not get together and find common ground.

Clark Schooler was somewhat jealous of Bonnie Kanecton, who got to sit in on many of the morning staff meetings as a member of Senator Dirksen's legal staff. But Bonnie was careful to reassure Clark that no great damage was being done to the civil rights bill.

"Every staff member in the room has been given the go-ahead by his or her boss to produce a good civil rights bill," Bonnie explained to Clark soothingly. "There's no sense that the Humphrey people are for the bill and the Dirksen people are against it. Everyone is determined to write a good, strong bill. And there's equal determination to work out our differences amicably so that the entire nation, the United States of America, ends up with a workable civil rights program."

But there were occasional fireworks when senators Humphrey and Dirksen were negotiating directly. On one occasion, Senator Humphrey asked a strong civil rights supporter, Senator Joseph Clark of Pennsylvania, to attend one of the negotiating sessions in Dirksen's office. Humphrey secretly arranged for Senator Clark to throw a political tantrum. Just at the moment when Senator Dirksen was being particularly demanding on a crucial part of the bill, Senator Clark jumped to his feet, pointed an accusing finger at Humphrey, and yelled: "This is a wholesale sellout." Senator Clark then stalked angrily out of the meeting.

Senator Humphrey then turned to Senator Dirksen with a somewhat helpless look on his face. "See what pressures I'm up against, Ev. I just can't concede any more on this particular point." [97]

Senator Clark's little ruse worked perfectly. The mood of the meeting improved markedly. Senator Dirksen conceded a point here and there. Amicable agreement was soon reached on that particular part of the civil rights bill.

As negotiations moved slowly but steadily forward in Senator Dirksen's office, the filibuster continued to drag along on the Senate floor. The Southerners were becoming fearful that Senator Dirksen really was going to support cloture and enable the Senate to produce a strong civil rights bill. As a result, the Southern senators began filibustering late into the evening. The senators from Dixie also became more vehement in their condemnation of the civil rights movement in general and the civil rights bill in particular.

Early one evening in late spring, Clark Schooler was observing the action on the Senate floor. He decided to take a short break from the endless Southern speech making and stepped out on the front portico of the Senate wing of the Capitol to get some fresh air.

The weather was warm. It was quite pleasant to be outdoors. Standing amidst the marble pillars, Clark suddenly heard music playing. He glanced over at the center section of the Capitol building.

There, on the front steps of the Capitol, with the Capitol dome rising above and behind them, sat a crowd of people listening to an outdoor band concert. The band was playing on the sidewalk just below the marble steps on which the people were seated. At the moment Clark gazed upon this somewhat idyllic scene, it was the "sing along" portion of the program. The audience, which was almost exactly half-white and half-black, was lustily singing "America The Beautiful."

Clark was almost overwhelmed by the contrast between the two differ-

ent worlds he was observing that evening. Inside the Capitol building, on
the floor of the U.S. Senate, the Southerners were fighting fiercely to
preserve legal racial segregation in the United States. But no more than 100
yards from these Southern senators, on the Capitol steps, a racially integrated audience was enthusiastically singing about "brotherhood from sea
to shining sea."

The two different groups were completely unaware of each other. Clark
listened to the singing for awhile, became somewhat inspired by it, and then
returned to his primary responsibility of witnessing the action on the Senate
floor.

In early June of 1964, word began to spread through the Senate, and
the nation, that senators Humphrey and Dirksen had reached agreement on
a compromise version of the civil rights bill. Apparently there was a critical
breakthrough when a top aide to Senator Dirksen proposed that the bill only
be enforced where there was a "pattern or practice" of racial discrimination.
Senator Dirksen had been fearful that single individuals, or small individual
business companies, would be punished under the law for very slight, almost
unprovable acts of racial discrimination. The new compromise provided for
U.S. Government action only where a distinct pattern or practice of discrimination could be readily documented.

As senators Humphrey and Dirksen walked out of their final meeting
together, they were suddenly surrounded by a group of newspaper reporters
assigned to cover Capitol Hill. The members of the press had camped out
at the meeting room door in hopes of being the first to learn if the deal had
actually gone through.

Clark Schooler had camped out with the reporters. He thus was able
to observe the impromptu press conference held in the hallway by Humphrey and Dirksen. Standing arm in arm and waving the text of their
agreed-upon amendments, the two senators announced their joint support
for this new version of the civil rights bill.

Several of the reporters asked to see the text of what would soon be
known as the Humphrey-Dirksen amendments. As Senator Dirksen passed
his copy to the reporters for them to share, Dirksen quietly intoned: "The
lid is on, gang!" That was Dirksen's way of telling the reporters that, until
the text was officially announced and published, the exact wording of the
amendments was off the record. [98]

It was interesting to Clark Schooler that a group of aggressive newspaper reporters were the first Americans to see the actual text of the
Humphrey-Dirksen agreements. The national news hounds got to see the
detailed text even before most of the United States senators who would have
to vote on those agreements.

Also present at this impromptu press conference was Ralph Shepard, Senator Humphrey's special assistant for civil rights. When the press conference broke up, Ralph Shepard stopped to chat for awhile with Clark Schooler.

"These really have been amazing events," Ralph ruminated to Clark. "When else has major legislation of national importance been written in the back office of the Senate minority leader? Dirksen is a Republican, and the Democrats are in the majority in this Senate. It's incredible that could have happened." [99]

"The Southerners brought it on themselves," Clark replied. "Senator Eastland of Mississippi refused to hold hearings on the bill before the Senate Judiciary Committee. Senator Eastland thus failed to have a Senate standing committee review the bill and mark up the final form of the legislation. In essence, the negotiations between Dirksen and Humphrey took the place of committee consideration and mark-up of the bill. Senators Humphrey, Dirksen, and Kuchel became a three person ad hoc committee that wrote the detailed language of the final version of the bill before it went to the Senate floor."

"I hate to admit this to a Republican," Ralph Shepard said to Clark, slowly shaking his head, "but the Democratic leadership in the Senate was delighted to negotiate with Dirksen and give him a major role in writing the bill. The other option would have been to consider Dirksen's amendments when he introduced them for a formal vote in the Senate. The arguing would have taken place in public on the Senate floor. There would have been much less opportunity for quiet negotiation and compromise." [100]

"In other words," Clark replied, "it wasn't just Senator Dirksen who benefitted from the private negotiations in his office. The Democratic leadership benefitted greatly as well."

With the Humphrey-Dirksen negotiations successfully completed, a date could be set for a cloture vote on the civil rights bill. The date chosen was June 10, 1964. To many people, that day was just another early summer day in the nation's capital. Similar to so many summer days in Washington, D.C., it was sunny and warm and humid with a light and cool breeze blowing. It was a super pleasant day on which to be outdoors.

But to those following the fate of the civil rights bill, June 10, 1964, was anything but an ordinary day. The public galleries of the Senate chamber had been packed tight with important people since early morning. Senatorial aides, such as Clark Schooler and Ralph Shepard, were banned from the Senate floor to lessen the noise and confusion. Ironically, young men and women staff members, who ordinarily could go on the Senate floor to work with their senators, had to find a way to learn about the progress of the cloture vote from the news media.

Thus it was that Clark Schooler and Bonnie Kanecton found themselves walking across the east lawn in front of the Capitol on cloture day. They were headed for an outdoor television location that had been set up by CBS News. Standing on the lawn, with the white marble Capitol dome for a backdrop, was CBS news reporter Roger Mudd. Beside him was a large scoreboard with the names of all 100 senators and a place to mark their votes for or against cloture.

Senate rules at that time forbade live television coverage of debates and roll call votes on the Senate floor. CBS was going to make do by having a reporter in the press gallery in constant telephone contact with Roger Mudd. As each vote was cast on the motion to cloture the civil rights bill, Roger Mudd would make the appropriate mark on his scoreboard. With one television camera trained on Roger Mudd, and a second camera focusing on the scoreboard, CBS flashed each senator's vote to the American people.

With Clark and Bonnie that morning were Carl Brimmer and Vonda Belle Carter. "Yes," Carl Brimmer had previously told Clark, "I cannot hide it any longer. Vonda Belle and I are a twosome, an item, going steady, making time, going out, dating, sparking it up . . ."

"That's enough," Clark had interrupted Carl. "All I did was ask why you and Vonda Belle were holding hands so tightly when you walked away from the Carriage House in Georgetown. You don't have to give me every possible synonym for what the two of you are up to."

The four young people were able to get a good spot from which to stand and watch Roger Mudd report the cloture vote as it happened. Clark said to the other three: "Can you believe this? When else has a record vote in the U.S. Senate been reported live, vote by vote, on national television? We're probably witnessing one of the great moments in the history of the American news media, and a great moment in the history of Congress."

As Clark, Bonnie, Carl, and Vonda Belle waited expectantly on the Capitol lawn, various senators were delivering their final speeches on the civil rights bill prior to the cloture vote. The situation was ready made for flowery speech making and calls to serve historical necessity. In other words, the situation was ready made for a senator with the speaking abilities of Everett McKinley Dirksen of Illinois.

"I shall quote the great writer Victor Hugo," Dirksen said, standing in his customary spot in the well of the Senate. "Hugo wrote, 'Stronger than all the armies is an idea whose time has come.'"

"The time has come for civil rights in America," Dirksen expounded. "The time has come for equality of opportunity. It must come in government, in education, in employment. This moment will not be stayed or denied. It is here."

"On the civil rights issue," Dirksen intoned, "we must rise with the occasion. The issue is essentially moral in character. It must be resolved. It will not go away."

"I appeal to all senators," Dirksen concluded, raising his arms in a gesture of openness to new ideas and necessities. "Let us not be found wanting. Let us give whatever it takes in the way of moral and spiritual substance to face up to the civil rights issue. Let us vote for cloture." [101]

Precisely at 11:10 A.M., the sound of bells and buzzers echoed throughout the Senate side of the Capitol. The senators were being summoned to one of the most important Senate votes in American History.

Senator Hubert H.Humphrey, the Democratic whip in the Senate, sat at his desk in the front row on the Democratic side of the aisle. Ironically, seated right next to him, was Senator Harry Byrd of Virginia, one of the most committed of the filibustering Southern Democrats. Just a few seats behind them, at a desk on the aisle, perched Richard Russell of Georgia, the Southern leader. Russell was arched forward over his desk, his hand cupped to his ear, straining to hear every vote as the roll call got underway.

In the first desk in the first row on the Republican side of the aisle sat Senator Everett Dirksen of Illinois. He was being hailed as the man of the hour. He was praised as the legislative wizard who found both the formula and the votes to make a successful cloture vote possible. Next to Dirksen was Senator Thomas H.Kuchel, the Republican whip in the Senate.

A pall of total silence, a rare event in the Senate, was interrupted only by the mechanical sounding voice of the clerk calling the roll. The clerk droned through the list of senators in alphabetical order. Each of the Senate leaders had a tally sheet on his desk on which to record the vote of each senator. Humphrey, Dirksen, and Kuchel were checking to see that, vote by vote, every senator who had pledged to vote for cloture was delivering. Richard Russell, on the other hand, was hoping for enough surprise switches and jumping ship for the cloture vote to fail.

As would be expected for such a crucial vote, all 100 senators were on the Senate floor. A big moment came when the clerk spoke the name "Dirksen." An instantly recognizable voice, as mellifluous as ever, said "Aye."

When the clerk called "Humphrey," the response was somewhat weary but tinged with an aura of success. "Aye," said Hubert Humphrey, sounding as if he had waited throughout his entire political career to cast this one vote.

And when the clerk intoned "Russell," the Southern leader virtually bellowed a sharp and defiant "No." [102]

Out on the Capitol lawn, there were feelings of tension but a growing sense of success. Clark, Bonnie, Carl, and Vonda Belle cheered when a Democratic fence sitter, Howard Cannon of Nevada, cast his vote for cloture. There was more good news when J. Howard Edmondson of Oklahoma, another Democratic holdout, voted to end debate.

"I'll bet Lyndon Johnson did some of his classic arm-twisting on senators Cannon and Edmondson to get their votes," Carl Brimmer said. "And we all know that no one can do arm-twisting like our president."

Cloture seemed definitely assured when Bourke Hickenlooper of Iowa, a wavering Republican, stayed loyal to Senator Dirksen and voted for cloture.

And, near the end of the roll call, there was icing on the cloture cake when Ralph Yarborough of Texas, another Democratic undecided, voted to end the filibuster.

Suddenly the roll call vote was over. The results were announced. The final count was 71 yeas and 29 nays. The civil rights bill had been successfully clotured with four more votes than the 67 required by Senate rules.

At that moment, Clark Schooler later realized, simultaneous celebrations took place all over Capitol Hill and throughout the nation. The pro-civil rights senators milled about the Senate floor, loudly congratulating each other. The small crowd on the Capitol lawn watching Roger Mudd on CBS TV, which included Clark and his three friends, clapped and cheered loudly. These expressions of joy were picked up by Roger Mudd's microphone and broadcast across the country as enthusiastic background noise.

But also, Clark knew, in homes, and offices, and schools, and factories, and colleges, and even while driving along listening to their car radios, civil rights supporters throughout the United States were experiencing and expressing both joy and relief.

It was June 10, 1964. It was Wednesday. It also was the 75th day of Senate debate on the House-passed civil rights bill. It was the day on which, for the first time in American history, the United States Senate invoked cloture on a civil rights bill.

Subsequent events took place like clockwork. The cloture vote had assured that certain things would happen, and happen they did.

Senate Rules provided that, following a cloture vote, each senator had one more hour of time to debate. Some of the more avowedly segregationist Southerners, such as Senator Sam Ervin of North Carolina and Senator Strom Thurmond of South Carolina, used their full hour of time to further excoriate the bill. But the clock ticked away each senator's last 60 minutes of speaking time with a grim, inevitable certainty.

Finally, when every Southern senator who wanted to do so had used up an hour of time, a final vote was held on the civil rights bill. It passed the

Senate by a vote of 73 to 27. But now, because it was not a cloture vote, only a simple majority was required. The civil rights forces had more than 20 votes to spare.

Having successfully passed the Senate, the bill immediately returned to the House of Representatives. Clark Schooler quickly reminded himself that, to avoid going to conference committee, the Senate version of the civil rights bill would have to be re-adopted by the House without amendment. If the bill were sent to a conference, the conference report would have been subject to a second filibuster when it came back to the Senate for final passage.

But Clark knew that Nicholas Katzenbach, the deputy attorney general for civil rights, had been a regular attender of the Humphrey-Dirksen negotiations on the Senate version of the civil rights bill. Nick Katzenbach had made it a point to keep the House leadership, both Democratic and Republican, fully informed on the changes that Humphrey and Dirksen were making to the bill. Katzenbach stayed particularly in touch with Representative William McCulloch of Ohio, the foremost Republican authority in the House on civil rights matters.

"In essence," Clark liked to say to anyone who would listen to him, "the conversations between Katzenbach and McCulloch were an ad hoc House-Senate conference committee on the civil rights bill. Whenever Humphrey and Dirksen started to do something that McCulloch and the House Republicans did not approve, Katzenbach would carry the word back to the Humphrey-Dirksen negotiations. Appropriate changes would be made in the Senate version of the bill."

"When else," Clark would exclaim with an extra dose of theatrics, "have just two men, Katzenbach and McCulloch, wielded so much power? Those two guys were the House-Senate conference committee for one of the most important bills in congressional history. And they conducted their ad hoc conference committee while the bill was being filibustered in the Senate." [103]

The House of Representatives wasted no time in bringing the Senate-amended civil rights bill to a final vote. The night before, Clark Schooler and Carl Brimmer and Greg Netherton were enjoying their customary late dinner at Mike Palm's Restaurant on Capitol Hill. Greg Netherton livened the meal up by announcing that, as of the next day, he would be joining Clark and Carl in supporting the civil rights bill. Greg Netherton explained:

"My boss, Representative Charles L. Weltner of Atlanta, Georgia, is thinking of voting for the Senate version of the civil rights bill," Greg said. "Weltner voted against the original House bill. But he believes the bill really was improved and made considerably less coercive on the South by the changes implemented by Senator Dirksen."

Carl Brimmer had a ready reply to this shocking announcement. "Weltner also has noticed," Carl said sarcastically, "that about 1/3 of his House district in Atlanta now is black. He can make a real play for those black voters by supporting the final version of the bill."

"The growing black vote in Atlanta is a factor in this decision," Greg replied. "But it's not the only factor. Weltner thinks its morally right to support civil rights. And he believes the South must discard its old segregationist social structure if its going to modernize and expand its economy."

"It will really raise some news media eyebrows if he does it," Clark Schooler said. "Most of the Southern Democrats in the House have been as defiant as the Southern senators in the face of the civil rights bill."

Just as Greg Netherton had speculated, Representative Charles Weltner told the House of Representatives the next day that he was voting for the Senate-passed version of the civil rights bill. Weltner was famous for often referring in his speeches to the song "Dixieland," the anthem of the Confederate states during the Civil War. Weltner noted that the last line of the song was: "Look away. Look away. Look away. Dixieland."

Then Weltner would add: "But we in Dixieland cannot 'look away' forever. We cannot 'look away' from the reality of the civil rights demonstrations. We cannot 'look away' from the continuing pleas of the South's black population for equal rights." [104]

Just prior to the House vote on the Senate amendments to the civil rights bill, Representative Weltner said with great emotion: "Change, swift and certain, is upon the South. I will add my voice to those Southerners who seek reasoned and conciliatory adjustment to this new reality. I would urge my fellow Southerners to leave the past behind and move on to the task of building a new South. We must not remain forever bound to another lost cause." [105]

Unamended in any way, the Senate version of the civil rights bill passed the U.S. House of Representatives by a vote of 289 to 126. President Kennedy's and President Johnson's civil rights bill was now an Act of Congress. The signature of President Lyndon Baines Johnson would make it a United States law.

President Johnson wasted not one second of time. Within hours of House passage of the final version of the bill, the president held one of the most elaborate bill signing ceremonies in the nation's history. Under ordinary conditions, the president signs bills in the Oval Office with only a few of the bill's congressional supporters looking on. Lyndon Johnson moved the ceremony to the East Room of the White House, a large and ornate reception hall that could accommodate more than 100 observers.

The president invited almost every notable person who had been associated with the passage of the bill. Heading the guest list were the key leaders of the civil rights movement, in particular the Reverend Martin Luther King, Jr. Also on hand were several Cabinet members, including Attorney General Robert Kennedy. Important foreign ambassadors were present, particularly those from African nations. And the party leaders from the House and the Senate were placed right next to the president. Prominent among them was Everett McKinley Dirksen, Republican from Illinois.

Clark Schooler and his two house mates watched the signing ceremony, live on national network television, in the living room of their home on Sixth Street South East on Capitol Hill. It felt good to Clark that, at this final moment, he and Carl Brimmer and Greg Netherton were united in support of the final version of the civil rights bill. Clark also was delighted to see his boss, Senator Kuchel, very much part and parcel of all the signing ceremony hoopla.

President Lyndon Baines Johnson signed the civil rights bill at 6:45 P.M., Eastern Daylight Time, on July 2, 1964. The bill was now the Civil Rights Act of 1964. It was also the law of the land.

The president, who had given so many speeches and talks urging that the bill be passed, shared his final thoughts on the bill with the people of the United States.

"Years ago I realized a sad truth," Lyndon Johnson said. "To the extent that black people were imprisoned by racial segregation, so was I. On this day, July 2, 1964, I have signed a bill that brings to us the positive side of that same truth. To the extent that American blacks are now really free, so am I. And so is our nation." [106]

In The Interim

The most immediate effect of the Civil Rights Act of 1964 was to almost instantly end legal racial segregation in the United States of America. Virtually overnight, African-Americans were granted access to restaurants, snack bars, swimming pools, ice skating rinks, hotels, motels, and other places of public accommodation engaged in interstate commerce.

The Civil Rights Act of 1964 also established the "cut-off" of U.S. Government funds as an effective way to get state governments to undertake specific actions mandated by Congress. Thus every state lowered automobile speed limits during the energy crisis of the mid-1970s rather than risk the cut-off of U.S. Government highway funds.

A variety of laws have been passed subsequent to 1964 that expanded protection from discrimination to other groups in addition to racial, reli-

gious, and ethnic minorities. For example, in 1967 Congress banned discrimination against workers or job applicants on the basis of age.

In 1972 Congress outlawed discrimination against women in educational programs receiving U.S. Government aid. One effect of this law was a major effort on the part of colleges and universities to bring women's sports programs up to the same level of activity and financing as men's programs.

And in 1973, and again in 1991, Congress passed laws requiring that handicapped and disabled persons be treated equally in the work place and be granted handicapped access to all public facilities and places of public accommodation.

Perhaps the greatest impact of the Civil Rights Act of 1964 was on employment opportunity. Because women were included in the equal employment sections of the new law, women as well as racial minorities began getting better jobs and being promoted more rapidly. The United States work force, previously dominated by white males, came to include substantially increased numbers of women and minority workers. Gains were particularly noticeable at professional and executive levels.

CHAPTER 14

PRESIDENTIAL ELECTIONS:
JOHNSON AGAINST GOLDWATER

Clark Schooler was genuinely surprised that the world did not stop spinning at the moment Lyndon Johnson signed the Civil Rights Act of 1964 into law. Clark had been only a bit player in that great legislative drama. But Clark had so pointed his every effort and every ability at getting the new law enacted that, it seemed to Clark, all human history should have ended when the long struggle for the civil rights bill at last was over.

But life did go on. On July 31, 1964, Clark's sojourn as a Capitol Fellow was over. To celebrate the end of their time in Washington together, the Capitol Fellows and their spouses and friends boarded a "party boat" on the Chesapeake and Ohio Canal. Operated by the National Park Service, the boat was a former canal barge that had been converted from hauling freight to hosting a stand-up social gathering and a buffet dinner. A real live mule hauled the old tow boat through the C. and O. Canal Park on a lovely summer's night.

The old Chesapeake and Ohio Canal was one of the things Clark liked best about life in Washington, D.C. The actual canal, which stretched from Georgetown to Cumberland, Maryland, had been abandoned as a working canal in the 1930s. The old canal bed paralleled the Potomac River, so walking the old canal included beautiful river scenery along with canal scenery.

The tow path on the canal, along which mules had walked pulling canal boats up and down, had been converted by the National Park Service into one of America's best and most scenic biker-hiker trails. Clark loved to be out walking or bicycling on the old canal. He particularly enjoyed inspecting the ruins of old stone locks, the gated portions of the canal that were used to lift the canal boats from one water level of the canal to another.

So Clark was delighted that a dinner party on a barge ride on the old Chesapeake and Ohio Canal was going to be the final social event of his year as a Capitol Fellow. Clark took Bonnie and Carl brought Vonda Belle to this final event of the Capitol Fellows program. Clark experienced both joy and melancholy that evening. He was joyous because his year as a Capitol Fellow had been unusually challenging and exciting. But he also felt melancholy, because he was going to greatly miss working on Capitol Hill with Senator Kuchel.

Upon returning to his job in the Washington bureau of the Patriot Press newspaper chain, Clark was immediately assigned to a Patriot Press News Squadron covering the 1964 Democratic National Convention. The party confab was to be held in Atlantic City, New Jersey, in late August of 1964.

The convention delegates would be able to enjoy the famous beach and more than six miles of boardwalk in Atlantic City. In between lavish parties at the city's famous row of ocean front hotels, the delegates would formally vote Lyndon Johnson as the 1964 Democratic nominee for president.

Clark dutifully pointed out to his superiors at the Patriot Press newspapers that he was a Republican and perhaps could not be trusted to cover the Democratic Convention. His journalistic bosses would have none of it. "This is your chance to test your objectivity as a newsman," said Jim Senitall, the Patriot Press organization's top Washington correspondent. "You can work on training yourself to keep your partisan biases out of your reporting."

By 1964, the national conventions were no longer true nominating conventions. Budding political analysts such as Clark Schooler referred to them as ratifying conventions. One of the major candidates for the party nomination for president always had enough delegate votes to win the nomination even before the national convention began. Careful spade work at state conventions and winning most of the presidential primaries usually enabled one candidate to quickly wrap up a majority of the convention delegates.

"It's not like the good old days," Jim Senitall told Clark wistfully. "As recently as 1952, just twelve years ago, national conventions often began with no one candidate having a majority of the delegates lined up. During convention week, the various candidates would promise things like Cabinet posts and seats on the Supreme Court in order to get key delegates to give them their votes. Or sometimes the candidates would promise big U.S. Government projects for a delegate's home state. It was really exciting. You often didn't know until the last day who was going to actually win the nomination."

"But that seems to be all over now," Jim Senitall continued. "John F.

Kennedy really furthered the trend in 1960. He lined up lots of delegates at the state conventions and then won six presidential primaries. Kennedy already had five votes more than he needed when the convention chairperson banged down the gavel and called the 1960 Democratic National Convention to order."

Clark listened dutifully to Jim's little lecture. "It sounds to me," Clark commented, "as if I'm on my way to a coronation rather than a convention."

Clark Schooler drove up to Atlantic City in his 1951 Ford Victoria hardtop convertible. He took one of the nation's oldest highways, U.S. 40, which also was known as the National Road. U.S. 40 stretched all the way from Atlantic City to San Francisco, California, and passed through Baltimore on its way west. With every window in his automobile open, Clark drove through the incredible heat and humidity of a hot and sunny East Coast August day.

With Lyndon Johnson already having the nomination safely in hand, Clark thought, this would probably be one of the dullest week's of his life. Clark was genuinely fearful that there would be virtually no news for him to report and write up for the millions of readers of Patriot Press newspapers.

Clark was saved from that fate by a civil rights struggle. The white politicians who were firmly in control of the Mississippi Democratic Party had sent a state delegation to the Democratic National Convention that was composed of white persons only. Despite the passage of the Civil Rights Act of 1964 in early July, Mississippi's white Democrats had refused to put even one or two token blacks in the Mississippi delegation.

Inspired by the recent gains of the civil rights movement, a group of black Mississippians formed the Mississippi Freedom Democratic Party. The key word in that name was "Freedom." This group elected an all-black delegation to the Democratic National Convention and raised the money to send those delegates to Atlantic City for convention week. This rival organization demanded that the national Democratic Party, in the spirit of racial equality, seat the black delegation from Mississippi, rather than the white delegation, on the convention floor.

Suddenly Clark found himself at the epicenter of a major national news story. With the presidential nomination already decided, the national press corps was gleeful to have something really exciting to cover. Suddenly the members of the Mississippi Freedom Democratic Party were all over the newspapers and network television news. The boardwalk and the grand hotels in Atlantic City suddenly turned into a stage on which Mississippi blacks cried out for justice and highlighted the inequities of living in one of the nation's most segregated states.

Out on the boardwalk in front of the Atlantic City convention center, a group of black and white demonstrators marched in silent protest against racial segregation in the all-white Mississippi Democratic Party. These protesters were visible to all the delegates as they entered and left the convention hall. The demonstrators also were photographed for the nation's newspapers and televised for the evening network news.

The Mississippi Freedom Democratic Party presented a very difficult problem to President Johnson. The white delegation from Mississippi had, after all, been elected according to Mississippi state law. The blacks in the Freedom Democratic Party delegation had moral credentials but no legal credentials. And, as long lines of delegates marched past the boardwalk demonstrators on their way into the convention hall, there was a growing sentiment among Northern and Western delegates to recognize the Mississippi Freedom Democratic Party in some highly visible and rewarding way.

To Lyndon Johnson, the obvious solution to the problem was compromise. The president sent two of his most trusted allies, Hubert Humphrey and Joseph Rauh, Jr., to try to broker a deal between the white and black Mississippians. Humphrey was to try to appease the white Southerners. Rauh was to work with the black Mississippians. It was a sensational break for Clark Schooler. Because the two men knew him from the civil rights bill struggle, Humphrey and Rauh both gave Clark personal interviews as they struggled to find a solution to the "Mississippi problem."

National conventions are organized under a committee system, exactly as Congress is. Major committees hold hearings and make policy recommendations to be adopted by the full membership of the convention on the convention floor. An example of a national convention committee is the Resolutions Committee, which debates the Party Platform and then recommends specific language to be voted upon by the entire convention.

The Credentials Committee's task was to listen to the pleas of those persons who contended they should be seated as bona fide delegates to the convention with the privilege to vote. It was not unusual for contested delegations to appear at national conventions in the early 20th Century. Often, in a heated race between two strong candidates, one delegation from a particular state would appear supporting Candidate A. Then another delegation would arrive from the same state committed to Candidate B. The job of the Credentials Committee was to recommend to the entire convention which delegation should be seated.

Thus the Credentials Committee at the 1964 Democratic National Convention became the arena in which the battle between the white Mississippians and the black Mississippians was fought out. Joseph Rauh negotiated strongly on behalf of the Mississippi Freedom Democratic Party, but eventually he was forced to acknowledge that the current laws of Mississippi had to be followed and all of the white delegates recommended for seating on the convention floor. The best deal that Rauh could get for the Mississippi Freedom Democratic Party was that two black Mississippians would be admitted to the national convention as at-large delegates with one vote each.

That deal, when it was announced, came nowhere near satisfying the demands of the black Mississippians. In an open act of defiance against President Lyndon Johnson and the Democratic Party, many of the Freedom Democrats stealthily made their way on to the convention floor. Most of them simply got entrance tickets from sympathetic white delegates from the North and the West. Once on the floor, the black Mississippians took the seats reserved for the white delegates from Mississippi. They sat with their arms locked together and stubbornly resisted all efforts by the sergeant at arms at the convention to get them to leave.

At ratifying conventions, where the nominee for president has been determined long before the national convention begins, the name of the game is stage management. Properly controlled and orchestrated, a national convention can be a week of free advertising for the presidential nominee and the political party. There are speeches by leading members of the party, supportive demonstrations on behalf of the party presidential candidate, and tons of exposure for the candidate and the candidate's spouse and children. All of this, with Hollywood style production values, can be presented via the mass media to the American people.

But, by the same token, unruly protests on the convention floor, or in the streets outside the convention hall, can turn a national convention into a public relations disaster for a political party. And, with the invasion of the convention floor by the Mississippi Freedom Democratic Party and their illegal occupation of the white Mississippians' seats, the 1964 Democratic National Convention was well on its way to being bad advertising, not good advertising.

Clearly the national convention, by 1964, had metamorphosed from a political event into a media event. In fact, the more than 5,500 news reporters and television and radio technicians present outnumbered the convention delegates.

Clark Schooler had a bird's eye view of the proceedings from the Patriot Press desk in the press section of the convention hall. Bernard Martin, the black reporter who had covered the riot at Ol' Miss with Clark, had risen steadily in the Patriot Press organization during the year that Clark was working as a Capitol Fellow in Washington, D.C. As a result, Bernard Martin was in charge of the Patriot Press News Squadron covering the 1964

Democratic National Convention.

Clark had been the first Patriot Press reporter to spot the black Mississippians coming into the convention hall and heading for the seats of the all-white Mississippi delegation. "Hey, Bernard," Clark said. "It looks like some blacks are trying to take over the Mississippi section of the convention floor. What do you want to do about it?"

Bernard Martin did exactly what Clark thought he would do. He hurried down on to the convention floor to try to interview the invading black Mississippians personally. As he hurried away, however, Bernard Martin yelled an order back to Clark: "Go outside and see if things have also gone berserk in the streets or down on the boardwalk."

The time of day was early evening, just before the eight o'clock hour when the convention was scheduled to begin. Back when national conventions were true nominating conventions, the conventions met during the daytime. And sometimes, when there was a real fight over who would win the presidential nomination, a convention might last well into the night. But by 1964, in the age of television, the most important sessions of national conventions were scheduled in the evening. That way, the convention proceedings would be covered on prime time television when the largest TV audiences were watching.

It was twilight when Clark walked out of the convention hall, which was located right on the boardwalk in Atlantic City. The first thing Clark did was check the streets immediately surrounding the convention center. Traffic was moving normally, and the sidewalks were filled with tourists and vacationers. There was not a protester or a demonstrator to be seen. Clark then checked the boardwalk where, for more than three days, the silent vigil had been going on to support the Mississippi Freedom Democratic Party.

The protesters had situated themselves on a portion of the boardwalk close to the beach in Atlantic City. Behind them, across a broad stretch of some of the best beach sand in the United States, the waves of the Atlantic Ocean pounded upon the New Jersey shore. The breakers looked good, Clark noticed as he hurried to the site of the ongoing demonstration. His mind slipped into the vernacular. Surf's up, he thought. Because it was summertime, the entire scene was bathed in the warm pinkish and orangish glow of a setting summer sun.

The demonstrators were mainly black males. They were dressed in white cotton shirts and dark blue overalls. They looked exactly like Mississippi tenant farmers who had come to Atlantic City to fight for their right to be represented equally at the convention.

At the moment Clark walked up, the protesters were standing listening to a speech. One of the protesters was James Farmer, a black man who was the national leader of CORE, the Congress of Racial Equality. Farmer had an injured eye and wore an eye patch over it. He made an inspiring sight, standing with the ocean to his back and with his eye patch catching the fading light of the setting sun.

"The Freedom delegation is on the convention floor," Clark heard a demonstration leader say. "Our delegates are sitting in their deserved seats as black representatives of the state of Mississippi. We shall support them out here with our silence and our commitment."

In front of the protesters, some 50 feet away, delegates were lined up to enter the convention hall. They could clearly see the demonstration. Some of the delegates occasionally yelled words of encouragement.

When the demonstration leader had finished his pep talk, the protesters began slowly walking in a circle on the boardwalk. Some of them carried small lighted candles which they carefully shielded from the light breeze blowing in off the ocean. As the demonstrators came by him along their circular path, Clark noticed for the first time that there were two women participating in the protest, one black and one white. Unlike the men in their overalls, the two women were dressed in blouses and wraparound skirts.

Clark did a double take when he recognized who the women were. The black woman was Vonda Belle Carter. The white woman was Bonnie Kanecton.

"You two are certainly full of surprises," Clark said as Vonda Belle and Bonnie walked past him.

Clark then began walking along with the two of them so he could talk to them. In all sincerity, Clark asked:

"Are your fellow demonstrators really Mississippi tenant farmers?"

Bonnie Kanecton smiled. "If you'll look closely," she said, "those white shirts and blue overalls are all brand new. We've talked with these particular demonstrators. Many of them are black lawyers and businessmen from New York and New Jersey pretending to be Mississippi tenant farmers."

"It didn't take us long to figure that out," Vonda Belle said, also smiling. "Hardly a one of them has a Southern accent."

Before Clark could ask anything more, one of the black men in overalls said to him: "It certainly is nice to have a white man in a suit coat and necktie join our demonstration."

The man's comment seemed to be sincere, and that sincerity embarrassed Clark. "I'm actually a newspaper reporter," Clark stammered back. "I'm just interviewing these demonstrators for the Patriot Press newspapers."

Clark took out his pencil and his reporter's tablet to make it look like he really was interviewing Bonnie and Vonda Belle as he walked along beside them. Clark asked a question that emphasized his amazement at finding his two friends in Atlantic City.

"How did you get here?"

"We drove up together from Washington," Vonda Belle said matter-of-factly. "According to the newspapers, this obviously is the place for anyone who truly believes in civil rights." She said the word "truly" in such a way that Clark felt like a rabid segregationist for not grabbing a candle and marching all night long.

"But you're actually hurting the cause," Clark said, sounding a great deal like Lyndon Johnson. "Holding protest demonstrations right after we passed the greatest civil rights bill in American history is folly. All it's doing is driving white voters into the arms of Barry Goldwater, the Republican nominee for president. The voters all know that, as a states' rights conservative, Senator Goldwater voted against the civil rights bill."

"We black people always get nervous when white people start saying stop, or wait, or slow down," Vonda Belle replied. "The civil rights bill did not end all forms of racial discrimination in the United States. The situation with the Mississippi freedom delegation clearly illustrates that point."

Clark continued to argue. "But why not wait until after the November election? Then, after President Johnson's won and Barry Goldwater and his states' rights ideology have been repudiated by the voters, the civil rights movement can get underway again."

At this moment, Bonnie Kanecton decided to get into the conversation.

"Be realistic, Clark," she said with an earnestness that revealed concern for both the civil rights cause and Clark Schooler. "The quest for liberty and freedom for minority Americans is going to be a continuous and ongoing task. Our beloved Civil Rights Act was a beginning, not an ending. It's been a mighty battle, and great gains have been made. But many more battles lie ahead, and much remains to be done."

The conversation ended abruptly when the protesters began to sing a few verses of "We Shall Overcome," the unofficial anthem of the civil rights movement. It was just as well, Clark thought. Clark was in Atlantic City to work for the Patriot Press organization, not conduct theoretical discussions on minority rights with Vonda Belle and Bonnie.

Clark quickly bade the two young women goodbye and hurried back into the convention hall. As he left the boardwalk, he cast one last glance back at Bonnie. She waved and smiled at him, as if to say that it was all right for the two of them to see this situation somewhat differently.

When Clark returned to the Patriot Press desk in the press section, he found the situation on the convention floor still out of control. The Mississippi freedom delegates refused to voluntarily leave their seats. By the same token, the Lyndon Johnson forces controlling the convention were reticent to use force to eject the freedom delegates from the convention hall. Finally, on the direct orders of President Johnson himself, the black Mississippians were pulled out of their chairs by security personnel and dragged or carried away.

In the end, the black Mississippians left Atlantic City, blaming their failure to get seated at the convention on Lyndon Johnson. But others left as well. The Mississippi and Alabama delegations, both of them all-white, marched indignantly and conspicuously out of the convention hall. They claimed that offering even two at-large delegates to the black Democrats of Mississippi was an unacceptable recognition of "illegal" delegates.

Once that disruptive scene was completed, however, the convention began to run as planned by Democratic Party leaders. The delegates played their assigned role of providing a background of enthusiastically cheering individuals in front of which Lyndon Johnson could accept the party nomination for president. The delegates had become so unimportant by 1964 that Clark Schooler mockingly referred to them as "movie extras" and nothing more.

There was the requisite ballot for president, but the roll call of the states was merely a formality since everyone knew that Lyndon Johnson was going to win. And, the night after the balloting made it official, Lyndon Johnson concluded the convention by giving his acceptance speech during prime time on national television.

Clark Schooler returned to Washington, D.C. He was immediately assigned to a Patriot Press News Squadron covering the 1964 presidential election campaign. The race was expected to be an interesting one. The Republican presidential nominee challenging incumbent Democratic President Lyndon Johnson was U.S. Senator Barry Goldwater of Arizona. Goldwater was an outspoken conservative Republican who took strong right wing stands on a variety of domestic and foreign issues.

When he first heard he would be covering the 1964 presidential election, Clark visualized himself traveling with Lyndon Johnson or Barry Goldwater, flying around the nation on the press plane that accompanied each candidate from state to state. Clark also saw himself riding on the press bus that took the reporters from campaign event to campaign event within a particular state. In this particular daydream, Clark spent much of his time chatting and socializing with David Broder of the *Washington Post*, James Reston of the *New York Times*, and other leading political reporters and commentators of the time.

But that was not the case. Clark was assigned to remain in the nation's capital and cover the more intellectual aspects of the presidential election, such as the influence of the Electoral College and the television spot ads that Johnson and Goldwater were running against one another.

"The Electoral College is found in the United States Constitution," Clark pointed out to Carl Brimmer one day when the two young men were discussing the campaign. "The Founders did not trust the people to elect the president directly. They provided for each state to select electors who would do the actual voting for president. Each state was assigned one elector for each seat it had in the U.S. House of Representatives. In addition, each state received two more electors for its two seats in the U.S. Senate."

Carl Brimmer listened politely to Clark and then said lightheartedly: "Somehow, Clark, you turn any subject we discuss into a lecture."

"I can't help it," Clark replied. "I think that, similar to most Americans, you don't really understand how the Electoral College works."

"Sure, I do," Carl answered back. "Because the Electoral College is based mainly on the House of Representatives, the states with the largest populations have the largest number of electoral votes. In almost all states, when a state votes for a particular candidate, that candidate wins all of that state's electoral votes. The way to win a presidential election is to just win the big states with the largest numbers of electoral votes."

Now it was Carl who was lecturing. "Presidential candidates concentrate their efforts in states such as New York, Pennsylvania, Ohio, and Illinois," Carl said with an air of great authority. "Most of these states are located in the Northeast quadrant of the United States bounded by St.Louis, Milwaukee, Boston, and Washington. The only other place that's big and important is California."

Carl was on a roll. "The result is a theory called the Quad-Cali Theory," Carl explained. "To win the Electoral College, presidential candidates concentrate on the Quad, the Northeast quadrant of the United States, and on Cali, the state of California."

Clark Schooler smiled the smile of one who possessed superior knowledge. "Close, but no cigar," Clark said. "It's more subtle than that. When public opinion polls show New York or California to be voting strongly for one candidate or the other, neither candidate will bother to campaign in that state, even though it has a giant pot of electoral votes. Furthermore, a presidential candidate often will campaign in a middle-sized state, a state with a middle-sized population, when polls show that the race is close and either candidate might win that state and all of its electoral votes."

"So the general rule," Clark said with a tone of triumph, "is that presidential candidates campaign in the largest states, population wise, where polls show the race to be close."

Carl Brimmer absorbed all this weighty information and then said: "All right! Your analysis is more subtle than mine. So tell me, Mr. Republican know-it-all, is that how Barry Goldwater is going to win this race for the White House. Is he just running in states where the polls show the contest to be close?"

"No," Clark responded. "He's pursuing a completely different strategy. He calls it a Southern strategy. Goldwater seems to be giving the Northeast quadrangle of New York, Pennsylvania, Illinois, etc., to Lyndon Johnson without a fight. Goldwater proposes, with his conservative ideology, to steal the entire South from the Democratic Party and get it to vote Republican. He plans to add in the more conservative states in the Rocky Mountain West plus California. He thinks he can carry California because of all the conservative Republican voters in Orange County in the Los Angeles suburbs."

"As a U.S. senator, Barry Goldwater voted against the 1964 civil rights bill," Clark continued. "It was part of his Electoral College strategy to win the South. He plans to pry the South away from its normally Democratic leanings with his opposition to civil rights."

"Sometimes," Clark rambled on, "you hear Goldwater's Southern strategy referred to as the Sunbelt strategy. The Sunbelt is the strip of states across the southern United States which have experienced rapid population growth since the end of World War II. Three of those states are California, Texas, and Florida. Those states are already populated enough for each to have a large number of electoral votes. And those three states are attracting more people and growing larger all the time."

"Sunbelt theorists," Clark concluded, "look with disdain on the Rustbelt, the old industrial states of the Northeast and Midwest that are filled with worn-out and rusted-out old factory buildings. They argue electoral power in the United States is shifting from the Rustbelt to the Sunbelt, and that will help elect Goldwater to the presidency."

Carl Brimmer listened to all this high-powered Electoral College logic and then shook his head in wonderment. "OK," he said. "You're a veritable political Sherlock. But what's Lyndon Johnson doing to head Barry Goldwater off?"

Clark was more than happy to strategize for the Democrats as well as the Republicans. "As far as I can tell," Clark said, "Lyndon Johnson and the Democrats are playing it straight Quad-Cali. President Johnson is willing to let Goldwater have the South, but that's all right if Johnson can hold the Quad and California together. It's now clear the state each of them has to win to make his Electoral College theory work is California."

In addition to writing articles for the Patriot Press newspapers on the

Electoral College, Clark Schooler covered the political strategy of the Johnson and Goldwater campaigns for president.

Lyndon Johnson, Clark told his readers, was running a standard liberal Democratic campaign. Johnson was emphasizing the "deal me in" strategy, the idea developed during President Franklin Delano Roosevelt's New Deal that the U.S. Government should share the great wealth of the United States with less fortunate groups in the society. Thus New Deal programs such as Social Security and unemployment compensation and public welfare collected taxes from the middle class and well-to-do and shared this money with the elderly, the out-of-work, and the economically destitute.

Among intellectuals, it was fashionable to refer to this particular method of winning votes as "redistribution politics." Money was redistributed from the wealthy to the poor in return for votes.

Lyndon Johnson called for a U.S. Government program to provide health care for the elderly. In addition, Johnson promised to undertake a series of U.S. Government poverty programs to reduce economic hardship throughout the nation. Johnson referred to his package of proposed government subsidies as the Great Society.

The political strategy of President Johnson's opponent, Republican nominee Barry Goldwater, was considerably different. Goldwater pledged to cut U.S. Government welfare programs rather than expand them. Goldwater called for more individual responsibility in the United States and for less dependence on the government.

And, with great fervor, Goldwater called for freeing the state governments from rules and regulations forced upon them by the U.S. Government in Washington, D.C. That position was a thinly-veiled attack on all the rules and regulations imposed on the states by the recently enacted Civil Rights Act of 1964.

Clark reminded his readers over and over again that these were the traditional ideologies of the Democratic Party and the Republican Party. Ever since Franklin Roosevelt and the New Deal, Clark emphasized, the Democrats had been strongly pro-government and the Republicans had called for less government. The Democratic Party had been for collective responsibility, Clark wrote, while the Republicans had hammered away in favor of individual initiative.

The most interesting thing about the 1964 presidential election, Clark emphasized in his writing, was that the ideologies of the two political parties were so frankly and clearly stated. The choice between the Democratic candidate and the Republican candidate in 1964 was an unusually clear one.

In the post-World War II years, the political weapon of choice in the United States was the 30-second television spot ad. The Johnson forces were aided in their advertisement writing by Barry Goldwater's tendency to take strong stands on controversial political issues.

For instance, although U.S. troops were serving in South Vietnam only as military advisers in 1964, there was considerable debate as to whether United States troops should be serving in Vietnam at all. Barry Goldwater stepped into the middle of this controversy by stating that, if elected president, he would give the authority to use tactical nuclear weapons to U.S. military commanders in Vietnam. Up to this time, it had been assumed that nuclear weapons would never be used by the United States except upon the direct orders of the U.S. president.

That statement by Goldwater was all that the Johnson forces needed. A TV spot ad came out picturing a little girl, about five years old, playing in a field and picking the petals off a daisy. The camera focus was intentionally fuzzy, giving the impression that the little girl was having an enjoyable, almost dream-like experience.

Suddenly, the peace and happiness of the scene was shattered by a male voice giving the backward countdown of a missile launching. "Three. Two. One. Zero," the voice said sharply, and suddenly the screen erupted into the rising mushroom cloud of a nuclear explosion. Then another voice spoke softly and convincingly, articulating the main message of the ad:

"There is a man running for president who supports the free and easy use of nuclear weapons in Vietnam. Peace loving Americans cannot let that happen. Be certain to vote in this presidential election. The stakes are too high not to."

The ad concluded visually with the words: "Lyndon Johnson for President."

That one television spot ad set off a storm of controversy in the print press. Was it fair to imply that Goldwater wanted to start a nuclear war that would kill little American girls? Was picturing an actual nuclear explosion going too far in criticizing Goldwater's position?

All at once Clark Schooler found that his assignment to cover campaign advertising was a juicy one. Clark's stories were the one's getting on page one of the Patriot Press newspapers. The reporters actually covering the candidates were having their stories demoted to page two or page three inside the newspaper. The situation inspired Clark to come up with Schooler's First Law of Presidential Campaigns. To wit: What the ads are saying is more important than what the candidates are saying.

The anti-Goldwater ad with the nuclear explosion in it was eventually pulled off the air by the "Johnson For President" campaign. But by that time, Clark carefully pointed out to his readers, that 30-second spot had been played over and over again on news programs reporting the controversy over the ad. That resulted in millions of dollars of free advertising for Lyndon Johnson. And the entire incident firmly established in millions of voters' minds that Barry Goldwater was the war candidate and Lyndon Johnson was the peace candidate.

In his effort to emphasize individualism and personal responsibility in his campaign for president, Barry Goldwater proposed that the Social Security retirement system be made voluntary rather than compulsory. Goldwater wanted to let people invest their Social Security money in the stock market, if they wanted to, rather than be forced to give it to a government-managed program.

Here was another opportunity for a Lyndon Johnson 30-second television spot ad. The ad writers took a very simple approach. The ad opened with a picture of a Social Security membership card. The announcer's voice accused Goldwater of trying to sabotage the Social Security system by letting wealthy people invest their Social Security funds in the stock market. That would leave no money for poor and middle-class persons, the announcer said, who only had Social Security to support them in their old age.

Just before the end of the ad, two human hands appeared and tore the Social Security card in half. The hands proceeded to tear the Social Security card into little bits. The announcer's voice concluded: "There is a man running for president who wants to take away our Social Security retirement plan. Average Americans cannot let that happen. Be certain to vote in this presidential election. The stakes are too high not to."

And, on the screen, the final words: "Lyndon Johnson for President."

Although he was a Republican, Clark thought the Social Security ad was stunning. "Every working American has a Social Security card in his or her wallet," Clark wrote. "Virtually all citizens of the United States are depending on that card to provide for them financially in their later years of life. Having two human hands, ostensibly Barry Goldwater's hands, tear up the Social Security card brought the gravity of this issue home to the average voter in a highly visual and compelling way."

The 1964 presidential campaign ended up being a very rich one for innovative television spot ads. In the end, Clark's favorite turned out to be a Lyndon Johnson ad based on an offhand comment by Barry Goldwater. The Republican nominee had stated for the record that, in his opinion, the United States would be a better country if someone "sawed off" the East Coast and let it "float out to sea." That simple act, Goldwater implied, would eliminate large numbers of liberal Democratic voters from the national electorate.

Lyndon Johnson's ad writers saw another chance to further mine the electorate for votes. A 30-second spot ad opened with a map of the entire eastern half of the United States, starting at about the Mississippi River and going eastward to the East Coast and the Atlantic Ocean.

As the announcer's voice began reading the Barry Goldwater quote, a handsaw began sawing off the East Coast states. The saw worked its way down the western borders of New York, Pennsylvania, Maryland, Virginia and West Virginia. Eventually, when the saw had finished its work, the East Coast states began moving as if they were floating free of the rest of the nation. Then, as the ad concluded, the entire East Coast floated off into the Atlantic Ocean and, eventually, out of the television picture.

All that remained of the United States in the ad was a truncated nation that started with Ohio and Kentucky and Tennessee and went westward.

Once again Clark Schooler was impressed by the visual impact of the ad. "Residents of the East Coast immediately fixed their eyes on their home state," Clark wrote. "Or, more finitely than that, on the spot in which they lived in their home state. East Coast viewers were completely aware of when the saw went by their home state. And the viewers could feel the wave action when the East Coast was sawed free of the U.S. mainland."

The Johnson campaign saturated the East Coast with that particular 30-second television spot ad. And most of the states where the ad played, such as New York, New Jersey, Pennsylvania, and Virginia, were heavily populated states with large numbers of electoral votes.

Suddenly it was presidential election day 1964. The public opinion polls were all predicting a Lyndon Johnson landslide, and the polls turned out to be more than correct. The electoral slaughter of Barry Goldwater and the Republicans began in New England, where swing states such as Connecticut, Vermont, New Hampshire, and Maine went thunderingly for President Johnson.

The Democratic tidal wave surged across the American Midwest, that traditional breadbasket of the Republican Party. Ohio, Indiana, Wisconsin, and Missouri all voted for Johnson. Even Senator Everett Dirksen's home state of Illinois went heavily for the president. And the rising Democratic waters engulfed even the High Plains and Rocky Mountain states, where such Republican diehard strongholds as Kansas and Nebraska and Wyoming and Idaho repudiated Goldwater-style conservatism and voted instead for Lyndon Johnson's brand of liberalism.

When it was all over, the 1964 presidential election had redrawn the map of American politics. Barry Goldwater carried only six states. One was his own home state of Arizona. The others were the five Deep South states of Louisiana, Mississippi, Alabama, Georgia, and South Carolina. All the rest of America, 44 states in all, had voted for Lyndon Johnson.

"It's incredible," Clark Schooler grumbled, as much to the television set as to anyone else in the room. "The Republicans have always dreamed of stealing away the Solid South from the Democratic Party. Tonight, with Barry Goldwater as their presidential candidate, the Republicans succeeded in winning the five states of deepest Dixie. But it cost them almost all the rest of the United States to do it. That's no way to restructure and rebuild a political party."

Clark was watching the election returns with the three people who had become his closest friends in Washington. They were Bonnie Kanecton, Carl Brimmer, and Vonda Belle Carter. The four young people were on the election night equivalent of a double date. They had gathered together at an election night party in Georgetown to, as Clark put it, "watch the voters of America paint an electoral picture of the nation."

The electoral picture that soon emerged was one of Lyndon Johnson having unusually long presidential coattails. Large numbers of Democrats were being elected to the U.S. Senate and the U.S. House of Representatives, some of them from states and districts that were considered heavily Republican.

Carl Brimmer, an ever loyal member of the Democratic Party, was particularly delighted by the large numbers of Democrats who were winning Senate and House seats from the Republicans. "With each new report," Carl gloated to Clark, "we seem to mine another nugget of electoral gold for the Democratic Party."

Carl's enthusiasm was shared by Vonda Belle Carter. "My parents," Vonda Belle said at one point in the evening, "are like many older blacks. My parents were born and raised Republicans. After all, the Republican Party is the party of Abraham Lincoln and the emancipation of the slaves. And I always kind of thought of myself as a Republican. But this election tonight has won me over to the Democratic Party. Totally!"

The results of the 1964 presidential election were hardest of all on Bonnie Kanecton. A lifelong Republican from the Chicago suburbs, she was watching her chosen political party suffer one of the worst defeats in its history.

"It's all so unfair," Bonnie said, sounding as if she might burst into tears at any moment. "Senator Dirksen worked so hard on the civil rights bill. He really thought his efforts to get his fellow Republican senators to vote for cloture would win support for the Republican Party among black voters. But then Barry Goldwater came along and nullified Dirksen's efforts by voting against the civil rights bill and winning the Republican nomination for president."

"Dirksen did such a good, good thing for American blacks," Bonnie concluded sorrowfully. "But now Dirksen's been completely overshadowed by Goldwater. Dirksen's good deeds for American blacks are being totally ignored."

Vonda Belle Carter replied to Bonnie's sad lament with some measure of sympathy. "Sorry," Vonda Belle said, "but I'm one of those American blacks you just referred to. For me, stopping Barry Goldwater and his conservative ideology was a ten-times higher priority than rewarding Senator Dirksen for his laudable efforts on the civil rights bill."

Clark Schooler was amazed that so many Republican candidates for Congress had gone down with Goldwater's ship. Lyndon Johnson was not just going to remain the American president. Johnson was going to be a Democratic president with some of the largest majorities the Democratic Party had ever enjoyed in the U.S. Senate and the U.S. House of Representatives.

In The Interim

National conventions are as stage managed in the 2000s as they were in the 1960s, only more so. In 1992 the Democratic Party called upon two Hollywood television producers, Harry Thomason and his wife, Linda Bloodworth Thomason, to script virtually every detail of the Democratic National Convention. The Thomasons played down political speeches and strongly played up warm and fuzzy TV scenes of William Jefferson Clinton, the Democratic Party nominee-designate, dancing with his wife, Hillary Rodham Clinton, and talking with his teenage daughter, Chelsea Clinton. The result was the kind of warm and fuzzy television that draws and enchants audiences but has very little to do with the more practical realities of American politics.

Hollywood style at national conventions also means tightly controlling the convention so that there are no negative images such as those presented by the Mississippi Freedom Democratic Party at the 1964 Democratic Convention. The only people who are allowed to appear on the official television coverage of the national convention are supporters of the designated party presidential nominee.

And, whenever possible, glitzy well-known Hollywood celebrities who support the political party are put on television. These nonpolitical headliners take the place of important elected party politicians, such as U.S. senators and members of the U.S. House of Representatives, whose political speeches and complex political proposals tend to bore audiences.

The high spot of the year 2000 national conventions came when Albert Gore, Jr., the Democratic Party nominee-designate, gave a warm and meaningful kiss to his wife, Tipper Gore. Although Gore narrowly lost the

2000 presidential election to Republican candidate George W. Bush, Gore's emotional kiss for his spouse, before a sizeable national television audience, was said to have energized his presidential campaign more than any other event at the national convention.

Presidential election campaigns remain much the same in the 2000s as in the 1960s. The Electoral College is still in effect. Therefore Republican and Democratic presidential nominees continue to concentrate their efforts in states where the public opinion polls show the race to be close. Even a populous state with a large number of electoral votes, such as California or New York, will receive minimal attention from presidential candidates if polls show the state going solidly for one candidate or the other.

And television advertising, particularly 30-second spot ads, continues a big part of campaigning for president of the United States. In fact, it is the high cost of television ads that causes both political parties in the 2000s to put a heavy emphasis on raising large sums of money to pay for those television ads.

A major change has been the rise in importance of presidential television debates. Ever since 1976, the Democratic and Republican presidential nominees have met in a series of two or three face-to-face television debates in the October before the November presidential election. These debates are conducted in an even-handed style with officially nonpartisan journalists serving as moderators and question askers.

These formal television debates can have an effect on a presidential campaign, particularly when one candidate makes a particularly pointed and memorable statement. More importantly, presidential candidates need to avoid a major gaffe when debating. Incumbent Republican President Gerald Ford greatly weakened his 1976 campaign for reelection to the White House when he erroneously stated that Poland was no longer a Communist country under the control of the Soviet Union. That statement would not become true until 13 years later, in 1989, when the Berlin Wall was torn down and the Soviet Union lost control of its Eastern European satellite nations.

The most important change in presidential elections since the 1960s has been the shift of the South from the Democratic to the Republican Party. This quantum change in United States voting behavior took place slowly and steadily throughout the 1970s and the 1980s. As the Southern states, and their large pot of electoral votes, slipped away from the Democratic Party, the Democrats were forced to rely more heavily on the votes of racial minorities, particularly African-American voters in East Coast, Midwest, and West Coast cities. The new Democratic base became the populous states in the Northeast and the Midwest, with occasional help from the most populous state of all, California.

But the shift of the old South to the Republican Party continued relentlessly in the 1990s. In the 2000 and 2004 presidential elections, Republican candidate George W. Bush carried every one of the states that seceded from the Union during the Civil War. The old Solid South of the Democratic Party appeared to be gone forever.

By the early 2000s, there was a new Republican base consisting of the entire South plus the heavily Republican High Plains and Rocky Mountain states. It closely resembled the electoral coalition that Barry Goldwater had attempted to assemble in 1964, but which Goldwater only carried in part. The Southern strategy, a losing strategy in 1964, had become a winning strategy by the time of the 2000 and 2004 presidential elections.

CHAPTER 15

THE SUPREME COURT:
THE CONSTITUTIONAL TEST

"The fight over the civil rights bill isn't over yet!"

Bonnie Kanecton said those words to Clark Schooler with genuine concern. "The Civil Rights Act of 1964," Bonnie said, "will not truly be the law of the land until the Supreme Court declares it constitutional."

"Ah, yes," Clark replied. "Judicial review. In the landmark Supreme Court case of *Marbury v. Madison*, the Supreme Court won for itself the power to declare laws of Congress constitutional or unconstitutional. That makes approval by the Supreme Court the final step in the legislative process."

"Well," Bonnie said, "that's not true for every law passed by Congress. But it's true for almost all the major pieces of legislation. Someone almost always files suit charging that some aspect of a new law doesn't conform to the Constitution. And the Supreme Court decides whether that person is right or not. If the person who files the suit is supported by the Supreme Court, the new law, or a key section of the new law, is declared unconstitutional and is no longer in effect."

"And one more thing," Bonnie added. "The United States Supreme Court does not give advisory opinions. It does not sit in that giant marble building across from the Capitol and answer theoretical questions. The United States judicial system is an adversarial system. It is competitive and confrontational. There has to be an actual conflict, which begins in a state court or a lower U.S. court, that makes its way, on appeal, to the U.S. Supreme Court."

"I'm a little uncomfortable," Clark said, "with the fate of my civil rights bill being in the hands of nine older people dressed in black robes."

Bonnie immediately rose to the defense of her chosen profession of the law. "They're not just nine older persons," Bonnie said. "They are, at any given time in history, some of the finest jurists the United States legal system can produce."

"Each one is appointed by the United States president with the 'advise and consent' of the United States Senate," Bonnie continued. "'Advise and consent' means that the Senate has to approve the president's choice by a majority vote. The president usually gets whom he wants on the Supreme Court, but not always. Sometimes the Senate does turn down the president's Supreme Court appointments."

"Sometimes, but not very often," Clark interjected.

"But it makes such a difference just who the justices are," Bonnie said. "The nine persons sitting on the Supreme Court at the present time mainly were appointed by three presidents. Those presidents were Franklin D. Roosevelt, Harry Truman, and Dwight Eisenhower. Roosevelt and Truman's appointees are essentially liberal Democrats, so I am expecting them to uphold the Civil Rights Act of 1964. Eisenhower's appointees were more moderate, as one would expect from a Republican president, but I'm also expecting them to support civil rights."

One morning in the late fall of 1964, Clark and Bonnie were waiting in line to get into a session of the United States Supreme Court. They were in the main hall of the Supreme Court building, located on 1st Street Northeast, just across the street from the Senate wing of the Capitol.

Bonnie had invited Clark to come with her to see and hear the opening arguments in a case involving the Civil Rights Act of 1964. The owner of a motel in Georgia filed suit to have the Supreme Court declare the public accommodations section of the new law unconstitutional.

"This is an interesting case," Clark said. "The business in question is named the Heart of Atlanta Motel. It's situated just off Peachtree Street in downtown Atlanta, Georgia. Can you believe it? Peachtree Street is where Scarlet O'Hara and Rhett Butler spent much of their time in the great Southern novel 'Gone With The Wind.' And just a little way away, in the Auburn section of Atlanta, is the boyhood home of Martin Luther King, Jr. Atlanta is the perfect city from which the civil rights struggle should be moved into the courts."

"And it's not much of a motel, either," Clark rattled on. "Only 216 rooms. And not nationally known, like a Holiday Inn or a Quality Court or one of those new motel chains that are popping up all over the place."

"And they don't rent rooms to black people there," Clark continued. "They never have. They hope they never will. And, the ownership is so biased, they didn't wait for the Justice Department to come after them. They filed suit first, seeking a declaratory judgement from the U.S. courts that

Title Two, the public accommodations title, of the Civil Rights Act of 1964 is unconstitutional."

Bonnie listened politely to this oration and then said softly: "Your description of this case contains every last colorful detail except for the most relevant facts. Only a journalist would describe a Supreme Court case and bring in so many irrelevant details."

"All that really matters," Bonnie said with mock exasperation, "is that the Heart of Atlanta Motel is readily accessible to Interstate highways 75 and 85. Also, about 75 percent of the people who stay at the Heart of Atlanta Motel are from outside the state of Georgia. To add insult to injury, the motel buys advertising in national magazines. The motel also maintains over 50 billboards along Interstate highways and U.S. highways that solicit business for the motel. The Heart of Atlanta Motel is totally involved in interstate commerce."

At that moment, the doors to the Supreme Court chamber opened and the line of people waiting to observe the court proceedings began filing in. Clark loved the architectural appearance of the Supreme Court building. He particularly loved the marble columns that graced both the front entrance and a number of the interior spaces in the court building. To Clark, those columns were an instant tutorial in Greco-Roman architecture. There were marble columns topped with the square angles of the Doric style. There were columns topped with the curving curlicues of the Ionic style. And, most prevalent of all, marble columns topped with the leafy look of the Corinthian style.

Clark and Bonnie found good seats about five rows deep in the audience. Before them, the polished wooden bench of the Supreme Court rose into the air. From behind that high bench, in almost Jovian fashion, the nine justices would hear and weigh the various arguments in the case. The nine high-backed leather chairs which the nine justices would soon be occupying were visible behind the bench.

The Supreme Court chamber was opulent in terms of decor. Marble columns lined all four walls. A rich red rug covered the entire floor. On the wall behind the justices, luxurious red tapestries hung from the ceiling to the floor. It was, in Clark's eyes, a judicial throne room rather than just another courtroom.

"It certainly is majestic and quiet in here," Clark said to Bonnie with a touch of awe in his voice.

"Don't let the quiet mislead you," Bonnie replied, "This is only the calm before the storm. Some of the most powerful political and economic forces in American society come together to fight it out in this courtroom. The conversation and the overall mood may be civilized and polite, but the stakes are very high, and the decisions of the Supreme Court have far-reaching effects."

The quiet was suddenly interrupted by the voice of the clerk of the Supreme Court. "The honorable chief justice and associate justices of the Supreme Court," the clerk intoned. The audience was asked to stand as the nine justices, all dressed in black robes, paraded to the bench and sat down in their chairs. Following that, the lawyers that would be arguing cases that day filed in and sat at highly polished wooden tables in front of and below the bench. The lawyers for the Justice Department were dressed in formal morning clothes. The other lawyers were dressed in dark conservative business suits and neckties.

Clark Schooler was impressed by and supportive of the elaborate pomp and ceremony of the United States Supreme Court. These regal proceedings were more than appropriate, Clark thought, given that these nine judges were the constitutional guardians of the United States.

"It really is awe inspiring to be here," Bonnie whispered softly to Clark. "In its own unique way, the Supreme Court is a recreation of the Constitutional Convention held in Philadelphia in 1787. The Supreme Court tells us what the Constitution means, but those meanings can be changed by the court from one epoch to another."

For the next two hours, Bonnie and Clark watched and listened as each set of lawyers argued the case strongly. The lawyers for the Heart of Atlanta Motel hammered away on state's rights and private property rights. The U.S. Government answered back with the interstate commerce clause.

A number of days later, the justices of the Supreme Court published the decision in the *Heart of Atlanta Motel* case. As Bonnie had predicted, it was a unanimous decision for civil rights by a vote of 9 to 0. The justices reaffirmed the decision of a lower U.S. Court that Title Two of the Civil Rights Act of 1964 was constitutional and that the motel must begin serving "transient black persons."

The Supreme Court noted in the decision that the American people had become increasing mobile over the years and that black Americans in particular had been subject to discrimination in "transient accommodations." Travel conditions for blacks had become so difficult, the court said, as to necessitate the listing of available lodging for black Americans in a special tour book, which was itself "dramatic testimony" to the difficult problems black people encountered when traveling.

And then came the part of the decision that Clark liked best. In one pithy sentence, the Supreme Court of the United States declared the public accommodations provisions of the Civil Rights Act of 1964 to be constitutional.

The exact words were: "We, therefore, conclude that the action of the Congress in the adoption of the act as applied here to a motel which serves interstate travelers is within the power granted to it by the commerce clause of the Constitution, as interpreted by this court for the past 140 years."

And there was a bonus for Clark Schooler with this particular decision by the Supreme Court. In a companion case to *Heart of Atlanta Motel*, the Court took up *Katzenbach v. McClung*. This suit, filed by the U.S. Department of Justice, concerned racial discrimination at Ollie's Barbecue, a family owned restaurant in Birmingham, Alabama.

Ollie's specialized in serving barbecued meats and homemade pies to a predominantly local clientele. Although 2/3 of the employees at Ollie's Barbecue were African-Americans, Ollie's was segregated and served only white customers. Furthermore, the restaurant's lawyers argued, Ollie's had a Southern white clientele that would stop eating at Ollie's if the dining area were racially integrated.

"The owners of Ollies's Barbecue have a much better case than the owners of the Heart of Atlanta Motel," Clark explained to Bonnie as he read the text of the decision to her. "Their barbecue pit and pie ovens are eleven blocks away from the nearest Interstate highway. They get virtually no business off the Interstate. They rely almost completely on local trade. And, knowing the prevailing sentiments in Birmingham, Alabama, on race mixing, I find it believable that Ollie's will lose lots of customers if they start serving black people there."

Bonnie gave Clark a condescending look and said with false sweetness: "Sometime I'll have to tell you about the love affair between the U.S. Supreme Court and the commerce clause of the United States Constitution."

Bonnie got it right. In a second unanimous decision, the Supreme Court ordered Ollie's Barbecue to racially integrate its eating facilities. The court noted that approximately half of the meat that was cooked and served at Ollie's moved in interstate commerce. That was all it took. In the exact words of the court, which Bonnie savored as she heard Clark read them: "The only remaining question, one answered in the affirmative, is whether the particular restaurant serves food, a substantial portion of which has moved in interstate commerce."

When he had absorbed the decision on Ollie's Barbecue, Clark Schooler's thoughts raced back to the day, some six years earlier, when Clark had observed the unsuccessful attempt to integrate the White Dinner Plate restaurant at the Monarch Shopping Center in Baltimore. It was the same day that Clark, without realizing it until much later, had met Bonnie Kanecton, who was leading the demonstration. On that day, Clark ruminated, the men and women protesting racial segregation had stood virtually alone and unsupported. But now, on this day, just a little more than half a decade later, the U.S. president, the U.S. Congress, and the U.S. Supreme Court were solidly behind the goal that Bonnie and the other White Dinner Plate demonstrators had set out to achieve.

"Well, that's it," Clark said to Bonnie, putting down the text of the court's two decisions. "The deed is done. The play is finished. We have reached completion. The third of the three branches of the United States Government, the judicial branch, has given its blessing to the Civil Rights Act of 1964. The final 'i' has been dotted. The final 't' has been crossed."

"Not quite," Bonnie replied, but in a friendly and happy manner. "Many other provisions of the Civil Rights Act of 1964 will be tested before the Supreme Court. But the court will do its job. The court will fill in the blanks left by Congress. The court will apply specifics to the more general rules and regulations made by the Congress and signed into law by the president of the United States."

Shortly thereafter, four young people set off on a double date of a somewhat different sort. Clark Schooler and Bonnie Kanecton and Carl Brimmer and Vonda Belle Carter were all driving up to Gettysburg, Pennsylvania, to see the Civil War battlefield there. It was late December of 1964, just a few days before Christmas. Both the work level and the news intensity in Washington, D.C., were quieting down as political newsmakers and their assistants began leaving the nation's capital for extended holiday vacations.

"This really is the wrong time of year to visit Gettysburg," Clark said to no one in particular. "The battle was fought in early July of 1863, with southern Pennsylvania at its hottest and stickiest. But, by going in December, we will be a lot more comfortable, albeit a little chilly, than the Union and Confederate soldiers were."

It was a typical East Coast winter's day. The sky was filled with low hanging, wall-to-wall clouds. But no snow or rain was falling or predicted to fall. And the outside temperature was in the high 40s, a pretty good temperature for walking around an old battlefield.

The four young people had wanted to celebrate the successful enactment of the Civil Rights Act of 1964 and the upholding of the public accommodations section by the Supreme Court. In one way or another, all four of them had worked hard for the bill to be passed. It was Clark who suggested they go to Gettysburg. That was partly because Gettysburg was an interesting place to visit. It was also partly because of Gettysburg's historical significance in the struggle for racial equality.

Because he grew up in Baltimore, Maryland, which was only a one-hour drive from Gettysburg, Clark had visited the battlefield many times in his life and knew it well. When he learned that none of his three companions had ever been to Gettysburg, Clark offered to both drive them up there and give them a personal tour of all the significant battle sites.

"Carl and I have something to tell you," Vonda Belle Carter said from the back seat of Clark's car. She and Carl were sitting back there holding hands.

Vonda Belle draped her left hand over the front seat where Bonnie could see it. Just as Vonda Belle had intended, Bonnie's eyes widened and then Bonnie half screamed: "It's a ring. It's an engagement ring. You're getting married!"

"That's right," Carl Brimmer said from the back seat. "We don't really love each other," he added sarcastically. "We just want to strike one more blow for American civil rights by having a racially mixed marriage."

"That's our Carl," Clark chimed in. "I should have known Carl would plan a wedding night with more politics than romance involved."

"Hey, you guys," Vonda Belle said in a complaining tone. "We're serious about this. And it's not going to be easy to pull off, either."

Clark continued the lighthearted approach to the upcoming event. He asked: "What's the problem? Did Senator Richard Russell of Georgia refuse to give the bride away?"

Carl quickly picked up on Clark's sarcastic political humor. He quipped back: "Russell wouldn't do it, so we had to get Senator Eastland from the Judiciary Committee instead."

Vonda Belle insisted on treating the subject seriously. "We've just been through a heavy-duty round of telling our respective families," she said. "It was hard to tell who was more upset. Carl's family because he's going to marry a black woman, or my family because I'm going to marry a white man."

"I have to give them all credit," Carl Brimmer added. "They all struggled mightily to be nice about it, congratulate us, and say that everything would be fine. That was the problem. You could tell they were all struggling mightily."

"I hate to say it," Vonda Belle lamented, "but my fine, upstanding, all-for-civil-rights black family was more upset than Carl's family was."

"The worst part comes later," Carl commented. "One of your beloved family members gets you alone for a serious conversation. They ask: 'You're not really going to do it, are you?' Then they start winking their eye at you and say: 'I'm sure it's a lot of fun to be playing around with a black woman, but (wink) a little bit goes a long way (wink). Fun's fun, but (wink) do you think it's a very good idea to marry one of them?'"

"Oh, yeah," Vonda Belle said. "And then they start on the children bit.

I'm not talking about diehard Southern segregationists here. I'm talking about our all-out liberal family and friends who sincerely believe in racial equality. They whisper softly to me over in a corner: 'Have you thought about your children? The poor things won't be either black or white. They'll be unwanted in both worlds. It's not you and Carl we are worried about. It's your half-black, half-white children growing up in a mentally and emotionally segregated society.'"

Clark Schooler felt his jaw clenching and his hands gripping the steering wheel of his car more tightly. Clark was suddenly embarrassed. He realized the things that Vonda Belle's and Carl's family and friends were saying were things that Clark Schooler himself might have said, and wanted to say.

Interracial marriage was a very emotional and challenging subject, even for people who considered themselves total liberals on the civil rights issue.

"You just did me a big favor," Clark said to Carl and Vonda Belle with great seriousness. "You headed me off at the pass from saying all those things myself. I just might have taken Carl to one side and asked: 'Have you thought about this carefully?'"

But Clark also realized that logic impelled him to give his all-out support to Vonda Belle and Carl and their marriage plans. Clark spoke out: "The ultimate argument of the racial segregationists was always, 'Would you want your son or daughter to marry one of them?' Blacks and whites will never totally be free until they can marry one another with no fears or regrets whatsoever, both on their part and the part of their friends and relatives."

"I wouldn't worry about the children," Bonnie added. "The Civil Rights Act of 1964 is really going to change things. At least legal equality is now the law of the land. Your children will grow up in a much more racially integrated world than the segregated one we all grew up in."

By this time they were driving around the battlefield in Gettysburg. In his best reportorial and professorial manner, Clark began his lecture on the great Civil War conflagration. "General Robert E. Lee, the Southern commander, was making a major drive into the North," Clark began. "His goal was to capture Harrisburg, Pennsylvania, a major railroad center, and then drive toward Philadelphia. General Lee hoped that a quick string of Confederate victories on Northern soil would frighten President Lincoln into ending the Civil War and letting the Southerners secede in peace."

Clark took his three friends to all the major battle locations at Gettysburg. At Little Round Top, Clark pointed out how the Confederates almost captured this significant piece of high ground. Only quick action and hard fighting by Union troops prevented the Southerners from taking this major hilltop and using it to fire artillery shells at the Northern soldiers arrayed along the ridge line below.

Clark drove his friends along Seminary Ridge, the point from which General Lee launched Pickett's Charge, an all-out, go-for-broke infantry assault on the Union line. Then Clark drove around to the other side of the battlefield, to where the Union Army was waiting for its Confederate attackers.

Clark had his three friends get out of the car. He marched them to a spot on the Gettysburg battlefield known as the Angle.

"This is what I really wanted you to see," Clark said, standing by a bend in a low stone wall. "This is as far as the Southern attack got at Gettysburg. It was also as far North as General Lee's Southern army ever advanced. This spot has been called, 'The high water mark of the Confederacy.'"

"The fighting here was particularly fierce," Clark went on. "The toll in lives lost, for both the North and the South, was enormous. But the Union soldiers drove back the rebels. From that point on, the end of the Civil War and the freeing of the slaves were inevitable."

"I often think about the Union soldiers who fought here at the Angle," Clark continued. His friends appeared to be more than interested in what he was saying. "It was just by accident that those particular soldiers were here. A real twist of fate. But those Northern soldiers got the job done at the critical moment. For one day, fighting desperately for this piece of ground, those particular men were living on the forward edge of their time."

"I thought about this spot a lot when the Civil Rights Act of 1964 was enduring the challenge of the Senate filibuster," Clark said. "All of you have heard me say many times that the civil rights movement was a refighting, almost exactly 100 years later, of the American Civil War. If that idea has merit, then the Southern filibuster of the civil rights bill was the 1960s version of Pickett's Charge at Gettysburg. In both instances, the Southerners were giving it all they had. They were making one final attempt to preserve the Southern way of life, whether that way of life was human slavery in 1863 or racial segregation in 1964."

"And, in conclusion," Clark said, realizing he was subjecting his friends to quite a lengthy oration, "the cloture vote on June 10, 1964, was the modern equivalent of what happened here at the Angle at Gettysburg. The Southerners tried desperately to defeat the cloture vote on the Civil Rights Act of 1964. But the Southern senators were defeated and thrown back on cloture day, just as the Southern army was defeated and thrown back at this spot on this battlefield."

"A number of historians have called the fighting here at the Angle the turning point of the Civil War," Clark added. "In the same way, I regard the cloture vote on the civil rights bill as the turning point in the civil rights movement. From that day on, June 10, 1964, the defeat of racial segregation as a legal part of American life will become inevitable."

The four young people had been standing in a circle facing each other while Clark had been speaking. At one point during Clark's oration, without anyone actually suggesting it, they had all four taken each others' hands. They remained that way when Clark finished speaking.

It was Bonnie Kanecton who broke the sentimental and endearing silence. "I think I agree with you, Clark," she said. "In a legislative rather than a military way, we have been like the brave soldiers who fought here at the Angle at Gettysburg. All of us, each in his or her own way, worked hard for the Civil Rights Act of 1964 and sought to counter its opponents in any way possible. And, these past few years, like the soldiers here at Gettysburg, we have all four lived on the forward edge of our time."

In The Interim

The Civil Rights Act of 1964 was the first of three major civil rights bills to be passed by Congress and signed into law by President Lyndon Johnson during the 1960s.

The Voting Rights Act of 1965

One aspect of racial discrimination that had not been corrected by the Civil Rights Act of 1964 was denial of voting rights. Large numbers of Southern blacks were prevented from voting by legal devices such as literacy tests. Early in 1965, Martin Luther King, Jr., attempted to lead a march from Selma, Alabama, to Montgomery, Alabama, to protest the various Southern stratagems that prevented African-Americans from registering to vote and casting a ballot on election day.

Martin Luther King and his supporters began their march by walking across a bridge over the Alabama River leading out of Selma. This peaceful, nonviolent demonstration was met by Alabama state troopers, some of them mounted on horseback, who fired tear gas into the crowd of protesters and began beating people with billy clubs. The resulting television images and front-page newspaper photographs instantly produced a nationwide demand for legislative action by Congress.

President Lyndon Johnson jumped at the chance to exploit such a golden opportunity. Johnson gave a speech to a joint session of Congress in which he called for national voting rights legislation. Under Johnson's proposal, U.S. Government registrars would go into the South to register blacks to vote. Johnson concluded his speech with words from a song being sung by civil rights workers throughout the nation. Those words were: "We shall overcome!"

Quickly beating back a Southern filibuster with a cloture vote, the Senate joined the House in rapidly enacting President Johnson's voting rights proposal. The speed with which cloture was attained in the Senate was credited to the precedent set by the victorious cloture vote on the 1964 civil rights bill.

The Voting Rights Act of 1965 had immediate effects in the American South. African-American voter registration increased to more than 50 percent of those eligible to vote in six Southern states. Most important, there was a dramatic increase in the number of blacks winning elected offices, such as city mayor and county sheriff, throughout the South.

The Housing Rights Act of 1968

In the spring of 1968 in Memphis, Tennessee, African-American garbage collectors went on strike against the city government for higher wages and better working conditions. The strike was hard fought. The black sanitation workers ran into a solid wall of opposition from Memphis city officials, most of whom were white.

Martin Luther King, Jr., heeded the call to come to Memphis and give his moral support to the garbage men and their economic demands. On April 4, 1968, while standing on the balcony of the motel where he was staying in Memphis, Martin Luther King, Jr., was killed by a rifle bullet. As news of King's assassination spread throughout the nation, outraged citizens, most of them black, took to the streets to protest the willful killing of America's renowned civil rights leader. There were riots in over 130 U.S. cities, with 46 persons killed and over $100 million in property damage.

Once again a dramatic national news event generated a legislative opportunity. A housing rights bill, which had been slowly working its way through Congress, was immediately put on the fast track to enactment. The bill prohibited racial, religious, and ethnic discrimination against minority groups in the sale and rental of housing. The bill was universally viewed as a fitting final legislative memorial to the slain Martin Luther King, Jr.

After being passed in the Senate, the final version of the bill was passed in the House of Representatives after only one hour of debate. The date was April 10, 1968, just six days after Martin Luther King, Jr., was killed. President Johnson signed the Housing Rights Act of 1968 into law on the following day.

The Minority Bill of Rights

Looked upon as a group, the three great civil rights acts of the 1960s can be characterized as the Minority Bill of Rights. In the four decades from the 1960s to the 2000s, these three laws protected all United States minorities, not just blacks, from most overt and clearly identifiable forms of legal discrimination. The Civil Rights Act of 1964, the Voting Rights Act of 1965, and the Housing Rights Act of 1968 are the enduring legislative fruit of the civil rights movement of the 1960s.

School Busing

In 1971 the United States Supreme Court ruled that it was constitutional for black students to be bused to white schools and for white students to be bused to black schools. The purpose of such crosstown school busing was to try to end de facto segregation of public schools.

This court decision, Swann v. Charlotte-Mecklenburg, was hailed by civil right supporters as a way of partially overcoming the reality that white students tended to live in exclusively white neighborhoods and black students resided in all-black neighborhoods.

But school busing met tremendous resistance from white parents who did not want their children bused across the city to black schools in black neighborhoods. In a number of cities, most notably Boston, Massachusetts, hostile whites took to the streets to protest school busing. Often white parents would stage a school strike by keeping their children home rather than having them bused to distant schools with large numbers of minority students.

One effect of court-ordered school busing was to encourage white families to move out of central cities, where their children would be bused, and relocate in surrounding suburbs, where school systems remained predominantly white.

To compensate for this white flight to the suburbs, city school systems began creating magnet schools. These were center city schools designed to attract students who wanted a specialized curriculum, such as an emphasis on advanced science classes or classical music courses. Magnet schools were relatively successful at attracting white students from the suburbs to go to center city schools with significant numbers of minority students.

The Bakke Case

In 1978 the Supreme Court once again rendered a major decision *concerning American civil rights. In the case of University of California Regents v. Bakke, the court ruled that a college or university could not set specific quotas for the number of minority students who were to be admitted to the college or university. In other words, an educational institution could not designate a specific number of spots in an entering class of students that would automatically go to minority applicants.*

The Bakke case, as it is popularly known, stirred up a storm of protest from civil rights advocates. But at the same time the Supreme Court outlawed quotas in the Bakke decision, the court also ruled that colleges and universities could take race, religion, and ethnicity into consideration when making admission decisions. Only specific numerical quotas for minority groups were outlawed. The Bakke decision thus gave institutions of higher learning the flexibility to continue to make extra efforts in attempts to attract and admit minority students.

An Enduring Struggle

The proper role of the United States Government in the protection of minority rights remains a subject of continuing debate in American society.

As was true of Clark Schooler and his friends and acquaintances, every generation of Americans must contend with the reality of racial discrimination and find appropriate solutions "on the forward edge of our time."

NOTES

1. George Gallup, guest speaker, graduate course in American Politics, Johns Hopkins University, c. 1958, by recollection of the author.

2. *Congressional Quarterly Almanac 1963*, p. 336.

3. Michael Dorman, *We Shall Overcome* (New York, NY: Dial Press, 1964), p. 143. Dorman gives a journalistic account of major events in the civil rights movement in the early 1960s.

4. *Washington Evening Star*, May 14, 1963.

5. *Washington Post*, May 28, 1963.

6. Joseph L. Rauh, Jr., "The Role of the Leadership Conference on Civil Rights in the Civil Rights Struggle of 1963-1964," in Robert D. Loevy, ed., *The Civil Rights Act of 1964: The Passage of the Law That Ended Racial Segregation* (Albany, NY: State University of New York Press, 1997), p.53.

7. Theodore C. Sorenson, *Kennedy* (New York, NY: Harper and Row, 1965), p. 489.

8. Charles and Barbara Whelan, *The Longest Debate: A Legislative History of the 1964 Civil Rights Act* (Cabin John, MD: Seven Locks Press, 1985), p. 33.

9. For a detailed description of U.S. Government efforts to integrate the University of Alabama, see Dorman, *We Shall Overcome* (New York, NY: Dial Press, 1964), Ch. IX, "Tuscaloosa," pp. 270-334.

10. *Congressional Quarterly Almanac 1963*, p. 967.

11. Daniel M. Berman, *A Bill Becomes A Law: Congress Enacts Civil Rights Legislation*, 2nd ed. (New York, NY: Macmillan, 1966), pp. 64-65.

12. For testimony and comments of senators Sam J. Ervin and Kenneth Keating to the Senate Judiciary Committee, see *Congressional Quarterly Weekly Report*, July 26, 1963, p. 1318.

13. Robert D. Loevy, *To End All Segregation: The Politics of the Passage of the Civil Rights Act of 1964* (Lanham, MD: University Press of America, 1990), p. 49-50. Also see *Congressional Quarterly Weekly Report*, July 12, 1963, p. 1131.

14. Charles W. and Barbara Whelan, *The Longest Debate: A Legislative History of the 1964 Civil Rights Act* (Cabin John, MD: Seven Locks Press, 1985), p. 26.

15. Charles W. and Barbara Whelan, *The Longest Debate: A Legislative History of the 1964 Civil Rights Act* (Cabin John, MD: Seven Locks Press, 1985), p. 26.

16. *Congressional Quarterly Weekly Report*, September 20, 1963, p. 1632.

17. *Congressional Quarterly Weekly Report*, September 20, 1963, p. 1633.

18. *Congressional Quarterly Weekly Rept.*, September. 20, 1963, pp. 1632-1633.

19. *Congressional Quarterly Weekly Rept.*, September 20, 1963, pp. 1632-1633.

20. Recollection of the author.

21. Joseph L. Rauh, Jr., life history and comments from Joseph L. Rauh, Jr., interview by the author, August 15, 1983, Washington, D.C.

22. Joseph L. Rauh, Jr., "The Role Of The Leadership Conference On Civil Rights In The Civil Rights Struggle Of 1963-1964," in Robert D. Loevy, ed., *The Civil Rights Act Of 1964: The Passage of the Law That Ended Racial Segregation* (Albany, NY: State University of New York Press, 1997), pp.

52, 54. Also see Memorandum #2, August 5, 1963, and in succeeding memoranda, Series D, Box 4, Leadership Conference on Civil Rights Collection, Library of Congress.

23. The field trip to the Baltimore, Md., National Association for the Advancement of Colored People (NAACP) is by recollection of the author.

24. This account of passage of a civil rights bill in Congress is from Joseph L. Rauh, Jr., interview by the author, August 15, 1983, Washington, D.C. Also see Joseph L. Rauh, Jr., "The Role Of The Leadership Conference On Civil Rights In The Civil Rights Struggle Of 1963-1964," in Robert D. Loevy, ed., *The Civil Rights Act Of 1964: The Passage of the Law That Ended Racial Segregation* (Albany, NY: State University of New York Press, 1997), pp. 56-65.

25. This account of passage of a civil rights bill in Congress is from Clarence Mitchell, Jr., interview by the author, August 17, 1983, Baltimore, Md.

26. Joseph L. Rauh, Jr., "The Role Of The Leadership Conference On Civil Rights In The Civil Rights Struggle Of 1963-1964," in Robert D. Loevy, ed., *The Civil Rights Act Of 1964: The Passage of the Law That Ended Racial Segregation* (Albany, NY: State University of New York Press, 1997), p. 55.

27. Joseph L. Rauh, Jr., interview by the author, August 15, 1983, Washington, D.C.

28. For Representative Arch Moore's view, see *Congressional Quarterly Weekly Report*, October 25, 1963, p. 1863. Also see *Congressional Quarterly Weekly Report*, November 29, 1963, p. 2105.

29. For Representative William McCulloch's view, see *Congressional Quarterly Weekly Report*, October 11, 1963, p. 1749. Also see Nicholas Katzenbach, interview, November 11, 1968, p. 18, Oral History Collection, Lyndon Baines Johnson Library, University of Texas, Austin, Texas. Also see Theodore C. Sorensen, *Kennedy* (New York, NY: Harper and Row, 1965), p. 501.

30. Joseph L. Rauh, Jr., "The Role Of The Leadership Conference On Civil Rights In The Civil Rights Struggle Of 1963-1964," in Robert D. Loevy, ed., *The Civil Rights Act Of 1964: The Passage of the Law That Ended Racial*

Segregation (Albany, NY: State University of New York Press, 1997), p. 12.

31. *Congressional Quarterly Weekly Report*, October 11, 1963, p. 1749.

32. *Congressional Quarterly Weekly Report*, October 18, 1963, p. 1814.

33. *Congressional Quarterly Weekly Report*, October 18, 1963, p. 1814.

34. All quotes excerpted from a transcript of a White House meeting. See Jonathan Rosenberg and Zachary Karabell, *Kennedy, Johnson, And The Quest For Justice: The Civil Rights Tapes* (New York, NY: W. W. Norton, 2003), pp. 184-191.

35. Recollection of the author.

36. *Public Papers of the Presidents, Lyndon B. Johnson, 1963-64*, vol. 1 (Washington, DC: U.S. Government Printing Office, 1965), p. 1.

37. *Congressional Quarterly Weekly Report*, November 29, 1963, p. 2089.

38. Joseph L. Rauh, Jr., interview by the author, August 15, 1983, Washington, D.C. See also Joseph L. Rauh, Jr., "The Role of the Leadership Conference on Civil Rights in the Civil Rights Struggle of 1963-1964," in Robert D. Loevy, ed., *The Civil Rights Act of 1964: The Passage of the Law That Ended Racial Segregation* (Albany, NY: State University of New York Press, 1997), p. 61.

39. Lyndon B. Johnson, "Off The Record Remarks To Governors," November 25, 1963, p. 4, Appointment File (Diary Back-up), Box 1, Lyndon Baines Johnson Library, Austin, Texas.

40. *Congressional Quarterly Weekly Report*, December 6, 1963, p. 2118. See also *Congressional Quarterly Weekly Report*, December 13, 1963, p. 2150.

41. *Congressional Quarterly Weekly Report*, December 6, 1963, p. 2118.

42. *Congressional Quarterly Weekly Report*, January 10, 1964, p. 48.

43. *Congressional Quarterly Weekly Report*, January 24, 1964, p. 157.

44. *Congressional Quarterly Weekly Report*, January 24, 1964, p. 157.

45. *Congressional Quarterly Weekly Report*, January 24, 1964, p. 157.

46. *Congressional Quarterly Weekly Report*, January 24, 1964, p. 157.

47. Joseph L. Rauh, Jr., "The Role of the Leadership Conference on Civil Rights in the Civil Rights Struggle of 1963-1964," in Robert D. Loevy, ed., *The Civil Rights Act of 1964: The Passage of the Law That Ended Racial Segregation* (Albany, NY: State University of New York Press, 1997), p. 61.

48. Joseph L. Rauh, Jr., "The Role of the Leadership Conference on Civil Rights in the Civil Rights Struggle of 1963-1964," in Robert D. Loevy, ed., *The Civil Rights Act of 1964: The Passage of the Law That Ended Racial Segregation* (Albany, NY: State University of New York Press, 1997), p. 61.

49. Daniel M. Berman, *A Bill Becomes A Law: Congress Enacts Civil Rights Legislation*, 2nd ed. (New York, NY: Macmillan, 1966), p. 95.

50. Clarence Mitchell, Jr., on civil rights problems in the Committee of the Whole, is from Clarence Mitchell, Jr., interview by the author, August 17, 1983, Baltimore, Md. Also see Clarence Mitchell, Jr., interview, April 30, 1969, Tape 1, p. 28; Tape 2, pp. 1-2; Oral History Collection, Lyndon Baines Johnson Library, Austin, Texas. Also see "How Supporters 'Got out the vote' on Key Amendments," *Congressional Quarterly Weekly Report*, February 21, 1964, p. 365.

51. *Congressional Quarterly Weekly Report*, February 14, 1964, p. 293.

52. *Congressional Quarterly Weekly Report*, February 14, 1964, pp. 293-294.

53. *Congressional Record* 110, Pt. 2 (February 8, 1964), p. 2577. See also *Congressional Quarterly Weekly Rept.*, February 14, 1964, p. 296. See also *Time*, February 21, 1964, p. 22.

54. *Congressional Record* 110, Pt. 2 (February 8, 1964), p. 2581. See also *Congressional Quarterly Weekly Report*, February 14, 1964, pp. 296-297. See also *Time*, February 21, 1964, p. 22.

55. *Congressional Record* 110, Pt. 2 (February 8, 1964), p. 2578-2580. Also see *Congressional Quarterly Weekly Report*, February 14, 1964, p. 296.

56. *Congressional Record* 110, Pt. 2 (February 8, 1964), p. 2581. Also see *Congressional Quarterly Weekly Report*, February 14, 1964, p. 296. Also see *Time*, February 21, 1964, p. 22.

57. Jo Freeman, *The Politics Of Women's Liberation* (New York, NY: Longman, 1975), pp. 53-54. Also see *Congressional Record* 110, Pt. 2 (February 8, 1964), pp. 2581-2582.

58. Joseph L. Rauh, Jr., "The Role of the Leadership Conference on Civil Rights in the Civil Rights Struggle of 1963-1964," in Robert D. Loevy, ed., *The Civil Rights Act of 1964: The Passage of the Law That Ended Racial Segregation* (Albany, NY: State University of New York Press, 1997), p. 63.

59. *Congressional Record* 110, Pt. 2 (February 7, 1964), p. 2503. Also see Joseph L. Rauh, Jr., "The Role of the Leadership Conference on Civil Rights in the Civil Rights Struggle of 1963-1964," in Robert D. Loevy, ed., *The Civil Rights Act of 1964: The Passage of the Law That Ended Racial Segregation* (Albany, NY: State University of New York Press, 1997), p. 65.

60. Joseph L. Rauh, Jr., "The Role of the Leadership Conference on Civil Rights in the Civil Rights Struggle of 1963-1964," in Robert D. Loevy, ed., *The Civil Rights Act of 1964: The Passage of the Law That Ended Racial Segregation* (Albany, NY: State University of New York Press, 1997), p. 64. Also see Clarence Mitchell, Jr., interview, April 30, 1969, Tape 1, pp. 30-31, Oral History Collection, Lyndon Baines Johnson Library, Austin, Texas.

61. *Time*, February 28, 1964, p. 22.

62. *Congressional Record* 110, Pt. 3 (February 17, 1964), p. 2882.

63. Recollection of the author. See Robert D. Loevy, *To End All Segregation: The Politics of the Passage of the Civil Rights Act of 1964* (Lanham, MD: University Press of America, 1990), p. 169.

64. *Congressional Record* 110, Pt. 5 (March 26, 1964), p. 6431.

65. *Congressional Quarterly Weekly Report*, March 27, 1964, p. 597. Also see Stephen Horn, "Periodic Log Maintained During Discussions Concerning the Passage of the Civil Rights Act of 1964," unpublished notes, p. 23.

66. *Congressional Record* 110, Pt. 3 (February 17, 1964), p. 2882-2884. Also see Peter E. Kane, "The Senate Debate on the 1964 Civil Rights Act," unpublished Ph.D. dissertation, Purdue University, 1967, pp. 68-69.

67. *Time*, April 17, 1964, pp. 35-36.

68. Recollection of the author.

69. *Congressional Record* 110, Pt. 5 (April 4, 1964), p. 6863.

70. Joseph L. Rauh, Jr., "The Role of the Leadership Conference on Civil Rights in the Civil Rights Struggle of 1963-1964," in Robert D. Loevy, ed., *The Civil Rights Act of 1964: The Passage of the Law That Ended Racial Segregation* (Albany, NY: State University of New York Press, 1997), p.68.

71. Stephen Horn, "Periodic Log Maintained During Discussions Concerning the Passage of the Civil Rights Act of 1964," unpublished notes, p. 77.

72. *Time*, April 24, 1964, p. 18.

73. For a detailed description of U.S. Government efforts to integrate the University of Alabama, see Michael Dorman, *We Shall Overcome* (New York, NY: Dial Press, 1964), Ch. IX, "Tuscaloosa," pp. 270-334.

74. Recollection of the author.

75. Lyndon Baines Johnson, *The Vantage Point: Perspectives On The Presidency 1963-1969* (New York, NY: Popular Library, 1971), p. 29.

76. *Time*, April 17, 1964, p. 37.

77. *Congressional Quarterly Weekly Report*, May 8, 1964, p. 905.

78. Daniel B. Brewster, interview by the author, August 1982, Glyndon, Md. Also see Robert D. Loevy, *To End All Segregation: The Politics of the Passage of the Civil Rights Act of 1964* (Lanham, MD: University Press of America, 1990), pp. 216-223, 261-266.

79. Daniel B. Brewster, interview by the author, August 1982, Glyndon, Md.

80. Recollection of the author.

81. *Congressional Quarterly Weekly Report*, May 22, 1964, pp. 1000-1001.

82. *Congressional Quarterly Weekly Report*, May 22, 1964, p. 1001.

83. *Congressional Quarterly Weekly Report*, March 20, 1964, p. 580.

84. *Congressional Quarterly Weekly Report*, April 10, 1964, p. 701.

85. *Congressional Quarterly Weekly Report*, April 24, 1964, p. 797.

86. Merle Miller, *Lyndon: An Oral Biography* (New York, NY: G. P. Putnam's Sons, 1980), p. 368.

87. Hubert Humphrey, "Memorandum on Senate Consideration of the Civil Rights Act of 1964," in Robert D. Loevy, ed., *The Civil Rights Act of 1964: The Passage of the Law That Ended Racial Segregation* (Albany, NY: State University of New York Press, 1997), pp. 86-87.

88. Merle Miller, *Lyndon: An Oral Biography* (New York, NY: G. P. Putnam's Sons, 1980), pp. 368-369.

89. Merle Miller, *Lyndon: An Oral Biography* (New York, NY: G. P. Putnam's Sons, 1980), p. 370.

90. John G. Stewart, "Thoughts on the Civil Rights Bill," in Robert D. Loevy, ed., *The Civil Rights Act of 1964: The Passage of the Law That Ended Racial Segregation* (Albany, NY: State University of New York Press, 1997), p. 95.

91. Stephen Horn, "Periodic Log Maintained During Discussions Concerning the Passage of the Civil Rights Act of 1964," unpublished notes, pp. 92-94. Also see Joseph L. Rauh, Jr., "The Role of the Leadership Conference on Civil Rights in the Civil Rights Struggle of 1963-1964," in Robert D. Loevy, ed., *The Civil Rights Act of 1964: The Passage of the Law That Ended Racial Segregation* (Albany, NY: State University of New York Press, 1997), p. 70.

92. These comments by Clarence Mitchell, Jr., on being addressed by his first name, are by recollection of the author.

93. For a complete history of Richard Russell's opposition to civil rights, see David Daniel Potenziani, "Look to the Past: Richard B. Russell and the Defense of Southern White Supremacy," unpublished Ph.D. dissertation, University of Georgia, Athens, Ga., 1981.

94. John G. Stewart, "Thoughts on the Civil Rights Bill," in Robert D. Loevy, ed., *The Civil Rights Act of 1964: The Passage of the Law That Ended Racial Segregation* (Albany, NY: State University of New York Press, 1997), p. 97.

95. Neil MacNeil, *Dirksen: Portrait of a Public Man* (New York, NY: World Publishing Company, 1970), pp. 128, 6.

96. Annette C. Penney, *Dirksen: The Golden Voice of the Senate* (Washington, DC: Acropolis Books, 1968), pp. 62-69.

97. Winthrop Griffith, *Humphrey: A Candid Biography* (New York, NY: William Morrow, 1965), pp. 281-282. Also John G. Stewart, "Thoughts on the Civil Rights Bill," in Robert D. Loevy, ed., *The Civil Rights Act of 1964: The Passage of the Law That Ended Racial Segregation* (Albany, NY: State University of New York Press, 1997), pp. 119-120. Also see John G. Stewart, "The Civil Rights Act of 1964: Tactics I," in Robert D. Loevy, ed., *The Civil Rights Act of 1964: The Passage of the Law That Ended Racial Segregation* (Albany, NY: State University of New York Press, 1997), pp. 258-259.

98. Stephen Horn, "Periodic Log Maintained During Discussions Concerning the Passage of the Civil Rights Act of 1964," unpublished notes, p. 179.

99. John G. Stewart, "Thoughts on the Civil Rights Bill," in Robert D. Loevy, ed., *The Civil Rights Act of 1964: The Passage of the Law That Ended Racial Segregation* (Albany, NY: State University of New York Press, 1997), pp. 123-124.

100. John G. Stewart, "The Civil Rights Act of 1964: Tactics I," in Robert D. Loevy, ed., *The Civil Rights Act of 1964: The Passage of the Law That Ended Racial Segregation* (Albany, NY: State University of New York Press, 1997), p. 260.

101. *Congressional Record* 110, Pt. 10 (June 10, 1964), pp. 13319-13320.

102. Winthrop Griffith, *Humphrey: A Candid Biography* (New York, NY: William Morrow, 1965), p. 284.

103. Robert D. Loevy, *To End All Segregation: The Politics of the Passage of the Civil Rights Act of 1964* (Lanham, MD: University Press of America, 1990), p. 281.

104. *Congressional Quarterly Weekly Report*, October 11, 1963, p. 1749.

105. *Congressional Quarterly Weekly Report*, July 3, 1964, p. 1331.

106. Lyndon Baines Johnson, *The Vantage Point* (New York, NY: Popular Library, 1971), p. 160.

ABOUT THE AUTHOR

Robert D. Loevy was born in St. Louis, Missouri, on February 26, 1935. He received his A.B. from Williams College in 1957 and his Ph.D. from Johns Hopkins University in 1963. While at Johns Hopkins he conducted research and wrote position papers for the House of Representatives Republican Policy Committee. During the 1963-1964 academic year, he served as an American Political Science Association Congressional Fellow in the office of United States Senator Thomas H. Kuchel, of California, the Republican floor manager in the Senate for the civil rights bill that later became the Civil Rights Act of 1964. In 1968 Loevy joined the faculty at Colorado College in Colorado Springs, Colorado, where he currently serves as professor of political science. His major research interests include Congress and civil rights, presidential elections, and Colorado politics and government. He is the author of *To End All Segregation: The Politics of the Passage of the Civil Rights Act of 1964*, and he is the editor of *The Civil Rights Act of 1964: The Passage of the Law that Ended Racial Segregation*. He also wrote *The Flawed Path to the Presidency 1992: Unfairness and Inequality in the Presidential Selection Process*, as well as *The Manipulated Path to the White House 1996: Maximizing Advantage in the Presidential Selection Process*. His Colorado publications include *The Flawed Path to the Governorship 1994: The Nationalization of a Colorado Statewide Election*, and, with Thomas Cronin, *Colorado Politics and Government: Governing the Centennial State*. He also is the co-author of a high school civics text, *American Government: We Are One*.